SUSTAINING EXPORT-ORIENTED DEVELOPMENT

Ideas from East Asia

TRADE AND DEVELOPMENT

A series of books on international economic relations and economic issues in development

Edited from the National Centre for Development Studies, Australian National University

Advisory editors
Ross Garnaut, *RSPAS, Australian National University*
Reuven Glick, *Federal Reserve Bank of San Francisco*
Enzo R. Grilli, *The World Bank*
Mario B. Lamberte, *Phillipine Institute for Development Studies*

Executive Editor
Maree Tait, *National Centre for Development Studies, Australian National University*

Other titles in the series
Helen Hughes (ed.), *Achieving Industrialization in East Asia*
Yun-Wing Sung, *The China–Hong Kong Connection: The Key to China's Open Door Policy*
Kym Anderson (ed.), *New Silk Roads: East Asia and World Textile Markets*
Rod Tyers and Kym Anderson, *Disarray in World Food Markets: A Quantitative Assessment*
Enzo R. Grilli, *The European Community and the Developing Countries*
Peter G. Warr (ed.), *The Thai Economy in Transition*

SUSTAINING EXPORT-ORIENTED DEVELOPMENT

Ideas from East Asia

ROSS GARNAUT

Division of Economics, Research School of Pacific and Asian Studies
The Australian National University

ENZO GRILLI

World Bank
The Paul H. Nitze School of Advanced International Studies
Johns Hopkins University

JAMES RIEDEL

The Paul H. Nitze School of Advanced International Studies
Johns Hopkins University

CAMBRIDGE
UNIVERSITY PRESS

*This book is dedicated to Helen Hughes, Professor of Economics and
Executive Director of the National Centre for Development Studies,
The Australian National University, 1983–93.*

CAMBRIDGE UNIVERSITY PRESS
Cambridge, New York, Melbourne, Madrid, Cape Town, Singapore,
São Paulo, Delhi, Dubai, Tokyo

Cambridge University Press
The Edinburgh Building, Cambridge CB2 8RU, UK

Published in the United States of America by Cambridge University Press, New York

www.cambridge.org
Information on this title: www.cambridge.org/9780521121361

First published 1995
This digitally printed version 2009

A catalogue record for this publication is available from the British Library

National Library of Australia Cataloguing in Publication data

Sustaining export-oriented development: ideas from East Asia.
Bibliography.
Includes index.
1. Foreign trade promotion – East Asia. 2. East Asia –
Economic policy. 3. East Asia – Economic conditions.
4. East Asia – Commercial policy. I. Garnaut, Ross.
II. Grilli, Enzo R. III. Riedel, James. (Series: Trade
and development).
382.6095

Library of Congress Cataloguing in Publication data

Sustaining export-oriented development: ideas from East Asia/
[edited by] Ross Garnaut, Enzo Grilli, James Riedel.
    p.   cm. – (Trade and development)
Includes bibliographical references and index.
1. Exports – East Asia. 2. East Asia – Commercial policy.
3. Foreign trade promotion – East Asia. 4. East Asia – Economic
conditions. 5. International trade. 6. Economic development.
I. Garnaut, Ross. II. Grilli, Enzo R. III. Riedel, James.
IV. Series: Trade and development (Cambridge, England)
HF3820.5.Z5S87 1995
382'.6'095–dc20   95–3729

ISBN 978-0-521-48304-9 Hardback
ISBN 978-0-521-12136-1 Paperback

Contents

Figures

Tables

Symbols used: ··   not available.   –   zero.
                     *   insignificant.   ha   hectare.
                n.a. not applicable.

Contributors

HEINZ ARNDT, MA, Oxford University, is Emeritus Professor of Economics, The Australian National University, Editor, *Asian-Pacific Economic Literature*.

KYM ANDERSON, PhD, Stanford University, is Professor of Economics and Director of the Centre for International Economic Studies at the University of Adelaide.

PHILIPPA DEE, PhD, Simon Fraser University, is Assistant Commissioner, Industry Commission, Australia.

PETER DRYSDALE, PhD, The Australian National University, is Professor of Economics and Executive Director of the Australia–Japan Research Centre, The Australian National University.

RON DUNCAN, PhD, The Australian National University, is Professor of Economics and Executive Director of the National Centre for Development Studies at The Australian National University.

CHRISTOPHER FINDLAY, PhD, The Australian National University, is Associate Professor in the Department of Economics at the University of Adelaide and an Associate of the Australia–Japan Research Centre.

ISAIAH FRANK, PhD, Columbia University, is William L. Clayton Professor of International Economics, The Paul H. Nitze School of Advanced International Studies, Johns Hopkins University.

ROSS GARNAUT, PhD, The Australian National University, is Professor of Economics and Head of the Department of Economics and Division Convenor, Research School of Pacific and Asian Studies, The Australian National University.

ENZO GRILLI, PhD, Johns Hopkins University, is Director of Development Policy and Executive Director for Italy at the World Bank and Professorial Lecturer in International Economics and European Studies at The Paul H. Nitze School of Advanced International Studies, Johns Hopkins University.

ANNE O. KRUEGER, PhD, University of Wisconsin, is Professor of Economics, Stanford University.

E.S. LEUNG, PhD, Johns Hopkins University, is Director, Graduate Studies in Economics of Development, National Centre for Development Studies, The Australian National University.

JAMES RIEDEL, PhD, University of California, is Professor of International Economics, The Paul H. Nitze School of Advanced International Studies, Johns Hopkins University.

DAVID ROBERTSON, PhD, University of Reading, is Senior Research Fellow, National Centre for Development Studies, The Australian National University.

RICHARD H. SNAPE, PhD, London School of Economics, is Professor of Economics and Chairman, Department of Economics, Monash University.

NANCY VIVIANI, PhD, The Australian National University, is Professor of Politics and Dean of Students, Griffith University.

YONGZHENG YANG, PhD, The Australian National University, is a Research Fellow, National Centre for Development Studies, The Australian National University.

CHIA SIOW YUE, PhD, McGill University, is Professor of Economics and Head of the Department of Economics, National University of Singapore.

Dedication to Helen Hughes

Helen Hughes, in a long and distinguished career as an academic and an international public servant, has made important contributions to the subject of this book.

Her list of publications contains 13 books written or edited by her, 38 chapters in books and occasional papers, 26 journal articles and five government reports. From this massive output, there appear to be five significant contributions:

- emphasis on sound infrastructure, rather than financial incentives, to attract foreign direct investment;
- the case for export-oriented, instead of import-substituting, industrialisation;
- the importance of efficient capital utilisation in developing countries;
- the key role, even in export-oriented industrialisation, of sound domestic, especially macroeconomic, policies; and
- demonstration of the fallacy of 'export pessimism'.

Attracting foreign direct investment

Helen Hughes came to development economics from economic history, particularly the history of manufacturing. Her first book was a history of the Australian steel industry (Hughes 1964). Her active involvement in economic development came with her appointment to a senior fellowship at The Australian National University to embark on a major study of industrialisation in Southeast Asia. In the next few years, she undertook extensive fieldwork in what are now the ASEAN (Association of Southeast Asian Nations) countries, making contacts at the Asian Development Bank in Manila and ECAFE (Economic Commission for Africa and the Far East) in Bangkok. One offshoot was an annual teaching appointment at the Asian Development Institute. Another was a study of direct foreign investment in Singapore, first surveying Australian investors then, in cooperation with You Poh Seng, organising a collective study of direct foreign investment from all sources.

At that time, there was increasing competition among the governments of Southeast Asia (other than Singapore) and industrialising countries generally, each outbidding the other with tax concessions and other financial incentives. The main conclusion of the Hughes–You study was that this competition, while depriving the competing governments of revenue, had little effect on the overall rate of direct foreign investment or even on each country's share. As Helen put it again recently, 'direct foreign investment flowed into the economy of [Singapore] to take advantage of its low costs, excellent infrastructure and macroeconomic stability. The absence of tax holidays and other incentives was no deterrent' (Hughes 1993). She was not the only one to say this. But her book and contribution to the 1972 PAFTAD (Pacific Trade and Development Conference Series) volume on direct foreign investment helped spread the message and its policy implications.

Export-oriented industrialisation
By the time the Hughes–You book appeared, Helen had moved to the World Bank, initially as senior economist in the Industry Division. She began working with Béla Balassa and, after initially feeling compelled to reprimand him for his 'free trade prejudices' (Hughes 1968–71), found collaboration with him fun and soon joined him in the cause of export-oriented industrialisation. Increasing evidence that import-substitution had failed to promote development in Latin America, South Asia and elsewhere had begun to stimulate a shift of opinion towards outward-looking policies. While Little, Scitovsky and Scott were working on their seminal OECD (Organisation for Economic Cooperation and Development) study on *Industry and Trade in Some Developing Countries: a Comparative Study*, she got an opportunity to present the case persuasively as member of a team assembled by the Asian Development Bank to report on Southeast Asia's economy in the 1970s. She observed:

> The further pursuit of import-substituting industrialisation strategies will lead to more high costs and balance of payment difficulties. In the Philippines, industrial growth has already slowed down in the 1960s, and in Malaysia

and Thailand ... industrial growth is in danger of slowing down in the 1970s, because the relatively easy import-substitution possibilities have been exhausted. An alternative, outward-looking industrialisation strategy, already adopted with remarkable success in Singapore, entails a difficult and painful adjustment of policies (Hughes 1971).

Hla Myint, in his overall report in the same volume, endorsed her recommendation that 'the Asian countries should move away from import-substitution' (Myint 1971:19).

Again, Helen Hughes was not the first to put this view and it would probably have prevailed without her help. But her tireless support for outward-looking policies, inside the World Bank and on many other platforms for a quarter of a century has undoubtedly been influential in Southeast Asia and other parts of the Third World (not least in Australia).

Efficient capital utilisation

From 1969 until 1983, as she rose in the World Bank from Chief Economist to Division Chief in the Industry Division, to Deputy Director and then Director of the Economic Analysis Department, collaborating and occasionally sparring with Hollis Chenery, sometimes writing something that caught McNamara's fancy (Hughes 1968–71), she travelled incessantly, on missions to Brazil, Indonesia, Iran, Thailand, Cambodia, the Philippines, and Papua New Guinea, as well as to conferences all over the world. Each mission brought new insights, sparked new ideas. One idea which germinated around 1970, not unrelated to the new emphasis on the export of labour-intensive manufactures, was the widespread waste of capital in developing economies through inefficient utilisation.

Partly because the early postwar literature emphasised capital accumulation as the chief determinant of economic growth, industrial development policies in the 1950s and 1960s had a strong capital-intensive bias. Investment incentives, low interest rates, exemption of capital goods from tariffs, as well as an ideological preference for heavy industry, all contributed to this bias. Underutilisation of capital through single-shift working and other limitations on hours worked not only wasted capital but also restricted employment opportunities for labour. Plant layout and other managerial aspects of 'X-efficiency' further detracted from the intensity of capital utilisation.

In early 1972, Helen Hughes organised a conference on this subject. The report on the resulting research project, which collected data on capital utilisation in manufacturing in four countries in 1972/73, did not finally see the light of day until 1981 (Bautista et al. 1983), but in the meantime the attention that had been drawn to this aspect of industrialisation had made a considerable impact on policy, both in the World Bank and in individual developing countries.

The key to success in good domestic policies
During the 1960s the development debate was increasingly dominated by social objectives—employment, basic needs, growth with equity—and in the 1970s by the Non-Aligned Movement's campaign for a New International Economic Order. Helen Hughes, inside and outside the Bank, threw her weight behind the neoclassical view that the key to success was good domestic policies. Certainly, poverty alleviation and greater equality of opportunity are desirable, but both depend on rapid and sustained economic growth. 'Only countries that grow rapidly have the means to redistribute income' (Hughes 1985:5). Since all developing countries face the same international economic order, why were most of the countries of East Asia doing so much better than those of Latin America, Africa and South Asia?

The explanation is obviously not natural resource endowment: some of the most rapidly growing countries were least well endowed with natural resources. 'Cultural characteristics are also poor indicators of growth capacity' (Hughes 1985:14). The Confucian culture, which some were giving the credit for East Asian success, had been blamed for China's stagnation in the nineteenth century. Nor does the political system appear to be decisive. 'Some democratic and some autocratic countries are development-oriented. But many are not ... Governments have an essential role to play in establishing social and political cohesiveness and the rule of law' (Hughes 1985). But the key economic policies are monetary, financial and associated exchange rate policies which set the parameters; trade policies which largely determine the efficiency and competitiveness of domestic industries; fiscal policies which determine the resources available for physical and social infrastructure; and manpower policies which determine the real cost of labour.

This summary is taken from Helen Hughes' 1985 paper for the Group of Thirty, but the paper merely restated the sermon she had preached for a decade and more. It inspired much of her academic writing and promotion during the 1980s, about *Achieving Industrialisation in East Asia* (Hughes 1988a), about 'Explaining the differences between the growth of developing countries in Asia and Latin America in the 1980s' (Hughes 1988b) and, more generally, about 'Development policies and development performance' (Hughes 1993b).

Fighting export pessimism

In 1983 Helen Hughes returned to Canberra as Director of the ANU Centre which she soon elevated into the National Centre for Development Studies. The highlights of the decade since then have been academic entrepreneurship and influential reports for the Australian government rather than studies in development economics. However, she has continued to expound her views, with one new twist which deserves to be listed as a contribution. This is her denunciation of 'export pessimism'—the notion that export-oriented industrial development is bound to fail sooner or later because markets for labour-intensive manufactures are limited and increasingly constrained by protectionist policies in the industrial countries.

She has argued vigorously that this pessimism flies in the face of the empirical evidence and ignores the dynamics of world trade. The East Asian developing countries have steadily and rapidly increased their exports of manufactures to the United States and Japan and, more particularly, to one another in the form of burgeoning intra-industry trade. In 1989 she organised a conference on the dangers of export pessimism, the proceedings of which she edited (Hughes 1992). She stated the thesis in her introduction:

> Export pessimism—the belief that exports from developing countries cannot successfully penetrate the industrial market economies of the developed nations—has undermined the export performance of many developing countries. It has been proved wrong in practice by rapidly growing developing countries. Yet many developing countries continue to take a pessimistic view of their export potential, only half-heartedly liberalising their trade policies. Export pessimism thus becomes a self-fulfilling prophecy ... Despite the increase in the number of

countries opting for export-orientation and despite the diversification of their export products, the countries of destination have proved flexible enough to adjust their economic structures to growing competitiveness. The export pessimists continue to be, as they always have been, the losers (Hughes 1992:1, 8).

H.W. Arndt, Canberra

Editorial Preface

A little over three decades ago the world began to notice that something unusual was happening in Japan. Japan had shared strong economic growth with a number of European countries in the process of reconstruction in the early postwar period. But whereas growth had eased elsewhere, it was continuing unabated in Japan. Observers in the West began to talk about a 'Japanese Miracle'.

Since then, 'economic miracles' have become commonplace in East Asia. Taiwan and Hong Kong began their period of rapid growth at about the same time as Japan—a little awkwardly in Taiwan until it groped its way to the export-oriented strategies that were to sustain strong growth of the 1960s, 1970s and 1980s. Korea joined the process with its adoption of more internationally open policies from the early 1960s. Others were to follow later.

Gradually, it became widely recognised that there was nothing miraculous at all about sustained rapid growth in poor countries such as China, Singapore, Indonesia and Korea. Many countries are capable of it, if they adopt export-oriented policies, supported by sound policies in other areas. However, there may be economic, political and social preconditions that exclude this possibility in some countries through some periods in their histories; that is an important matter for speculation and research.

Heinz Arndt (in the Dedication) has identified Professor Helen Hughes as the first person to recognise the phenomenon of export-oriented growth, and to profess its value as a growth strategy. At the time, Helen was working in the Economics Department of the Research School of Pacific Studies at The Australian National University. Her subsequent career at the World Bank and then as the founding Executive Director of the

National Centre for Development Studies, gave her plenty of scope for encouraging research and proselytising on the character and virtues of export-oriented growth.

These essays, by Helen Hughes' colleagues and friends from various stages of her career, are about the model of export-oriented growth that emerged in East Asia in the third quarter of the twentieth century, and its sustainability in its home region and beyond.

The collection begins with an essay by Anne Krueger, on the way that the experience of export-oriented growth in East Asia and elsewhere has forced modification of our ideas and development. Open trade influenced growth in the directions anticipated by the old theory, but much more powerfully. The reasons include the competitive disciplines that outward-oriented strategies apply to domestic enterprises, institutions and policies.

Enzo Grilli and Jim Riedel ask how widely we can expect the East Asian growth model to apply. What are its preconditions, and where, outside East Asia, can we expect them to be met? With some qualifications, they conclude that there are reasonable contemporary prospects in, at least, South Asia, Latin America, Eastern Europe and parts of North Africa.

Richard Snape in Chapter 3 traces the development of ideas about the role of trade in development, and their absorption (in varying degrees) into the policies and practices of the international agencies with relevant responsibilities. The special role of the World Bank as an agent of communication of policy ideas is identified and discussed.

Chia Siow Yue in Chapter 4 looks across the East Asian experience—including that of the newcomers in Southeast Asia—and seeks to draw some general conclusions about the role of government in the success of export-oriented growth in East Asia. Some aspects of government's role stand out as necessary conditions: macroeconomic policies that deliver stability in reasonable degree; provision of a range of public goods that are essential for development. 'Industry policy' interventions to influence private resource allocation have been extensive—more so in some successful countries than others—but there is no consensus on whether they have helped or hindered development.

Isaiah Frank in Chapter 5 examines the remarkable phenomenon of globalisation of production that has emerged over the recent past, alongside the consolidation and extension of export-oriented growth in East Asia. It has been associated with rapid expansion of direct foreign investment—faster than international trade—and growth in services. The pay-offs to open policies (and the penalties for inward-looking policies) have increased. It has become necessary to extend the rules governing international trade to new areas. The Uruguay Round is a start, but there is an important agenda of outstanding issues. The difficulties of managing negotiations on this agenda on a global basis have contributed to the factors driving recent interest in regional economic groups.

Ross Garnaut and Peter Drysdale (Chapter 6) discuss the ideas about regionalism that have emerged around East Asian trade expansion in the period of rapid growth. There has been a substantial increase in the proportion of East Asian trade that is intra-regional. This reflects the operation of market forces and the expansion of trade opportunities that have accompanied economic growth, rather than any discrimination in official policy. Ideas about regionalism that have emerged in East Asia and the Western Pacific emphasise cooperation to reduce transaction costs of international commerce and reduction in tariff barriers on a non-discriminatory basis, and not regional discrimination along the lines of a free trade area. There is now a challenge to the traditional support for the region's unconditional most-favoured-nation status arising out of the increasing interest in free trade areas in the United States, as reflected in the North America Free Trade Agreement. These ideas are intruding into the discussions of Asia Pacific Economic Cooperation (APEC), through the participation of North America, alongside Western Pacific economies. This is potentially damaging to the sustenance and expansion of East-Asian-style growth.

E.S. Leung (Chapter 7) focuses on the important role of the exchange rate and exchange control regimes in East-Asian-style export-oriented growth. Flexible and open exchange regimes have become more important with increasing international capital markets. Sound exchange rate policies support open trade policies and require disciplined fiscal and monetary policies.

Nancy Viviani (Chapter 8) examines the role of development assistance in development. It is now of great importance only for relatively poor and small economies, such as Australia's neighbours in the Southwest Pacific. In these, donors typically balance development against trade, political and other objectives. The value of the aid for growth and development depends on where the balance is struck.

Philippa Dee and Christopher Findlay (Chapter 9) discuss the relationship between population growth and export-oriented growth. There is no reason to think that rapid population growth will reduce the prospects for export-oriented growth, so long as other preconditions and the appropriate policy settings are in place. Neither are there likely to be limits in the export markets that are available to developing countries embarking on export-oriented growth, especially because rapid growth in other countries expands opportunities for any single country.

Yongzheng Yang (Chapter 10) focuses more narrowly on the sustainability of rapid export growth in the largest of the East Asian developing countries: China. There is no evidence that limits on the size of the external markets will block export-oriented growth in China. Further domestic reform is necessary to sustain rapid growth.

The instability and secular deterioration of export markets has raised questions about the sustainability of export-oriented growth in countries whose comparative advantage lies in primary commodities. Ron Duncan (Chapter 11) shows that the severity of problems of instability depends a great deal on domestic policy responses. The use of modern price risk management mechanisms can reduce further the cost of primary commodity price instability in countries with open foreign exchange regimes.

Kym Anderson (Chapter 12) examines the intriguing question of why countries with comparative advantage in agricultural industries have grown relatively slowly. Part of the problem is that insulation of agriculture from world markets in industrial and developing economies alike has increased the instability and reduced the relative level of agricultural prices. These influences are likely to be less important in the future.

David Robertson (Chapter 13) examines environmental limits to growth. He concludes that whatever the limits imposed by environmental deterioration itself, the means of addressing environmental problems that are favoured by political activists and the international community of developed countries are likely to impose important costs and constraints.

The essays are meant to illuminate and illustrate issues that arise in relation to the sustainability of export-oriented growth. They are not meant to cover the whole field, and room has been left for others to follow. Some of the essays contain strong assertions of views for which Helen Hughes herself was well known. That is what the reader should expect from close associates of Helen, to whom the volume is dedicated.

The editors owe a huge debt to Maree Tait, for organising the Festschrift Conference from which the book emerged, for anchoring communications between authors and editors scattered across the earth, and for much highly professional work on the manuscript. We are also very grateful to Lou Will for finalising this book. Our thanks go also to the Australian International Development Assistance Bureau for its financial and other support of this undertaking.

Finally, our thanks to Helen, for lots of stimulation over many years, and for agreeing that colleagues and friends should know her in this way.

Ross Garnaut, Canberra
Enzo Grilli, Washington, D.C.
Jim Riedel, Washington, D.C.

I

The Role of Trade in Growth and Development: Theory and Lessons from Experience

ANNE O. KRUEGER

At the end of the Second World War, the governments of a large number of poor economies declared rapid economic growth and rising standards of living to be a major, if not the predominant, policy objective. Some of those economies, such as Korea and India, were newly independent after years of colonial rule. Some had long been sovereign states, but low living standards distinguished them from the industrialised economies although their political objectives were similar.[1]

Most political leaders and economists rapidly came to differentiate between developed and developing economies. Economics as a discipline had a number of precepts which were fairly widely accepted. Among the most widely accepted was that of comparative advantage: if each country's resources were allocated to the goods which that country could produce relatively cheaply, living standards in each country would be higher than if each country took measures to produce all goods domestically. And, although the Great Depression and the advent of Keynesian economics had introduced the idea that a legitimate function of government was to maintain full employment and macroeconomic stability, economic theory nonetheless suggested that microeconomic interventions in the absence of market failure would not improve welfare.

The reaction of most development economists and policy-makers, when confronted with the political mandate to achieve rapid growth in output and living standards and by these precepts of economics, was to conclude that developing economies' economics were 'different', and that, therefore, the economics of development was different from the economics of industrialised economies.

Several ideas were central to this conclusion. On the one hand, there was a widespread belief that there were 'structural' rigidities in developing economies. That, in turn, was taken to mean that responses to price signals were very slow and weak, if indeed they occurred at all. That conclusion was buttressed by experience in the Great Depression and a deep-seated suspicion of markets and their functioning, especially in ex-colonial economies where it was widely believed that colonialism had served to 'exploit' the resources of the country to enrich those in the imperial country.

For those believing that markets did not function effectively in developing economies, a natural conclusion was that government intervention would be necessary to achieve desired growth goals.[2] Policymakers therefore supported the establishment of state-owned enterprises, including manufacturing ventures and financial services provision, historically undertaken by private groups in industrialised economies. There was frequent use of direct controls over private economic activity, and little reliance on incentives and markets to achieve desired economic objectives.

Nowhere was this set of views more evident than with respect to trade and exchange rate policy in developing economies. Almost all developing economies at that time had very similar economic structures, with a very high percentage of their GDP originating from, and their labour force engaged in, agriculture. They were heavily reliant on exports of primary commodities and imported most of their manufactures, as few were produced domestically.

As Bates (1983) explains so well, it was almost universally concluded that rapid industrialisation was synonymous with rapid growth. Equally, it was thought that the only way to achieve rapid industrialisation was to protect fledgling domestic industries against foreign competition. It seemed evident to those in developing economies that their newly established industries would be unable to compete on world markets.[3] In addition, it was anticipated that establishment of new industries would require imports of machinery and equipment, while there was general pessimism about the prospects for growth of export earnings from primary commodities. It was concluded that import substitution would be necessary in order to free foreign exchange from some traditional uses, such as imports of consumer goods, to enable purchases of capital equipment, intermediate goods and raw materials to support industrialisation.

To the arguments of economists who pointed out the principles of comparative advantage, development economists advocating import substitution had several rebuttals. They noted, *inter alia*, that the notion of comparative advantage was static, concerned with maximising real incomes at each point in time, and did not focus on the dynamic aspects of the ways in which comparative advantage might change with growth. It also seems to have been implicitly assumed that developing economies would remain specialised in primary commodity production in the absence of intervention to promote import substitution. This assumption was also flawed: it is inevitable that rising productivity in agriculture and additional investment will generate resources for development of non-primary industry. The question is the allocation of new resources among new industries. They also reiterated the view that primary commodity prices would decline secularly, and that, therefore, comparative advantage had to shift. This argument is theoretically flawed. If all market participants anticipate the future path of the terms of trade, private investors will appropriately invest without additional incentives.

Regardless of the intellectual merits of the case for comparative advantage or the case for import substitution, the views which prevailed were of those advocating automatic protection for new industries, government establishment of state-owned enterprises to manufacture industrial goods previously imported, and other means of inducing industrialisation outside normal market mechanisms. In fact, the automatic protection and other government measures for import-substitution production constituted a highly powerful incentive for private producers. For later reference, the real difficulty was that these incentives were certainly not uniform and across-the-board, i.e. awarding approximately the same returns for activities which utilised equal resources in earning or saving foreign exchange. Instead, the system quickly evolved into one with very high variation in the domestic resources employed per unit of foreign exchange in different activities.

During the 1950s, virtually all developing economies whose governments formulated development policies began utilising exchange controls in order to regulate their payments regimes. The stated motive was to maintain the exchange rate at a level that made capital goods imports 'cheap'. It was not recognised that cheapness implied excess demand and therefore rationing.

With rationing of scarce foreign exchange, some investment projects were highly subsidised and both investment and foreign exchange were then misallocated. Simultaneously, these economies adopted measures to encourage investment in new, import-substitution industries. Quickly, however, inflationary pressures began to erode the real exchange rate, resulting in unanticipated shortfalls in foreign exchange earnings, as producers of traditional exports responded to appreciated real exchange rates.[4] The shortfall in foreign exchange earnings, combined with pressures to increase investment (and therefore imports of machinery and equipment) rapidly created considerable excess demand for foreign exchange. Import licensing measures therefore became more stringent and were, themselves, a major factor in inducing domestic investment in import-competing activities. What had started as a drive towards industrialisation through selective import substitution rapidly evolved into indiscriminate high-cost protection for any and all new products produced domestically.

From the mid-1950s, however, some economies in East Asia began following a different development strategy. Among the components of that strategy, as is now well known, was a reliance upon the international market for industrialisation through exporting. The subsequent experience of those economies, and others adopting the outward oriented strategy, contrasts sharply with the experience of economies which have maintained import-substitution policies.

Interestingly, the lessons are both pragmatic and theoretical. They provide a deeper understanding of the role of trade than does the traditional comparative advantage dictum, although they simultaneously reinforce the policy prescriptions emanating from that dictum.

In the remainder of this discussion, the focus is on those lessons. The experience of the East Asian economies after they abandoned import substitution and adopted outward-oriented trade strategies is reviewed briefly. The current theoretical understanding of the direct role of trade in growth, as learned through the contrasting experience of economies adopting import substitution and those adopting outward orientation, is then considered. The discussion concludes with a sketch of current understanding of the relationship between alternative trade policies and forms of government intervention.

East Asian growth[5]

By now, the salient characteristics of East Asian growth have received so much attention that a very brief review will suffice. In broad terms, Korea, Singapore, Taiwan and Hong Kong have all experienced sustained rates of economic growth well in excess of those earlier thought attainable. In the 1960s, Chenery and others developed the 'two-gap' model of developing economies' growth, in which either the rate of savings or the availability of foreign exchange was thought to be the binding constraint on overall growth. As they developed that model, Chenery and Strout (1966) assumed there was a third constraint, which they described as the maximum attainable rate of growth, and suggested that the number was between 6 and 8 per cent. All East Asian economies exceeded that rate for extended periods of time, with Taiwan and Korea each achieving periods of a decade or longer with rates in excess of 10 per cent.

Each East Asian economy started from a relatively low per capita income; each adopted policies which resulted in rapid growth of exports; each had fairly conservative monetary and fiscal policies; each government provided infrastructure consistent with rapid growth; the educational attainments of the labour force rose rapidly; there was a rapid shift of the labour force from agricultural to industrial employment; and once rapid growth began, savings and investment rates rose. All were, and are, regarded as resource-poor economies, although Taiwan and Korea were net exporters of primary commodities in the 1950s.

For present purposes, it suffices to start with an overview of the economic growth experience and structure of these economies, and then to discuss some of the aspects of their recent economic history that have provided lessons for the analysis of the role of trade in growth.

Comparative growth and structures

Data on comparative growth rates and per capita gross domestic product (GDP) over the 1965–90 period are provided in Table 1.1. All four East Asian economies have grown exceptionally rapidly by world standards. Middle-income economies

Table 1.1: Economic growth of East Asian newly industrialised economies

	GDP per capita (1990 US dollars)		Average annual rate of growth of per capita income
	1965	1991	1965–90
Hong Kong	2,544	13,430	6.2
Korea	970	6,330	7.1
Singapore	2,312	14,210	6.5
Taiwan	995	8,800	8.1
All middle-income	1,353	2,220	2.2

Note: 1976 (data were converted to 1990 prices by using the IMF Index of Dollar Export Unit Values) from the International Monetary Fund, *International Financial Statistics.*
Sources: For Hong Kong, Korea and Singapore: World Bank, *World Development Report 1992*, Oxford University Press, New York, 1992 and *World Bank News*, 29 April 1993, for 1991 data. For Taiwan, 1965 per capita income data were derived from: International Monetary Fund, *International Financial Statistics*, May 1976, IMF, Washington, D.C. 1991 per capita income for Taiwan is in current dollars from: *Economist*, Survey, 19 October, 1992:5.

as a group are estimated by the World Bank to have experienced per capita income growth of 2.2 per cent over the same period, while other Organisation for Economic Cooperation and Development (OECD) economies grew at 2.4 per cent, compared with more than 6 per cent in each of the newly industrialised economies.

Data on rates of growth of GDP and exports in each country are presented in Table 1.2. In general, the rate of growth of exports exceeded that of GDP for each country and in each time period. The exceptions were Hong Kong in the period right after the oil price increase of 1973 and between 1953 and 1962, and Singapore in the 1963–72 period. Data on the share of exports in each country's GDP for selected years over the 1953–90 period again reflect the growing importance of trade as growth took place (Table 1.3). Exports can exceed 100 per cent of GDP because GDP is a value added concept and exports are measured in value of output. In Singapore's case, there is very large *entrepôt* trade and, in addition, oil refining is a large industry as petroleum is imported and re-exported in various refined forms. In Hong Kong's case, the rapid growth in exports in the 1980s reflects the rapid increase in imports from the

Table 1.2: Growth of real GDP and exports by country, 1953–91

	1953–62	1963–72	1973–80	1981–91
Hong Kong				
GDP	12.8[a]	11.7	10.1	6.7
Exports	6.9[a]	14.0	9.8	13.6
Korea				
GDP	3.9[a]	9.1	8.3	9.3
Exports	16.1	30.3	17.6	11.6
Singapore				
GDP	..	10.3	8.1	7.1
Exports	0.3	6.1	29.1	9.5
Taiwan				
GDP	7.3	11.0	8.4	7.8
Exports	17.9	27.7	22.6	9.3

[a] average nominal change without 1952–53.
Sources: For Hong Kong: United Nations, *Yearbook of National Accounts Statistics*, various years, United Nations, New York. For Korea and Singapore, IFS CD-Rom.IMF. For Taiwan, data kindly provided by Dr J. Chou and Dr T.-S. Yu of Chung-Hua Institution for Economic Research.

People's Republic of China for re-export. Singapore did not separate from Malaysia until 1965, biasing Singaporean statistics for the 1963–72 period.

As rapid growth of exports (and the policies under which it took place) is a central feature of the East Asian economies, it is worthwhile to examine this phenomenon more closely. Inspection of the growth of Korean exports will suffice (Table 1.4).

The dramatic increase in exports shows up even more clearly when the very small base from which they began is taken into account. From US$33 million in 1960, Korean exports grew by more than 20-fold to US$882 million in 1970, and then grew almost 20-fold over the following decade, reaching US$17 billion in 1980. Growth tapered off still more over the 1980s, with exports 'only' increasing by a factor of 3.8. It should be noted that imports also rose dramatically, although the size of Korea's trade deficit as a proportion of GDP fell sharply over time. Nonetheless, imports as a percentage of GDP rose from around 10 per cent in the mid-1950s to over 30 per cent by the late 1980s (Table 1.3).

Table 1.3: Share of exports and imports in GDP, (per cent)

	1953	1963	1973	1980	1990
Hong Kong					
Exports	109.13	67.14	89.26	95.71	135.15
Imports	154.61	99.74	85.53	100.61	129.72
Korea					
Exports	2.11	4.76	29.13	34.03	30.96
Imports	9.92	15.91	32.12	41.47	31.52
Singapore					
Exports	..	124.55	87.28	165.21	149.52
Imports	..	153.41	122.62	204.67	172.81
Taiwan					
Exports	8.64	15.22	41.60	47.76	42.70
Imports	12.00	16.60	35.35	47.71	34.86

Sources: For Hong Kong: United Nations, *Yearbook of National Accounts Statistics,* various years; United Nations, New York, and *Economic Survey of Asia and the Far East 1954,* for 1953; and United Nations, *Economic Survey of Asia and the Far East 1964,* United Nations, New York, for 1963. For Korea and Singapore, IFS CD-Rom.IMF. For Taiwan, data were kindly provided by Dr J. Chou and Dr T.-S. Yu of the Chung-Hua Institution for Economic Research.

Phenomenal growth was, of course, accompanied by a major change in the economic structure of each country. Not only did the importance of trade increase markedly as a share of GDP but the relative importance of urban activities increased greatly in Korea and Taiwan, while that of the rural areas diminished. Over the 1965–90 period, agriculture's share of GDP fell from 38 to 9 per cent in Korea, and 24 to 4 per cent in Taiwan. As Hong Kong and Singapore were city-states, there was little agriculture at the beginning of the period. Some analysts have contended that the absence of a rural sector provided a major advantage for Hong Kong and Singapore. It is true that the growth of agricultural output was slower than that of industrial output in the other two East Asian economies (in Korea, agricultural output grew at an average annual rate of just under 3 per cent over the 1965–90 period, while industrial production grew at an average annual rate in excess of 14 per cent). Over the same period, manufacturing as a percentage of GDP rose from 25 to 45 per cent in Korea, 22 to 24 per cent in Taiwan

Table 1.4: Evolution of Korean exports and imports, 1960–90 (US$m)

	Exports	Imports
1960	33	306
1965	175	416
1970	882	1,804
1975	5,003	6,674
1980	17,214	21,598
1985	26,442	26,461
1990	63,123	65,127

Note: Both exports and imports are reported f.o.b and are from balance of payments data. Exports and imports cover both goods and non-factor services. Shares of GNP were calculated from the national income accounts.
Source: International Monetary Fund, 1990 and 1991, *International Financial Statistics Yearbook*, IMF, Washington, D.C.

and 24 to 37 per cent in Singapore, but fell from 40 to 26 per cent in Hong Kong.

In all economies, savings and investment rose as a percentage of GDP, at least until the 1980s (Table 1.5). The most dramatic increases were in the poorest economies. Taiwan and Singapore financed rates of investment above those of savings by relying heavily on private foreign investment. Korea relied more on borrowing, first from official sources in the early 1960s, and then increasingly from private commercial banks.

Evolution of economic policies in East Asian economies

As with any description of the overall features and growth experience of East Asian economies, any account of economic policies encounters both similarities and key differences. Economic histories for these economies are significantly different, and provide important clues as to the interpretation of growth experiences.

The Korean experience is the best documented among the East Asian developing economies (Cole and Lyman 1971; Frank, Kim and Westphal 1975; Kim 1991; Krueger 1980a; Mason et al. 1980). The period prior to 1960 had been one of political and economic shocks, accompanied by fairly chaotic policies, including import substitution, multiple exchange rates, and inflation rates that were among the world's highest at that time. As an accompaniment to those policies, economic growth

Table 1.5: Savings, investment and the current account balance in GDP, 1953–90 (percentage)

	1953	1963	1973	1980	1990
Hong Kong					
Savings	..	..	..	..	..
Investment	..	..	20.61	30.61	28.53
Current account balance	..	..	..	..	..
Korea					
Savings	..	..	16.44	15.08	..
Investment	15.61	18.23	25.50	31.73	36.95
Current account balance	−3.23	−3.72	−2.25	−9.23	−0.90
Singapore					
Savings	..	..	27.11	30.46	..
Investment	..	17.46	39.20	46.34	39.13
Current account balance	..	−11.85	−15.25	−16.63	8.46
Taiwan					
Savings	14.46	19.06	34.36	32.23	29.88
Investment	14.04	18.28	29.09	33.80	22.40
Current account balance	0.40	0.78	5.28	−1.56	7.47

Sources: For Hong Kong: United Nations, *Yearbook of National Accounts Statistics*, various years, United Nations, New York; United Nations, *Economic Survey of Asia and the Far East 1954*, United Nations, New York, for 1953; and United Nations, *Economic Survey of Asia and the Far East 1964*, United Nations, New York, for 1963. For Korea: 1973 savings from United Nations, *Yearbook of National Accounts Statistics*, 1974, Vol. 3, United Nations, New York; 1980 from *1986 Korea Statistical Yearbook*; others from IFS CD-Rom.IMF. For Singapore: savings from United Nations, *Yearbook of National Accounts Statistics*, various years, United Nations, New York; others from IFS CD-Rom.IMF. For Taiwan: data were kindly provided by Dr J. Chou and Dr T.-S. Yu of the Chung-Hua Institution for Economic Research.

rates after 1953 (the year the Korean War ended) averaged only 3 to 4 per cent annually, very low for a country with possibilities for reconstruction.

In 1960, South Korea was among the poorest economies in Asia. With few natural resources and the highest ratio of people to arable land of any country in the world, outside the city-states, there seemed little prospect for economic growth. Indeed, the domestic savings rate was close to zero, and only large inflows of US foreign aid had permitted some investment. The current account deficit, financed by foreign aid, equalled around 10 per cent of GDP in each year from 1954 to 1959, with exports fluctuating at around 3 per cent of GDP annually.

It is noteworthy that Korean economic policies were typical of many developing economies at that time; if anything, they were slightly worse than most. Between 1958 and 1963, however, policies changed markedly. The government undertook a series of policy reforms. Incentives for exporting were greatly increased both through a change in the nominal exchange rate greater than that in prices and through the creation of export subsidies and incentives (which applied to all commodities which were exported) to offset the bias toward import-competing industries inherent in the trade regime.[6] Quantitative controls on imports were significantly relaxed (and then dismantled further in discrete steps over the next 30 years), with exporters able to import needed inputs without significant restriction. In the early 1970s the Korean authorities began protecting domestic agriculture. The rate of protection rose and, by the 1980s, was high by any standard. This set of policies was not adopted in order to promote economic growth, and was probably detrimental to it. For the purposes of the present discussion, however, policies towards the agricultural sector have little relevance and are not further discussed here.

Budgetary reforms resulted in much smaller fiscal deficits starting in the mid-1960s, and inflation fell from its earlier levels to an average of around 10 per cent in the late 1960s.

These and other reforms have been thoroughly analysed elsewhere, as have their consequences (Mason et al. 1980). As already noted, savings and investment rates rose markedly, the current account became positive for a period in the late 1980s and rapid growth continued.

For present purposes, there are two key points. First, all analysts agree that the change in policies was a key variable in permitting the rapid rate of growth that Korea experienced over the next three decades. Second, and equally important, opening up the trade regime played a key role in that transformation. If one were permitted to name only one characteristic of South Korea's rapid growth from 1960 to the present, it would have to be the phenomenal growth of exports.

In most regards, Taiwan's economic growth has been similar to Korea's, and more rapid (Table 1.2). Taiwan's economic circumstances in the late 1940s were as unpromising as Korea's appeared to be a decade later, although Taiwan's endowment of agricultural resources per capita was greater than Korea's. Both governments had significant security concerns, receiving sizeable American support but also devoting considerable national resources to defence expenditures.

Policy reforms in Taiwan began in the early 1950s, and rapid growth started half a decade earlier than in Korea. Again, a realistic exchange rate and an outward-oriented trade regime were hallmarks of economic policy, and export growth was a key feature of Taiwan's spectacular performance (Table 1.2). Taiwan's rapid export growth began by the mid-1950s, as liberalisation of the trade regime and other markets proceeded.

Much less attention has been paid to Hong Kong and Singapore because most observers believe that their status as city-states somehow renders their experience less relevant for other developing economies. For present purposes, suffice it to note that Hong Kong remained a British colony and grew quickly, despite rapid immigration from the People's Republic of China, under a *laissez-faire* regime. Singapore's growth was equally dramatic, with reliance upon export-led growth starting in 1965 after an earlier period where the focus was on import substitution. As with Korea, Taiwan and Hong Kong, export earnings grew rapidly, and there was little doubt that Singaporean growth was 'outward-oriented', along with the other three Asian newly industrialised economies. Young (1992) has carried out an analysis of the comparative growth of Hong Kong and Singapore. He found that much of Hong Kong's growth (like that of Korea and Taiwan) was accounted for by increases in total factor productivity. In Singapore, by contrast, most of the growth is explicable by rapid accumulation of factors of production. In that regard, Singapore's rapid growth appears to be less sustainable than that of Hong Kong or the other newly industrialised economies, unless structural changes occur.

Trade and payments regimes

Common to all East Asian policy regimes was the commitment to integration with the world economy and, subsequently, to facilitating exports. Although a variety of policy measures (preferential access to rationed credit, tax breaks, etc.) were designed to stimulate export growth, especially in the early years as the policy reforms were started, incentives were almost entirely uniform and across-the-board, in the sense that they applied to any would-be exporter. The hallmark of trade policy, therefore, was a lack of discrimination among export activities. Policymakers in each country seem to have been committed to increasing exports, with little regard for the nature of the commodity or service to be exported.

Moreover, as exports grew in importance in each of the East Asian economies, policymakers increasingly found that it was costly to rely on tax credits, credit rationing, or export subsidies, and there was a tendency to place increasing reliance on a uniform realistic exchange rate as the principal means of encouraging exports. In the Japanese case, Corden once described the strategy as being one of 'export promotion' through 'exchange rate protection' (Corden 1985), which meant the maintenance of an 'undervalued' exchange rate. The term might apply as well to the East Asian newly industrialised economies.[7]

Outward-oriented trade policies were, of necessity, accompanied by exchange rate regimes which provided exporters reasonable assurance that the real value of their export earnings, relative to domestic costs, would not be affected by the vagaries of exchange rate policy. In Korea, as has already been seen, this policy was effected in the early years by adjusting tax credits, interest subsidies and export subsidies, but increasingly the exchange rate came to be used for this purpose. In Singapore and Hong Kong, a unified exchange rate was used throughout the period under study. Taiwan by the early 1960s had achieved a unified and realistic exchange rate (Kuo 1983).

On the import side, there was more variability. Hong Kong, of course, always maintained a free trade regime. Singapore, too, rapidly achieved very low tariffs on all imports. At the opposite end of the spectrum was Korea, which began the export-oriented drive with a highly restrictive import regime. Starting as early as 1960, however, mechanisms were established so that exporters could import duty-free intermediate goods and other commodities and services used in the production of exportables (Krueger 1980a). Thereafter, the import regime was liberalised: quantitative restrictions were liberalised, and then abandoned except on luxury goods imports where there was no competing domestic industry, and tariff rates fell over time (Kim 1991). Because exports were growing rapidly, the East Asian newly industrialised economies were deemed creditworthy on international capital markets and, as already noted, inflows of capital supplemented domestic savings to permit very high rates of investment. Liberalisation of capital account transactions also took place in all the East Asian economies except Hong Kong (which never had any restrictions), although at varying paces. In general, inward capital flows were liberalised earlier and more completely than outward flows. Korea tended to discourage direct foreign investment, while Singapore explicitly encouraged direct foreign investment as a key component of its development strategy (Aw 1991).

The broad picture, then, is that all East Asian exporters had fairly uniform incentives for exporting across virtually all industries and activities. Although occasional episodes of intervention can be found (some of which proved to be major policy mistakes), the degree of intervention was small compared with that in inward-oriented developing economies.

As noteworthy as the uniformity of incentives for exporting is the trend towards greater liberalisation over time of both imports and capital flows. All the newly industrialised economies have liberalised imports over time, although the pace and extent of liberalisation varied. Capital controls were gradually relaxed on capital inflows, with positive inducements for those flows in some instances. In more recent years, those controls, too, have been liberalised. Except in Hong Kong, the process of liberalisation continues but is not yet complete.

Other policies

A detailed exploration of other East Asian policy regimes is well beyond the scope of this discussion. Briefly, the share of government expenditures was fairly small relative to most other developing economies. Government expenditures constituted less than 20 per cent of GDP in Hong Kong and Korea after 1980 (government expenditures as a percentage of GDP in Hong Kong were 6.6 per cent in 1980 and 7.9 per cent in 1990). Likewise, fiscal deficits were comparatively small during the rapid growth era: after 1960, none of the East Asian economies' governments incurred a fiscal deficit larger than 2 per cent of

GDP, and there were more surpluses than deficits. As a counterpart to this fairly conservative macroeconomic policy, inflation rates were well below those experienced in most developing economies and, by the mid-1980s, were also below those in industrialised economies.

All four economies are regarded as having had fairly egalitarian distributions of income over the years of rapid growth. The authorities seem to have paid considerably more attention to equity issues than have those in some other developing economies. Income distribution was, and remained during rapid growth, relatively more equal in Taiwan and Korea than in other countries at comparable stages of development (Kuznets 1988; World Bank 1993f). Except for Korea in the 1970s there is no evidence of increasingly unequal distribution of income and, indeed, real wages rose rapidly in all four economies. Over the two decades following 1970, real earnings per employee rose at average annual rates of over 8 per cent in Korea, 7.4 per cent in Taiwan, 4 per cent in Singapore and 5.5 per cent in Hong Kong.

Although the growth experience has been similar among the East Asian newly industrialising economies, there have been significant differences in other variables. Taiwanese firms tend to be small whereas Korean *chaebol* (conglomerates) are large. Hong Kong experienced rapid population growth through immigration whereas Korea, Singapore and Taiwan seem to have gone through a demographic transition to much slower population growth.

One final set of policies should be mentioned. They have to do with the composition of government expenditures and investments. Most East Asian economies have focused heavily on education, and on improving the quality of the labour force (Kuznets 1988). The rapid increase in the general level of workforce education, along with the flexibility of the labour markets, has clearly contributed to economic growth. All East Asian governments have invested in the provision of adequate infrastructure—telephone networks, mail services, port capacity, power provision, railroads and roads—to support rapid increases in manufactured output and exports. Most visitors in the 1960s and 1970s were impressed by the quality of infrastructure in Korea, Taiwan and Singapore relative to other developing economies.

Lessons for other economies' development efforts

Because the transition from controlled, inward-oriented economies to more liberal, outward-oriented economies was a continuing process, with changes in a large number of policy instruments, analysis of the precise composition and magnitude of 'essential' policy ingredients for success of the East Asian model is difficult. Questions as to how rapidly initial policy reforms must be undertaken in order for them to be viable cannot be definitively answered based on the East Asian experience. The comparative success of Poland, however, is giving additional credence to the proposition that 'faster is better'. Among other things, all East Asian economies were resource poor and had relatively low per capita incomes; whether their experience generalises at all to economies with different characteristics (significantly different factor endowments, or initially higher level of per capita income) is an open question. Nor can analysts assert with any conviction that there is, for example, a certain rate of inflation, a particular size of the fiscal deficit, or a specified maximum average rate of protection, above which rapid growth is impossible. There is, therefore, a great deal more to be learned both about the interrelationships between policy regimes, and the nature of policy reforms that provide the basis for rapid economic growth.

Nonetheless, the experience of the East Asian newly industrialised economies has demonstrated clearly that an outward-oriented trade strategy is not only viable, but essential for prospects for rapid growth. There are two groups of conclusions, or lessons. The first has to do with why an outward-orientation is so important, and how it contributes to growth. The second has to do with the 'supporting' policies that must be in place for a genuine outward-oriented trade strategy.

What does an outward orientation contribute to growth?

For developing economies, starting as they did with highly specialised rural production, trade policy decisions were also decisions as to the domestic allocation of resources. And, if resource allocation ever mattered, it did so in developing economies bent upon growth. It was the allocation of new resources that would affect the future structure of the economy.

Decisions to follow import substitution were decisions to allocate new resources to import-competing sectors, in the anticipation that additional output of import-competing goods would satisfy domestic demand sufficiently to release foreign exchange for other imports. Thus, consonant with the thinking outlined in the introduction, it was anticipated that rapid growth would entail sharply rising demand for capital goods which would be imported (and therefore call for foreign exchange availability). That demand would be met, it was thought, not so much by rising foreign exchange receipts as by falling demand for foreign exchange for other goods previously imported.

In any case, there were a number of problems with following this strategy. First, it should be noted that the strategy became more difficult to follow the longer it was pursued: 'easy' import-substitution opportunities were quickly undertaken. As new investment followed new investment, the remaining imports were more difficult and costly to replace with domestic substitutes.

Difficulties took several forms. First, for many imported commodities in all developing economies, volumes were very small. Establishing domestic production facilities often involved a scale of plant too small to utilise capital or labour efficiency when output was directed only towards the domestic market. That became even more true as import substitution progressed, as initial import-substitution activities were normally in mass consumption goods where volumes consumed domestically were larger.

Second, import substitution turned out to be import-intensive, with the result that the demand for foreign exchange for imports shifted upward more rapidly than foreign exchange was saved by import substitution. This led Diaz-Alejandro (1965) to discuss the 'import-intensity' of import substitution, in which he called attention to the fact that import-substitution industries seemed to be more import intensive than export industries. In addition, the incentives provided for import substitution (particularly including the maintenance of the nominal exchange rate to provide 'cheap' capital goods imports in the face of domestic inflation) proved to be more of a disincentive to exports than had been anticipated. In country after country, foreign exchange earnings rose more slowly than anticipated, resulting in the necessity for increasingly stringent import licensing. The disincentive effect for exports was so strong that developing economies as a group lost shares in world markets for their traditional exports. Whereas developing economies accounted for almost one-half of all primary commodity exports in world markets in the 1950s, that share had fallen to less than one-quarter by 1973. Stringent import licensing, in turn, increased exporters' costs, and further increased the attractiveness of import substitution. This gave rise to indiscriminate incentives for import substitution, regardless of cost. It also explained the so-called 'stop–go' cycles, in which policymakers found themselves unable to maintain rates of investment because of balance of payments difficulties. The general scenario was that growth slowed, imports were reduced, and a stabilisation program was undertaken, during which time economic activity was stagnant or only growing very slowly. Export earnings increased, permitting some increase in imports, and then growth to resume. Stop–go cycles themselves were costly in terms of economic performance.

But the perceived necessity for stringent import licensing, combined with the small size of domestic markets, had yet another set of effects on the domestic economies. That is, in most instances, one or a few factories could provide output for the entire domestic market. Usually, there came to be only one or two producers of a given product, and even then, their market share was often determined by the import licences each received for imports of the necessary raw materials and intermediate goods used in production.

Hence, many newly established import-substitution industries were facing incentives much more like those of a monopolist than those of a competitive firm. They had little incentive to cut costs or to improve quality, as their market share was assured. There was also no mechanism to weed out high-cost firms, or to increase the market share of low-cost firms. Usually, even those firms that might have exported under an alternative incentive structure found the domestic market too profitable (so that new investments were directed into still further lines of import substitution rather than expansion for export) and the returns from exporting too unattractive (because of the unrealistic nominal exchange rate and the high cost of domestic inputs and even of import-competing goods compared with those confronting their competitors on world markets). Moreover, poor quality or unreliable deliveries in some industries meant that industries using those goods as inputs were at a large competitive disadvantage and thus precluded from exporting.

Yet another widely observed consequence, which followed most efforts to control economic activity rather than to provide incentives, was the increased importance for individual firms' managers of contacts in government bureaucracies. Profits depended more on receiving the appropriate licences and permission than on efficient engineering and to inducing officials to react favourably to applications, with consequent losses in the efficiency with which new resources were employed.

The upshot, as is well known, was a gradual slowing in the rate of economic growth. While some economies attempted to offset this by borrowing more from abroad for a period of time, their ability to borrow eroded quickly in the debt crisis of the early 1980s. Either way, the lesson was learned that import substitution was not a strategy that could be maintained indefinitely.

But, at the same time, as negative lessons were being learned from import-substitution regimes, the experience of East Asian economies provided some positive lessons. The first, and perhaps the most important, was that the export pessimism that had provided one part of the intellectual underpinning for the import-substitution strategy was wrong. It was possible for developing economies to increase their exports at very rapid rates. To be sure, sceptics remain. Some have argued that Korea and Taiwan were 'lucky' in adopting their strategies during the boom years (for international trade) in the 1950s and 1960s, and that high rates of growth of exports are not possible today. The force of that argument, such as it was, is greatly diminished, both by the continued rapid growth of East Asian exports from a much larger base and by the entry of other economies whose policies have been reformed. The most dramatic case is Turkey, whose exports and export earnings grew at an average annual rate in excess of 20 per cent during the 1980s (with growth starting during the worldwide recession of the early 1980s).

Chile, Mexico, and a variety of other economies whose policies were changed also experienced greatly improved export performance.

Once it is recognised that exports can grow, then questions of resource allocation become central. Moreover, much of the growth of exports in East Asia took place in non-traditional items. Questions of allocation of new resources therefore had to focus on alternatives within new activities: the potential of exporting industries could not be overlooked.

A second important lesson, derivative from the first, was that while the comparative advantage argument was undoubtedly correct, the dynamic arguments also led to an outward orientation. Not only were the earlier advocates of import substitution mistaken when they claimed that there were dynamic reasons for ignoring comparative advantage, dynamic arguments reinforce comparative advantage arguments! Rates of total factor productivity growth (an important element of accelerated growth) have been much faster in economies with outward-oriented trade strategies than in economies with import substitution. The World Bank (World Bank 1993f) notes the rapid accumulation of factor inputs in East Asia, as rates of investment in both physical and human capital were high and rising. Total factor productivity growth rates, however, were also very high and account for about 3 percentage points of growth. In addition, of course, high rates of total factor productivity growth (and therefore growth of income) permitted rising rates of savings, and therefore of investment.

Reasons for more rapid total factor productivity growth may be several. They include:

- the ability of low-cost producers to increase their share, and expand beyond the scale, of the domestic market (this includes the ability of producers to concentrate their production in a few lines in which they are able to compete on world markets, rather than attempting to fabricate a broad array of products);
- the increasingly competitive environment, and the incentives provided by it for finding more efficient ways of combining inputs; and
- the more productive utilisation of newly accumulated resources and with it, the rapid shift of the labour force towards more productive employment.

In addition, there is at least a once-and-for-all increase in output per unit of input as firms increase their rate of capacity utilisation. This occurs both because import licensing regimes under import substitution constrained firms to fewer intermediate goods than would have been purchased had firms not been quantity constrained and because some firms are enabled to concentrate their production in one or a few lines, and produce profitability (at least covering marginal cost) for export.

Recently, some economists have turned their attention to 'technological catch-up' by which is meant learning about modern production methods in general (Grossman and Helpman 1991). They point out that imports may be important, both in quantity and in variety, in permitting rapid learning about what is happening in the rest of the world. For example, producers in economies in which only 'essential' imports of capital goods are permitted may not learn about new developments pertaining to their product (either in output or in inputs) in other economies as rapidly as would producers when imports are freely permitted. The more important is this set of phenomena in explaining more rapid productivity growth under an outward-oriented strategy, the more costly are practices such as restricting business travel, almost universally encountered under import substitution.

A final set of factors has to do with economic policy itself. By now, it is widely recognised that sustained growth under an outward-oriented trade strategy will occur only under circumstances in which producers have the appropriate incentives (and supportive infrastructure), and are confident that those incentives will be maintained. Achieving that set of policies requires not only that they be approximately 'right' at a moment in time, but that they will be stable over time. Hence, stability of the policy framework appears to be important.

Once that is recognised, it must then be noted that the presence of export interests is likely to be an inducement to policymakers to maintain appropriate incentives. This, in turn, increases credibility and stability. But stability of incentives, in turn, provides an environment in which productivity growth is likely to be more rapid: producers will respond more quickly to small changes in relative prices when those changes are infrequent, and not dwarfed by changes in the policy regime itself!

What set of policies is desirable or essential for an outward-oriented trade strategy?

It seems clear that economies that have adopted sustained outward-oriented trade strategies have experienced economic performance superior to those which have not. Equally, an outward-oriented trade strategy seems a *sine qua non* for the type of rapid growth experienced by East Asian economies. Among the other lessons provided by the East Asian newly industrialised economies, perhaps a key one, is that a development strategy that relies on integration with the world economy, rather than insulation from it, is not only feasible, but preferable.

There remains, however, the troublesome issue that during this period of rapid growth in the East Asian economies a variety of policies changed with the shift to an outward-orientation. It is reasonable to assume that, for example, more efficient functioning of financial markets, positive real interest rates, and other policy changes also contributed to the environment in which rapid growth was possible.

An important question concerns the lesson that may be learned from the East Asian economies about the policies which are more or less essential concomitants, and necessary for the success, of an outward-oriented trade strategy, and which policies conducive to better economic performance are complementary with those supporting rapid growth through integration with the world economy.

Several points are generally accepted. The first is the role of the exchange rate. While it is probably possible to embark on an outward-oriented trade strategy by adding (uniform, across-the-board) export subsidies of various kinds to the nominal exchange rate to offset the discrimination against exports inherent in the protection of imports, it does not appear possible to sustain growth without a shift towards increasing reliance on a realistic exchange rate. Moreover, exchange rate policy must be such that producers can anticipate reasonable real exchange rate stability. One of the hallmarks of the East Asian policy regimes has been the relatively narrow range in which real exchange rates have fluctuated.

The need for a stable and realistic real exchange rate derives, in part, from the second lesson: an outward-oriented trade strategy can succeed only if exporters have reasonably free access to the world market, in which supplies may be obtained more cheaply (or in preferred specifications or quality) than in the domestic market. Free access of this kind is not possible if there are high rates of protection for the inputs because incentives for misrepresentation become so great that the authorities find it necessary to check all incoming shipments carefully, causing delays for exporter-users. If the authorities then attempt to limit exporters' access to inputs from the world market, their competitiveness abroad suffers commensurately.

A variety of techniques has been used to provide free access at early stages of an outward-oriented trade strategy. Korea allowed duty-free importation of materials used in export production with little or no red tape on the condition that exporters export within the year. Estimates of imported inputs per unit of export were made for various industries with generous 'wastage allowances' which, in effect, permitted exporters to obtain imports for the domestic market duty-free. Of course, when protection has been negligible, as in Hong Kong and Singapore, the problem does not arise. In addition to the argument made above, high rates of protection also provide incentives for domestic production of the inputs, diverting resources from (more economically efficient) export industries.

In turn, free access implies that the exchange rate must be reasonably realistic and whatever protection is in place at the beginning of an outward-oriented trade strategy must either be in the form of, or else be quickly transformed into, tariffs. Quantitative restrictions on many imports appear to be inconsistent with an outward-oriented trade strategy. There may be an exception for goods that are truly final consumer goods with few or no intermediate uses. In Korea, for example, imports of ladies' fur coats and wines were quantitatively restricted. Most items, however, are both intermediate and final goods.

Many of those who earlier advocated import substitution, when acknowledging the success of the outward-oriented trade strategy, have attempted to argue that appropriate policy can permit 'some' export-oriented activities combined with 'some' import substitution activities. While this is undoubtedly true, in that the optimal allocation of resources clearly entails the sale of newly produced goods on the domestic market as well as internationally, it is highly misleading on two counts.

First, even when the East Asian economies did countenance the emergence of new activities with government support (more often in the form of access to credit and tax incentives than in the form of protection), it was always expected that those industries would become competitive exporters. Indeed, the signal to the Korean government that the heavy and chemical industry drive was not achieving its intended results was that the new industries could not, with few exceptions, profitably export. Thus, there were few activities within the domestic economy for which producers could anticipate continued shelter from international competitive pressures. In a sense, the ability to export competitively became the 'market test' that was used by the authorities.

Second, when activities are likely to make economic sense, it is certainly possible, but probably unlikely, that they make sense at a scale of production which satisfies the domestic market but does not also produce enough for export. It could, of course, happen that with rising marginal costs, firms' optimal levels of output were such that they produced to meet all or part of domestic demand, but found it unprofitable to produce additional units for export. The higher are transport costs relative to the price of the good, the greater the range in which such a result could occur. Given the low transport costs associated with most tradeable commodities, however, the empirical importance of this possibility is questionable. There were even cases in the East Asian newly industrialised economies where production began completely destined for exports. The more likely case, however, is one in which production capabilities for products competing with imports are used partially for export and partially to satisfy domestic demand.

What seems clear is that the expectation that firms will, if not immediately, reasonably quickly be expected to export, provides a clear discipline on businessmen and government officials alike. If exceptions are made for some commodities, the diversion of resources from potential export industries itself constitutes a cost. Perhaps more important, however, is that other producers who are competitive in international markets must be able to acquire their inputs at internationally competitive qualities and prices. Once a sheltered import-competing sector is established, the inevitable pressures to induce domestic firms to purchase output from it are virtually irresistible.

Thus far, discussion has focused on the central features of the trade and payments regime; uniformity of incentives, exchange rate appropriateness and stability; free access by exporters to the world market for their inputs; and so on. Regarding these policy instruments and their importance, there is little, if any, disagreement.

Moving to other policies, however, there is somewhat more uncertainty. For example, all the East Asian newly industrialised economies had relatively free labour markets, in the sense that wage determination seems largely to have been the result of market forces, and not government controls or strong union bargaining power.

Employment and real wages both rose quickly during the rapid growth years. An important question is whether or not labour market flexibility simply contributed to growth, or was instead a prerequisite for the success of the outward-oriented trade strategy.

One can define the limits of the debate. At one extreme, there could have been sufficiently restrictive regulations surrounding wages and conditions of work that, especially in the early years of the outward-oriented trade strategy, the Asian newly industrialised economies' comparative advantages in manufacturing processes, which were relatively intensive in the use of unskilled labour, would have been largely choked off. A sufficiently high real wage would clearly have made it unprofitable to export unskilled labour-intensive commodities. There are economies in which minimum wage legislation is in force, but in which the minimum wage established is below that prevailing in virtually all activities. In such an instance, it is evident that the legislation is not a restrictive factor. At the other extreme, labour market flexibility quite clearly permitted even more rapid growth than would have been possible without it.

That said, however, it is difficult to define precisely the necessary amount of labour market flexibility required in order for an outward-oriented trade strategy to achieve the intended results.

A second question relates to financial markets. From a policy perspective, many developing economies have imposed ceilings on nominal interest rates that have kept them below the rate of inflation. Therefore, the real rate of interest paid by borrowers has been negative.

In these circumstances, if credit is then allocated to any activity through rationing, there are two effects. First, the allocated credit represents an implicit subsidy to the recipient. If rationed credit is allocated to activities that would not be profitable at appropriate positive real rates of interest, there is a loss in economic efficiency. In so far as credit is allocated to those activities which are in any event most profitable, there may be no resource allocation consequences across activities. Even in that case, however, the second effect may be significant. That is, depending on the criteria for the quantitative allocations of credit, recipients may treat their cost of capital as being equal to the real rate of interest they are paying in their rationed credit. To the extent that they do so, techniques of production may be relatively more capital-using than would occur under positive real interest rates and the real marginal product of capital be lower.

In the East Asian newly industrialised economies, reforms in financial markets were sufficient that there was little extension of credit at negative real interest rates after the early years of the outward-oriented trade strategy. Real interest rates were largely positive although, especially in Korea, they were below market-clearing rates. Whether positive real interest rates were a prerequisite to the rapid growth performance of the newly industrialised economies, or only increased growth still further, is an open question. Clearly, maintenance of positive real interest rates cannot fail to improve resource allocation. The only questions are by how much, and whether that margin is sufficiently large to render the potential for growth greatly reduced in the presence of negative real interest rates.

One last aspect of policy must be noted: as indicated above, the East Asian newly industrialised economies' governments all appear to have focused their attention on the provision of adequate infrastructure to support the growth of exports. Communications and transport linkages between domestic exporters and their foreign customers were never reported to be a bottleneck. Indeed, most anecdotal evidence suggests that the standards of availability and quality in these areas were much higher than in other developing economies and may even have exceeded those of some Organisation of Economic Cooperation and Development economies.

Clearly, these linkages are a necessary precondition for the success of an outward-oriented trade strategy. Taking that as a 'lesson' for policy, however, is difficult. There is, as yet, no widely accepted means for quantifying the 'goodness' or 'adequacy' of infrastructure.

Interrelationships among policies

For all of those attempting to analyse or quantify the relationships between different policy stances and economic growth, there are a number of unresolved challenges. One, in particular, deserves attention here. There appears to be a positive correlation between 'goodness' of policy across various policy instruments. Some of that correlation, such as between fiscal deficits and the rate of increase of the money supply, or between the realism of the exchange rate and the restrictiveness of quantitative controls over imports, has an obvious economic basis. Some of it, however, does not.

To make the point more concrete, a broad generalisation will suffice. That is, economies that adopted import-substitution policies also tended to rely on government controls and government pursuit of economic activity, and to suppress and regulate markets. They tended to discriminate more against agriculture, to control the banking system and rely more on credit rationing at negative real rates of interest, to regulate wages and conditions of work (often at unrealistic levels with consequent emergence of an informal sector), to neglect infrastructure investment and maintenance, and to use intervention instruments that permitted wide disparities in incentives for different activities.

By contrast, economies following outward-oriented trade strategies tended to have less regulated labour markets, less discrimination against agriculture, smaller fiscal deficits and hence lower inflation, more realistic exchange rates, positive real interest rates, and more satisfactory infrastructure. They all allocated more resources to education, and increased their stock of human capital more rapidly than did economies following import-substitution policies.

This raises a number of issues. First, of course, there is the question already discussed of the relative contribution of each policy, or set of policies, to growth. Second, however, it raises important questions about political–economic interactions in policy formation and evolution (Krueger 1993). Controls do seem to beget controls, and liberalisation of markets seems to have a cumulative aspect to it as well.

Finally, there are important issues surrounding the process of policy reform. If there were no political constraints, it might make sense in all circumstances to proceed with policy reforms as rapidly as possible. Even then, it takes time to formulate laws, decrees, and other policy changes. Some things, such as changing the exchange rate, can normally be done very quickly; others, such as tax reform, require a considerable technocratic input if they are to be done well, even in the absence of political pressures. In the real world, however, politicians use up their 'political resources' when making unpopular changes. Since policy reforms normally require several years before their benefits are fully evident, a politician intent upon achieving reforms might rationally decide to delay some of them until the benefits from earlier policy changes had begun to be widely felt. Here, the issue of the 'minimum critical effort' necessary for any success becomes highly relevant.

While the lessons from East Asia are valuable, there is a great deal of uncertainty surrounding many of the issues. Clearly, not everything that is a desirable part of a strategy for rapid growth can or need be done at once. What items may be delayed without jeopardising the success of the entire program, and what items require immediate action is not so clear. Given the present state of knowledge, decision-makers embarking upon policy reforms are still relying on their intuition and knowledge of the situation in their own country to form these judgments. Hopefully, further analyses will begin to shed light on these questions.

Notes to Chapter I

The author is indebted to Matthew Raiff for valuable research assistance in preparation of this chapter.

[1] It has even been argued by some leaders in developing economies that low living standards and dependence on primary commodity exports led to *de facto* dependence on the rich industrialised economies prior to the Second World War, even when there was titular independence. This argument is regarded as especially applicable to Latin America *vis-à-vis* the United States.

[2] It should be recalled that part of the Keynesian legacy was to challenge the efficacy of markets in general. Even among economists in industrialised economies it was believed that there was little to choose between government and private ownership and management. See Tinbergen (1984) for a statement.

[3] In economic theory, there was (and is) an exception to the policy prescription of free trade that emanates from comparative advantage. That is the infant industry case. It has long been accepted that under highly restrictive circumstances (there must be sufficiently rapid productivity growth so that the industry will eventually become profitable enough to repay the losses incurred in the early stages and there must be externalities so that some of the profitability will occur outside the producing firms, because otherwise private producers would find it profitable to incur losses in order to reap the profits at a later date) government protection of industry may be welfare improving.

In practice, however, the measures taken to encourage industrial development in developing economies went far beyond those that would have been sanctioned under the infant industry rubric. Protection became virtually automatic for almost all industries, and there was little test as to whether they would ever become viable. Many of them became senescent without ever becoming competitive. See Baldwin (1969) and Krueger (1990), respectively, for critical analyses of the theory and of experience.

[4] After the Korean War, world prices were fairly stable until the late 1960s. Developing economies with rates of inflation of even 5 to 10 per cent were therefore experiencing fairly rapid real appreciation of their currencies when they held their nominal exchange rates constant over periods of five years and longer. In addition, many developing economies had increased imports markedly during the early postwar years (when reserves built up during the Second World War and high commodity prices provided for ample foreign exchange). When commodity prices fell after 1952 and sterling balances had been run down, cuts in expenditure and an exchange rate change would, in any event, have been necessary. Maintaining a constant nominal exchange rate thus resulted in rapidly intensifying restrictiveness of the trade and payments regime.

[5] This section draws heavily on Krueger (1993). All data in this section for which a source is not otherwise indicated are taken from the World Bank (1992a), *World Development Report, 1992: Development and the Environment*.

[6] For an analysis of the impact of all interventions on the rates of effective protection received by various Korean industries in the

late 1970s see Nam (1980). See also the comments by Corden on that paper, in which he puzzles over the apparently 'low' rates of protection reported by Nam.

[7] It should be recalled that even Japan was perceived as a poor country in a large international economy in the 1950s and 1960s, and followed the same general policies in an outward-oriented trade regime. It is often forgotten that Japanese exports were not always as important on the world stage as they are now: indeed, as late as 1952, the value of Japan's exports was less than that of India's.

2

The East Asian Growth Model: How General is it?

ENZO GRILLI AND JAMES RIEDEL

East Asia has been the fastest growing area of the world for the past three decades (Table 2.1) and is now becoming the bari-centre of world economic activity. East Asia has also been more resilient to global recessions than most other areas, achieving stable growth even in the midst of global economic turbulence. The dramatic gains made by this region over the years have not been confined to economic growth, but have also been accompanied by notable improvements in health and education, by large increases in life expectancies and, perhaps most strikingly, by substantial reductions in absolute poverty. All this is well documented and factually incontrovertible (Riedel 1988; World Bank 1993c; Grilli 1994).

What remains open to controversy, however, is the origin or causes of East Asia's relative success. Many factors have been identified—outward orientation, macroeconomic discipline, good public policy and high rates of savings and investment—

Table 2.1: Growth of production in developing areas, (average annual growth, %)

	GDP		Agriculture		Industry	
	1965–80	1980–90	1965–80	1980–90	1965–80	1980–90
East Asia	7.3	7.8	3.2	4.8	10.8	10.2
South Asia	3.6	5.2	2.5	3.0	4.3	6.3
Middle East and North Africa	6.7	2.0	4.3	4.3	6.3	0.7
Latin America	6.0	1.6	3.1	2.0	6.6	1.2
Sub-Saharan Africa	4.2	2.1	2.2	2.1	7.2	2.0

Source: World Bank, 1993c, *Sustaining Rapid Development in East Asia and The Pacific*, World Bank, Washington, D.C.

but the relative weight of each in explaining the region's success is still a matter of considerable debate.

No matter how the various pieces of the East Asian success story are put together and relative weights assigned, a core model of export-oriented industrialisation has emerged from the East Asian experience, spearheaded by the 'early tigers' (Taiwan, Korea, Singapore and Hong Kong) and brought forward in time, with adaptations, by Thailand, Malaysia and more recently China and then Indonesia. In this chapter the preconditions for export-oriented growth in the style of the East Asian 'tigers' and the policies required to launch and sustain that strategy are examined. Having identified 'what worked', and at what stage, in the economic development of these economies, the questions of how relevant and adaptable their strategies are to other developing economies are considered. Simply stated, the questions are as follows. Can the East Asian model of export-oriented industrialisation travel outside the region? If so, where will it work and in what way, compared with the areas of origin?

These are obviously complex questions to which definitive answers cannot be provided, though some plausible hypotheses concerning the replicability of the East Asian growth experience in other developing areas can be advanced. In the first part of the paper the main characteristics of the growth model followed by the East Asian economies are summarised, and some of the key stages through which it evolved are identified. The second part examines in more detail the preconditions for success of an export-oriented growth strategy of the kind experienced by the East Asian tigers and the extent to which they currently appear to be satisfied in the major developing regions of the world, including Eastern Europe. The third part of the chapter focuses on the role played by economic policies in the process of East Asian development and in the last part some conclusions are drawn about the significance and applicability of the East Asian model to other parts of the developing world.

Key features of the East Asian growth model: an overview

The starting point of the analysis is the identification of the export-oriented growth strategy successfully followed by three

East Asian economies in the period since the Second World War—Taiwan, Thailand and more recently China.[1] These economies constitute an interesting sample, representative of three fairly distinct realities that coexisted in East Asia: the small and natural resource-poor economies (like Taiwan), the small-to-medium-sized natural-resource-rich economies (like Thailand) and the large and previously insular economies (like China), whose opening to the outside world through international trade and capital flows is a relatively recent phenomenon.

In looking at the period during which economic take-off occurred (Taiwan from 1960 to 1975, Thailand from 1970 to the present and China from 1980 to the present) certain key features of their shared experience emerge. First, all three economies at the time of their take-off had an abundance of low-wage labour, residing for the most part in the rural sector. Second, during their early phases of export-oriented industrial growth, all experienced significant increases in agricultural productivity. This generated a surplus extractable by government through taxation to be used to develop infrastructure and sustain industrial investment. Third, all three experienced rapidly rising and ultimately relatively high rates of domestic saving, which financed the bulk of their domestic investment. Fourth, neither the abundance of natural resources nor the size of the pre-existing industrial base appears to have been especially important to their success, as the main growth-generating activity—manufacturing labour-intensive goods for export—was started and developed as a 'footloose' activity, with very few linkages to pre-existing industrial bases.

Thus, the essence of the East Asian model is manufacturing (and exporting) labour-intensive goods by combining low-cost labour, drawn for the most part from the rural sector, with imported intermediate inputs and capital goods. The rapidly growing export-oriented industrial production did not initially replace the inward-oriented industries built up during the previous import-substitution phase of industrialisation, but instead grew up alongside the existing industrial base. It is only after the vast reservoir of low-wage labour was exhausted, as it was in Taiwan after 1975, that it became necessary, in order to maintain a high growth rate, to rationalise the industrial structure by removing subsidies and protection of the relatively inefficient import-substituting industries in favour of further expansion of the relatively efficient export-oriented industries. Before the reservoir of low-wage labour in the rural sector is depleted and wages begin to rise rapidly a country can, more or less, have it both ways: that is, it can promote efficient export-oriented industrial growth and at the same time maintain, and even expand, the inefficient heavy industrial base through high protection and heavy subsidies, as China is currently still doing and Thailand has done until recently.

The dualistic nature of industrial growth in the early phase of rapid economic expansion in the East Asian economies has created a good deal of confusion among those who have tried to interpret the East Asian experience and draw out policy lessons for other economies. Some have focused on the measures which made exporting of labour-intensive manufactures profitable, including devaluing and unifying the exchange rate and removing barriers to the import of intermediate and capital goods, discounting the importance of the previous phases when heavy industry development was sought through government intervention. For these analysts (Little 1989; Riedel 1988), government thus played a supporting role in the economic take-off of these economies (mostly removing obstacles to exporting and providing a conducive environment for private savings and investment) rather than a starring role in their industrial development. Others (Wade 1988, 1990) have tended to focus more on the importance of direct support given by government to the heavy, import-substituting industries, even during the period of export-oriented growth, and have concluded that continued government intervention was a significant factor in the East Asian success. What the latter analysts have failed to recognise, however, is that in East Asia, the protection and subsidies given to heavy industry were, because of the footloose nature of manufacturing for export, largely irrelevant to their success, at least up until the point at which the reservoir of low-wage labour in the rural sector began to dry up and real wages began to rise rapidly.

Thus, to summarise, the policy prerequisites for emulating the first phase of the East Asian model are, first, to remove the obstacles to exporting and, second, to provide a conducive environment for private sector savings and investment. The first requires that governments set a realistic exchange rate and remove barriers to imports of intermediate and capital goods. The second requires that the government supply essential public infrastructure and maintain macroeconomic stability.

This is, of course, no small order, and still means that government has a crucial role to play if the East Asian model is to succeed. Such a role, however, differs in nature and specific content from that implied in the traditional government-led industrialisation paradigm, which many developing economies still followed in the 1960s and 1970s when the early tigers of East Asia were already, and radically, moving away from it.

Preconditions of the East Asian growth model

It is not suggested here that there is any precise set of preconditions to rapid growth *à la* East Asia. The premise is simply that if conditions in other regions of the world are not grossly different from those which existed first in Taiwan (or in Korea) and subsequently in Thailand and China when they shifted from an inward-looking to an export-oriented growth strategy, then that same path should be open to them. Neither is it suggested here that the East Asian model is generally optimal, or even highly desirable, for developing economies everywhere else in the world. The aim is to verify, however simply, the conditions under which other developing economies could entertain the hope of replicating it, if they decided that such a model of growth was desirable.[2]

Quality of human resources

After the city-states of Hong Kong and Korea, the first to adopt what has become the East Asian growth model—Taiwan and Korea—are relatively small and very densely populated countries. Twenty-five to 30 years ago, when they began to grow rapidly, population densities were very high: around 300 persons per square kilometre. Densities were obviously even higher in the city-states of Hong Kong and Singapore. Total population was around 11 million in Taiwan and 30 million in Korea. Ten years later when rapid growth started in Thailand, its population was around 40 million, but with a density one-third that of Taiwan and Korea. Population density in China

Table 2.2: Population: size, density and growth

Region/ Country	Total population[1] (million)	Population density[1] (Pop./ sq. km)	Total population growth[2]	Urban population growth[2]	Rural population growth[2]
					% per annum
Latin America	··	21	(1.8)	3.0	−0.1
Brazil	150	18	2.2	3.2	−0.3
Mexico	86	44	2.3	3.3	0.3
Argentina	32	12	1.3	1.8	−0.9
Colombia	32	28	2.0	3.0	−0.1
Peru	22	17	2.3	3.1	0.8
Venezuela	20	22	2.7	2.8	−1.1
Sub-Saharan Africa	··	22	(3.0)	5.0	2.2
Nigeria	115	124	3.3	6.0	2.8
Ethiopia	51	42	2.5	5.0	1.7
Zaire	37	16	3.2	4.5	2.2
Sudan	25	10	2.7	3.9	1.3
Tanzania	25	26	3.8	8.5	3.0
Kenya	24	42	3.8	5.9	3.2
Uganda	16	69	3.7	6.4	3.0
Ghana	15	62	3.4	4.2	2.3
Cameroon	12	25	3.0	5.9	1.8
North Africa	··	50	2.7	3.8	0.8
Egypt	52	52	2.4	3.1	2.1
Morocco	25	56	2.6	4.3	0.4
Algeria	25	61	3.0	4.8	0.4
Tunisia	8	49	2.5	3.9	−1.1
Eastern Europe	··	92	(0.8)	1.4	−3.5
Poland	38	122	0.7	1.6	−2.6
Romania	23	97	0.4	1.7	−3.8
Czechoslovakia	16	123	0.3	0.8	−3.2
Hungary	11	114	−0.3	0.5	−4.7
Bulgaria	8	80	0.1	0.8	−3.8
South Asia	··	222	(1.8)	3.9	1.8
India	850	258	2.1	3.7	1.5
Pakistan	112	140	3.7	4.8	2.8
Bangladesh	107	743	2.7	5.1	1.8

Table 2.2: *continued*

Region/ Country	Total population[1] (million)	Population density[1] (Pop./ sq. km)	Total population growth[2]	Urban population growth[2]	Rural population growth[2]
					% per annum
East Asian comparators					
Taiwan (25–30 years ago)	11	300	3.1	5.7	1.5
Thailand (15–20 years ago)	41	108	2.7	5.2	2.2
China (15–20 years ago)	916	96	1.8	2.3	−6.0

Note: Figures in parentheses are regional averages that include all countries. The exception is North Africa, where they are averages of the countries shown in the table.
[1] Population: size and density figures refer to most recent year available (typically 1990).
[2] Population growth figures refer to latest 10 years period available (typically 1980–90).
Sources: World Bank, 1990b and 1992b, *Social and Economic Indicators*, Johns Hopkins University Press, Baltimore; Food and Agriculture Organisation, 1992, *Production Yearbook*, FAO, Rome; Riedel, J., 1993, 'Vietnam: on the trail of the tigers', *The World Economy*, 16(4):401–22.

was about the same as in Thailand when rapid growth started (about 100 people per square kilometre), though total population was more than 20 times larger. In all these countries, however, the rate of expansion of population was fast (somewhere between 2 and 3 per cent per annum) when rapid growth of output began. More importantly, in all these countries urban population grew much faster than overall population, nearly twice as fast in Thailand and Taiwan, and appreciably faster even in China, despite the legal and administrative constraints on migration to cities (Table 2.2). The strength of the population pressures in these countries was an important ingredient in their early success in that it allowed their agricultural sectors to maintain output, and even generate surpluses, while at the same time releasing a heavy and growing flow of labour to the expanding export-oriented manufacturing sector.

Table 2.3: Health, nutrition and education indicators

Region/ Country	Infant mortality rate[1] (per 1000 births)	Life expect- ancy (years)	Daily calories per capita (numbers)	Enrolment rates[1] Primary/Secondary (% of age group)		Illiteracy rate[1] (%)
Latin						
America	48	68	2,721	107	50	16
Brazil	37	66	2,751	105	39	19
Mexico	39	70	3,052	114	53	13
Argentina	29	71	3,163	111	74	5
Colombia	37	69	2,598	107	52	13
Peru	69	63	2,186	123	67	15
Venezuela	34	70	2,582	105	56	12
Sub-Saharan						
Africa	107	51	2,122	68	18	50
Nigeria	98	52	2,312	70	19	49
Ethiopia	132	48	1,667	38	15	· ·
Zaire	94	52	1,991	78	24	28
Sudan	102	50	1,974	· ·	· ·	73
Tanzania	115	48	2,206	63	4	· ·
Kenya	67	59	2,163	94	23	31
Uganda	117	47	2,153	77	13	52
Ghana	85	55	2,248	75	39	40
Cameroon	88	57	2,217	101	26	46
North Africa	61	64	3,086	93	55	45
Egypt	66	60	3,336	97	81	52
Morocco	67	62	3,020	68	36	51
Algeria	67	65	2,866	94	61	43
Tunisia	44	67	3,121	115	44	35
Eastern						
Europe	30	70	3,433	102	73	· ·
Poland	16	71	3,505	99	81	· ·
Romania	27	70	3,155	95	88	· ·
Czechoslovakia	12	72	3,632	95	80	· ·
Hungary	15	71	3,644	94	76	· ·
Bulgaria	14	73	3,707	97	75	· ·
South Asia	93	58	2,215	90	38	53
India	92	59	2,229	98	43	52
Pakistan	103	56	2,219	38	20	65
Bangladesh	105	52	2,021	70	17	65

Table 2.3: *continued*

Region/ Country	Infant mortality rate[1] (per 1000 births)	Life expect- ancy (years)	Daily calories per capita (numbers)	Enrolment rates[1] Primary/Secondary (% of age group)		Illiteracy rate[1] (%)
East Asian comparators						
Taiwan (25–30 years ago)		63	2,390	97	30	70
Thailand (15–20 years ago)	55	60	2,285	83	26	7
China (15–20 years ago)	46	65	2,070	135	47	27

Note: Figures in parentheses are regional averages that include all countries. The exception is North Africa, where they are simple averages of countries shown in the table.
[1] Data refer to latest year available (typically 1989 or 1990).
Source: World Bank, 1990b and 1992b, *Social and Economic Indicators*, Johns Hopkins Press, Baltimore; Riedel, J., 1993, 'Vietnam: on the trail of the tigers', *The World Economy*, 16(4):401–22.

Health and education standards were already quite developed in East Asian economies during their take-off stage. Infant mortality was around 50 per 1,000 births and life expectancy above 60 years. Enrolment in primary education was nearly 100 per cent, and about one-third of pupils of the relevant age group were enrolled in secondary education. By 1965, the intake of calories was, on average, already above the minimum level of 2,000 a day in Taiwan, as it was in both Thailand and China by 1970. The quality of human resources was thus relatively high (and improving) in East Asian economies when they initiated their export-oriented growth path.

Conditions similar to those of East Asian economies 20 to 25 years ago prevail today in much of the developing world in regard to population pressures and trends in urbanisation (Table 2.2). In most developing economies, total population growth is still high (2 to 3 per cent per year) and urbanisation rates even higher (5 to 6 per cent per year), although there are significant differences between developing areas. Overall population growth is fastest in Africa and lowest in Latin America, with South Asia in an intermediate position. The only exception to these trends, in the developing world (broadly defined), is in Eastern Europe, where population growth is nearly zero in the major countries and urbanisation rates are quite moderate (at about 1 per cent per year, as against 3 to 6 per cent in the traditional developing areas of the world). Rural population growth continues strong in South Asia, Egypt and throughout Sub-Saharan Africa, while it is already declining in most Latin American countries and Eastern Europe.

While at least overall population growth rates are similar to those which existed in East Asia, health and education conditions today differ significantly in much of the developing world from those of East Asian economies 20 to 25 years ago; there are also significant differences in physical infrastructure, see Krueger (this volume) for the importance of this (Table 2.3). Infant mortality rates, for example, are somewhat lower in Latin America than they were in the East Asian economies when they started on the road to export-led growth but not in South Asia and Africa (both South and North of the Sahara) where they remain much higher. The same is generally true for life expectancies and school enrolment rates, even though in these two areas the North African economies today are at about the same levels as their East Asian counterparts several decades ago, with life expectancy at 60 to 65 years and school enrolment rates at near 90 per cent for the primary and above 35 per cent for the secondary level.

Noteworthy also are the positions of India among the Asian economies and of Egypt in the North African context. In both of these countries education indicators are significantly better today than in most of their neighbours, standing at about the same level as (or above) those of the East Asian nations when they initiated their export-oriented growth strategy. As would be expected, given per capita incomes and development priorities, today's educational standards in Eastern Europe are systematically above those of East Asia 25 or so years ago. The same is true for per capita intake of calories, more than one-third higher in Eastern Europe on average than the Asian standard at take-off.

Availability of natural resources

Physical size is only a rough, and often imprecise, indicator of resource endowment. East Asia contains some small countries, such as Taiwan and Korea, with areas of less than 100,000 square kilometres, medium-sized ones, such as Malaysia, Thailand and the Philippines, of about 300,000 to 500,000 square kilometres and a few large ones, such as Indonesia and China, which are four to 20 times larger than the average of the medium-sized group.

Non-renewable natural resources, such as minerals (including oil) and tropical woods, are more abundant in Malaysia, Thailand, Indonesia and China than in Korea and Taiwan, with the size of the Philippines' endowment somewhere in between. Geological estimates of mineral resources (including oil) are not only unreliable, but also say very little about their economic value (which depends on factors such as location, accessibility and extraction costs that vary greatly within and across economies, even for the same material). Nevertheless, a closer look at the value per capita of mineral resource endowments does not much change first impressions.

The availability of agricultural land is another commonly used resource indicator. When expressed in per capita terms (Table 2.4), the relative availability of agricultural land is shown to vary widely across countries. Taiwan and Korea are at a clear disadvantage compared with their Asian neighbours, while the per capita availability of land in Thailand and China (around 4,500 square metres per person) is seen to be between one-half and one-third smaller than in North Africa (with the exception of Egypt) and in several countries of Sub-Saharan Africa (like Cameroon, Ethiopia, Tanzania and Kenya). It is also apparent that Latin America is a region of relatively abundant agricultural land, in per capita terms, compared with the majority of developing economies today and much better endowed than the tigers of East Asia 25 years ago. The Eastern European economies also appear to be less endowed than other developing economies in Latin America and Africa in terms of per capita land availability.

East Asian economies made good use of the agricultural land available to them. Production of cereals (especially rice—the staple food) was raised considerably in Taiwan, Korea and China through increases in yields brought about by improved

Table 2.4: Physical size and resource endowment indicators

Region/Country	Land area (1000 sq. km)	Forest land/ total land[1] (% shares)	Agricultural land per capita (sq. m)
Latin America			
Brazil	8,512	65	16,423
Mexico	1,958	23	11,597
Argentina	2,737	22	231,841
Colombia	1,139	44	14,105
Peru	1,280	54	14,211
Venezuela	912	33	10,870
Sub-Saharan Africa			
Nigeria	924	13	6,186
Ethiopia	1,222	22	11,549
Zaire	2,345	74	6,098
Sudan	2,506	19	44,029
Tanzania	945	43	16,200
Kenya	570	4	16,799
Uganda	236	24	5,226
Ghana	230	35	5,197
Cameroon	465	53	12,961
North Africa			
Egypt	1,101	—	500
Morocco	446	18	12,069
Algeria	2,382	2	15,244
Tunisia	163	4	9,397
Eastern Europe			
Poland	313	28	4,924
Romania	238	27	6,370
Czechoslovakia	125	37	4,305
Hungary	92	18	6,115
Bulgaria	111	35	7,013
South Asia			
India	3,287	20	2,130
Pakistan	796	5	2,295
Bangladesh	144	14	942

Table 2.4: *continued*

Region/Country	Land area (1000 sq. km)	Forest land/ total land[1] (% shares)	Agricultural land per capita (sq. m)
East Asian comparators			
Taiwan (25–30 years ago)	36	58	785
Thailand (15–20 years ago)	511	28	4,204
Korea (25–30 years ago)	121	39	1,444
China (15–20 years ago)	9,561	15	4,571

[1] Data refer to latest year available (typically 1989).
Source: World Bank, 1993a, *World Development Report 1993*, Oxford University Press, New York; Riedel, J., 1993 'Vietnam: on the trail of the tigers', *The World Economy*, 16(4):401–22.

irrigation and increasing applications of fertiliser, together with adoption of green revolution techniques. Rice production also expanded in Thailand during take-off, but entirely because of increasing land area under cultivation, i.e. at constant (if absolutely high) yields per hectare (Table 2.5).

In most of South Asia and Latin America, rates of growth of cereals production are now as high, or higher, than they were 25 years ago in East Asia, although only the South Asian economies, like their East Asian neighbours, are large producers of rice. As in Taiwan and Korea during their take-off period, improvements in yields are today the main source of agricultural output growth in South Asia and Latin America, the source of these gains being improved irrigation and green revolution technology (Johnson 1983).

The role of agriculture and industry

Agriculture played a major role in the economies of Taiwan, Thailand and China when they launched their export-led industrialisation drives. In each of these countries, agriculture then accounted for about one-third of value added and for about one-half to one-third of employment. In Thailand, agriculture also accounted for the bulk of exports (Table 2.6).

At the start of their export-oriented growth, Taiwan, and later Thailand and China, also had sizeable industrial sectors, accounting for one-quarter or more of value added, and, with the exception of Thailand, nearly 20 per cent of employment.

Table 2.5: Agriculture: production, yields and fertiliser use

Region/Country	Cereal				Tubers				Fertiliser consump'n/ha
	Yields[1] ton/ha	Product growth[2]	Yield growth[2]	Area growth[2]	Yields[1] ton/ha	Product growth[2]	Yield growth[2]	Area growth[2]	
		% per annum				% per annum			
Latin America									
Brazil	2.0	3.4	1.5	1.9	12.5	-1.0	-0.6	-0.4	43
Mexico	2.2	3.0	2.8	0.2	14.7	3.1	2.0	1.1	73
Argentina	2.1	1.8	2.4	-0.6	20.4	0.3	2.9	-2.6	5
Colombia	2.5	3.3	2.7	0.6	11.9	3.7	2.1	1.6	90
Peru	2.5	2.5	2.2	0.3	8.5	0.0	1.0	-1.0	41
Venezuela	2.2	4.9	2.8	2.1	8.3	0.8	0.4	0.4	151
Sub-Saharan Africa									
Nigeria	1.2	2.2	3.2	-1.0	12.4	2.7	1.2	1.5	12
Ethiopia	1.2	1.7	2.0	-0.3	3.3	2.7	-0.2	2.9	7
Zaire	0.8	3.9	0.6	3.3	7.5	2.6	0.4	2.2	1
Sudan	0.4	2.6	-2.4	5.0	2.2	-2.4	-1.4	-1.0	4
Tanzania	1.5	6.9	3.6	3.3	7.3	3.6	2.7	0.9	9
Kenya	1.7	0.9	1.0	-0.1	8.6	2.2	0.3	1.9	48
Uganda	1.5	-0.6	-1.6	-1.0	6.3	3.7	2.0	1.7	—
Ghana	1.8	2.1	-0.3	2.4	10.1	1.7	-0.7	2.7	3

North Africa									
Egypt	5.4	1.6	1.3	0.3	23.1	7.0	1.5	5.5	404
Morocco	1.3	1.9	1.4	0.5	16.7	6.5	3.1	3.4	34
Algeria	0.7	0.3	0.9	-0.6	8.6	6.8	1.1	5.7	28
Tunisia	0.6	0.2	0.6	-0.4	11.2	5.0	2.2	2.8	23
Eastern Europe									
Poland	3.2	1.8	1.9	-0.1	18.5	-1.5	0.2	-1.7	205
Romania	3.0	2.0	2.4	-0.4	12.6	3.1	3.0	0.1	133
Czech.	4.9	2.8	3.0	-0.2	18.6	-2.3	1.1	-3.4	321
Hungary	5.5	3.1	3.8	-0.7	18.6	-1.9	3.5	-5.4	246
Bulgaria	4.4	1.4	1.8	-0.4	13.8	0.9	-0.3	1.2	195
South Asia									
India	2.0	3.2	2.8	0.4	15.7	3.8	2.2	1.6	69
Pakistan	1.8	4.0	2.8	1.2	10.1	6.2	0.1	6.1	89
Bangladesh	2.6	2.3	1.7	0.6	10.0	1.8	0.3	1.5	99
East Asian comparators									
Taiwan (25–30 years ago)	2.5	2.5	2.6	0.1	n.a.	n.a.	n.a.	n.a.	n.a.
Thailand (15–20 years ago)	3.0	1.7	—	1.7	13.1	11.7	0.5	11.2	37
China (15–20 years ago)	1.9	3.7	4.0	-0.3	11.2	1.0	1.9	-0.9	262

[1] Data refer to 1989.

[2] Growth rate is for the period 1965–1990.

Sources: World Bank, 1992a, *World Development Report 1992*, Oxford University Press, New York; Riedel, J., 1993, 'Vietnam: on the trail of the tigers', *The World Economy*, 16(4):401–22.

Table 2.6: Share of agriculture and industry in employment, value added and exports

Region/ Country	% Share of agriculture in:			% Share of industry in:		
	Employ- ment	Value added[1]	Exports[2]	Employ- ment	Value added[1]	Exports[2]
Latin America						
Brazil	24	10	31	23	39 (26)	53
Mexico	23	9	13	20	39 (23)	54
Argentina	13	13	59	34	41 (32)	36
Colombia	26	17	42	21	32 (21)	25
Peru	35	7	29	16	37 (27)	16
Venezuela	12	6	2	25	50 (20)	11
Sub-Saharan Africa						
Nigeria	45	36	2	4	38 (7)	2
Ethiopia	80	41	94	8	17 (11)	3
Zaire	72	30	37	13	33 (13)	7
Sudan (1965)	82	54	94	5	9 (4)	1
Tanzania	86	59	84	5	12 (10)	11
Kenya	81	28	70	7	21 (11)	11
Uganda	86	67	97	4	7 (4)	0
Ghana	59	48	64	11	16 (9)	1
Cameroon	74	16	55	5	28 (13)	16
North Africa						
Egypt	34	17	20	12	29 (16)	39
Morocco	46	27	30	25	33 (18)	42
Algeria	14	13	0	17	47 (12)	4
Tunisia	22	16	12	16	32 (17)	69
Eastern Europe						
Poland	26	14	15	37	36	68
Romania	29	18	··	40	48	··
Czechoslovakia	11	8	6	44	56	··
Hungary	18	12	26	37	32 (27)	66
Bulgaria	18	13	··	44	47 (12)	··
South Asia						
India	63	31	19	11	29 (19)	73
Pakistan	50	26	29	12	25 (17)	70
Bangladesh	56	38	25	10	15 (9)	73
East Asian comparators						
Taiwan (1960)	50	18	9	18	25 (17)	41
Thailand (1970)	77	38	67	11	25 (16)	23
China (1980)	70	37	25	18	45 (33)	53

Table 2.6: *continued*

---

[1] Data refer to 1989 (value in parenthesis refers to share of manufacturing in value added).

[2] Data refer to 1990; export data are for non-fuel primary commodity (agriculture) and machinery and equipment plus their manufactures (industry).

Sources: World Bank, 1992a, *World Development Report 1992,* Oxford University Press, New York; World Bank, 1976, *World Tables 1976,* Johns Hopkins University Press, Baltimore; United Nations Development Program, 1992, *Human Development Report 1992,* Oxford University Press, New York; International Labor Organisation, *Yearbook of Labor Statistics 1992,* ILO, Geneva; Riedel, J., 1993 'Vietnam: on the trail of the tigers', *The World Economy,* 16(4):401–22.

However, the manufacturing components of industry, which resulted for the most part from state-led, import-competing industrialisation efforts in previous decades, were much smaller, limited as they were by the size of national markets and by concentration in relatively heavy industry (typically steel and chemicals).

With the exception of China, where 30 years of central planning had promoted industry above everything else, the manufacturing sectors of the main East Asian economies generally accounted for only 15 per cent of domestic value added at the start of their outward-oriented growth. The situation in Korea was similar to that of Taiwan and Thailand.

Agriculture contributed significantly to the success of export-oriented industrialisation in East Asia. It provided the bulk of domestic savings which financed industrial investment and it initially supplied much of the foreign exchange needed for capital goods imports. Agriculture also provided industry with the surplus labour that was the very basis of the international competitiveness of export-oriented manufacturing in East Asia. In order to make these contributions, agriculture itself had to be fundamentally transformed. Increases in agricultural labour productivity allowed a steady transfer of labour resources to the expanding industrial sector. Savings generated in agriculture were made available to support, directly and indirectly, investments in industry through both financial channels and taxation. Rice production, for example, was heavily taxed in Taiwan through land taxes, compulsory rice purchases and rice for fertiliser barter programs, through which government

authorities manipulated prices paid and received by farmers.
The 'hidden rice tax' yielded a revenue equivalent to about
2.5 per cent of GDP or about 20 per cent of total government
budget revenue throughout the 1950s (Kuo 1983). Similarly,
direct taxation of the two key agricultural exports—rice and
rubber—generated revenue in Thailand of more than 1 per cent
of GDP (or about 10 per cent of total government revenues) in
the early 1970s (Siamwalla and Setboonsarng 1989). Agriculture
was for many years the main source of finance of government
subsidies of heavy industry in China.

South Asian economies today have reached a balance
between agricultural and industrial development very similar
to that of East Asia at the start of outward-oriented industrialisation (Table 2.6). Both India and Pakistan have agricultural
and industrial sectors that account for one-third and one-fifth
of value added, respectively. Manufacturing in Bangladesh has
considerably less weight in the total economy than in either
India or Pakistan, but it is growing rapidly and is being diversified from jute processing to other non-traditional manufactures. In all these countries a modest process of outward
orientation had already started in the 1980s, after decades of
mostly inward-looking industrialisation. The 1990 figures
already reflect the effects of some change in policies, but neither
the direction of policies nor the extent of their effects has been
significant enough to reverse the inward course of their development to date.

Morocco, Tunisia and (less so) Egypt also exhibit an economic
structure which is similar to that of East Asia at the outset of
its export-oriented industrialisation. The main outlier in North
Africa is Algeria which, after the first boom in oil prices, followed a mode of industry-led, centrally-planned development
similar to that of India during the first five-year plans and of
China in the initial phases of socialist development. The effects
of this strategy are reflected in the much lower share of value
added accounted for by agriculture, and in the correspondingly
higher share of industry, as compared with other countries of
the region (Table 2.6). Characteristically, however, the manufacturing sector of Algeria is little different in size from those
of its neighbours.

Sub-Saharan African developing economies today are much
more dependent on agriculture than their counterparts in Asia
20 years ago or in Latin America today. The large size of the

agricultural sectors in terms of both employment and value added reflects the paucity of economic diversification and structural transformation. Except for the few oil and mineral-rich economies such as Nigeria, Cameroon and Zaire, the shares accounted for by industrial value added are relatively small, in the 10 to 20 per cent range. Even smaller is the size of their manufacturing sectors. Employment in industry is minuscule accounting, in most cases, for only about 5 per cent of the total. The apparent exceptions turn out not to be real exceptions at all. Much of their industrial sector is merely an extension of their extractive industries, refining of crude oil in Nigeria and Cameroon, and production of intermediate copper products in Zaire. The small employment shares of industry confirm this conclusion.

Latin America, on the contrary, seems to have already a larger manufacturing sector than the economies of East Asia when they launched their export-oriented industrialisation drives or, for that matter, the rest of the developing world today (Table 2.6). Industry generally accounts for 40 to 50 per cent of domestic value added and, in some cases, even more in terms of exports. Manufacturing alone constitutes 25 to 30 per cent of domestic value added. Mexico and Brazil are, therefore, rightly regarded as part of the group of rapidly industrialising economies, together with Taiwan, Korea, China, Thailand, Singapore and Hong Kong. Even for such land-rich and traditionally agriculture-based economies of Latin America as Argentina and Colombia, industrial output constitutes more than one-third of the national product, industrial employment accounts for one-quarter of the total, and manufacturers make up one-quarter to one-third of total exports. In the main, Latin America has already achieved considerable industrialisation, even though current levels were in most cases reached with only a limited degree of export-orientation (Hughes 1988b; Corbo 1992). The exceptions are Brazil and Mexico.

Finally, much of Eastern Europe by all standard indicators also appears to be already highly industrialised, though this result was obtained by following a model that emphasised heavy industry and close integration with the former Soviet Union. It is well known that industrialisation in Eastern Europe was not only bloc-autarkic, and thus only marginally reflective of global comparative advantage, but also heavily distorted by a very complex system of incentives and disincentives rooted more in ideology than in economics. As a consequence, the main challenge facing Eastern European economies today is fundamentally different from that of most developing economies: it is the transformation of the existing industrial sectors and not the creation or the expansion of industry (Hughes and Hare 1992). Of course there are exceptions to this general pattern in Eastern Europe—Bulgaria and Albania, for example, which have relatively small manufacturing sectors and face a challenge to industrialise that is more similar to that of traditional developing economies than to the industrial transformation problems of their neighbours.

Domestic savings and investment

When they adopted the export-oriented growth strategy, the East Asian economies had relatively high domestic savings rates and, in most cases, also benefited from sizeable inflows of foreign savings. Taiwan, Thailand and Korea at that stage saved about 20 per cent of GDP, with foreign savings amounting to an additional 2 to 5 per cent of GDP. In the early 1970s, China was something of an exception, with no access to foreign savings, but with a share of domestic savings much higher than its neighbours, at around 30 per cent of GDP. On the whole, however, domestic and foreign savings allowed an investment in these economies at the outset of export-oriented industrialisation, equivalent in size to about 20 per cent of GDP (Table 2.7).

Savings and investment ratios, moreover, increased rapidly in East Asia during the early stages of outward-oriented growth, reaching 26 per cent of GDP in Taiwan in the mid-1970s, 32 per cent in China and 35 per cent in Thailand by the late 1980s. This is characteristic of the 'virtuous circle' between savings, investment and growth that occurred in East Asia after the start of the outward-oriented growth process. As observed by Collins (1991) for a sample of these economies, saving leads to investment, investment to growth, and growth to saving, producing a wholly virtuous circle.

Today, India and Pakistan, among South Asian economies, have overall savings–investment ratios only slightly lower than those of East Asian economies at the beginning of rapid growth. Pakistan, however, has much lower domestic savings, relative to GDP, than India (and the East Asian economies 20 to 30 years ago), relying much more than its neighbours on foreign savings.

Bangladesh is an even larger exception to the South Asian trend when it comes to savings. With a much lower per capita income than those of its neighbours, and a much lower rate of domestic saving, Bangladesh still finances the bulk of domestic invest- ment with foreign aid and resources. This situation closely par- allels that of the low-income, non-oil African economies.

The North African economies, with the exception of Egypt, also exhibit domestic savings ratios that are as high as those of the East Asian economies at the beginning of their outward- oriented growth. Algeria's domestic savings ratio is, in fact, double the average of the region. In addition, all these econo- mies have the capacity to attract very large inflows of foreign savings, largely in a form of private transfers (worker remit- tances), which allows them to achieve investment rates between 25 and 30 per cent of GDP, as high or higher than those of the economies of East Asia when they initiated outward-oriented growth.

Current savings ratios are much lower in Latin America than in East Asian economies. Savings to GDP ratios in Latin America today only match those prevailing in East Asia 20 to 30 years ago. High investment and growth rates in Latin America were underwritten during the 1970s by heavy foreign borrowing. When this source of savings waned in the 1980s, both investment and growth rates suffered. Indeed, with domestic savings ratios at around 22 to 23 per cent of GDP in most Latin American economies, domestic investment fell sig- nificantly below domestic savings.

In Sub-Saharan Africa, savings ratios are still very low, a reflection of low (and in many cases falling) per capita incomes. The variance among these countries is quite high, but with the exception of oil-rich Nigeria domestic savings in lower-income African countries are generally at or below 10 per cent, and only slightly above in higher-income economies (Cameroon, Ghana, Kenya). Most of the lower-income economies of this region (indeed the majority, if the entire population is consid- ered) depend on foreign aid for most of their investments. This is exemplified by Ethiopia, Uganda and Tanzania, among those whose data are reported in Table 2.7. Yet, despite relatively large inflows of foreign (especially public) savings, investment ratios are still generally low, at around 15 per cent of GDP or about 10 percentage points lower than the average of East Asia at take-off.

Table 2.7: Gross domestic savings and investment as a percentage of GDP

Region/Country	Investment[1]	Savings	
		Domestic	**Foreign[2]**
Latin America	(19)	(22)	(−3)
Brazil	22	23	−1
Mexico[3]	23	22	1
Argentina	9	16	−7
Colombia	19	25	6
Peru	23	23	0
Venezuela[4]	21	24	−3
Sub-Saharan Africa	(16)	(12)	(4)
Nigeria	15	29	−14
Ethiopia	13	6	7
Zaire	11	(10)	(1)
Sudan	10	9	1
Tanzania	25	−6	31
Kenya	24	18	6
Uganda	12	−1	13
Ghana	15	11	4
Cameroon	13	12	1
North Africa	(22)	(22)	(0)
Egypt	23	10	13
Morocco	26	20	6
Algeria	33	38	−5
Tunisia	27	19	8
Eastern Europe	(25)	(2)	(3)
Poland	31	39	−8
Romania	34	27	7
Czechoslovakia	30	28	2
Hungary	23	27	−4
Bulgaria	29	28	1
South Asia	(21)	(19)	(2)
India	23	20	3
Pakistan	19	12	7
Bangladesh	12	2	10
East Asian comparators			
Taiwan (1960)[5]	20	18	2
Thailand (1970)	26	21	5
China (1980)	29	29	0

Table 2.7: *continued*

Notes: Figures in parentheses are regional averages that include all countries. The exception is North Africa where they are simple averages of the countries shown.
[1] Data refer to 1990.
[2] Residually estimated as the difference between total gross domestic savings and domestic investment.
[3] Data refer to 1985–87 (average).
[4] Data refer to 1989–91 (average).
[5] Taiwan's investment and savings rates in 1970 were both at 26 per cent of GDP.
Sources: World Bank, 1992a, *World Development Report 1992*, Oxford University Press, New York; Riedel, J., 1993, 'Vietnam: on the trail of the tigers', *The World Economy*, 16(4):401–22.

In Eastern Europe domestic savings and investment ratios, at about 30 per cent of GDP, are as high or higher than those prevailing in East Asia when fast economic growth began. These economies suffer from misallocation of investments, not from insufficient investment resources, a problem that lies at the core of their economic transformation process.

The policy framework for export-oriented growth

The experience of East Asia suggests that to launch an export-oriented growth strategy three sets of policy requirements must be fulfilled: governments must maintain a reasonable degree of macroeconomic stability; they must provide an adequate supply of economic and social infrastructure; and they must remove the major obstacles to exporting, by establishing and maintaining a realistic exchange rate and by giving exporters free access to imported intermediate and capital goods.

Strictly speaking, macroeconomic stability is not a necessary condition for achieving economic growth. There are numerous instances of growth in unstable economic environments. Some have even hypothesised that economic growth must co-exist with inflation in developing economies (Hirshman 1957), but the sustainability of growth in highly inflationary conditions is nearly impossible, as such circumstances all too often generate crises which bring the growth process to a halt, or worse. For many reasons, stop–go economic progress occurs during periods of high inflation. Consumption and investment become unstable, either because of speculative responses to fast and sustained price changes or as reaction to real appreciations of the exchange rate. Appreciating exchange rates often follow high inflation rates and lead to loss of external competitiveness. Policy responses to high inflation and financial instability can also exacerbate the stop–go movements of the economy. The recent examples of Argentina and Peru in the mid-1980s and of Brazil from the mid-1980s to the early 1990s are cases in point (Dornbusch and Edwards 1989; Kiguel and Liviatan 1990). In these cases the growth which occurred in unstable environments, while initially rapid, soon collapsed into stagnation and even retrogression.

Comparison of the inflationary experience of various groups of developing economies during the past three decades with that of East Asian economies shows quite clearly how the latter group maintained a strong record of relative price stability while the former, with the exceptions of South Asia and (in part) North Africa, did not (Table 2.8). In the East Asian economies, inflation was low at take-off and remained low throughout the period of fast growth that followed. In the other groups, with the noted exceptions, inflation rose sharply in the 1970s and exploded in the 1980s. A measure of price stability is only now being maintained in the Latin American economies (excluding Brazil), while in much of Sub-Saharan Africa inflation rates remain unacceptably high. High inflation rates in much of Eastern Europe during the second half of the 1980s were, to some extent, inevitable in a phase when prices were liberalised after decades of rigid controls and production processes were reshaped.

An adequate supply of a range of public goods that includes physical infrastructure and administrative services is also an important condition for sustaining rapid growth. The experiences of Taiwan, Korea and Thailand indicate that these economies had, at take-off, an adequate supply of electric power, transport facilities and the means of communication to support growth. Also, the supply of these essential services was more or less kept in line with the growth in their demand as their economies expanded (Christensen et al. 1992).

The supply of infrastructure today is only marginally adequate in most of South Asia (with electric power still a problem in India and Pakistan), though it is generally good in

Table 2.8: Inflation rates by developing country regions

Region	1965–80	1980–90
East Asia and Pacific	9.3	6.0
South Asia	8.3	8.0
Middle East and North Africa	13.6	7.5
Sub-Saharan Africa	11.4	20.0
Latin America	37.4	192.1
Eastern Europe	13.9	38.8

Source: World Bank, 1992a, *World Development Report 1992*, Oxford University Press, New York.

North Africa, with Egypt showing relative weakness in some of its most densely populated parts. Transport and communications infrastructure is woefully inadequate in most of Sub-Saharan Africa, and is suffering from a decade of near neglect in much of Latin America. Eastern Europe has a relatively sound economic infrastructure, compared with most developing economies, though heavy reliance on coal-generated electric power and on nuclear energy has created serious conversion problems. In addition, housing shortages are pervasive in much of the urban areas of Eastern Europe.

Unshackling export growth requires that the government establish and maintain competitive exchange rates and give exporters free access to imported intermediate and capital goods. Real devaluation and at least partial import liberalisation are necessary to counter the inhibiting effect of previous import-substitution policies and to even out incentives for export and import-competing industries. Other measures, such as those aimed at actively promoting certain industries or exports through direct or indirect subsidisation, do not appear to have been decisive in East Asia. The evidence does not support the view that the East Asian tigers succeed by 'picking winners', except in so far as they picked exporting as a winning strategy. Even in the case of 'picking exports', the key policy condition was to remove biases against exports.

Real exchange rate devaluations did not occur systematically in other developing economies until the 1980s. They were most general and sustained in Latin America (with the exceptions of Brazil and Peru for a period) and in North Africa, but not in Sub-Saharan Africa, where high rates of inflation caused numerous reversals of attempts to devalue real exchange rates to sustain exports. In much of South Asia significant devaluations were also resisted until the late 1980s or early 1990s, but when introduced they were generally sustained. The same occurred in Eastern Europe. Exchange rate volatility, moreover, was much greater in Latin America than in East Asia during much of the 1970s and 1980s (Harberger 1988).

Liberalisations of import regimes were also resisted in much of the developing world outside of East Asia until the 1980s and, in some cases, until the early 1990s. Liberalisation became more frequent and radical during the 1980s in both Latin America and North Africa (Dean, Desai and Riedel 1993). In several Sub-Saharan African economies import liberalisation also occurred during the 1980s, but it was generally less sustained through time, and in some instances, was rendered ineffective by adverse fluctuations in real exchange rates. The South Asian nations resisted the impulse to liberalise their closed import regimes until the second half of the 1980s and proceeded very cautiously along this road even when the process started, fearful of balance of payments problems. India is still lagging in the liberalisation of its imports, except for intermediate goods, which were liberalised in the early 1990s. Domestically produced capital goods and agriculture are still very protected. In Eastern Europe, trade liberalisation also started late but was swift and radical after it began, fostered by the desire to integrate quickly with Western Europe and by the need to reorient trade after the collapse of the Council for Mutual Economic Assistance (COMECON).

The relevance of East Asian experience to other countries

The merits of an outward-looking development strategy and the shortcomings of an inward-looking one are now almost universally recognised in the developing world. Most, if not all, developing economies have adopted more competitive exchange rates and a set of 'export promotion policies', usually consisting of duty drawback schemes and various direct and indirect subsidies to exports. In spite of this, the export-oriented growth strategy has nowhere produced the high and sustained rates of growth it did in East Asia. Why is that? Is it because no other region enjoys (or enjoyed) the preconditions required to make it work, or because no other region has adopted the policy framework for an export-oriented growth strategy? If neither of these is the answer, then perhaps it is some other, more elusive ingredient, like culture, that differentiates the economic performance of East Asia.

The evidence presented in this chapter, and summarised in Table 2.9, suggests that it is not necessary to resort to these kinds of exotic explanations. The data in Table 2.9 suggest the reasons for other regions' inability to match East Asia's success with the export-oriented growth strategy have often been a combination of factors, varying from region to region, for example, missing preconditions and/or failure to adopt the requisite policies.

A distinction has been drawn between the early and late phases of the export-oriented growth strategy *à la* East Asia, the early phase being characterised by a situation in which a surplus of low-wage labour exists in the rural sector that can be drawn into export-oriented manufacturing with almost no opportunity cost to the economy.

In East Asia, only Taiwan and Korea (excluding from our analysis the rather special cases of the city-states of Hong Kong and Singapore) have progressed very far beyond the early phase, though Malaysia and Thailand have perhaps crossed the boundary between the two phases in recent years. In the early phase, it was argued, rapid export-oriented growth can be achieved without a broad liberalisation of the trade regime, though sustainable growth still requires a stable macroeconomic environment and an adequate supply of social and economic infrastructure in this phase. However, sustaining rapid export-oriented growth beyond the early phase of the export-oriented growth strategy, after the reservoir of low-wage labour is exhausted, does require a general liberalisation of the trade regime and a rationalisation of the industrial structure—essentially what Taiwan and Korea have been engaged in since the second half of the 1970s.

As indicated in Table 2.9, conditions in Latin America and Eastern Europe more closely resemble those of the East Asian economies in the later phase rather than the early phase of the export-oriented industrialisation strategy. Neither the population pressure nor the wage level in these regions is comparable

Table 2.9: Matching of East Asian growth conditions by other groups of developing economies (today with respect to 20–30 years ago)

	Population pressure (overall)	Social conditions			Resource endowment	
		Health	Nutrition	Literacy (school enrolments)	Land available for agriculture	Agricutral land per capita
South Asia	Yes	No	Yes (weak)	India only	Yes (except Bangladesh)	No
North Africa	Mixed (No on density, Yes on growth)	Yes	Yes (strong)	Yes (strong)	No (except Tunisia)	Yes (weak)
Sub-Saharan Africa	Mixed (No on density, Yes on growth)	No	No	No	No (except Nigeria)	Mixed
Latin America	No	Yes	Yes (strong)	Yes (strong)	No	Yes
Eastern Europe	No	Yes (strong)	Yes (strong)	Yes (strong)	Yes	Yes

| | Economic structure | | | | Policy stance | |
	Agricultural production	Industrial base	Savings	Investment	External competitiveness	Liberalisation
South Asia	Yes (except Pakistan)	Yes (except Bangladesh)	India only	Yes (except Bangladesh)	Yes (weak)	No
North Africa	Yes	Yes	Yes (except Egypt)	Yes	Yes	Yes (weak)
Sub-Saharan Africa	No	No	No (except Nigeria)	No	No (weak)	No (weak)
Latin America	Yes	Yes (strong)	Yes	Yes (weak)	Yes (except Brazil)	Yes
Eastern Europe	Yes	Yes (strong)	Yes	Yes (strong)	Yes	Yes

with those in East Asia in the early phase. For the Latin American and Eastern European economies, as for Taiwan and Korea at present, rapid growth requires overall liberalisation as well as the solid policy fundamentals of macroeconomic stability and adequate provision of public goods. Fortunately, in many Latin American and Eastern European economies, these requirements are at long last being addressed.

In much of the rest of the developing world, principally Africa and South Asia, per capita income is not much lower than it was in the East Asian economies when they launched the export-oriented growth strategy. In Sub-Saharan Africa, while wages are low, population pressure is not nearly as great nor are the indicators of the quality of human resources as high as was the case in East Asia. Domestic savings and investment are much lower than in East Asia during the first phase of fast growth and the existing industrial base is smaller. In South Asia and some parts of North Africa, on the other hand, population density is as high and education systems and other essential infrastructure are as developed as they were at the outset in the East Asian economies and the agricultural sector still has a sizeable supply of labour. What is generally missing in these economies is the necessary policy framework to make the export-oriented growth strategy work. Many governments in these regions have not made a sufficient commitment to maintaining competitive exchange rates and to giving exporters free access to imported intermediate and capital goods. In the larger South Asian economies such commitment has been lacking more than in the smaller economies, given the greater weight of protected sectors in the domestic economies. Most of the South Asian and North African economies have had export in place promotion schemes which were nonetheless insufficient to counterbalance the disincentives existing on the import side and the ingrained commitment to protection of domestic production from import competition.

Export-oriented industrialisation is, in essence, industrialisation according to comparative advantage. Historical experience suggests that no country can industrialise against its comparative advantage without paying a heavy price. So, in an important sense, the East Asian experience is relevant to every country. But that is not to say that every country can replicate the experience of the East Asian economies in adopting the export-oriented industrialisation strategy, especially the early phase of that model. Some economies in the developing world are far advanced beyond that stage (Latin America and Eastern Europe) while others (principally in Sub-Saharan Africa) lack some of the necessary ingredients to make it work the same way as it did in East Asia. However, the model is highly relevant to South Asia and some parts of North Africa, where conditions are not dissimilar to those which prevailed in the East Asian economies when they launched the strategy. To date, the South Asian economies (except briefly, or completely, in the case of Sri Lanka) have failed to adopt the policies needed to make the model work as it did in East Asia, but there are indications that India, in addition to Pakistan, has begun to recognise the merits of a more outward-looking strategy, encouraged by the experience of the East Asian economies. This augurs well for the future of South Asia. In much of North Africa the overall policy stance of governments has become progressively closer to what is needed to launch, or successfully sustain, export-oriented industrialisation and signs of success are already evident in Tunisia and Morocco. With conducive policy frameworks in place, fast growth *à la* East Asia can be maintained in these economies as well. The East Asian model appears, therefore, capable of maintaining relevance inside Asia and acquiring additional significance also for other regions.

Notes to Chapter 2

[1] This approach follows Riedel (1993) which examined the applicability of the model to Vietnam alone.

[2] We are grateful to Peter McCawley for highlighting the need to make this distinction clear.

3

Interrelationships Between Economic Ideas and Policy in the International Institutions

RICHARD H. SNAPE

Recent history of ideas and practice

If progress in science is viewed as the testing of hypotheses, then ideas and experience in the relationship between international trade and economic growth have provided a fertile arena for progress in economic science. There have been competing hypotheses which, albeit imperfectly, have been reflected in markedly different policies. And there have been excellent empirical analyses which have attempted to identify the key factors which might account for differential economic performance across countries. Finally, many countries have changed their policies markedly, so that examination of the same country's performance under different policy regimes is possible.

Trade policy and economic development during the middle decades of this century were intertwined with colonial independence, Keynesianism and state planning—Marxist or otherwise (Arndt 1987). National independence was riding high outside the industrial world. The conflicts of the first half of the century brought internationalism in their wake to the industrial rather than the developing world, though even in the industrial world Keynesian and other national *dirigiste* thought imposed limits on this internationalism. The political imperatives in the developing world were nationalist rather than internationalist and the analysis of most development economists reinforced the national bias.

Thus it is very difficult to disentangle the separate contributions to development policy of economic ideas on the one hand, and political ideology (including nationalism) on the other.

Of course, this is not surprising for ideology and economic logic are intertwined, even at the individual level. Nevertheless there were distinctive economic threads dominant in the development thinking of economists in the postwar period.

The influence of a combination of economic and political ideas (some of which are outlined below) resulted in the widespread adoption of import substitution and extensive planning as the road to development.[1] This entailed:

- export pessimism. The view that only through industrialisation could developing economies achieve an equality of economic bargaining power with industrialised economies;
- Keynesian concerns with unemployment;
- infant industry views which, in one form or another (for example, linkages or interdependences), encompassed the industrial sectors of developing economies; and
- nationalism.

The economic ideas were not just the product of populist amateur economics. Professional economists were at the forefront of this thinking: the inward-oriented policies of Latin America and India, for example, were at least as much the product of the ideas of professional economists as they were of political ideology. Never before had so many trained economists influenced economic policy so much and, as far as development policy was concerned, the professional advice promoted inward-oriented economic development.

During the late 1950s and 1960s, and following the Haberler Report of 1958, emphasis turned more from import substitution to export opportunities for developing economies, particularly export opportunities in the industrial world (Finger 1991:210; Hudec 1987:40–52). Considerable emphasis was given to industrialised economies offering non-reciprocal trade preferences, even to the extent of ranking these above non-discriminatory reductions in trade barriers (Finger 1991:214).

From the early 1970s it came to be appreciated that production which focused solely on the home market was not the road to development and that whatever harm was being inflicted by industrialised economies on the developing world by restrictions on access to industrialised-economy markets, the harm was not going to be redressed by import-substitution policies in developing economies. As many have pointed out, it was not that this had not previously been suggested by a number of economists; Viner and Haberler were early dissenters in the context of development policy (Little 1982). Rather, the evidence of the connection between outward-oriented trade regimes and rapidly developing economies triumphed. The evidence appeared in a well-known series of studies undertaken by Little, Scitovsky and Scott, Bhagwati and Krueger, Krueger, Donges, and by Balassa at the World Bank, in particular.

Thus ideas relating to linkages between trade and economic growth have been subjected to significant testing, and the dominant paradigm has changed from inward to outward-oriented. Taking on board the lessons of successful export orientation has required adjustment of much more than trade policies in many countries. Importantly, trade policy constrains other policies: meeting a competitive world market requires an ability to adjust to prevailing competitive conditions.[2]

Trade policy and development

While ideas of import substitution as a road to sustainable growth and development have been tested and are now rejected by most of the economics profession and by economic policymakers in most countries, the profession, and policymakers, are still divided on what ideas are supported by the evidence. Krueger (1980b) asked why substantial differences in rates of growth should be associated with export promotion as compared with import substitution. Krueger questioned whether the differences arose:

- from technological–economic factors (for example, scale economies, indivisibilities, competition, etc.);
- from the excesses of import substitution as actually implemented; or
- from the fact that export-oriented trade policy cannot in practice depart as much from neutral industry policies as can import-substitution policy.

In a survey eight years later, Bhagwati (1988) raised similar questions. To a significant degree these questions remain. Although provision of incentives for general import substitution is now ruled out by the evidence, the desirable industry policy stance for government, including selective import substitution as a transition to, or a basis for, export orientation, is still under contention, at least in some quarters.

The focus in recent years has been on East Asia. Many have questioned why the East Asian economies have performed so much better than most other developing economies. Hughes (1993a) pointed out correctly that there is not a single East Asian model. Rather there have been, and are, substantial differences in the policies of the successful East Asian economies, not just between Hong Kong and Singapore on the one hand, and South Korea and Taiwan on the other, but also between Hong Kong and Singapore and between South Korea and Taiwan. And authors at the World Bank (1991), and elsewhere, have reminded us that economic growth and development are the product of many factors and not just of a single magic ingredient. Getting the prices (or, more generally, the economic signals) right requires macroeconomic stability, including real exchange rate stability, not to mention government and property rights stability. It also includes building externalities into the framework of those who make economic decisions. On these matters there is little argument.

The dispute at essence is over whether, in trade and industry policy, it has been the general acceptance of the disciplines of the international market as such (as compared with import-substitution development strategies) that has been important, or whether, having committed the country to meeting international competition, government interventions have been an essential element of success in this competition. Given commitment to the international market, have government industry interventions on balance improved or worsened economic performance?

It is notable that the new growth theory stresses the international interdependence of industries, particularly through the transmission of ideas, in contrast to the linkages and interdependencies literature of an earlier generation which concentrated on the national economy.[3] The earlier literature was used to justify protection of the industrial sector; the current literature supports integrating it into the world market. Nevertheless, the evidence is still not able to discriminate among many hypotheses regarding sources of growth in those economies which have committed to the international market, nor regarding the net contribution of government industry policies.

Development policy and international institutions

What is clear, however, is that there is nothing like competition as a discipline on inefficiencies, and international competition provides the toughest and, in some cases, the only source of discipline on the policies of governments as well as of enterprises. Commitment to the international market is the essential ingredient which governs governments.

Three of the international bodies with strong interests in development, the United Nations Conference on Trade and Development (UNCTAD), the World Bank and the General Agreement on Tariffs and Trade (GATT), represent three very different ways in which economic ideas have been able to affect policy.

United Nations Conference on Trade and Development

UNCTAD was very clearly established on the basis of the dominant development ideas of the 1950s, and the principal ideas have not stood up well. Apart from various forms of technical assistance, the dissemination of information, and exhortation, UNCTAD's main effects on policy have been wrought through its influence on the GATT in the 1960s and, more recently and less importantly, through mechanisms aimed at commodity price stabilisation. Effects on the GATT are considered below.

The World Bank

The World Bank has been in a much stronger position than either UNCTAD or the GATT to have direct influence on policy; it has money to dispense. Institutionally it is in a much stronger position also. The staff of UNCTAD and the GATT comprise secretariats; decisions are taken by the Trade and Development Board of the United Nations on the one hand and by the CONTRACTING PARTIES (in capital letters, that is the Contracting Parties acting together) on the other. The equivalent at the Bank would involve the annual meeting of the Board of Governors making lending decisions and setting the conditions for loans. Instead, the Bank is established as a decision-making organisation in its own right, the decisions being taken by the Board of Directors. In addition, nationality considerations are not as important in the staffing of the Bank as they are at UNCTAD or even at the GATT, though they are not irrelevant.

The World Bank, particularly through the influence of Béla Balassa, Anne Krueger and Helen Hughes, has exerted the major international institutional influence on the trade and industry policies of developing economies and their transformation. The institutional structure of the Bank has facilitated the professional economic analysis of ideas and policies, and the conversion of these ideas into policy action. Particularly in the last decade or so, the *World Development Report* has clearly enunciated and developed the intellectual basis for the main thrust of the policy line of the Bank. This is not to say that the lines have always been consistently followed or that there are not many strands of thought within the Bank. Nevertheless the Bank has proved to be the most important avenue for the development and implementation of new ideas.

The General Agreement on Tariffs and Trade

In an important sense the GATT does not reflect the views of twentieth-century economists and never has done: the exchange of trade barrier concessions is at best in the realm of political economy rather than straight economics. On the other hand, the foundations of the GATT—that reductions in trade barriers are beneficial, that tariffs are preferred to quantitative or other restrictions, that trade barriers should not discriminate between foreign countries, and that trade barriers should be transparent—are fairly sound from an economic perspective.

The concessions framework, however, has many costs: it is often held that it reinforces mercantilist views of international trade. It encourages the idea that other countries' trade barriers are a greater burden than one's own (even that one's own barriers are not a cost at all), and that exemptions from the disciplines of the GATT are benefits, so that granting exemptions is a form of aid. The Secretariat and CONTRACTING PARTIES of the GATT have, on occasion, argued the case for special and differential treatments for developing economies, not as concessions from other countries necessary to induce developing economies' membership of the GATT, but as actions which are desirable in themselves. Thus, as many have pointed out, 'a somewhat surrealist situation—the world's leading organisation in the field of international trade explaining its policies to the world in terms of voodoo economics rejected by virtually every professional economist in the field' (Hudec 1987: 143–4) has developed.

Should developing economies be offered membership of the GATT with lower constraints than industrialised economies? Three supporting reasons can be put forward.

- There may be fewer policy weapons available in developing economies to pursue economic or non-economic goals so that it was, and is, more important to retain sovereignty with respect to trade policy.
- The domestic political cost of accepting constraints on national sovereignty may be higher in developing than industrial economies.

In principle these two reasons could justify a lower GATT membership payment, but the case is not strong, and could not justify the very slight constraints which GATT membership imposes on developing economies.

- Industrial economies, in so far as their trade policies *vis-à-vis* developing economies are concerned, have been relatively unconstrained, agriculture and clothing and footwear being prime examples.

This argument, in the context of the concessions framework which inevitably is the essence of the GATT, may have more substance, though it is overdone. The non-discriminatory provisions of the GATT have, in fact, disciplined the actions of industrial economies and the GATT provides for trade relations between developing economies as well as between those economies and industrial economies. The main point is not whether special and differential treatment is necessary to induce membership of the GATT club, but that the old trade and development orthodoxy held that these provisions were desirable in themselves.

Has the GATT been altered by the change in the prevailing trade and development orthodoxy? Mike Finger has addressed this question in his usual incisive manner. He takes the view that the GATT die has been cast and remains intact. 'The institutional structure, having been established without incorporating the "new" ideas and facts about trade and development, now serves to keep these concepts out. Thus proposals based on the experiences of the successful developing economies are excluded from consideration.' Further, the GATT 'as an institution designed to nudge countries toward the best choice of trade policy should receive a low score' (Finger 1991:203, 216).

Finger points out that most of the provisions of the GATT which specifically affect developing economies were informed by the prevailing orthodoxy in the three decades prior to 1970. The original GATT provided for exemption from some GATT constraints for measures directed towards infant industry assistance in developing economies and also for less stringent constraints for developing economies in the use of trade policy for 'balance of payments' reasons. The position was softened further by changes to the GATT undertaken after the GATT Review of the mid-1950s, with positive endorsement of infant industry and other exceptions for developing economies (Finger 1991:210; Hudec 1987:27). Further wide-ranging provisions for developing economies, more in the form of exhortations than of substance, are contained in Part IV of the GATT which was added in 1965 at a time when the GATT was in institutional and membership competition with the newly established UNCTAD (Finger 1991:208). Provisions for preferences for developing economies were first allowed for Australia under a GATT waiver, in 1965. They were then adopted on a much broader basis in 1968 under the Generalised System of Preferences (GSP), to be administered by UNCTAD, again under waiver until the so-called Enabling Clause, which was agreed to in 1979 as a part of the Tokyo Round of multilateral trade negotiations, made the waiver unnecessary.

Trends in the evolution of the GATT (for example, some of the new issues included in the Uruguay Round), in GATT rhetoric and in the formulation of the draft General Agreement on Trade in Services (discussed below), however, suggest that developments in economic ideas have had their impact, despite the constraints of the concessions framework.

Have attitudes towards the GATT changed? As a consequence of the change in views towards trade and development one could expect to see a greater readiness on the part of developing economies to join the GATT, less demand for (and supply of) special and differential treatment, greater readiness to take on constraints to import barriers, and fewer voodoo economics justifications for special and differential treatment emanating from the GATT Secretariat and the CONTRACTING PARTIES.

As far as preferences are concerned, one could hardly expect that developing economies would voluntarily forsake the preferences which are accorded by industrialised economies, unless they were to be traded off for something better. Although the effort that went into negotiating preferences may have been better spent in other directions, for example in securing greater adherence by all contracting parties to the general rules of the GATT, the preferences now exist, the costs of securing them are sunk and the costs of maintaining them are generally low. The vested interest in preference retention, even when it is at the expense of other developing economies, is well illustrated by the current banana dispute, European Union preference for the bananas of European ex-colonies being hotly challenged (under the GATT) by other banana exporters (GATT 1993:2).

So it is to aspects of GATT policy other than preferences to which most attention should be directed. Developing economy membership of the GATT and some Agreement Codes has been steadily increasing (albeit with few constraints on the members in many cases) and the propagation of voodoo economics by the GATT has decreased.

For further evidence on the impact of recent ideas on trade and development on international institutions it is instructive to examine the draft General Agreement on Trade in Services. Although the General Agreement on Trade in Services was negotiated under the same auspices as the Uruguay Round GATT negotiations, it has addressed a new set of problems. This new focus has allowed some release from entrenched positions.

Development policy in the General Agreement on Trade in Services

Despite the not unexpected initial opposition from India, Brazil and some other developing economies, negotiations for a multilateral trade agreement in services, officially on a separate track from the GATT negotiations, have been undertaken as part of the Uruguay Round. To the surprise of many, given the initial hostility, developing economies have stayed with the negotiations. The document tabled by the Director-General of the GATT in December 1991 is an agreement negotiated by more than 100 participants.

In many regards the tabled General Agreement on Trade in Services parallels the GATT. There are general obligations regarding transparency of barriers, non-discrimination (with an exception in the context of economic integration) and other matters. These general commitments cover all the service industries (with a very wide definition of services) for all signatories (Parties).[4]

As well as general obligations there are specific commitments relating to market access and national treatment. The specific commitments are undertaken only with respect to those services industries listed in a Party's schedule: market access for other Parties can be no less favourable for these industries than is specified in these schedules. In addition, unless specified in these schedules, Parties cannot impose a number of listed quantitative restrictions.

There are several provisions for developing economies. The preamble expresses the desire 'to facilitate the increasing participation of developing economies in international trade in services and expansion of their services exports, *inter alia*, through the strengthening of their domestic services capacity and its efficiency and competitiveness' while taking 'particular note of the serious difficulty of the least developed economies'. In Part II, which covers general obligations and disciplines, developing economies are allowed flexibility under the provision that Parties have to supply 'enquiry points' under the transparency provisions and again with respect to meeting the criteria (paralleling Article XXIV in the GATT) specified for economic integration. The latter provision presumably would allow as much flexibility as does the Enabling Clause of the Tokyo Round agreements, that is, a great deal of flexibility. Again in Part II, the General Agreement on Trade in Services has an article which covers 'restrictions to safeguard the Balance of Payments' in much the same way as do Articles XII and XVIIIB of the GATT. This was perhaps inevitable, given Article XII in the GATT, and the improbability that it would be revoked. Allowing the possibility of restrictions being placed on goods trade and not on services trade, in the presence of financial crises it would have been a brave move as it would have undermined the GATT provision. Taking its cue from Article XVIIIB of the GATT, the General Agreement on Trade in Services Article XII recognises 'that particular pressures on the balance of payments of a Party in the process of economic development or economic transition may necessitate the use of financial restrictions', and in the incidence of such restraints,

'Parties may give priority to the supply of services which are more essential to their economic or development programs'. Such restrictions have to be non-discriminatory and consistent with the Articles of the International Monetary Fund (for members of the Fund).

The General Agreement on Trade in Services does not have provisions for applying countervailing duties on subsidised services trade, though it does provide for negotiations with a view to developing multilateral disciplines on subsidies and 'to address the appropriateness of countervailing procedures'. These negotiations 'shall recognise the role of subsidies in relation to the development programs of developing economies and take into account the needs of Parties, particularly developing economies, for flexibility in this area'. This is in line with provisions of the Tokyo Round Code covering subsidies on goods. (There are no provisions in the General Agreement on Trade in Services with respect to dumping or anti-dumping actions.)

The Article which addresses developing economies most fully is Article IV, titled Increasing Participation of Developing Countries. It provides that such participation should be facilitated by scheduled commitments of Parties to help developing economies' services capacity through, *inter alia*, access to technology on a commercial basis, improving access to distribution channels and information networks and liberalising market access in sectors and modes of supply of export interest to developing economies. Contact points should also be established for information on commercial and technical aspects of services supply, on acknowledgement of professional qualifications and on the availability of services technology. Least developed economies would be given special priority and latitude.

Thus while there are particular provisions for developing economies, there are no preferences for products as such. (Article IV refers to service products of interest to developing economies, not to preferences for developing economies.) It is particularly notable that technology transfer is to be on a commercial basis. There is a strong emphasis on the supply of information.

What parts of the General Agreement on Trade in Services, in so far as they affect developing economies specifically, would be inconsistent with the new trade and development

economics? The greatest hangovers of the old development ideology are those parts of the General Agreement on Trade in
Services which have been brought over from the GATT or the
Tokyo Round Enabling Clause; the provisions regarding economic integration and balance of payments problems. Apart
from these provisions there is little to which exception can be
taken, and the tone of the General Agreement on Trade in Services is to facilitate the participation of developing economies
into international services trade, not keep them at bay. It may
be concluded that the export orientation of the new trade and
development economics has had some influence on the draft
agreement.

The General Agreement on Trade in Services is consistent
with Part II (relating to services) of the Ministerial declaration
which launched the Uruguay Round:

> Negotiations in this area shall aim to establish a multilat-
> eral framework of principles and rules for trade in
> services ... with a view to expansion of such trade under
> conditions of transparency and progressive liberalisation
> and as a means of promoting economic growth of all
> trading partners and the development of developing
> economies.

The tone here differs significantly from that of the much
longer Part I of the Declaration, referring to negotiations for
goods under the GATT itself, which stated that 'the principle
of differential and more favourable treatment embodied in Part
IV and other relevant provisions' of the GATT and in the Tokyo
Round Enabling Clause should apply to the negotiations, and
that 'developed countries do not expect reciprocity for commitments made by them to reduce or remove other barriers to
the trade of developing countries'. Thus some enlightenment
may have been present at the conception of the General Agreement on Trade in Services, and it did not disappear during
gestation.

Having noted the positive tone of the General Agreement on
Trade in Services towards the participation of developing economies, and that developing economies participated extensively
in the negotiation of the General Agreement on Trade in Services, one must acknowledge that the real tests are in which
countries join and which specific commitments they undertake.

The slow conversion of ideas into policy

The trade and development orthodoxy has changed sharply over the past five decades: economic ideas have been tested and some have been rejected. The ideas of economists have been of major significance in the formation of the postwar development orthodoxy and in its overthrow. The evidence strongly supports incentive systems which reflect commitment to the world market, though there is still dispute as to the actual sources of growth and the role of governments in industry policy. A key ingredient is that international markets discipline decision-makers in general, both within governments and business enterprises.

International institutions have played an important role in the conversion of ideas to policy. The GATT is particularly important given the emphasis on outward-oriented trade regimes. Governments join the GATT in order to constrain the trade policies of other governments as well as their own, a framework in which concessions are exchanged is more or less inevitable in international agreements, and this has encouraged some poor economics. The development orthodoxy of the 1950s and 1960s affected the GATT Articles and rhetoric significantly in ways not consistent with the new trade and development orthodoxy. There is some recent evidence that the new development orthodoxy may have had some impact, though one must agree with Finger (1991) that change is very difficult.

Notes to Chapter 3

1 And not just in low-income countries, the midway doctrine, a sort of generalised infant industry concept, dominated the thinking of Australian trade policymaking until the end of the 1960s (Arndt 1965). Australian representatives were leading proponents of Keynesian considerations in negotiations for the International Trade Organization, and probably were responsible for the inclusion of 'ensuring full employment' as an objective of trade policy in the preamble of the GATT. They also pressed for the inclusion of infant industry exemptions from the GATT. In his memoirs, Dr Coombs argues that domestic demand could only be sustained at a high level in Australia if export income or capital inflow remained high. This depended on the United States maintaining high consumer spending and imports. 'Logically the

proposed conference on trade and employment was the opportunity to persuade the United States, particularly, to commit itself to policies likely to provide these prerequisites, and the "Keynesian" approach was the intellectual basis for that persuasion. Our objective [was] to ensure a United States economy which would, by its consumption pressure, power the demand for internationally traded goods, and which would open its markets to the products of other countries' (Coombs 1981:90–1).

[2] In a recent survey, Dornbusch (1992) sees the shift of developing economies from 'severe and destructive protection to free trade fever' as stemming from four overlapping sources: anti-statism, poor economic performance, information about opportunities in other countries, and World Bank pressure and evidences of success.

[3] 'Until other politically viable institutions for fostering development can be discovered, the only safe piece of advice to offer developing countries is that integration with world markets offers large potential gains. The gains from using someone else's ideas come from a source that is different from the classical gains from trade. The gains [China] receives from interaction with Hong Kong and Taiwan (China) far outweigh the small and risky gains that might be achieved through a more tightly controlled industrial policy' (Romer 1992:88).

[4] A limited exemption from according most-favoured-nation treatment for particular measures may be granted at the time of entry into force of the agreement. The exemptions are to be for five years or less, are to be reviewed within five years and can be renewed. This exempting provision was introduced following pressure from the US maritime and telecommunications industries, the former fearing the thin edge of the wedge in terms of increasing foreign competition, the latter fearing constraints on the use of Section 301 type actions (that is, targeted policies designed to open foreign markets through penalising non-opening) against telecommunications industries abroad.

4

Government's Role in East Asia's Economic Success

CHIA SIOW YUE

The rapid growth and structural transformation of the East Asian newly industrialised economies since the early 1960s has sparked considerable interest among development economists and policymakers. In the past decade, interest in this East Asian 'economic miracle' has broadened to encompass the ASEAN (Association of Southeast Asian Nations) economies, dubbed the second tier of Asian newly industrialised economies. This chapter examines the role of government in the four resource-poor Asian newly industrialising economies of Hong Kong, South Korea, Taiwan and Singapore, and the three resource-rich ASEAN economies of Indonesia, Malaysia and Thailand. These economies constitute the world's most dynamic grouping of the past three decades. For simplicity, the term 'East Asia' is used to cover these countries.

The determinants of the East Asian economic success have been a matter of active debate in the economic development literature (Amsden 1989; Wade 1990; Islam 1992). Neoclassical development economists interpret the success in terms of the efficiency of the market mechanism and policies emphasising openness, private enterprise and the minimal role of government. Statists drew a different conclusion, however, explaining the East Asian success in terms of effective state intervention. A growing number of empirical studies show that government intervention in the Asian newly industrialised economies (except Hong Kong) has been extensive, though there appears to be no consensus on its benefits.

Governments in East Asia undertake multifaceted roles of providing public goods, promoting industrial growth through incentives and regulations, and acting as entrepreneur in owning and operating business enterprises. There are considerable variations, however, in the level and nature of government intervention among countries and at different stages of economic development.

In the Asian newly industrialising economies, economic success is associated with both a minimal role of government in Hong Kong and an extensive role in South Korea, where industrial policy is aggressively pursued, with the government targeting specific industries and conglomerates (*chaebols*) for promotion through selective credit and other forms of assistance. In Singapore, unlike Hong Kong, economic success is associated with a government which is actively involved in every facet of the Singaporean economy, ranging from ensuring a favourable business climate for investors to the establishment of highly successful state-owned enterprises and administrative guidance on wage increases, but refraining from the South Korean policy of providing subsidised credit to selected industries and firms. Like Singapore, Taiwan has a large and successful state-owned enterprise sector, but unlike South Korea, its private sector is dominated by small and medium-sized enterprises. Among the ASEAN economies, Malaysia and Indonesia have achieved strong economic growth in spite of poor performances of their extensive state-owned enterprises. Thailand's excellent economic performance of recent years is associated with a weak government sector and a strong private sector.

The objective in the following discussion is to examine the role played by governments in the economic success of the East Asian economies. If success can be attributed largely to the policy framework, then the East Asian development experience holds useful lessons for other developing regions.

Reasons for government intervention

Modern-day governments take on responsibilities far beyond those advocated by Adam Smith, and are held responsible not only for defending the country, maintaining law, order and justice, and protecting property rights, but also for economic management to promote growth and ensure macroeconomic stability.

Economic intervention occurs for a variety of reasons. The primary reason is to combat market failure. East Asian governments had to play an active role in promoting economic development and industrialisation in the 1950s and 1960s because of serious market failure and unfavourable socio-political climates. Markets fail in the presence of large externalities, as in the case of public goods, or in the presence of imperfect competition. Correcting market failure using government intervention, however, may lead to government failure from economic mismanagement or rent-seeking by private interest groups.

Some areas of government intervention are widely accepted while others are controversial. Activities which are non-controversial include:

- the provision of public goods characterised by externalities and indivisibilities;
- government information gathering and dissemination as this reduces the transaction costs of the private sector; and
- government provision of physical and social infrastructure as such goods are crucial for economic development and tend to be underprovided if left to the private sector.

Highly controversial is government intervention to anticipate or alter market outcomes, that is, trying to pick winners. Government may not have the know-how to pick industries which can become internationally competitive and contribute to economic growth and structural transformation.

A second reason for government intervention is to alter both the interpersonal distribution of incomes and the intertemporal allocation of resources. All governments are committed to improving income distribution, alleviating poverty and providing basic needs such as education and health. Such interventions are justified not only on equity grounds, but also have a growth rationale, as provision of basic needs can improve labour productivity and extreme income inequalities can disrupt the growth process. There is some trade-off, however, between growth and distribution. Countries which emphasise distribution, without paying sufficient attention to growth, eventually face the problem of unsustainability. Mushrooming welfare expenditures burden government budgets and reduce resources available for productive investment. The past decade is witness to attempts by various governments to cut back such welfare commitments. Increasingly also, governments are called upon to act as custodian of the interests of future generations by conserving natural resources and protecting the environment.

Neoclassical versus statist views on government intervention

Neoclassical development economists agree that governments should intervene to overcome inherent market failure. They argue, however, that such failures are uncommon and that most market failures are policy induced. The proper role of government is to help create and maintain an environment in which price signals can effectively determine resource allocation. This entails a neutral policy regime and a small public sector.

The neoclassicals drew empirical support from the contrasting economic performances of East Asian and other developing economies. Costly government failures in a large number of developing economies led to the 1980s phenomenon of deregulation, liberalisation and privatisation; largely spearheaded by international and regional agencies such as the World Bank, the International Monetary Fund and the Asian Development Bank.

In recent years the neoclassical position has come under increasing attack from statists, who also draw on the East Asian experience to buttress their arguments (Amsden 1989; Wade 1990). First, it is pointed out that the Asian newly industrialising economies have not been pursuing non-interventionist or neutral policy regimes, except in the case of Hong Kong. Governments in South Korea, Taiwan and Singapore have intervened extensively in their economies and actively promoted the development of new industries, including many which have since become internationally competitive. Second, it is argued that neoclassical development economists have ignored differences in the capacity of governments to guide the market. Governments in South Korea and Taiwan have an unusually well-developed capacity for selective intervention to promote economic growth and restructuring. This capacity is attributable to a powerful set of policy instruments at their disposal and to certain institutional structures and relationships. The East Asian experience shows that active and selective government intervention in a market economy can co-exist with outstanding economic performance. Third, it is argued that the theoretical foundation for a *laissez-faire* approach towards industrial development policy reflects the neoclassical emphasis on trade rather than technological change as the centrepiece of industrialisation. If the focus is shifted to technological change, a strong economic rationale exists for selective industrial promotion. National comparative advantage can be created, as government policies promote capital accumulation and skill acquisition. Industries with external economies, scale economies and learning curve economies can benefit from government support, and economic restructuring would be too slow if left to market forces.

The capacity for economic management

East Asian governments vary in their capacity to supply public goods, especially infrastructure, and they have intervened in both product and factor markets with very different results. East Asian governments, however, appear more capable of successful economic intervention than most other developing economies, as evidenced by their more successful economic performance.

Wade (1988) identifies three aspects of East Asian leadership which have contributed to successful government intervention:

• The economic bureaucracy in these economies had the wisdom to ensure that protected industries became competitive. In South Korea, the government strongly encouraged infant industries to export, thus exposing them directly to international competition, even when exports had to be sold at a loss; subsidies to firms were tied to export performance. In Taiwan, the government appeared to put less direct pressure on infant industries to export, and relied more on the threat of import competition to ensure productive efficiency from both private and state-owned enterprises. As a result, import substitution did not saddle South Korea and Taiwan with inefficient and non-competitive industries, as in the case of many economies in Latin America and South Asia.

• The policy instruments adopted were deliberately selective rather than across-the-board. Protection and assistance were given primarily to infant industries and to those industries perceived to be the 'commanding heights' of the economy. Intervention focused on sunrise industries with potential competitiveness rather than on sunset industries which had lost their competitiveness.

• The government interventions had a high degree of policy and implementation coherence, pulling in the same direction and resulting in cumulative impacts. For example, activities that received help through trade controls were also assisted through financial subsidies and fiscal incentives.

The capacity for successful government intervention depends not only on appropriate policy instruments but also on the competence and goals of decision-makers and on the institutional framework.

- The central decision-making structure has to be staffed by the best administrative and managerial talents. The bureaucracies of the Asian newly industrialising economies are generally noted for their competence and efficiency, a reflection of a meritocratic recruitment system and remuneration and career paths which are competitive with those offered by the private sector.
- The central decision-makers need to be relatively insulated from pressure groups, be they the legislature, a farm lobby or a trade union movement. Authoritarian regimes in many of the East Asian economies have ensured such insulation.
- Decision-makers have to be imbued with growth-oriented goals and have a centralised structure through which to order and coordinate priorities. In the various East Asian economies, there is generally close coordination between various ministries and statutory boards responsible for economic policy formulation and implementation.
- A credit-based financial system enables the government to directly influence the sectoral and firm-level allocation of credit. It has been argued that such a financial system not only provides the government with a powerful lever for promoting particular industries and firms, but also makes available more funds for economic growth than is possible under an alternative capital-market system.
- Success requires a high degree of public–private cooperation and information sharing.

The economic success of the ASEAN economies, particularly Malaysia and Thailand, reduces the case for an authoritarian regime. More important than authoritarianism is political continuity which enables both the political leadership and the bureaucracy to have a long-term vision and to develop and implement policies to that end. Democratic processes that result in frequent changes of government and policy direction are generally constrained in planning and acting long term.

The governments of East Asia also have institutional mechanisms which ensure that they act responsibly. In several economies, governments are constrained in their ability to incur and finance budget deficits. Singapore has gone to great lengths to ensure financial and fiscal prudence. Following political independence, the colonial currency board system was retained to ensure that the Singapore dollar was fully backed by external reserves. A 1993 constitutional amendment constrains the ability of an elected government to use the country's accumulated official reserves to finance budget deficits.

The East Asian experience has also shown that when policy mistakes are made, as in South Korea in the late 1970s and Singapore in the mid-1980s, corrective measures can be quickly put in place so that economic downturns and loss of competitiveness are only temporary.

Areas of government involvement

Minimal functions of government

The East Asian economies have performed the minimal functions of government reasonably well. First, these economies have enjoyed political stability and law and order for the greater part of the past three decades, notwithstanding the problems of a divided Korea and the two Chinas. The ASEAN economies (including Singapore) have successfully overcome the threat of communist insurgency and established ethnic harmony. The absence of wars and civil strife and the enforcement of property rights have conserved scarce economic resources and promoted private investment.

Second, until recently the East Asian economies have generally provided the physical infrastructure (telecommunications, transportation, utilities) necessary for private investment, economic growth and quality of life. Singapore has been most successful in infrastructure development, considering it a crucial prerequisite for maintaining its competitive edge as a regional commercial, transportation and financial hub, and for attracting foreign investment. In the other economies, rapid economic growth and investment have strained infrastructure. Taiwan has embarked on an ambitious multi-billion-dollar plan to develop its increasingly inadequate infrastructure. Malaysia has had a good record of infrastructural development until lately, when shortages in utilities and transportation bottlenecks have become a matter of investor concern. Thailand's phenomenal urban growth and delays in developing the land transportation network are choking Bangkok, and investors are offered incentives for regional dispersal of industries. Traditionally, infrastructure development in East Asia has been regarded as a government responsibility. Massive infrastructural needs, however, have necessitated new forms of partnership between private sectors and foreign investors.

Third, an important feature of East Asian industrial capability and competitiveness is the quality of its human resources. The Asian newly industrialising economies have invested heavily in education and training, providing a well-educated labour force. These economies have placed a strong emphasis on engineering, technical and vocational education. South Korea and Taiwan, benefiting from the Japanese and American heritage of mass education, started earlier, so that the bulk of their populations are well educated, and a sizeable percentage has tertiary education. Singapore and Hong Kong followed the British model and pursued a more elitist educational policy for a considerable period. As a result, Singapore's educational stock is poor relative to its per capita income. In the past decade, the government has placed top priority on education and training. The ASEAN economies have low secondary school enrolment ratios and are increasingly experiencing skill shortages. They need to expand educational and training facilities rapidly.

Macroeconomic management

As elsewhere, governments in East Asia have responsibility for macroeconomic management. As relatively open and small economies, the task of macroeconomic management has been rendered more difficult by various external shocks over the past two decades. This has been particularly so for the ASEAN economies which are dependent on primary commodity exports. Volatile commodity prices in international markets have created booms and busts in these economies. The external shocks started with oil price hikes in 1973 and 1980, coinciding with a period of high global interest rates. Global recession followed and oil and commodity prices slumped during the early 1980s. In addition, an appreciating US dollar led to major currencies realignments in Organisation for Economic Cooperation and Development (OECD) member economies in September 1985.

A World Bank report (World Bank 1993b) found that lack of macroeconomic stability is a serious obstacle to economic growth in developing economies. By and large, East Asian economies have a good record of macroeconomic stability, as evidenced by their low inflation rates and quick resolution of macroeconomic crises. Macroeconomic stability has been achieved through commitment to fiscal prudence, manageable domestic and foreign debt financing, and prompt and flexible responses to changing economic circumstances and external shocks.

Hong Kong and Singapore seldom run fiscal deficits. While the other East Asian economies do run into fiscal deficits, these have been within manageable limits and have not undermined macroeconomic stability. High growth and high private savings rates have eased the burden of fiscal deficits. In addition, institutional mechanisms have constrained the temptation of deficit financing, such as the balanced budget requirement in Indonesia and Thailand. And to reduce fiscal deficits and promote private sector savings and investment, governments have embarked on fiscal reforms—providing incentives to savings, improving the efficiency of the public sector, reducing income taxes, and shifting to consumption taxes including cost recovery through user-charges for goods and services provided by state-owned enterprises.

Hong Kong, Singapore and Taiwan have minimal external debts and are net capital exporters. The other East Asian economies have sizeable public or publicly guaranteed external debt. South Korea was the world's fourth largest debtor in 1980, while the external debt of Indonesia, Malaysia and Thailand mushroomed in the 1980s. These economies have not faced a serious debt crisis, however, and have avoided debt rescheduling, although the escalation of debt servicing has entailed structural adjustment policies. Rapid economic growth and high export performance have helped reduce the debt burden.

Pangestu (1991) examined the ASEAN economies' experience in the 1980s and found that often a crisis was necessary before governments would embark on policy reforms and structural adjustments. Prompt responses generally produced better results. For example, when confronted with the recession in

1985, the Singapore government undertook speedy policy reforms and the economy quickly rebounded, while in Indonesia and Thailand the policy responses were slower and economic recovery was delayed. Pangestu also found that monetary policy was ineffective and exchange rate policy became the main stabilisation tool for the small and open economies of ASEAN. Interest rates were usually needed to maintain exchange rates and could not be used to maintain monetary targets. Also, countercyclical budget deficits financed by foreign borrowing proved unsustainable unless attention was paid to long-term budgetary balance and loan productivity. Malaysia and Thailand pursued countercyclical policies, but the increased foreign borrowing led to higher debt burdens, current account deficits, budget deficits and inflation. Indonesia did not pursue a countercyclical policy in the recession of the early 1980s. Although demand management policies were undertaken, economic recovery did not occur because demand management was not accompanied by structural change policies. These were undertaken only after the rapid decline in oil prices in 1986. The ASEAN economies' experience suggests that macroeconomic stabilisation and structural adjustments go hand in hand. Macroeconomic stabilisation measures are needed to moderate inflation and maintain exchange rates at a realistic level, so that structural policies can work.

Industrial promotion

The East Asian economies have undergone rapid structural transformation, most evident in the rapid growth of the industrial sector. The pace of industrialisation has depended to an important degree on promotional policies and the regulatory environment. Governments were committed to promoting industrialisation in the 1950s and 1960s and intervened to initiate and quicken its pace and influence its direction and pattern. Industrial success is evident in the rising share of manufactures in GDP, employment and exports. In the Asian newly industrialising economies, the rapid growth in manufacturing output and employment resulted from early emphasis on labour-intensive manufacturing for export. The increased demand for labour and subsequent rise in wage rates helped spread the benefits of growth more widely. By the early 1970s, full employment had been reached. These economies have been experiencing labour shortages in the past decade. In the ASEAN economies, industrialisation began later and accelerated in the 1980s. Manufactures form a rapidly growing share of GDP, employment and exports. As in the Asian newly industrialising economies, employment absorption has been rapid and Malaysia is beginning to experience labour shortages.

Industrial policy broadly covers the range of government actions which directly affect the sectoral allocation of resources. In East Asia, it is associated with the promotion of new, sunrise or strategic industries, rather than the protection of ailing or sunset industries, and with the upgrading of existing industries and the promotion of technological development, exports and regional dispersal of industries. In some countries, industrial policy is more specifically identified with industrial targeting or picking winners.

The instruments of industrial policy are often discriminatory, favouring specific industries and firms. Pecuniary measures include tax incentives, tariffs, subsidies and loans, while regulatory measures include legal restrictions, administrative rules and guidelines, industrial licensing and controls of cartels. Governments usually have an advantage over the unorganised private sector in information and data-gathering and have better overall and long-term views of their economies. Governments can improve private sector decision-making and minimise risks by gathering, pooling and disseminating technical, commercial and market information. But they do not usually have a comparative advantage at the micro-level. Thus, while governments may provide special support based on the infant industry argument, they are not well equipped to pick national champions.

Does the need for industrial policy or government intervention vary with the stage of economic development? What is the relationship between stage of economic development and the type of industrial policy pursued? Some have argued that a country or industry's stage of economic development should be taken into consideration in judging whether a particular industrial policy is justifiable (Okuno and Suzumura 1986). An industrial policy appropriate for a country or industry at the infant stage may no longer be appropriate at the mature stage when the market is more developed and market failures are less pervasive. Also, government leverage to pursue industrial policy changes with the level of development. Some mandatory control measures that are within a government's discretion in an infant market economy may no longer be possible for a developed mature economy facing the threat of foreign retaliation.

As is observed in subsequent sections of this chapter, there is a wide range of experience with industry policy interventions in East Asia, across countries and over time. Generally, however, such interventions do less to discriminate between activities, and especially between import-competing and export activities, than is common in developing countries elsewhere. Hong Kong is the one economy in the world with almost no policy intervention. The resource-rich ASEAN economies have tended to apply incentive structures that are more strongly biased against exports than the others, although these biases have been reduced in the general trend of industry policy interventions right through the region since the early 1980s. There is much controversy over whether industry policy interventions, such as they have been in East Asia, have helped or hindered development.

The outcome would be more favourable if the policies were directed to facilitating the workings of the market, that is, correcting for market failures, rather than substituting for, or bypassing the market. Policies which go against underlying market trends, such as commodity restriction agreements or artificial price support programs, have inevitably ended in failure and at great cost. Similarly, while accelerating the acquisition of dynamic comparative advantage may be seen as a legitimate objective, the timing of policy can be crucial to the outcome. Implementing too far ahead, as in the case of South Korea's heavy industry program in the mid-1970s and Indonesia's aerospace thrust in the 1980s, runs counter to market fundamentals and can result in costly diversion of scarce resources.

East Asian experience of industrialisation

Except for Hong Kong, the East Asian economies embarked on industrialisation by first adopting an import-substitution strategy. Hong Kong and Singapore provide two contrasting paths to industrialisation. Both embarked on industrialisation in the early 1950s and early 1960s respectively, when their traditional *entrepôt* activities were disrupted. Hong Kong pursued a *laissez-faire* policy and industrial development was left to private sector initiative. Its *entrepôt* traders had experience in exporting China's manufactures and the influx of industrial capital and entrepreneurs from Shanghai (following the communist victory in China) provided the favourable supply conditions for industrialisation. The government played the minimalist role of maintaining a free trade and exchange regime with ready access to imports at world prices; provided infrastructure, education and training; and adopted a simple, low-rate tax system to promote private investment without discriminatory fiscal incentives. Singapore adopted a highly interventionist strategy. Unlike Hong Kong, Singapore did not experience an influx of industrial capital and expertise. Faced with the political instability and turbulent industrial relations of the late 1950s and early 1960s, the government felt it had to intervene to create a favourable investment climate. It provided infrastructure and wide-ranging investment incentives to attract foreign direct investment and its associated industrial and export marketing expertise.

Industrialisation in South Korea and Taiwan began after major political changes in the late 1940s and early 1950s following the retreat of the Kuomintang from mainland China to Taiwan, and the political division of Korea. In South Korea, government economic planners made extensive use of incentives and regulations, particularly the selective allocation of bank credit to pick winners. Industrial policy encouraged the development of *chaebols* (conglomerates) and pushed domestic investment well above domestic savings. Unlike Singapore, South Korea did not depend much on foreign direct investment, preferring to nurture domestic industrial entrepreneurship, borrow heavily from abroad to finance investments and promote technology transfer through licensing arrangements. The government did not directly involve itself in investment and production, except for public utilities and a few basic industries. In Taiwan, the Kuomintang government owned all large industrial concerns and banks, and controlled foreign aid and trade. Foreign direct investment was not encouraged.

Among the ASEAN economies, Malaysia and Thailand industrialised in the early 1960s and Indonesia somewhat later. For these resource-rich economies, industrialisation aimed at diversification away from their heavy dependence on primary products in production and exports, in order to provide less volatile and more dynamic sources of growth and to create employment for their rapidly expanding labour forces. For these geographically dispersed economies, industrial policy emphasises regional dispersal and support for indigenous small and medium-sized enterprises.

Selective assistance

The East Asian economies differ in their policies on industrial targeting. Hong Kong maintained a *laissez-faire* approach. South Korea was the most active in picking industries to nurture, moving quickly from labour-intensive industries in the 1960s to heavy industries in the 1970s and high-technology industries in the 1980s. Ng and Pang (1993) found that the quality of intervention was a critical factor in South Korea's success in industrial policy: a capable bureaucracy responsive to a determined government was able to direct a nationalist entrepreneurial class to new activities. Westphal (1990) and others, however, found that considerable policy mistakes were made during the 1970s when the South Korean government aggressively intervened in favour of heavy and chemical industries. For Taiwan, there is also evidence of failures in attempting to pick winners. For example, after more than two decades of government assistance, the Taiwan car industry has failed to produce a winner in export markets. The Singapore government does not explicitly identify national champions but has nonetheless invested directly in certain key industries as well as designed investment incentives to attract investors into particular industries, to accelerate the acquisition of dynamic competitive advantage and facilitate the market. As noted earlier, however, Singapore's high-wage policy contributed to a loss of investment and export competitiveness and was partly responsible for the severity of the 1985 recession.

Among the ASEAN economies, Indonesia and Malaysia actively practise picking winners. For example, the Indonesian government has committed extensive resources to developing an aircraft manufacturing industry, while Malaysia invested in heavy industries and in the automobile industry, including the Malaysian car. Ng and Pang (1993) found the economic contribution of these investments controversial.

Trade policy

In the pre-industrial phase, trade policy in East Asian economies was characterised by the promotion of primary commodity exports and import restrictions to protect agriculture and
the balance of payments, and as a source of government tax
revenue. Trade policy changed dramatically with the onset of
industrialisation in the 1950s and 1960s. Except for Hong Kong,
protection of the domestic market to foster industrialisation
was achieved via tariffs, quantitative restrictions and foreign
exchange controls. This protection was justified on infant industry grounds. Import substitution also received strong impetus
from:
* the need to restrict imports on balance of payments grounds;
* export pessimism regarding prospects for primary commodities;
* initial pessimism regarding the ability of developing economies to compete with industrialised economies for export
  markets in manufactures; and
* the need for government tax revenue.

Effective protection rates in all economies show wide dispersion across industries, with instances of exceptionally high rates
as well as negative protection. The effectiveness of the import
restrictions, however, was somewhat undermined by smuggling activities and by exchange rate policies.

Trade policy became more open as the East Asian economies
made the progressive shift from import substitution to export
manufacturing during the 1960s and 1970s. This move was basi-
cally occasioned by the growing evidence of problems with
import substitution as well as the advantages of export manufacturing (see Krueger:Ch.1). The export manufacturing strategy is not without problems however. Essentially, economic
vulnerability and volatility increase as the domestic economy
becomes exposed to external fluctuations and shocks. Also, it
is more difficult to initiate export manufacturing than import
substitution. Although, in principle, learning by doing in an
exporting industry should be no more difficult than in an
import-substituting industry, in practice, it is easier for financially strapped governments to protect infants in the domestic
market than to subsidise exports. Exporting also requires
knowledge and experience in marketing. In Singapore, export
marketing was facilitated by foreign multinational corporations

and in South Korea by specialised trading companies modelled after the Japanese *sogo shoshas*.

The rationale for import substitution in Singapore disappeared with political secession from Malaysia in 1965, and the policy response was a large-scale dismantling of tariffs and quantitative restrictions. Some tariffs were retained for tax revenue, to restrict consumption on social grounds, and for use in tariff negotiations, such as occurred under the ASEAN Preferential Trading Arrangement. Export capability was facilitated by the large-scale influx of multinational corporations with their technological and marketing expertise. For the other East Asian economies, the switch from import substitution to export promotion has been slower and less complete.

In Taiwan, the shift towards an export-orientation began in the late 1950s and in South Korea from the early 1960s. In both economies, measures comprised the dismantling or offsetting of earlier measures which discriminated against exports and the introduction of specific export promotion measures. They included abolition of multiple exchange rates, currency devaluation, establishment of export processing zones and bonded factories, remission of import duties, subsidised bank credit and tax exemptions and concessions. South Korea also aggressively adopted export targeting. The results achieved by these policies in both economies were spectacular. A United Nations Industrial Development Organisation study (UNIDO 1986) found that over the period 1965–81, exports from South Korea rose at an annual rate of 35 per cent and at 27 per cent from Taiwan, and that the balance of payments of both economies improved rapidly. The failure to liberalise imports more completely, however, has meant that both South Korea and Taiwan have been subject to market-opening pressure from the United States and the European Union.

Among the ASEAN economies, Malaysia and Thailand switched to export manufacturing in the late 1960s and Indonesia only in the early 1980s. Investment promotion agencies introduced various incentives for export manufacturing, including establishment of export processing zones, encouragement of foreign direct investment, offers of tax incentives, and duty drawbacks and exemptions on imports for export-oriented activities. In all these economies, however, protective measures co-existed with export promotion measures, and there was a second round of import substitution. These economies were able to maintain import substitution until the collapse in oil and commodity prices compelled them towards trade liberalisation. Malaysia and Thailand rapidly developed export competence in labour-intensive industries, particularly textiles, clothing and electronics assembly, as well as in resource processing of timber, rubber and precious stones. However, the discovery of major oil resources in Malaysia and natural gas in Thailand induced both economies to shift the emphasis of industrial policy in the early 1980s towards import substitution in heavy industry. In Indonesia, the switch to export manufacturing took place much later in response to a need to find new sources of export earnings to offset declining oil earnings in the early 1980s. The import liberalisation ratio (unrestricted imports to total imports) reached more than 95 per cent in Malaysia and Thailand in 1985 and 84 per cent in Indonesia in 1987 (World Bank 1987). Effective rates of protection remained quite high, however, even after import liberalisation reforms, at least in some product categories. Manufacturers producing for the domestic market, especially in intermediate and engineering goods industries, continued to enjoy tariff and non-tariff protection.

Industrial upgrading

Changes in factor endowment, industrial competence and cost structures provided the impetus for industrial upgrading in the Asian newly industrialising economies. Labour-intensive industrialisation became unsustainable as economic growth absorbed surplus labour and necessitated the shift into more skilled and capital and technology-intensive industries. The Asian newly industrialising economies' governments, except for Hong Kong, have been active in facilitating industrial upgrading. As both the South Korean and Singapore experiences show, however, while government intervention may be necessary to facilitate and ease adjustment, it should not contribute to further market distortions.

In the mid-1970s, South Korea and Taiwan readjusted their industrialisation strategies in response to external pressures from world trade slowdown, rising protectionism and to domestic pressures from rising wages. The industrial emphasis shifted towards heavy and technology-intensive industries, particularly machinery, basic metals and chemicals. South Korea embarked on the development of heavy and chemical industries through tariff protection and import controls on the one hand, and the provision of low-interest credit and direct government intervention through state-owned enterprises on the other. The interventions led to bottlenecks, large-scale debts and inflation, while labour-intensive industries were deprived of credit and exports faltered. In 1980 the economy experienced negative growth, as the cost of the heavy and chemical industries program was compounded by the second oil shock and a poor harvest which led to rising food prices. The economic crisis and social and political unrest led the new government to reassess the heavy and chemical industries program, reverse the credit allocation policies and devalue the currency. A greater role for the market mechanism led to financial and import liberalisation and reduced attempts to 'pick winners'.

Singapore's industrial upgrading policies offer a contrast to those of South Korea. To ease labour shortages, the government relaxed immigration restrictions and allowed massive inflows of foreign labour. The continuing influx, however, was seen to pose political and social costs. In the late 1970s, the government attempted to force the pace of restructuring through a series of measures:

- targeting investment promotion at non-labour-intensive industries and services;
- promoting labour-saving through a high-wage policy and through mechanisation, automation and computerisation; and
- accelerating human resource development through education and training.

The high-wage policy, however, contributed to a rapid loss of foreign direct investment and export competitiveness and, *inter alia*, helped push the economy into recession in 1985–86. This forced the government to re-examine its labour market policy and its role in the economy. Since then, policy responses to the labour shortage have focused on increasing the supply of labour through extension of the retirement age, encouraging more females to enter the labour market, improving labour productivity, continuing an emphasis on automation and computerisation, and relocating labour-intensive industries and processes offshore through outward investment. The revised strategy also focuses on developing Singapore into a total business centre, a regional service hub (finance, tourism, transportation, telecommunications and operational headquarters) rather than an industrial production base.

In Hong Kong, the authorities resisted pressure to allow large labour inflows from China and elsewhere on political and social grounds. Market forces have led to considerable industrial upgrading since the early 1980s and production and exports have become increasingly diversified. In the absence of an active industrial policy, however, and constrained by the scheduled return of the British colony to China in 1997, the shift out of labour-intensive activities was later than in the other Asian newly industrialising economies. Fortuitously, China's open door policy is helping Hong Kong to restructure without an industrial policy. Hong Kong's small and medium-sized enterprises are increasingly engaged in the phenomenon of outward processing and are shifting their labour-intensive industries and processes into the neighbouring Guangdong and Fujian provinces of southern China. This has led to the rapid de-industrialisation of Hong Kong, with industrial output and employment declining, a sharp shift of capital and labour resources into the booming service sector, and the growing integration of Hong Kong's economy with that of southern China.

The ASEAN economies possess not only abundant labour but also abundant natural resources, and so resource-intensive industries figured more prominently in their industrial structure in the early phase of industrial development. Nevertheless, over time the prominence of these industries has declined in response to a number of developments. Most important is the depletion of non-renewable resources and unsustainable exploitation of supplies of certain renewable resources such as tropical hardwoods. At the same time, labour-intensive export manufacturing has grown in importance, absorbing a growing proportion of surplus labour. The boom in export manufacturing has in turn generated strong demand for intermediate inputs and components, providing the basis for investments in physical capital-intensive industries (Chia 1993). These economies have all been tempted into heavy industry programs by their natural resource endowment, and when the commodities boom of the 1970s ended and growth faltered in the early 1980s, they faced serious budgetary and balance of payments problems and their external debt burdens rose significantly. They were forced to review their policies and adopt structural adjustment programs. Greater emphasis was given to the role of the private sector, manufactured exports and foreign direct investment.

Foreign investment and financial sector liberalisation

The East Asian economies have attracted a disproportionate share of the foreign direct investment that has flowed to developing economies in the past two decades, reflecting their economic dynamism as well as policy reforms to liberalise investment inflows. The share of foreign direct investment in total capital formation remains generally small, except for Singapore. Foreign direct investment in manufacturing activities is sizeable in most economies, however, and overwhelming in the case of Singapore. The resource-rich ASEAN economies also have sizeable foreign direct investment in minerals and energy activities while Hong Kong and Singapore have sizeable foreign direct investment in services, particularly in financial, business and distributive services.

Governments attempt to influence the level and direction of foreign direct investment inflows through policies which emphasise investment incentives on the one hand, and restrictions, regulations and performance requirements on the other. Policy reforms in the past decade have emphasised the former and reduced the latter. The selective application of incentives and restrictions means that foreign direct investment has influenced both the sector and interindustrial allocation of resources and the level of industrialisation. The mixture of incentives and restrictions reflects host country ambivalence. On one hand, it is recognised that foreign direct investment augments domestic investment while avoiding some of the risks of external borrowing, and incorporates management know-how, technology transfer and marketing expertise and linkages. On the other hand, there is fear that foreign ownership and control may undermine national sovereignty, limit government tax revenues because of tax concessions and transfer pricing, crowd-out domestic enterprise, introduce inappropriate technologies, and over-exploit domestic natural resources and pollute the environment.

Foreign direct investment policies show marked differences among East Asian economies, although there has been a policy convergence in the 1980s. At one extreme, Hong Kong practises *laissez-faire*. With free trade and free capital regimes, a low corporate income tax rate of 17.5 per cent, excellent geographical location, efficient administration and infrastructure, Hong Kong does not need special fiscal incentives to attract foreign direct investment. At the other extreme, Singapore adopted a liberal foreign investment policy regime in the early 1960s at a time when developing economies were sceptical about the benefits of foreign direct investment. Its foreign direct investment policy has remained consistently liberal. It offers a wide range of fiscal incentives and industrial facilities, imposes no restrictions on foreign ownership (except in mass media, defence and finance) and has no performance requirements. Fully foreign-owned enterprises are common, and there are no restrictions on repatriation of capital and income. The dependence on multinational corporations with their technological superiority and established marketing networks has enabled Singapore to industrialise quickly and efficiently without the high costs of infant industry protection for a small domestic market.

In South Korea and Taiwan, the foreign direct investment presence is smaller than in the city-states. In the 1970s, foreign direct investment accounted for about 8 per cent of investment in manufacturing in Taiwan, and even less in South Korea. Before the mid-1980s, foreign direct investment was restricted in South Korea and encouraged only on a highly selective basis. South Korea preferred foreign loans and technology licensing to foreign direct investment as a means of obtaining finance and technology, choosing to protect domestic industries and firms to promote the independence of the industrial sector and accelerate the assimilation of foreign technology. Since 1984, however, a more liberal policy towards foreign direct investment has been implemented. In Taiwan, because of the government's active and direct role in industrial development, there were many restrictions on foreign direct investment and incentives were given only selectively. Significant foreign direct investment liberalisation started in the 1980s with improvements in industrial competence, healthy balance of payments leading to relaxation of foreign exchange controls, and the objective of developing Taiwan as an international financial centre. Selective tax incentives, export processing zones and science and technology parks were important instruments in attracting foreign direct investment.

Foreign investment policies in the ASEAN economies were much more restrictive than in Singapore, particularly with regard to resource development and regulations and performance requirements. The past decade, however, has seen a growing realisation that foreign direct investment confers more benefits than costs and can contribute significantly to economic dynamism and export performance. With the collapse of oil and commodity prices in the early 1980s and the rising debt-service burden, these economies turned increasingly to export manufacturing and to foreign direct investment to spearhead manufactured exports. To attract foreign direct investment flows from traditional sources in North America and Western Europe and from new sources in Japan and the Asian newly industrialising economies, foreign direct investment policies were liberalised from the mid-1980s with the offer of a wide range of investment incentives and industrial facilities, and the more restrained application of restrictions and performance requirements, including allowing 100 per cent foreign ownership. The policy liberalisation has contributed to a significantly improved investment climate and an upsurge of foreign direct investment inflows into Indonesia, Malaysia and Thailand. More recently, infrastructural and skill bottlenecks, and intense investment competition from the emerging economies of China and Indochina have led to a slowdown in foreign direct investment inflows into these economies.

Apart from attracting foreign direct investment, the East Asian economies have been undertaking reforms to liberalise their financial markets in the 1980s, as part of overall policy reforms to improve economic efficiency, growth and domestic resource mobilisation, and to reduce the cost of financial intermediation and gain better access to global capital markets.

The financial systems in East Asia are characterised by different degrees of openness. Hong Kong and Singapore are major trading and financial centres, and have well-developed financial sectors and only minimal controls on financial flows. Financial developments have largely taken the form of financial deepening and widening, with a growing range of financial markets and instruments. Singapore has sought to promote its development as a financial centre with an array of financial incentives, and has not experienced any banking failures or financial crises because of its strong prudential regulatory and supervisory framework.

Traditionally, South Korea and Taiwan have had highly regulated and repressed financial markets and these conditions continued until the 1980s. Government control over domestic resource mobilisation and financial institutions was exercised through ownership of major banks, and control over credit allocation and interest rates. Allocation of funds was largely determined by government priorities, especially to support investment in export industries, heavy and chemical industries and for public utilities and infrastructure. In both economies the role of foreign financial institutions was severely circumscribed and strict regulations were maintained over external financial transactions.

With growing economic maturity, financial market liberalisation and the development of corporate securities and bond markets became critical in South Korea and Taiwan for continuing export competitiveness and industrial upgrading. Industries need access to a more efficient and sophisticated domestic capital market. Inward and outward investments help gain access to foreign technology and maintain global competitiveness. At the same time, rising incomes require domestic financial markets that provide a wide range of consumer-oriented financial services. Improvements in the balance of payments, pressures from the United States to open up the financial markets, as well as political pressure in South Korea to reduce the high concentration of economic power in the *chaebols*, contributed to financial liberalisation in South Korea and Taiwan in the 1980s.

Liberalisation measures included the privatisation of commercial banks, reduced administrative guidance on bank lending, the deregulation of interest rates and permission for the establishment of foreign financial institutions. After 1986 the pace of liberalisation accelerated. In Taiwan, interest rates were deregulated and restrictions on lending were abolished. The deregulation process was less comprehensive in South Korea, and preferential lending and interest rate control practices continued. In both economies, the stock markets expanded rapidly, enabling more domestic firms to meet capital needs through raising equity capital. Restrictions on capital flows were gradually relaxed. In Taiwan, controls on outward remittance of foreign exchange for foreign investment and for private purposes were relaxed in the late 1980s in the wake of current account surpluses and strong upward pressures on the exchange rate and on the prices of real estate and shares. At the same time a more open policy towards inward foreign investment was adopted. Similar liberalisation of external financial transactions was adopted in South Korea, but regulations on inward and outward investment remain somewhat more strict than in Taiwan.

In the ASEAN economies, prior to the 1980s, financial sectors were also repressed, with the absence of competition, credit and interest rate controls, and restrictions on inward and outward capital flows. Financial liberalisation and deregulation began in the 1980s to raise domestic savings and promote domestic and foreign investment. In recent years, the pace of financial reforms has accelerated. Indonesia adopted a wide-ranging program of financial liberalisation and deregulation in 1988, leading to a sharp growth in private financial institutions (including foreign participation), and deregulated interest rates. The proliferation of private financial institutions increased competition, led to the rapid expansion of bank credit in 1989–90, a deterioration of bank loan portfolios, shortage of professional financial personnel and a decline in prudential regulatory capability. Banking and stock market difficulties emerged, leading to the imposition of more stringent supervisory and regulatory measures. In Thailand, financial liberalisation reforms were also undertaken in the late 1980s, including deregulation of interest rates, removal of some barriers between bank and non-bank financial institutions and foreign exchange controls, and permission for domestic banks to offer foreign exchange accounts to private individuals. Malaysia had a fairly open financial sector. Some financial instability emerged in the mid-1980s, however, following prolonged low commodity prices and poor financial market regulations. Prudential regulations were tightened, while bureaucratic controls were relaxed.

Privatisation of state enterprises

The relative roles of the public and private sectors are undergoing reassessment and change in East Asia as the economies in the region seek to remain competitive in an increasingly borderless global economy characterised by growing capital and information flows and rapid technological change. Governments have begun to liberalise their economies and privatise state-owned enterprises in order to promote growth of the private sector. The extent of public investment and the public–private investment mix among East Asian economies depends on the economic ideology, the availability of budgetary resources (including access to external finance), and the competing needs for the development of infrastructure, human resources and technology. For some economies, implementation of International Monetary Fund structural adjustment programs is an added factor.

During the 1960s and 1970s the public sector played a major role in the development of East Asia. State enterprises proliferated and encroached upon the traditional areas of private enterprise to produce an ever-widening range of goods and services. In some economies, the extent of state ownership, measured in terms of share of output and employment and claims on the government budget, has been substantial. Until its takeover of two failed banks in the late 1980s, Hong Kong was the only East Asian country to confine government ownership to public goods and services (Riedel 1988). In other economies, government ownership is common in 'strategic' sectors and industries such as banking and capital-intensive industries.

These public investments were financed largely by domestic and external borrowings, resulting in heavy interest payments and ballooning budget deficits and external debts. Increasingly, state enterprises were perceived as laggards and obstacles. During the 1980s, most economies revamped their development strategies to stress the role of the market and of foreign investment as an engine of growth. Country after country undertook privatisation and marketisation programs to revive economic growth and promote industrial upgrading. These reduced the role of the state in manufacturing activities and in infrastructure and social services which were the traditional domain of the public sector. Increasingly, the role of the state is seen as establishing a framework that will ensure competitive market conditions and facilitate private sector investment.

State enterprises proliferated in East Asia largely as a pragmatic response to the need to achieve specific political, social and economic objectives. First, there was the belief that state enterprises would generate profits to finance development expenditures. As it turned out, their performance left much to be desired. Ariff and Hill (1985) found that, far from contributing to revenue, many state enterprises have required substantial government subsidies. Second, there was a common desire for state ownership of 'commanding heights' of the economy on nationalist and strategic grounds, and because of concern over private monopolies and foreign ownership. Third, there was the belief that many crucial industries would not emerge at all if left to market forces, due to poorly developed capital markets and the reluctance of the private sector to undertake risks in uncharted areas. State enterprises can play a catalytic role in spearheading private investment. For example, the absence of an industrial tradition in Singapore led the government to play a pioneering role in a number of industrial investments in the 1960s. When these ventures proved successful, some divestments took place. Fourth, state enterprises have also been established to achieve regional dispersion of industries and to create an indigenous entrepreneurial class. The latter has been particularly important in Malaysia and to a lesser extent in Indonesia and Thailand. In Malaysia, the rapid growth in state enterprises occurred after 1970 when the New Economic Policy was implemented to redress ethnic imbalances in economic power. The establishment of state enterprises was facilitated by the commodity and oil boom of the 1970s which boosted government revenues.

State enterprises have played an important role in the economic development of South Korea and Taiwan. They are found mainly in public utilities, mining, transport and communications and finance. They tend to be large firms operating as monopolies or in oligopolistic markets and controlled strategic sectors of the economy. In Taiwan in the 1950s the state owned all large industrial concerns and banks. It selected cronies to become industrialists and assisted them with capital, foreign exchange and labour (Gold 1986). The state continued to dominate the commanding heights of the economy, particularly banking, and accounted for a crucial portion of industrial production. In Singapore, state enterprises proliferated after the early 1960s because of the industrialisation objective, venturing into projects which domestic private enterprises were reluctant to enter because of the large capital requirements and long gestation period, and to counterbalance the increasingly dominant foreign multinational corporations.

In the ASEAN economies, state enterprises proliferated because of development and distributional objectives. State enterprises are found in various sectors of the economy including energy, transport, communications and public utilities.

They were not a drain on the national budget until 1973, but the sharp escalation in oil prices led to rapidly rising operating and fuel costs and heavy borrowings. According to Ng and Pang (1993), state enterprises in the ASEAN economies have not performed as well as those in Singapore, South Korea or Taiwan, partly because managers were chosen not on the basis of professional expertise but on political patronage.

Many state enterprises fail to live up to expectations and become a drain on the public budget, for a number of reasons:
• state enterprises often have to serve multiple objectives, and non-economic objectives and rent-seeking activities undermine economic efficiency; and
• state enterprises are managed by bureaucrats who usually do not make good entrepreneurs, lacking in motivation and inclination, sometimes also in competence.

The 1980s' movement towards privatisation is part and parcel of the general trend towards economic liberalisation and deregulation to improve competitiveness. The privatisation movement also affected state enterprises which were successful; where the state enterprises played a pioneering role, the maturing of industrial sectors and the emergence of private entrepreneurs have eroded the initial rationale for their emergence. Privatisation has also occurred in response to external pressures from major trading partners (particularly the United States) trying to open up the domestic markets of East Asia to secure a more level playing field, and from international agencies (such as the World Bank and the International Monetary Fund) as a condition for structural adjustment assistance. In the ASEAN economies, as government finances became increasingly constrained by the fall in oil and commodity prices, and as economic growth slowed and external debt servicing grew, the inefficiency of state enterprises became a matter of growing concern.

Another argument for privatisation is that where state enterprises engage in activities that are the traditional domain of the private sector, there is danger of crowding-out private enterprise. In Singapore, state enterprises have not been inefficient or a drain on the public purse. Privatisation was more in response to complaints by the private sector, particularly during the 1985–86 recession, of growing public sector encroachment and crowding-out of private sector activities, which was perceived to hinder the emergence of a dynamic local private sector.

According to the various country studies in Ng and Pang (1993), the privatisation process has been slow in East Asia. Progress has been hampered by lack of serious commitment, absence of developed capital markets and financing institutions, mobilisation of funds beyond the capacity of private investors, and lack of entrepreneurship and managerial skills. There are concerns over the appropriate valuation of assets of enterprises to be privatised, concentration of private ownership and emergence of private monopolies, possible lay-off of public workers, and continuing access of lower-income groups to basic goods and services. In some economies, privatisation has largely taken the form of divestment rather than the transfer of control to the private sector. In several economies, while reducing its equity stake in existing state enterprises, the government is increasing its involvement in new areas, particularly high-technology sectors.

Government intervention: hindrance or help?

In the past three decades, governments in East Asia (excepting the unique case of Hong Kong) have intervened extensively in their economies. In addition to serving minimal functions, these governments have intervened in three broad areas: maintaining macroeconomic stability, promoting industrialisation and structural transformation, and establishing state enterprises. The evidence on their performance is mixed. Generally, they have performed their minimal role of maintaining political and social stability and protection of civic and property rights well. They have also successfully pursued macroeconomic stability, in spite of the shock waves in the international economy of the 1980s. Macroeconomic stability has laid the foundation for the pursuit of growth and structural transformation by the private and public sectors.

Whether government intervention, particularly in the areas of industrial policy and production of private goods, has helped or hindered economic development remains a controversial issue. Empirical studies on East Asia thus far provide no definitive conclusions on the impact of government intervention. There have been successes and failures. While some attributed the East Asian success partly to government intervention, others argued that economic success was largely despite, rather than because of, government intervention. Where government intervention did play a positive role, it was in removing the obstacles to growth, which were often the result of government action in the first place. Neoclassical economists tend to judge government performance by the yardstick of the best performing market mechanism. In turn, pro-interventionists see only too clearly the weaknesses and limitations of rampant capitalism.

The dilemma can be highlighted by a comparison of the highly successful city-states of Hong Kong and Singapore, the former a model of *laissez-faire* and the latter of government intervention. The impact of the policy contrasts can be seen in two areas. On the one hand, Hong Kong's population is widely acknowledged to have a stronger entrepreneurial spirit than that of Singapore, even by no less a personage than Singapore's former Prime Minister Lee Kuan Yew. On the other hand, Singapore has put more resources into infrastructure, human resource and technological development and environmental protection, and its workers are better protected by labour laws and live in better quality and subsidised housing. A longer time frame is needed to assess the impact of different economic strategies in the two city-states on the sustainability of their economic growth and their resulting quality of life.

Perhaps what distinguishes East Asia from other developing regions is good governance, as measured by the pragmatism of leadership and the quality of economic management. Policies are pro-growth rather than ideological, and have not supplanted or distorted the market to the extent of stifling growth and private enterprise. Governments have also been flexible and have responded quickly and effectively to changes in the international economic environment, and have changed course where policies have adversely impacted on growth and private enterprise.

What is the appropriate role of government in the economy and the government–private sector nexus? It depends on the stage of economic development, the quality of government leadership and bureaucracy, the policy instruments available, and the domestic and external environment in which the country operates. Where markets are well developed and entrepreneurial spirit is strong, there is no need for government to play an entrepreneurial role, and its focus should be on the provision of public goods. This would imply that the role of government as allocator of resources and provider of private goods should diminish with economic progress. Where markets are not developed and private enterprise is weak, government may need to play a more pro-active role in providing economic leadership, including a direct hand in the allocation of resources and in the production and distribution of private goods. It is imperative, however, that government has the capacity for sound economic management and that such a pro-active role should not crowd-out private enterprise.

5

Trade Policy and the Globalisation of Production

ISAIAH FRANK

The changing world economy

More than ten years have passed since 1982 when the United States took the initiative to propose the agenda for an eighth round of the General Agreement on Tariffs and Trade (GATT) trade negotiations as a follow-up to the Tokyo Round that concluded in 1979. It is worth remembering that the United States' proposal was greeted with a notable lack of enthusiasm and even intransigence on the part of European and developing economies. Four years were required to bring those countries on board before the new round could be officially launched in 1986 at Punta del Este, Uruguay.

In the decade since the agenda for the Uruguay Round was put forward, the pace of change in the very nature of international trade has accelerated. No longer is international trade dominated by the simple nineteenth-century Ricardian model of an exchange of British cloth for Portuguese wine. The historic specialisation of national firms in particular products is being increasingly replaced by the globalisation of production in which different processes required for the production of individual goods and services are performed in different countries. An American automobile may be designed in Japan, assembled in Canada or Mexico and consist of parts manufactured in Taiwan, Brazil or just about anywhere.

Globalisation, therefore, means increased trade in parts, components and semi-finished goods. It also implies an increase in intra-firm trade as global companies move components and partially finished goods from their facilities in one country to those in another. In short, the traditional horizontal pattern of trade in final products is being overtaken by a form of vertical trade in which countries specialise in different parts or stages of the production chain for individual products.

The reasons for vertical specialisation vary by industry. For some parts and processes, low labour costs or the availability of particular skills may be crucial. For others, the main considerations may be low energy costs, or proximity to research centres, or the need to adapt products for key markets. Whatever the reasons, the globalisation of production has been made possible by two developments: transportation and communications technology (including data processing) advances have enabled managers to coordinate widely dispersed activities; and the steady reduction of trade barriers under the aegis of the GATT have made possible the movement of components and semi-finished goods across national frontiers with a minimum of penalties in the form of tariffs or other restrictions.

Another major development in international trade has been the rapid rise in the importance of trade in services. In addition to travel and transportation, services include a wide range of other activities such as advertising, accounting, financial, insurance, architecture, construction and engineering, education, medical and many others. Between 1986 and 1992, US exports of services more than doubled to US$179 billion, or 41 per cent of the value of US merchandise exports in 1992. Unlike trade in goods, the services sector has been generating sizeable trade surpluses. The US surplus in services trade in 1992 amounted to US$56 billion, offsetting 58 per cent of its merchandise trade deficit of US$96 billion (United States Department of Commerce 1993). Many types of services exports cannot be provided effectively through cross-border exports but only through the establishment of a local presence in the foreign countries in which the service is provided. In the services sector, trade policy and investment policy converge.

What globalisation implies, therefore, is the need to extend the horizon of international negotiations from the liberalisation of strictly border measures, to the coordination of various areas of domestic policy that substantially affect the ability of firms to conduct their operations worldwide. For example, it is difficult to conceive of a company producing parts of a complex product in different countries if each country accorded widely different treatment to intellectual property rights or mandated sharply divergent technical standards. Nor is it conceivable that international trade in a wide variety of services could flourish if firms encountered exclusionary business practices abroad, if they were subject to limitations on their right of establishment or they experienced discriminatory treatment as compared with domestic firms once they were established.

A successful Uruguay Round marks the culmination of the GATT efforts to integrate the global economy primarily by reducing barriers to trade in goods and services. Barriers reduced under the GATT's auspices have consisted mainly of border measures, such as tariffs and import quotas. In both the Tokyo and Uruguay Rounds a beginning has also been made in addressing non-tariff measures in the form of selective internal practices in areas of protection of intellectual property rights. The next and more difficult stage of negotiations will require that nations systematically address their internal regulatory and structural differences that distort international trade and investment and limit world output.

On a regional basis, the need to progress from shallow to deep integration has been recognised by the European Union. Initially concerned with eliminating border restrictions to trade among its members, the European Union realised that it could not achieve a truly integrated market without harmonising or reducing the internal regulatory, structural and institutional differences among its member states. Hence the far-reaching Europe 1992 initiative intended to complete the integration of its market by harmonising rules concerning a wide range of domestic policies.

On a bilateral basis, the Structural Impediments Initiative between Japan and the United States has also addressed the issue of the compatibility of domestic policies. The objective has been to ease tensions by reforming certain regulatory and structural features of the two economies that impede trade and balance of payments adjustment.

To what extent should regulatory and institutional structures be harmonised globally? After all, the basis for trade in accordance with comparative advantage lies in differences among nations, differences not only in resource endowments but in economic policies as well. Economic policies often reflect the distinctive social preferences of individual countries and should be accepted as legitimate determinants of comparative advantage rather than as subjects for international harmonisation.

The challenge, therefore, for the post-Uruguay Round global economy is to determine how to deal with international

competitive distortions arising from differences in national regulations and structures, while respecting to the maximum
extent the social preferences of individual nations. As any government policy can have some effect on trade and investment,
it would be essential to limit negotiations to measures which
substantially affect international competition.

Several areas where the intersection of trade and domestic
policies significantly affects the ability of firms to compete globally are discussed below. Specifically, the main trade-related
issues in competition policy, environment policy and investment policy are briefly highlighted.[1] Analysis of the extent to
which future trade negotiations should proceed on a multilateral, regional or some other basis concludes the discussion.

Trade and competition policy

International recognition of policy linkages

Trade policy regulates competition among firms across national
boundaries; competition policy regulates competition among
domestic firms. That trade and competition policies are related
has long been recognised. Indeed, competition issues were
covered in Chapter 5 of the stillborn *Havana Charter for an International Trade Organisation* negotiated in 1948. Although the
United States never ratified the charter, its commercial policy
provisions became the basis for the GATT. The rest of the
charter was dropped, but the inclusion of Chapter 5 in the original draft reflected recognition that trade liberalisation could be
undermined or nullified by the restrictive business practices of
private firms. Even if tariffs and other government obstacles to
imports were completely removed, market access for foreign
products and the efficiency of domestic production could be
severely impeded by monopolistic or cartel-like exclusionary
practices in the home market.

The link between trade liberalisation and competition policy
has also been recognised by the European Union. Its 1957 Rome
Treaty contains strong rules on restrictive business practices
(Articles 85–90) and endeavours to prevent state subsidies from
distorting competition (Articles 92–94). The Treaty's rules on
competition have been applied by the European Commission
with increasing vigour, as exemplified by the adoption in 1989

of a resolution defining, with greater precision, market concentrations likely to lead to a dominant position and the abuse of market power (European Community Council 1989). In 1991 the European Union and the United States entered into an agreement providing for cooperation between the competition authorities of the two parties in cases where they apply their competition rules to related situations.

The Organisation for Economic Cooperation and Development (OECD) has also been attempting to promote greater harmonisation of competition laws among countries and to reduce inconsistencies between trade laws and competition policy. At the June 1991 OECD ministerial meeting, an extensive program was launched to develop ways of bringing the two regimes into closer conformity.

A strong impetus for this endeavour was given by Sir Leon Brittan, the European Union Commissioner for Competition Policy, who called for a 'world competition initiative' at the 1992 Davos Symposium (Brittan 1992). He argued forcefully that an open world trading regime must be supported by international understandings on principles governing competition, subsidies and investment.

The most noteworthy bilateral consideration of competition policy in a trade-oriented context has been the talks between the United States and Japan under the Structural Impediments Initiative. The discussions on competition policy have focused on collusive behaviour among Japanese firms affecting the ability of foreign firms to penetrate the Japanese market; the adequacy of Japanese enforcement of anti-monopoly laws; access of foreign firms to existing distribution channels and the right to establish new channels; and impediments to foreign investment.[2]

Trade policies

The issues discussed in the Structural Impediments Initiative talks illustrate types of domestic restrictive practices and regulations that affect foreign trade. But the reverse effect also exists, that is, widely practised international trade policies can foster non-competitive behaviour among domestic firms. One example is the grey area of so-called voluntary export restraints which force a foreign country to limit its exports of particular products and to allocate its national export quota among competing firms in the domestic industry. To the extent that the allocative function is assigned to a private industry organisation, it encourages cartel-like practices of market sharing and price fixing.

The rules applying to dumping are another example of conflict between trade and competition policies. Both the GATT and US trade law permit an importing country to apply anti-dumping duties when material injury to domestic producers can be demonstrated as a result of a foreign company exporting a product at prices lower than those charged in its home market. Unlike the rules applying to foreign trade, however, US law does not regard price discrimination between different domestic markets as constituting unfair competition *per se*. Rather, the test is whether the pricing policy is predatory, that is, intended to put competitors out of business. Under the Robinson–Patman antitrust law, 'meeting competition' is a justification available to a defendant in a domestic price discrimination suit. As anti-dumping actions have become the principal modern instrument of trade protection, this inconsistency between the treatment of price discrimination in foreign and domestic commerce urgently needs to be resolved.[3]

Competition policies

All of the major OECD countries have antitrust laws and policies which reflect each country's individual history and distinctive social and economic institutions and attitudes. There are basic elements, however, that they have in common, for example, the prohibition of cartels and cartel-like practices such as the fixing of prices and the allocation of markets, and the surveillance of mergers and acquisitions. Where the countries differ is in the transparency of the systems of law and regulation and in matters such as principles of application, that is, whether certain practices are illegal *per se* or are subject to a rule of reason. Differences also exist with respect to remedies and penalties and to the scope of jurisdiction. Some countries apply their antitrust laws only to conduct occurring within their national territories. Others extend their jurisdiction to conduct abroad.

As a first order of business, agreed principles should be negotiated internationally as a basis for the adoption of more effective and convergent national competition laws and en-forcement mechanisms. At a later stage, existing international trade rules would need to be examined, and modified if nec-essary, to remove inconsistencies with the agreed competition principles.

Another area of competition policy that has increasingly been the source of trade disputes is domestic subsidies. Recent exam-ples include the continuing struggle in the Uruguay Round over the European Union's subsidisation of agriculture and US objections to the subsidisation of Airbus. These issues are dif-ficult to address because, unlike export subsidies, domestic sub-sidies are recognised in the GATT to be legitimate 'instruments for the promotion of social and economic policy objectives'. The GATT also acknowledges, however, that subsidies 'may cause adverse effects to the interest of other signatories'.

The domestic subsidies issue is becoming more important in such areas as the development of high-technology industries that have significant domestic spillover benefits in terms of pro-ductivity growth and high-paid jobs. The policy implication is that preferential treatment, subsidies, and/or trade restrictions may be warranted to promote the development of these industries.

The existence of such spillover benefits, however, is normally limited to the basic, generic and pre-competitive stages of research and development. History tells us that governments are all too willing to fund projects that the private sector rightly chooses to ignore; witness Europe's investment in the Concorde jet and Japan's in the next generation of computers. Moreover, these interventions may be quite vulnerable to political influ-ence. Nevertheless, domestic subsidies are a fact of life and can damage the competitive position of firms abroad. To the extent that this issue is not resolved in the Uruguay Round, further efforts to reach international agreement on government subsi-dies should be pursued.

Trade and environment policy

The subject of the relationship between trade and environment policy has burst to the fore in recent years as environmental groups have increasingly expressed strong opposition to new trade liberalisation agreements (the Uruguay Round and the North American Free Trade Agreement) on the grounds that they would impede progress towards national and global environmental goals. The opposition became especially strident in the atmosphere created by the 1992 Earth Summit in Rio.[4] Moreover, trade restrictions have become a major tool favoured by the environmental community to enforce environmental standards.

Several broad concerns have been expressed by environmentalists about the links between trade liberalisation and the environment. First, that the removal of trade barriers will lead to increased income and production, thereby promoting environmental degradation and unsustainable development. Second, that a successful Uruguay Round and the proliferation of free trade agreements will tighten existing constraints on the use of trade measures to protect the environment. And third, that the relaxation of controls on international trade and investment will encourage industrial flight from the industrialised economies to pollution havens in the Third World.

Improvement of the environment is a vital objective worthy of wide support. The implication that trade and development are somehow in conflict with environmental objectives, however, is highly questionable. Recent research has shown that, with the right policies and institutions, economic growth will provide the resources necessary for improved environmental management (World Bank 1992a). Growth and environmental objectives are, therefore, not only compatible but the former may well be a condition for achieving the latter.

Organisation for Economic Cooperation and Development guiding principles

Many of today's ardent environmentalists seem oblivious to the fact that some of the key issues in the relationship between trade and environment policy were addressed more than 20 years ago in the OECD. The result was a set of OECD Council recommendations adopted in 1972 in the form of *Guiding Principles Concerning the International Economic Aspects of Environmental Policies*. The three main principles, which are directly relevant to today's debate, deal with the allocation of pollution abatement costs, the harmonisation of environmentally related product standards and the desirability of using trade measures to offset differences in environmental control costs (Pearson 1992).

Pollution abatement costs

On the issue of pollution abatement costs, the guidelines enunciate the 'polluter-pays principle' as a way of avoiding trade distortions that might arise from differences among countries in the financing of pollution abatement. This eminently sound principle means that the producer, rather than the taxpayer, pays the cost of pollution abatement in the private sector. In practice, the producer can, of course, shift part of the cost forward to the user of the product to the extent that market conditions permit.

The economic rationale for the polluter-pays principle is twofold: by internalising pollution abatement costs, it ensures that product prices reflect the full social cost of production; and by harmonising, internationally, the way in which abatement is financed, it avoids a distortion of trade. Internalising costs results in a more efficient allocation of resources. And harmonising financing promotes the adoption of environmental protection measures by assuring firms that their competitors in other countries will not benefit from environmental subsidies.

What if a country does not follow the polluter-pays principle but instead pays for pollution abatement in the private sector out of public revenues? The implication of the polluter-pays principle is that exports benefiting from environmental subsidies should be subject to countervailing duties in the importing country on the same basis as any other subsidised export under Article VI of the GATT. Some environmentalists have argued against this position, however, on the grounds that it would discourage financial support by governments for environmental clean-up activities.

Harmonisation of product standards

The second guiding principle requires countries to avoid applying environmentally related product standards as covert barriers to trade. It also seeks to minimise the economic costs of differences in standards through harmonisation. Product standard harmonisation (for example, food purity requirements) will be difficult to achieve, however, in the absence of scientific consensus as to what the international standards should be.

Where differences in product standards do exist, a country should accord national treatment to 'like' imported products, that is, treatment identical to that accorded to domestic products. This principle is consistent with the general GATT obligation of national treatment for imports with respect to internal taxes, standards and regulations (Article III). Through recourse to this principle, Thailand, for example, was barred from restricting imports of US cigarettes on health grounds as Thailand imposed no comparable restriction on domestically produced cigarettes. The principle, however, would permit a country to impose the same labelling requirement on imports, for example, that it applies domestically regardless of whether or not that requirement exists in the exporting country.

International production processes

The third major component of the OECD guiding principles deals with the potential consequence for competition of national differences in environmental policies relating to production processes rather than to products. Should a country with stringent standards be permitted to adopt border adjustment measures (import tariffs, export rebates) to offset the trade advantage of the lower costs of complying with less stringent standards in another country? This question differs from the polluter-pays principle issue in that it addresses differences in the environmental standards themselves rather than differences in the way the enforcement of standards is financed.

The OECD guidelines expressed opposition to compensatory border adjustments on both economic and practical grounds. On economic grounds, it acknowledged the legitimacy of a diversity of environmental standards based on differences in countries' capacity to assimilate pollutants, economic structure and income levels. On practical grounds, the OECD believed that it was not possible to distinguish legitimate differences in standards and costs from non-legitimate differences resulting in artificial competitive advantage and trade distortion. To attempt to do so, and to sanction border adjustments, would encourage protectionist pressures and endless trade disputes.

The assumption underlying the OECD guidelines is that environmental damage is local. Increasingly, however, the focus of interest has shifted to the appropriateness of trade measures to deal with the adverse international environmental consequences of domestic economic activity, for example, transborder pollution, or damaging effects on global resources such as the ozone layer or endangered species.

Perhaps the most prominent recent example of a dispute over this issue is the United States' embargo on tuna caught by Mexico with drift nets that injure dolphins. A similar international dispute arose over the European Union's embargo on furs of animals caught with leg-hold traps. The underlying question in these and similar cases is whether a government should have a unilateral right to require foreign as well as domestic producers to make changes in their methods of production in order to minimise a perceived or actual adverse impact on environmental resources.

GATT rules and environmental issues

On this issue, the GATT rules are clear. They prohibit a country from making access to its market dependent on changes in the domestic production processes of the exporting country. The rationale is that to do otherwise would invite unending restrictions on imports as countries attempted to impose their own domestic environmental standards (or social policies) on other countries or used such attempts as a pretext for outright protection. Low-income economies would be especially vulnerable to imposed standards on minimum wages, health and safety.

The fact that the GATT rules bar the unilateral use of trade measures to dictate changes in the environmental policies of other nations does not imply that governments are powerless to advance international environmental goals. After all, GATT rules can be waived or amended by negotiation. The best option, however, is to negotiate specific multilateral solutions such as the Convention on International Trade in Endangered Species or the Montreal Protocol on Substances that Deplete the Ozone Layer. Both of these international agreements sanction trade measures as enforcement mechanisms.

Although the GATT came into force 45 years ago, it is not oblivious to the need to safeguard the environment. Article XX on general exceptions explicitly states that nothing in the agreement should be construed to prevent the adoption or enforcement of measures 'necessary to protect human, animal or plant life or health' (XX-b) or 'relating to the conservation of exhaustible natural resources if such measures are made effective in conjunction with restrictions on domestic production or consumption' (XX-g). Nevertheless, it makes sense for the members of the GATT to undertake an examination of the agreement's Articles with a view to determining whether changes are desirable that would advance the goal of mutually supportive liberal trade and environmental policies.

Trade and investment policy

Symbiosis between foreign trade and international investment

Foreign trade and international investment are inextricably linked. They can no longer be regarded simply as alternative means by which a producer can seek to penetrate a foreign market. As a result of the globalisation of production, trade and foreign investment have increasingly become integral elements in a firm's unified strategy for optimising the deployment of its resources worldwide. Firms operating in global markets are under strong competitive pressure to specialise vertically, that is, to carry out each separable operation in a production chain in the most advantageous worldwide location, whether in its own facilities or in facilities owned by subcontractors or independent suppliers.

The symbiotic relationship between trade and investment is reflected in the increasing proportion of foreign trade that takes place within individual multinational firms. A recent study showed that in 1986, 55 per cent of US exports consisted of intra-firm trade. Of this total, 32 per cent was made up of US exports by American multinationals to their foreign affiliates; and 23 per cent consisted of exports by foreign-owned firms in the United States to their parent companies abroad or to other affiliates (Julius 1990).

Another perspective on the trade–investment relationship is provided by a comparison of US exports to the European Union with sales to the European Union by the European affiliates of US multinationals. While US exporters shipped US$75 billion of American goods to the European Union in 1988, European affiliates of US firms sold some US$620 billion worth, or eight times as much, principally, but not exclusively, to European customers (Hufbauer 1990).[5]

The role of multinational corporations as organisers of economic activity in an increasingly integrated world economy has

expanded rapidly. Worldwide flows of foreign direct investment have risen at unprecedented rates in recent years. Annual
average investment growth of 34 per cent between 1985 and
1990 far exceeded that of exports (13 per cent) and nominal
GDP (12 per cent) (United Nations 1992).

Foreign direct investment accounts for an increasing share of
total investment in most economies, and for many economies it
has become the primary source of foreign capital. With the
decline of commercial bank lending to developing economies
in the 1980s, the share of foreign direct investment in total long-
term private capital inflows increased from 30 per cent in 1981–
85 to 74 per cent in 1986–90.

Data on foreign direct investment flows understate the
impact of multinational corporations in host countries. Associated with foreign direct investment are technology transfers
from parent firms to foreign affiliates in conjunction with both
equity investments and non-equity arrangements. International
transfers of technology are reflected in the payment of licensing
and other fees, most of which are made on an intra-firm basis.
In so far as technological change is a primary element in economic growth, the multinational corporation must be seen as
playing a crucial role in expanding the world economy.

The foregoing trends have profound implications for international economic governance in the future. Traditionally, trade
was considered the 'engine of growth' (Robertson 1938) in the
world economy, and a comprehensive international framework
was established in the GATT to reflect that perspective. Today,
however, with many foreign markets served more by foreign
affiliates' sales than by exports, with much of foreign trade
occurring as intra-firm transactions, and with technology flows
heavily associated with investment flows, foreign direct investment is increasingly the driving force of international economic
transactions.

A global accord on investment

Yet no global institution, comparable with the GATT, exists for
international investment. Given the widespread restrictions on
the free flow of foreign investment, it is essential to rectify this
asymmetry by negotiating a comprehensive international

accord on foreign direct investment that would include a binding set of rules, a dispute settlement facility and a mechanism for liberalising national policies and regulations regarding foreign enterprise.[6]

The absence of a global GATT-like accord on investment should not be taken to imply that no international investment agreements exist. Indeed, the United States is party to a number of bilateral investment treaties as well as bilateral Treaties of Friendship, Commerce and Navigation that include investment provisions. In addition, most industrial economies subscribe to a 1976 OECD 'soft law' arrangement in the form of non-mandatory guidelines for multinational enterprises.

The two major recent trade negotiations, the GATT Uruguay Round and the North American Free Trade Agreement (NAFTA), recognise the close link between trade and investment by including important provisions on investment. In the Uruguay Round, trade-related investment measures imposed on foreign enterprises are prohibited when they take the form of domestic-content or export requirements. The draft text also mandates the right of establishment and national treatment for trade in services in acknowledgement of the necessity for a foreign presence in order for many service industries to sell their services abroad.

More comprehensive provisions safeguarding the rights of foreign investors are contained in the NAFTA. They apply, of course, to investment in any one of the three member countries, Canada, Mexico and the United States, by investors from either of the other two. The NAFTA provides non-discriminatory treatment; eliminates the need for government approval of investments in most sectors; ensures freedom to remit profits and royalties and to repatriate capital; prohibits performance requirements in the form of local content or export mandates; protects against unjust or uncompensated expropriations; and grants access to international arbitration to enforce investor rights.

The most novel of the NAFTA provisions on investment relate to the protection of the environment. The treaty prohibits the lowering of environmental standards as a means of attracting investment and permits the parties to require environmental impact statements on new investments.

In summary, existing foreign direct investment agreements constitute a patchwork of intergovernmental arrangements.

Some are bilateral, others are regional, still others are multilateral; and they vary widely in scope and degree of binding force. Taken together, existing arrangements hardly qualify as a comprehensive and coordinated global regime for international investment.

The main elements of a new global accord on foreign investment have been spelled out by the author in some detail elsewhere (Frank 1991). The two pillars of an agreement would be the right of establishment and national treatment. The right of establishment would ensure that national markets are open to foreign firms through direct investment in both new and existing enterprises. National treatment would ensure that, once established, foreign investors would be treated no less favourably than domestic enterprises with respect to national laws, regulations and administrative practices.

The most difficult issue related to these basic principles is how to define permitted exceptions. For example, the United States and many other countries restrict the right of foreign establishment in certain sectors, such as telecommunications, shipping and nuclear power. And national treatment is circumscribed in some countries on a number of security or other grounds, for example, foreign-controlled enterprises may be barred from bidding on defence contracts or from joining government-subsidised research consortia. Because of the difficulty of negotiating a consensus on exceptions, consideration might be given to a limited reciprocity test for certain sensitive sectors under which national treatment would be accorded only to firms whose home governments also accorded national treatment to foreign enterprises.

An acrimonious issue that keeps recurring concerns conflicting assertions of jurisdiction over foreign enterprises by the governments of host and home countries. The problem has arisen mainly in the areas of antitrust, trade controls and banking and securities regulation. Here the basic principle should be that affiliates of multinational enterprises located in various countries are subject to the laws and regulations of those countries. In short, host country jurisdiction should normally take precedence over that of the home country.

Two other vexing issues have a special resonance among the concerns of developing economies about foreign direct investment. One is intra-corporate transfer pricing; the other is the question of tax holidays and other specific incentives to attract foreign investors.

The manipulation of prices in transactions among affiliates of individual multinational enterprises can distort the location of profits and lead to the underpayment of corporate taxes in some national jurisdictions and overpayment in others. An international investment accord should confront this issue and seek common principles to guide transfer pricing. Its manipulation as a device for the avoidance of taxes should be discouraged.

Use of special incentives to attract foreign investment should also be covered in a 'GATT for investment'. Especially when offered by developing economies, incentives, such as tax holidays, are often regarded by multinational enterprises as too transitory to induce location in a particular country, but the incentives result in a reallocation of the benefits to the detriment of the host. More generally, incentive schemes can result in mutually disadvantageous competition among developing economies to attract foreign investment and simply raise the returns to foreign firms that would invest anyway (Frank 1980). Just as the GATT limits the use of subsidies that distort international trade, a GATT for investment should attempt to constrain the use of incentives intended to distort the flow of foreign investment.

Multilateral versus alternative approaches

Since the end of the Second World War, the United States has been the staunchest supporter of an international trading system based on multilateralism and non-discrimination as epitomised by the GATT. The policy was a reaction to the prewar experience of bilateralism, Commonwealth and other preferences, and various spheres of economic influence that fragmented world trade and contributed to prolonging the Great Depression. Under the postwar regime of multilateral trade liberalisation, the world economy has expanded and prospered at an unprecedented rate.

Why, then, in the 1980s did the United States turn toward regional free trade agreements, first with Israel, then with

Canada, and now with both Canada and Mexico in the NAFTA that may ultimately be expanded to include other countries in the Western hemisphere. All of these arrangements are inherently discriminatory against non-members and represent sharp departures from the multilateral approach traditionally espoused by the United States.

Several factors have been at work in bringing about the shift in the United States' position. As successive rounds of GATT trade negotiations took place, the number of participants grew from the original 23 to more than 100 in the Uruguay Round. The task of forging a consensus among so many diverse participants became ever more difficult, so that each round took longer than the previous one.

Moreover, the negotiating dynamics of the GATT system have tended to slow the liberalisation process. Countries have been inclined to withhold concessions in the hope that they could benefit from the generalisation of others' concessions without making their own. The only way to prevent free riding of this type is for all participants to make concessions at the same time. As a result, the pace of progress in negotiations is determined by the most reluctant major participant, just as a convoy's speed is determined by that of its slowest ship.

As the relative economic position of the United States declined in recent years, it became less able to rally other nations and exert the decisive driving force needed to strengthen the international trade rules and step up the pace of liberalisation. This was dramatically demonstrated at the 1982 GATT Ministerial Meeting where, despite the strong urging by the United States and some other countries, the meeting failed to reach agreement on an agenda for a new round of multilateral trade negotiations.

The failure of the 1982 GATT Ministerial Meeting marked a watershed in US attitudes toward trade negotiations. The meeting occurred in the midst of a severe US recession when, as a result of flawed macroeconomic policies, the US dollar appreciated rapidly and the trade account turned sharply negative. Industry after industry came under severe pressure from imports, giving rise to strong protectionist pressures from the manufacturing sector, labour and the Congress. Suggestions that the United States should explore alternative methods of achieving trade liberalisation fell on fertile ground.

Other factors also encouraged US willingness to consider alternative approaches. The increasing globalisation of national economies exposed the need for negotiations to address not only border restrictions on trade, such as tariffs and import quotas, but a host of other domestic policies that have an impact on economic activity. To some extent, this realisation was reflected in the Tokyo Round and in the agenda ultimately adopted for the Uruguay Round, which included the protection of intellectual property and certain trade-related aspects of investment. But it has proved far more difficult to reach a consensus on sensitive areas of domestic policy in a global as compared with a more limited regional context. For example, the NAFTA goes well beyond the Uruguay Round in including comprehensive rules on the treatment of foreign investment as well as provisions on the protection of the environment.

Finally, the United States' turn to regional trade arrangements was bolstered by developments in Europe:

- the European Union's original reluctance to sign onto the agenda proposed by the United States for an eighth round of multilateral trade negotiations;
- the deepening of European economic integration foreshadowed by the signing of the Single European Act in 1986 with the goal of establishing a single market by the end of 1992; and
- the prospective widening of the Union by the inclusion of the European Free Trade Association countries and ultimately a number of Eastern European countries as well.

As the United States simultaneously pursues both multilateral and regional approaches to the liberalisation of trade and investment, the question naturally arises as to whether the two strands of policy are mutually compatible, or conflict. This issue was addressed analytically more than 40 years ago by the distinguished economist, Professor Jacob Viner, in his seminal treatise *The Customs Union Issue* (1950).

Viner demonstrated that preferential arrangements, such as customs unions and free trade areas, can have two types of effects. On the one hand, they may be trade-creating, as when the reduction of internal barriers results in a member country importing from another member what it previously produced itself. This effect brings about a reallocation of resources among the members that improves efficiency and raises incomes. On the other hand, such arrangements may also be trade-diverting when, because of the discriminatory treatment of outsiders, a member country simply shifts the source of its imports from a traditional foreign supplier to a new, higher-cost free trade area partner.[7] In this case, trade flows are rearranged in a way that reduces overall efficiency and incomes. Typically, a free trade area has both trade-creating and trade-diverting effects so that an evaluation of the arrangement depends on which effect is dominant.

If trade creation exceeds trade diversion, free trade areas are generally deemed to be beneficial. But beneficial for whom? The answer is that they are beneficial for their members collectively. The outside world, however, cannot gain in the short run regardless of whether trade creation or trade diversion is dominant. Non-member countries experience only trade diversion (Frank 1989).

The inherently negative effect of free trade areas on outsiders in the short run is related to the static nature of the trade-creation/trade-diversion framework. The consequences of once-and-for-all changes in the allocation of existing resources resulting from the formation of the free trade area are focused on. However, more important dynamic results flow from the growth induced by economies of scale and the stimulus to competition, investment and technological progress provided by the enlargement of the market.

When these dynamic effects are taken into account, they may not only overshadow the static results for the members, but may also have positive spillovers for outside countries. In short, whereas in purely static terms non-members cannot benefit from the formation of a free trade area, in dynamic terms they may well gain in the longer run from a secondary form of trade creation induced by a more rapid growth of the free trade area as a market for their exports.

This observation is consistent with the experience of the European Union in trading with non-member countries. The European Union's external trade declined initially as a percentage of gross national product (GNP). After 1978, however, its external trade as a proportion of its GNP was actually greater than it had been prior to the establishment of the common market. The initial trade-diverting effects were eventually overshadowed by the secondary trade-creating consequences of the dynamic forces put into motion by economic integration.

Although non-discrimination is a basic pillar of the GATT, the agreement recognises the potential contribution of free trade areas to world trade and therefore sanctions their formation (Article XXIV). The Article, however, lays down conditions reflecting Viner's insightful distinction between trade creation and trade diversion.[8] To improve the chances that trade creation will dominate trade diversion, barriers to outsiders may not be raised. Whatever trade diversion occurs as a result of a free trade area, therefore, would be a consequence of the removal of restrictions on trade among members rather than the imposition of new barriers against outsiders.

The other GATT condition requires that restrictions be removed on 'substantially all the trade' between the parties to an agreement. The logic here is that if countries are allowed to pick and choose among products, they would inevitably choose those that maximise trade diversion and minimise the painful domestic adjustments implied by trade creation.

Despite the safeguards in the GATT to ensure that free trade areas are outward-looking, there are legitimate concerns about the consequences for the international trading system of a proliferation of free trade areas. Countries left out of free trade areas, especially developing economies, rightly feel disadvantaged. Even the United States reflected this feeling when it objected strongly to the proposal by Prime Minister Mahathir of Malaysia for a regional arrangement in East Asia that would have excluded the United States.

The strong objection issued by the United States left people in East Asia puzzled: how could the United States, an architect of the NAFTA, object to movement toward an East Asian free trade zone? Moreover, the preoccupation with extending the two principal existing regional arrangements, the European Union and the NAFTA, to new members is bound to erode support for the multilateral approach to trade liberalisation. And, as demonstrated by provisions of the NAFTA with respect to the textile and auto sectors, rules of origin for free trade areas can be highly restrictive of trade with outsiders.

Several steps can be envisaged which would make regional approaches to free trade more compatible with an open world trading system. The GATT Article XXIV could be revised to require not simply that barriers to trade with outsiders not be raised, but that they be substantially reduced. Consideration might also be given to elimination of the free trade area option and requiring that all preferential arrangements take the form of customs unions. The common external tariff required by a customs union would eliminate the need for rules of origin which have become highly restrictive instruments of protection. Finally, countries negotiating regional agreements should be encouraged to include liberal terms of accession that would, in effect, leave the arrangement open to membership by any country willing to abide by its rules.

However, the most important way to ensure that regional arrangements become building blocks rather than stumbling blocks to an open global system of trade and investment would be to make sure that the Uruguay Round settlement is effectively implemented, and to begin negotiations soon that include the new issues of regulatory harmonisation that are becoming increasingly important for efficient global production. To the extent that multilateral negotiations reduce trade barriers and regulatory distortions globally, they decrease the margins of preference enjoyed by members of free trade areas so that the two strands of liberalisation, global and regional, will tend to converge. After all, the best free trade area is one that encompasses all trading nations.

Further requirements for an open international trading regime

The world is not standing still. The very nature of trade is rapidly changing from a horizontal exchange of finished products to vertical specialisation in which firms produce different parts and perform particular processes related to an individual product in different countries. In this new world, trade and investment are no longer alternative ways of penetrating a foreign market; rather, they are mutually supportive aspects of a unified strategy for optimising the worldwide deployment of a company's resources. Companies are concerned, therefore, not only about market access in terms of border restrictions to trade but also in terms of their ability to produce abroad as affected by domestic regulations and openness to foreign investment.

An agenda for future negotiations should therefore include, in addition to the traditional subjects, a number of domestic regulatory issues that have a direct impact on the ability of global companies to operate efficiently abroad.

Trade and competition policy are closely related. Even if tariffs and other obstacles to trade were completely removed, market access for foreign products can be severely impeded by monopolistic or cartel-like exclusionary practices of domestic firms. Principles should, therefore, be negotiated internationally that would serve as the basis for the adoption of more effective and convergent national competition laws.

Concern about a conflict between trade and environment policies has been widely expressed in recent years. Several principles, originally put forward by the OECD, are intended to reconcile conflicts between trade and environment policy.

The most prominent environmental issue recently concerns whether or not a government should have a unilateral right to require foreign as well as domestic producers to make changes in their production methods in order to minimise a perceived or actual adverse effect on the environment. On this issue, the GATT is clear. It prohibits a country from making access to its market dependent on changes in the domestic policies of the exporting country. A preferable solution is to negotiate specific international environmental agreements that sanction trade measures as enforcement mechanisms. The GATT Articles should be reviewed, however, for the purpose of determining whether changes would advance the goal of mutually supportive liberal trade and environmental policies.

Foreign direct investment is increasingly the driving force of international economic transactions. Yet no global institution comparable to the GATT exists that would provide a framework of norms and a mechanism for removing obstacles to, and resolving disputes associated with, international investment. A comprehensive international accord on foreign direct investment is needed. Among the most difficult issues an accord must address are the basis for exceptions to the right of establishment and to national treatment, and principles to guide transfer payments and investment incentives.

Although the United States has been the staunchest supporter of multilateralism and non-discrimination in trade, it turned in the 1980s towards regional free trade arrangements as a complementary policy. The question naturally arises as to whether the two strands of policy are mutually compatible or in conflict.

Legitimate concerns are noted about the consequences for the international trading system of a proliferation of free trade areas. To ensure that they become building blocks rather than stumbling blocks to an open global system of trade and investment, several suggestions are offered, including revision of the GATT Article on free trade associations. Most important, however, is the successful implementation of the Uruguay Round and the launching of new negotiations shortly to include regulatory harmonisation as well as the traditional forms of trade liberalisation. To the extent that multilateral negotiations result in a reduction in the preference margins enjoyed by free trade area members, the global and regional strands of liberalisation will tend towards convergence.

Notes to Chapter 5

[1] Other national regulatory structures meriting early efforts at harmonisation are the regulation of financial markets and state assistance to high-technology industries.

[2] Japan has been criticised for its permissive policy towards restrictive business practices. In reaction to the Structural Impediments Initiative talks, however, Japan has stated its intention to raise penalties under its anti-monopoly law, including the adoption of criminal charges.

[3] The ability of a firm to charge high prices and enjoy excessive profits at home is what enables it to sell at lower prices abroad. This pricing power in the home market is generally due to protection from imports or cartel-like practices among domestic firms, or both. Getting rid of these conditions would undermine a company's ability to dump in foreign markets.

[4] The following is a quotation from a full-page advertisement in *The New York Times* (20 April 1992) sponsored by 15 environmental groups. 'President Bush has been pushing for new international trade rules that give a secretive foreign bureaucracy vast new powers to threaten American laws that protect your food, your health, your wilderness and wildlife, and your job. It's part of the hidden agenda in the new GATT agreement in Geneva.'

[5] Of course, the economic significance of the two types of sales is not the same. Most of the US$75 billion in US exports represented

income for US workers and profits for US firms, whereas most of the US$620 billion in sales by US affiliates consisted of revenue paid to European factors of production.

6 A recent study by Mason (1992) delineates the domestic investment restrictions that historically have made it hard for United States' and other foreign firms to operate successfully in Japan.

7 The term free trade areas is applied both to customs unions and free trade areas. Although both require the elimination of trade barriers among members, only the former requires a common external tariff.

8 Jacob Viner was an adviser to the United States Department of State in the late 1940s and was influential in preparations for the United States' position during the formative stages of the GATT.

6

East Asia in the International System: Asia Pacific Economic Cooperation and the Challenge of Discriminatory Trade

ROSS GARNAUT AND PETER DRYSDALE

Sustained, rapid economic growth in East Asia has been the outstanding feature of world economic development in the last third of the twentieth century.

Rapid growth in East Asia has been strongly internationally oriented. Foreign trade has expanded more rapidly than output and expenditure—although less outstandingly so in Japan than in the region's developing economies. Since the mid-1980s, foreign trade growth has been concentrated in East Asia itself, increasing interest in the development of regional institutions to provide a range of public goods to reduce transaction costs in the rapidly expanding trade. At the same time, it is recognised that the trans-Pacific economic ties that were crucial to early export-oriented growth in East Asia retain considerable significance. As a result, the interest in regionalism has focused on a wider grouping, Asia Pacific Economic Cooperation (APEC), rather than narrowly on East Asia alone.

The most remarkable period of East Asian output and trade growth, and structural adjustment to accommodate increased specialisation, has occurred since the major realignments of nominal and real exchange rates in the mid-1980s (Garnaut 1994). Since the mid-1980s, more than one-half of the increase in world production of goods and services has occurred in East Asia. Between 1986 and 1991, growth in Japan added annual output equivalent to that of an economy the size of France. Internationally oriented growth became firmly entrenched in East Asia's most populous economies, China and Indonesia, and commenced in Vietnam. Most remarkably, strong growth in the region's developing economies continued undiminished in the early 1990s, despite deep and prolonged recession in the industrialised economies of the Northern hemisphere.

The East Asian economies that have grown rapidly through the postwar period have had very different initial relative resource endowments from those of the industrial economies. Japan, Hong Kong, Taiwan, Singapore, Korea and the coastal provinces of mainland China are all densely populated in comparison with the industrial economies of the North Atlantic, or the rest of the world. Their patterns of specialisation in international trade are therefore distinctive, both in the early stages of industrialisation when incomes are low, and later when they are high. This increases pressures for structural adjustment in the rest of the world, beyond those that are inevitably associated with the scale and pace of growth, at the same time as it expands the potential gains from trade. It also leads to criticism that East Asia does not behave 'normally' in its trade relations with the rest of the world, and to arguments that the old trade rules are not suitable for the new big players.

The emergence of East Asia as one of three major centres of production and trade alongside Western Europe and North America (and by early next century likely the largest) has placed great strain on the old rules of the international trading system. It was, of course, the liberal international trading system of the postwar period, built upon the rules of the General Agreement on Tariffs and Trade (GATT) that supported the emergence of internationally oriented growth, at first in Japan, and then in the newly industrialising economies.

Policy responses in the old industrial economies to the adjustment strains associated with East Asian growth, coming as they did at a time of slower growth and higher unemployment in the North Atlantic economies, fractured the system in several ways: most importantly, in relation to the huge exceptions in the rules on textiles, and the 'grey areas'. The exception for agriculture had different origins and, once created by the North Atlantic, was accepted readily as an excuse for avoiding adjustment in the newly rich Northeast Asian economies.

By the 1980s, the postwar rules were recognised by some as being inadequate and requiring development, for the management of areas of trade that had come to assume much greater importance, including in services, and the related matters of intellectual property rights.

Thus followed the Uruguay Round. It was supported by the United States and Japan (and some in Europe) to extend the rules to new areas, to bring in one old exception (agriculture) and to commit developing economies more tightly to the rules. The Uruguay Round was supported (and on some issues led) by Western Pacific economies, including developing economies, to constrain the exceptions related to manufactured goods and (for Southeast Asia and Australasia) to remove the exception for agriculture.

There is an important sense in which the weight and adjustment strain of East Asia's internationally oriented growth, and East Asia's comparative success through the 1980s and early 1990s, increased tendencies to discriminatory regionalism in Europe and North America. It was one factor in the acceleration of moves towards Western European economic integration, and, alongside frustration with slow progress in the Uruguay Round, towards the formation of the North American Free Trade Agreement (NAFTA). By the early 1990s, these and other moves towards discriminatory regionalism constituted threats to the liberal, multilateral trading system as important as those that the Uruguay Round had been established to remove. And the success of internationally oriented growth in East Asia, alongside weaknesses in economic policy and performance in the United States and, later, the European Union, began to undermine political and intellectual support for the postwar system in its old heartlands.

This chapter examines some of the factors behind the emergence of strains in East Asia's relations with the old champions of liberal, multilateral trade. The support that East Asia's own commitment to open trade and multilateralism can provide to the postwar system at this time of strain is discussed. Analysis of APEC as a form of non-discriminatory regionalism concludes the discussion. Asia Pacific Economic Cooperation can help bring the new legitimacy of regionalism in American discussion of trade policy to account in the strengthening of the principles of open trade upon which economic growth, including in East Asia, has been based over the past four decades. It also acknowledges the possibility and the danger that discussion of trade liberalisation within APEC will yet be captured by old-fashioned discriminatory forms of regionalism.

East Asia's economic growth

As the weight of East Asia and the Pacific in world affairs continues to increase, the commitment to the old verities of liberal
trade in this region could be crucial in holding back the new
tides of discriminatory regionalism in the old, North Atlantic
industrial economies.

Growth in East Asia is likely to be the primary influence on
world trade and economic growth in the next quarter century
and beyond, just as it has been in the last. The emergence of
East Asia has had a dramatic effect on the structure of world
output, and even more so on world trade (Figures 6.1 and 6.2).

East Asia accounted for just over 17 per cent of world production in 1980; at the end of the century it is expected to be
over 28 per cent. Already the region accounts for one-fifth of
world trade, a larger share than North America, and by the year
2000, we expect East Asia's share to be closer to one-third of
world trade. These ratios will not stop changing at the millen-
nium. One consequence is that, in the future, the rest of the
world will find itself reacting to the developments in economic
policymaking and the real economies in East Asia, as most of
the world has done to those in the United States for the past
half-century.

In East Asia in recent years, structural change and growth
have been mutually reinforcing; providing new markets, and an
increasingly sophisticated and dynamic regional economy. There
has been extensive unilateral market opening and deregulation
in most Western Pacific economies. Their remarkable growth
performance has confirmed the prediction of economic theory
that the greatest benefit from unilateral trade liberalisation
accrues to those who undertake it. The benefits for each economy
have been multiplied by the fact that many neighbouring economies have taken similar unilateral market-opening decisions.
The process of progressive trade liberalisation among Northeast
and Southeast Asian economies has been described elsewhere as
a game of 'prisoner's delight' (Garnaut 1991b; Drysdale and
Garnaut 1993) built around comprehension that each country's
own success in internationally oriented economic growth
depends on its own trade liberalisation.

Figure 6.1: Share of world output, 1980, 1990 and 2000

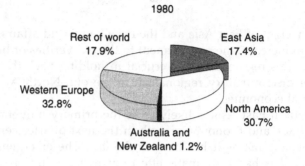

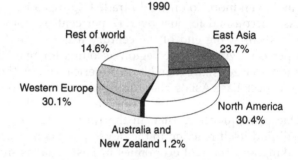

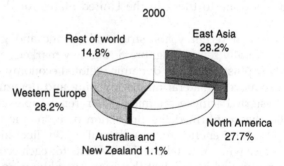

Source: Projections by the Australia–Japan Research Centre using data from the International Economic Databank, The Australian National University, Canberra, July 1992. Note that the China output numbers are 2.5 times those conventionally applied in the past by the World Bank (1992a), representing a conservative application of insights from recent research (Garnaut and Ma 1993b).

Figure 6.2: Share of world trade, 1980, 1990 and 2000

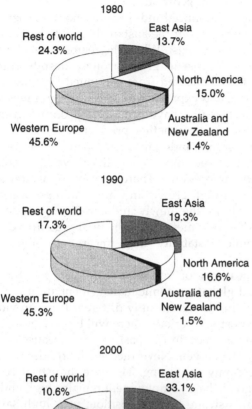

Source: Projections by the Australia–Japan Research Centre using parameters of output growth and trade intensities calculated using data from the International Economic Databank, The Australian National University, Canberra, July 1992.

While in recent years, East Asian developing economies have shown that they can grow strongly through recession in Japan as well as other advanced industrial economies, there are nevertheless anxieties about the sustainability of growth given the pattern of the recent past. While the region's developing economies have been able to grow strongly despite recession in Japan, they have benefited from continued Japanese industrial transformation, and expansion of direct foreign investment and imports in sectors that have been losing competitiveness. It is reasonable to wonder whether productive industrial transformation will continue indefinitely in Japan if there is slow economic recovery, especially if the political system becomes more open to popular pressure. There is also a question about the sustainability of high growth in China, so important to continued expansion in the newly industrialising economies and other ASEAN economies, under the dual pressures of domestic macroeconomic instability and uncertainty about external market access.

The implications of recession in Japan for the regional economy and global economic management are important. The current recession is significantly different from previous recessions in the postwar period—there will be no export-led recovery as there has been in the past, if only because of the large appreciation of the yen. Nevertheless, the fundamentals of the Japanese economy are strong. The core industrial economy in Japan is in good shape, employment remains high and inflation is low. Japan's strong budget position, very high savings rate and massive trade and current account surpluses provide space for further measures to expand domestic demand, and thereby encourage a recovery that is immediately helpful to export expansion in other countries. Political uncertainty in Japan will attenuate the process of recovery; however, it is likely that sustainable growth, slightly higher than the average for other industrial economies, will continue to be a feature of the Japanese economy for the remainder of the decade despite the ageing of the Japanese population and social change affecting attitudes to work and leisure.

The change in China is massive and unprecedentedly rapid, both in economic and political terms, and the commitment to reform in China has become more, not less, deeply entrenched since the political trauma of 1989. China is behaving increasingly like a market economy; undergoing industrial transformation in a manner not dissimilar to the historical experience of other East Asian nations. The macroeconomic stabilisation problems of a partly reformed economic system are formidable. There will be bumps in the road, one of the biggest yet through 1994, as yet another inflationary boom is brought to heel.

Getting the framework right for accommodating China is central to the future management of the global economy and polity. This is a huge challenge for the Asia Pacific Region as China's integration into the international economy moves forward rapidly. It is also a central, if not the central, political security interest in the Asia Pacific Region.

The ASEAN group has also developed its own growth momentum, most importantly with the entrenchment of export-oriented industrialisation since the mid-1980s. This has been boosted as Korea, Taiwan and Hong Kong have approached world industrial productivity frontiers and shed standard technology production to China and the ASEAN countries. There have been signs over the past two years of the direct investment flow to ASEAN diminishing with the greater attraction of China, but growth momentum in Southeast Asia remains considerable. The industrial transformation of the newly industrialising economies has added to the weight of Japan's role in the process of East Asian subregional economic integration.

International investment within the Asia Pacific economy has expanded even more rapidly than trade. The resulting relocation of production in line with changing industrial structures has led to the emergence of zones of intense economic interaction that transcend political boundaries. The largest case is the integrated zone of production in South China around Hong Kong; links are also strengthening across the Taiwan Straits, as well as across the Yellow Sea, and between Singapore and its neighbours. These subregional integrative processes are market-driven, generally with little formal government involvement in a regulatory sense. They are evolving in order to promote efficiency and competitiveness in global as well as domestic markets, rather than seeking to create a sheltered, discriminatory, subregional market (Lee 1991; Sung 1992).

Forging links with East Asia's growth

The intensification of intra-East Asian trade flows since the mid-1980s builds on strong established trade ties with North

Figure 6.3: North America's share in East Asia's and Japan's imports, 1970–93

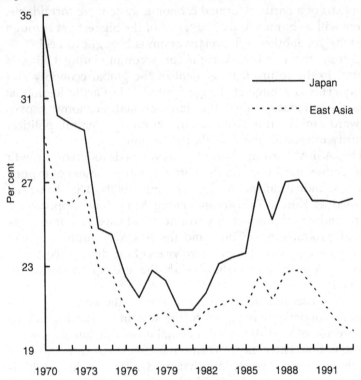

Source: International Economic Databank, The Australian National University, compiled from United Nations and International Monetary Fund statistics.

America and Australasia. As a result, the Asia Pacific is a region of intense trade ties (Frankel 1993; Drysdale 1988). In 1970, Asia Pacific economies (defined as the member economies of APEC) accounted for around 30 per cent of world trade, but their share in regional trade was around 55 per cent. In 1992, Asia Pacific economies accounted for 44 per cent of world trade, but 75 per cent of regional trade.

In 1992, intra-regional trade in Asia and the Pacific—at 75 per cent of the region's total trade—has already exceeded that within the European Union, despite the absence of comprehensive discriminatory economic arrangements such as those of Europe. Intra-regional trade in East Asian economies comprises 45 per cent of the region's trade (Drysdale and Garnaut 1993).

These crude trade shares are not reliable indicators of trade intensity as they take no account of differences in the value of total trade in various regions. Intensity of trade, properly measured, is similar in the APEC and Western European economies.

Expanding trade among APEC economies has continued to involve North America and Australasia, although these economies' weaker overall performance has in some periods led to declining shares in East Asian trade. Changes in the North American and Australasian regions' shares of the East Asian market between 1970 and 1993 are charted in Figures 6.3 and 6.4.

In the 1970s, North America's share in the principal East Asian markets declined sharply, for example, from over 30 per

Figure 6.4: Australia's share in East Asia's and Japan's imports, 1970–93

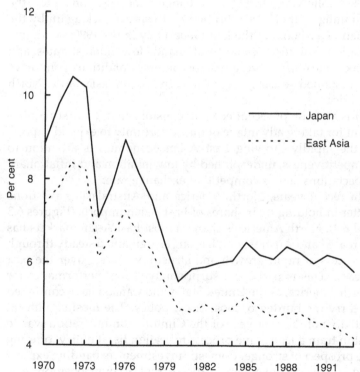

Source: International Economic Databank, The Australian National University, compiled from United Nations and International Monetary Fund statistics.

cent to around 20 per cent of Japan's total imports. This was also true of Australasia's share of East Asian markets: Australasia's share fell from over 9 per cent to around 6 per cent of Japan's total imports. These shares still represent very strong market penetration—but, importantly, the 1970s were a decade in which North American and Australasian export growth to East Asia did not keep pace with East Asian trade growth.

In part, the declining North American and Australasian shares in East Asian imports resulted from energy trade adjustments through the first and second oil shocks, when suppliers of oil from the Middle East and Southeast Asia secured a huge lift in the value of their exports to the region. The mismanagement of adjustment to changing international economic conditions, both in North America and Australasia, was one factor behind a decline in export competitiveness, affecting manufactures and services. Australian competitiveness rose in the mid-1980s following foreign exchange liberalisation and the beginning of trade liberalisation, but was set back again by the inflationary boom of the late 1980s. Only in the 1990s, with low inflation, subdued domestic demand, low interest rates and weaker currencies, were macroeconomic conditions conducive to sustained export expansion in Australasia and North America.

It is a lesson of recent economic history that the first requirement for taking advantage of the opportunity to expand exports to the rapidly growing East Asian economies is attention to competitiveness, underpinned by low inflation and inflationary expectations, and a competitive exchange rate.

In recent years, North America and Australasia have done better in holding their shares of East Asian imports (Figures 6.3 and 6.4). North America's share in most East Asian markets has increased and Australasia's has largely remained steady through a process of rapid growth and structural change over the past decade. This is perhaps a surprisingly strong performance for North America, as the United States and Canada have continued to carry the burden of loose fiscal policy. The most significant initiative of the first year of the Clinton Administration was to put in train a legislative process to realign fiscal policy, offering the prospect of stronger domestic investment, expanding exports and steady improvement in the current account position. It is also a more impressive achievement than it looks for Australasia in the face of low commodity prices over recent years.

The demonstrated relationship between export performance and competitiveness in East Asia underlines the importance of maintaining domestic effort in both North America and Australasia and not being diverted into shifting the blame for poor performance onto others. The key challenge over the next decade will be to harness the opportunity provided by the continued growth, structural change and interdependence of the regional economy to develop even more intensive trading relationships between Australasia, North America and East Asia.

At the same time, North America and Australasia have become proportionately much less important, and East Asia much more important, as destinations for Australian exports

Figure 6.5: North America's share in East Asia's and Japan's exports, 1970–93

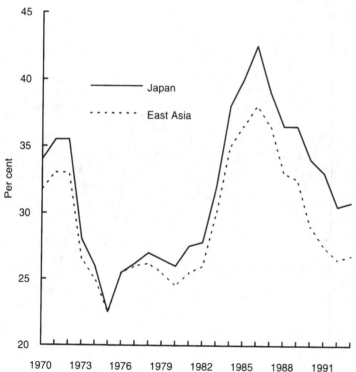

Source: International Economic Databank, The Australian National University, compiled from United Nations and International Monetary Fund statistics.

since 1986 (Figures 6.5, 6.6 and 6.7). More rapidly than is generally understood in the United States, the North American
market has become less crucial to overall export performance
in East Asia. Before many more years have passed, this geo-
economic reality will have an important effect on the extent to
which East Asian states are prepared to accommodate the idio-
syncrasies of US policymaking processes.

Underpinning this challenge is the importance of getting the
policy framework right to sustain industrial and trade penetration in East Asia and continued growth of market opportunities
in the region. The continuation of the game of 'prisoner's
delight'—beneficial trade liberalisation in the region—cannot
be taken for granted. It has proceeded rapidly over the past few
decades. It will continue if removal of barriers to deeper

Figure 6.6: Australia's share in East Asia's and Japan's exports, 1970–93

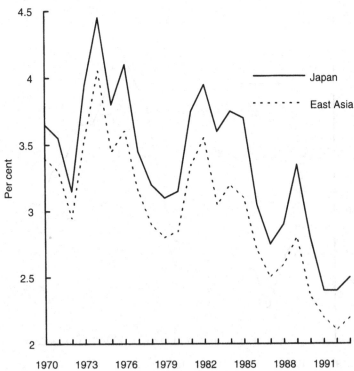

Source: International Economic Databank, The Australian National University,
compiled from United Nations and International Monetary Fund statistics.

Figure 6.7: East Asia's share in East Asia's exports and imports, 1970–93

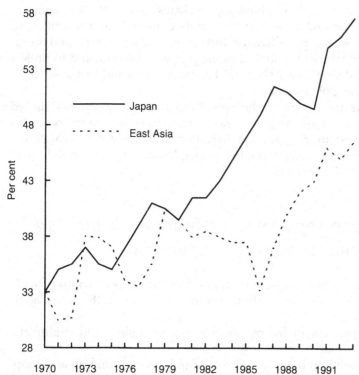

Source: International Economic Databank, The Australian National University, compiled from United Nations and International Monetary Fund statistics.

integration in the region is negotiated in a framework that creates confidence in the process, not tension and uncertainty. Trade arrangements that introduce discrimination by some regional economies against others could create serious divisions within the region. The 'invitation' in 1992, by the outgoing Bush Administration, for individual Western Pacific economies to enter separate, preferential trading agreements with the United States will, hopefully, never be reiterated, for it threatened to reintroduce the ideas into the region that have created the traditional trade policy 'prisoner's dilemma': leading each country, in narrow and ultimately mistaken pursuit of its own self-interest, through insisting on specific reciprocity and excluding outsiders, to take steps that lead all to be worse-off than they could be.

This means not only developing a favourable policy environment, but also establishing mechanisms for effective communication and coordination of policy interests and priorities, to exploit the potential for further economic growth and intra-regional trade in this dynamic part of the world, and to project and define East Asian and Pacific interests and responsibilities in the global arena.

As the centre of the world's economic gravity has shifted towards East Asia and the Pacific, there is a more powerful interest throughout the Asia Pacific in fostering Asia Pacific integration, based on the principles and policy objectives of open regionalism.

Open regionalism: a framework for Asia Pacific economic cooperation

The essential requirements of economic cooperation to provide a framework for continued trade expansion in the Asia Pacific region are:
• openness in international economic policy and diplomatic approach;
• evolution in the practice of high-level consultation and cooperation; and
• non-discrimination in growing economic partnerships among disparate polities.

The Pacific Economic Cooperation Council (PECC), established in 1980, was the first building block in the architecture of regional economic policy coordination. The Pacific Economic Cooperation Council—with its informal, tripartite structure, which includes participation at the official, industry and academic level—carried forward the process of fostering consultation and discussion of interests in regional cooperation through its Trade Policy Forum and other task forces.

An important policy achievement that grew out of consultations within the Pacific Economic Cooperation Council was the development of Asia Pacific support for the Uruguay Round of multilateral trade negotiations, and the facilitation of broader economic dialogue involving both China and Taiwan. The Pacific Economic Cooperation Council's semi-official processes also laid the groundwork for the next step in the development of outward-looking economic cooperation—the evolution of the Asia Pacific Economic Cooperation (APEC) group. APEC, through the establishment of regular ministerial-level meetings, brought the process of economic cooperation into the political arena.

APEC was initiated by Australia, with strong support from Korea, Singapore and Japan, in 1989, and has rapidly established itself as the main regional forum for discussion of trade liberalisation and expansion. The group has fostered consistency between regional economic policy objectives and multilateral international economic policy goals—and sought to strengthen the GATT-based multilateral trading system.

APEC could pursue these objectives most effectively if it were able to set positive examples of successful trade liberalisation and expansion. It is imperative that any joint economic or trade policy decisions by APEC be consistent with the fundamental principle of universal most-favoured-nation treatment of all trading partners as set out in Article I of the GATT, rather than explicitly discriminate against non-participants, seeking to rationalise discrimination by reference to Article XXIV. Any attempt to negotiate an APEC-wide preferential trading agreement is not only economically undesirable, given the trade and investment links of the East Asian economies outside the region, especially with the European Union; it is also destined to end in failure.

As argued by Yamazawa (1992) and Elek (1992a), if APEC is to establish itself as a promoter of open and multilateral trade, it must remain an open economic association:
- open in the sense of not discriminating against the rest of the world;
- economic in its primary policy focus; and
- an association in the sense of seeking voluntary understandings on principles and policy action that yield benefits to all participants, rather than imposing a supra-national authority on participants.

International policy concerns

A persistent theme in the discussion of international economic policy outcomes is the threat of inward-looking or closed regionalism. This was the context of East Asian commitment to the Uruguay Round.

The biggest danger for Asia Pacific economic expansion and political security is that the Pacific, under stress, might split down the middle. Regionalism and protectionism in North America and Europe invite a regionalist East Asian response, but a split makes no economic or political sense. That is why it is so important for Australia, Japan and other Western Pacific countries to articulate a clear and constructive response to the drift in trans-Pacific tensions. That is why strong commitment to the APEC framework for regional economic dealings is so important, because it encompasses both North American and Western Pacific economic and political interests and provides a vehicle for dealing with them in the post Cold War period. The APEC framework of open regionalism was conducive to the successful completion of the Uruguay Round, and to the continued viability of the multilateral system following the negotiations.

The North American Free Trade Agreement (NAFTA) is less threatening to traders and investors outside North America since the Uruguay Round was completed successfully. It is also important that the North American Free Trade area is engaged in open Asia Pacific regionalism, and that tensions between North America and East Asia can be settled within this framework rather than bilaterally (in ways that do not take into account the interests of other countries).

The framework of APEC and its inclusion of the world's two largest economic powers makes it a suitable forum for containing inclinations towards inward-looking policy developments within the Pacific region, encouraging the European Union towards outward-looking responses to East Asian dynamism and providing urgently needed leadership towards the further deepening of international economic integration after the implementation of the Uruguay Round.

Security issues require separate forum

Rapid economic growth has changed the structure of world economic power and challenges old definitions of political and security interests in East Asia and the Pacific in the post Cold War era. With the end of American economic hegemony, new regional and multilateral political structures are needed to define rules governing the relations between Asia Pacific states, to provide a framework for the emerging strategic significance of Japan and China, and ASEAN, and to establish a forum for discussing a wide range of regional and subregional security issues.

US–Japan economic tensions are more likely to be manageable so long as the established framework of security relations remains intact. The United States—a strong stabilising factor in regional security—is only likely to be induced to maintain a presence in the Western Pacific if there is a strong economic rationale for it to do so.

In political as well as in economic affairs, the pace of change must encourage experimentation with new structures to manage regional and subregional problems. To reflect the impact of economic policy on political and security arrangements, the aim should not be to develop a single overarching regional structure dealing with economic, political and security issues. Rather, separate structures are more realistic, but to be successful they need to reinforce each other.

The game plan

The challenge is to make the Asia Pacific economy a source of strength for a liberal international system, by facilitating the removal of barriers to trade among member economies without discriminating against non-regional nations. The GATT's most-favoured-nation-based trade rules have served the region well, and despite their limitations, they constrain the political threat of discrimination and provide a measure of security and political confidence in open international economic transactions.

Implementing the outcome of the Uruguay Round is the first task—not altogether straightforward given the far-reaching adjustments associated with the round. Yet, from the perspective of Western Pacific economies, the Uruguay Round is not the end of trade policy history, but the beginning, since it coincides with the region's continuing implementation of substantial reform and economic liberalisation programs. APEC is of critical importance in defining the international trade and economic policy agenda beyond the Uruguay Round.

Beyond the implementation of the Uruguay Round agreements, no issue is as important for the Asia Pacific and regional trading than securing Chinese membership of the GATT/World Trade Organisation and making its membership work within the established rules. APEC members are in a good position to lead wider international opinion on this issue.

It is obvious that 1994 was a very important year for APEC. In 1993, with the United States in the chair, a substantial agenda for regional cooperation and negotiation was defined around trade and investment facilitation. In addition, leaders committed themselves to building a region in which goods, services and investment moved freely, without defining the context of 'free trade'. The APEC meeting in Jakarta in late 1994 brought together the leaders of the nations that account for one-half of global production and 40 per cent of global trade. This was an important symbolic step in demonstrating the commitment of APEC economies to supporting the forum as the most appropriate vehicle for furthering their interests in the regional and global trading system, and focusing corporate attention and energies on regional developments.

It was important for the Jakarta Leaders' meeting to accomplish three things if APEC were to play a central role in sustaining internationally oriented growth in the Asia Pacific.

First, it had to give concrete form to regional cooperation on trade and investment facilitation. This agenda relates to provision and strengthening of the 'public goods' that facilitate international economic transactions. It includes a regional investment code and dispute settlement mechanism that needs to go further than the multilateral arrangements if they are to be useful for the region and as an example and model for the rest of the world. Other items encompass facilitation of trade-relevant information flows and reconciliation of standards where divergences had previously acted as a barrier to trade. This is an important, if apparently prosaic and uncontroversial, area of cooperation. In its nature, it need involve no discrimination against outsiders and should be designed to avoid deterrence of trade with non-APEC economies.

Second, it had to give substance to the Leaders' commitment to liberalise the flows of goods, services and investment in the Asia Pacific Region while avoiding the discrimination against outsiders that is inherent in free trade areas of the traditional kind, as well as to confirm its commitment to clear and timely implementation of the Uruguay Round agreements.

APEC Leaders needed to go beyond this, to a commitment to turn the Asia Pacific into a region of free trade, on a non-discriminatory basis, consistently with Article I of the GATT.

To be realistic, such a commitment would need to allow long periods for adjustment, to leave the pace and order of progress towards free trade to individual governments, influenced by APEC peer pressure but without threats of sanctions. Early steps would include agreements to go beyond Uruguay Round commitments to liberalise trade in sectors important to Asia Pacific trade, balanced to meet the interests of a range of member countries, But should discriminatory free trade, and agreement on the steps beyond the Uruguay Round be beyond regional consensus, it would be better to delay progress on trade liberalisation than to seek progress through discriminatory arrangements. The latter would have the effect of corroding the multilateral system, and would ultimately divide and weaken APEC itself.

Third, as a practical matter of the political dynamics of progress under Indonesian leadership in Jakarta, the relevance of APEC to development in the region's lower-income economies had to be demonstrated. This could be done most effectively through the linkage of development cooperation to the trade expansion agenda. In the event, the Leaders' Summit delivered handsomely on the trade and facilitation agenda, the commitment to free trade among Asia Pacific economies and, effectively, the extension of the APEC agenda to incorporate development cooperation. On the crucial question of whether free trade among Asia Pacific economies should be governed by Article I or Article XXIV of the GATT, the words from the Summit had the right flavour, but were insufficiently clear-cut in favour of non-discrimination to avoid the possibility of future debate and dispute. This is a threat to the future achievements of APEC, as a long debate about the form of Asia Pacific free trade would dissipate the momentum from Bogor that needs to be utilised fully if the Bogor commitments are to be effective.

The strong inclination of the Western Pacific members of APEC is towards non-discriminatory liberalisation, and this is explicitly embodied in APEC's commitment to open regionalism. Ironically, the pressures for discriminatory regionalism now come from North America, intellectually and politically the home of the postwar liberal multilateral system.

It now seems that the historic mission of East Asia and the Western Pacific in the international system is to sustain appreciation of the superiority of a multilateral framework of open trade. APEC has become the immediate arena of contests between discriminatory and multilateral versions of open trade. If the Western Pacific holds APEC to its recently established course, it will strengthen the sustainability of open trade on a global basis.

Notes to Chapter 6

The authors are very grateful to Yiping Huang and Ligang Song for their efficient assistance in producing the data and assembling the materials upon which the argument in this chapter is based.

7

Exchange Rate Regimes and Outward-looking Growth

E.S. LEUNG

In the past four decades, there has been a major change in thinking on the economics of development, akin to a paradigm shift. Governments of many industrial economies have come to recognise that reliance on world markets (outward orientation) gives much greater scope for economic growth than reliance on domestic markets (inward orientation). While there is much less agreement on the degree of government intervention necessary to bring about outward-looking growth, it is generally recognised that significant government interventions that run counter to market forces have been very costly in terms of misallocation of resources, resulting in retardation of economic growth. The adverse effects of repression in foreign trade and in the domestic financial sectors have been amply documented (Balassa 1985; Bhagwati 1978; Hughes 1985, 1989a; Krueger 1978; McKinnon 1973, 1991), while the theoretical foundations of the impact of outward-looking macroeconomic and trade policies on the rate of economic growth are currently being formally specified (Grossman and Helpman 1991; Khan and Villanueva 1991; Obstfeld 1992).

This paradigm shift has influenced exchange rate and monetary policy in the Asia Pacific Region.[1] Exchange and interest rates have become endogenised (that is, determined by market forces rather than by governments) in economies that have embarked on outward-looking growth. In the following discussion less attention is paid to the specifics of pegging arrangements. The distinguishing factor here between an independent float and a frequently changed 'crawling peg' is the degree and effectiveness of controls over trade and capital flows; that is, the influence of market versus administrative forces. During the

1980s many economies in the Asia Pacific Region undertook important structural reforms in the areas of government fiscal efforts, foreign trade and the domestic financial sector (Appendix 7.1). An important aspect of financial sector reform has been the movement away from the use of direct credit allocation rules and interest rates towards more market-oriented monetary policy instruments. Economies in the Asia Pacific Region have, over the past two decades, increasingly moved towards the flexible end of the spectrum in their exchange rate regimes and, while capital controls have been abolished in some countries, other countries retain administrative controls over short-term capital movements (Table 7.1).

Garnaut (1991a) expressed doubts about the effectiveness of capital controls as a continuing constraint on the choice of exchange rate regimes in the Asia Pacific region. Recent empirical evidence on short-term capital flows points to greatly increased mobility of short-term capital in the 1980s. This evidence is examined and it is argued that, among other factors, changes in foreign trade and domestic financial sector policies in economies of the Asia Pacific Region have brought about increased capital mobility, even in economies where capital controls are still in place.

Implications of increased capital mobility for choice of exchange rate regimes and monetary instruments are examined. The unsustainability of using exchange rate and credit allocation policies as instruments for promoting outward-looking growth and economic stabilisation, in an environment of mobile short-term capital is demonstrated. It is also argued that increasing sophistication and deepening in the financial and foreign exchange markets go hand-in-hand with outward-looking growth, and that government interventions must be consistent with developments in these markets.

Increased short-term capital mobility also affects the feasibility of following the sequencing of economic reforms as specified by McKinnon (1982), Edwards (1984) and Krueger (1984c). Some economies in the region have rapidly liberalised their domestic and external financial sectors while others have chosen to adopt a more gradual approach. The sequencing issue is re-examined in the light of the experience of some economies in the region, and guidelines are drawn for the future development of this debate.

Table 7.1: Exchange rate arrangements and capital controls for selected Asia Pacific economies

	Pegged to US$	Pegged to other currency or composite	Other flexible arrangements	Managed flexibility	Independent floaters	Capital controls Substantial	Capital controls Limited	Capital controls None
1975	3	6	1	2	1	10	2	1
1976	3	5	1	3	1	10	2	1
1977	3	4	1	3	2	10	2	1
1978	2	4	1	4	2	10	1	2
1979	1	4	1	5	2	9	2	2
1980	0	4	1	6	2	9	2	2
1981	0	3	1	8	1	9	2	2
1982	0	3	1	8	1	9	2	2
1983	0	3	1	8	1	7	3	3
1984	0	4	0	6	3	7	2	4
1985	0	3	0	5	4	6	3	4
1986	0	3	0	6	4	6	3	4
1987	0	3	0	6	4	5	4	4
1988	0	3	0	6	4	5	4	4
1989	0	3	0	6	4	5	4	4
1990	0	3	0	6	4	5	4	4
1991	0	3	0	6	4	5	4	4

Note: includes Australia, China, Hong Kong, Indonesia, Japan, Korea, Malaysia, New Zealand, Philippines, Singapore, Sri Lanka, Taiwan and Thailand.

Sources: International Monetary Fund, 1976–78, *Exchange Restrictions—Annual Report,* IMF, Washington, D.C.; International Monetary Fund, 1979–92, *Exchange Arrangements and Exchange Restrictions—Annual Report,* IMF, Washington, D.C.

Capital mobility in the Asia Pacific region

Most recent studies of capital mobility (Chinn and Frankel 1992; Faruquee 1991; Goldsborough and Teja 1991; Haque and Montiel 1990) make use of some form of the simple interest parity condition, $i = i^*$, where i represents the domestic interest rate on a financial asset and i^* represents the 'world' interest rate on a comparable financial asset. If capital is perfectly mobile, then arbitrage should equalise the two interest rates. This implies that, for a small country in world financial markets, domestic monetary policy can do little to affect domestic demand and levels of activity.

The simple interest rate parity can be broken down into its components:

$$i - i^* = (i - i^* - f) + (f - \Delta s^e) + \Delta s^e$$

where f represents the forward margin on the domestic currency and Δs^e represents the expected depreciation or appreciation of the domestic currency.

The first bracket on the right-hand side of the identity represents influences on the simple interest differential $(i - i^*)$ which are unrelated to currency factors, as the exchange rate is already covered forward. These influences are called country factors (Chinn and Frankel 1992) and they encompass the concept of political risks (Dooley and Isard 1980). These country factors chiefly comprise existing capital controls, prospects of future capital controls, default risks in a country, and localised information and transaction costs in transferring capital. Technically, this term is known as the covered interest differential. For any particular country, if the covered interest differential is equal to zero in a statistical sense, then the country factors are not important.

The second bracket on the right-hand side of the above identity represents the exchange risk premium of holding a currency. If expectations among market participants are rational, then the expected future spot rate should equal the actual future spot rate, on average. In any particular instance, however, there is a risk that the expected future spot rate may be wrong, in spite of rational expectations. In order to insure against expectation error in any particular instance, a market participant can cover forward. The difference between the forward rate and the expected future spot rate (or alternatively, the difference between the forward margin and the expected change in the future spot rate) could therefore be interpreted as a measure of the exchange risk premium. This exchange risk premium and the last term in the above identity, Δs^e, therefore constitute factors affecting the simple interest differential $(i - i^*)$ arising out of currency considerations. It can be seen that if country factors are not important (that is, the covered interest differential equals zero), and exchange risk is not important (that is, the exchange risk premium equals zero), then the simple interest rate differential $(i - i^*)$ will equal the expected change in the spot rate (Δs^e); that is, uncovered interest parity will hold.

Measures of capital mobility in the Asia Pacific Region derived from recent studies are presented in Appendix 7.2. Chinn and Frankel (1992) found that over the decade 1982–92, in the countries for which forward rate data were available (Australia, Canada, Hong Kong, Japan, Malaysia, New Zealand and Singapore), there was a significant trend towards zero in both the mean and the variance of the covered interest differential for three-month instruments. This means that country factors have become a great deal less important in impeding short-term capital flows over the course of the 1980s.

Using the LIBOR rate for three-month yen deposits instead of US dollar deposits as the proxy for the 'world' interest rate, Faruquee (1991) found that both the mean and the variance of the simple interest differential declined over the course of the 1980s for Korea, Singapore, Malaysia and Thailand. This implies that both country and currency factors became less important in affecting short-term capital flows in these countries over the past decade.

In another test of simple interest parity, Haque and Montiel (1990) found that for Indonesia, Malaysia, Philippines and Sri Lanka, perfect capital mobility cannot be ruled out for the period 1969–87. It is not clear, however, whether this study refers to short-term capital, and the conclusions do not say anything about changes in capital mobility throughout this period.

Finally, one part of the Goldsborough and Teja study (1991) confirms the Chinn and Frankel conclusion that there was a significant degree of financial integration with world capital markets in the seven Asia Pacific economies for which forward rate data were available. The other part of this study makes use of the savings–investment relationship and argues that, if capital is mobile, then there should be little correlation between a country's domestic savings and investment, the mismatch being taken up by capital flows (Feldstein and Horioka 1980). This test enables Goldsborough and Teja to examine Asia Pacific economies for which forward rates were not available. The results show that there was much lower correlation between domestic private savings and investment during the 1980s than in earlier decades, and that the correlation became weaker still in the period 1984–87 compared with the entire period 1980–87.

It is therefore reasonable to conclude that capital (particularly short-term capital) in the Asia Pacific Region has become a great deal more mobile in the 1980s than in previous decades. During the 1980s, capital mobility increased in the second half of the decade. This increased mobility occurred not only in economies that historically had little capital control (Hong Kong and Singapore), or in economies that abolished capital controls (Australia, New Zealand and Japan), but also in economies where significant controls are still 'on the books' (Korea, Philippines, Thailand, Sri Lanka and China). This last conclusion implies that capital controls (and country factors more generally) have become much less of an impediment to short-term capital movements. Why?

Advances in information technology have undoubtedly reduced the transaction costs associated with transfers of short-term capital. They have also substantially reduced gaps in knowledge due to localised information. Furthermore, liberalisation of domestic financial sectors in most Asia Pacific economies has revealed large differences in real rates of return previously hidden by repressed financial systems. This, together with various degrees of internationalisation of banking associated with domestic financial deregulation, has provided both the incentive and the mechanism for the international transfer of short-term capital.

In Australia, for instance, international interest arbitrage intensified throughout the latter part of the 1970s and early 1980s. Polasek and Lewis (1985) document the development of the private sector currency hedge market in Australia. Unlike the official hedge market where only certain trade-related transactions were permitted forward cover, the private hedge market allowed both trade and capital transactions to be hedged. The very rapid growth of this market in the non-bank sector led to pressure from banks to participate. By 1979, the government permitted the trading banks to develop their own 'interbank' hedge market, thereby formally creating a channel for international capital flows to take advantage of covered interest arbitrage.

In addition, with the opening up of foreign trade, the channels for evading capital controls increased (Mathieson and Rojas-Suarez 1992). For example, capital can be transferred via the underinvoicing and overinvoicing of trade transactions, including transfer pricing arrangements via leads and lags in commercial settlements; through timing changes in the repatriation of foreign earnings; and through forward exchange operations to cover trade transactions. A country's openness to international trade therefore gives rise to opportunities for the evasion of capital controls. This is consistent with Haque and Montiel's finding (1990) that between 1969 and 1987, capital was immobile between India and the rest of the world. India also had one of the most restrictive trade and financial regimes in the world.

It would appear, therefore, that the outward-looking growth-oriented policies adopted by Asia Pacific economies in the 1980s have brought about a deterioration in the effectiveness of capital controls, with resultant increases in capital mobility. This, in turn, has important implications for these countries' exchange rate and monetary policy regimes.

Exchange rate regimes and monetary instruments

Most theoretical literature on the optimal choice of exchange rate regimes focuses on the insulation properties of fixed versus flexible exchange rates for domestic prices and incomes (for a review of this literature see Moreno 1993). In general, for external monetary shocks, flexible exchange rates insulate better than fixed rates, but the reverse is true for external real shocks.[2]

In the following discussion it is argued that increased capital mobility has required economies in the region to move towards greater flexibility in both exchange rate regimes and monetary policy instruments. Both overvaluation and undervaluation of the nominal exchange rate become increasingly costly and unsustainable for economies increasingly integrated with world trade and financial markets. Internal credit rationing is incompatible with an open financial sector.

Exchange rate regimes

In theory, an exchange rate can be kept in disequilibrium for extended periods of time through foreign exchange interventions provided the magnitudes of such interventions are minimised by an effective system of controls over trade and capital transactions.[3] Economies in the Asia Pacific Region have been liberalising their trade and domestic financial sectors and restrictions on capital flows have become increasingly ineffective. These changes have rendered disequilibrium exchange rates more difficult and costly to maintain.[4]

The difficulty is obvious in the case of deficit countries where the volume of foreign exchange reserves and the country's international creditworthiness act as limits to extended periods of exchange rate overvaluation. Even in the case of surplus countries, however, problems arise because of the effect of an increasing inflow of foreign exchange reserves on the money supply. It is, of course, possible to sterilise, but the need to keep control of the money base or some kind of overall central bank credit limit would involve reducing the domestic credit of the central bank to offset the increases in international reserves. Particularly in economies where credit is rationed, this would result in quite severe financial constraints on firms that do not have access to external finance or to commercial domestic credit. In other words, the effect of constantly sterilising increasing foreign exchange reserves due, for example, to an exchange rate undervaluation, would be a sharp redistribution of financial resources in the private sector that could result in financial hardships and bankruptcies in many areas (Mathieson 1988). Thus, the difficulties caused by sterilisation increase significantly if capital inflow is maintained by a disequilibrium situation such as an exchange rate undervaluation. The alternative to non-sterilisation, however, is rapid expansion of the money supply, and inflation.

Taiwan faced this type of choice in the second half of the 1980s. Although Taiwan had moved from a currency peg to a managed exchange rate regime in 1979, the reality was that it had a crawling peg supported by capital controls and maintained by government interventions in the foreign exchange market. Some writers (Lee Sheng-yi 1990; Sachs 1987) claim that from 1981 to 1985, Taiwan used an undervalued exchange rate as part of its export promotion strategy. While there is some dispute about the strength of this claim (Liang and Liang 1981, 1988), there is no doubt that Taiwan amassed large current account surpluses, particularly between 1984 and 1988.[5] There is also no doubt that the Taiwan authorities intervened heavily in the foreign exchange market between 1985 and 1987 in an effort to prevent the New Taiwan (NT) dollar from appreciating sharply, for fear of an adverse effect on exports. The effect of this intervention in the face of large trade surpluses, however, was to generate expectations of further appreciation of the NT dollar. Speculative inflows of foreign capital entered the country through a loophole in the foreign exchange regulations that permitted exporters/importers to incur foreign currency debts via the commercial banking system. The trader would sell the currency for NT dollars in the expectation that when the debt fell due, the NT dollar would have appreciated sufficiently so that the foreign currency debt could be repaid using fewer NT dollars. Therefore, the gradual but delayed appreciation of the NT dollar did not have any apparent adverse impact on exports as exporters were able to continue quoting prices in foreign currencies prior to the NT dollar appreciation while offsetting their trade losses with speculative profits earned on the foreign exchange market. It was only when the freeze on commercial banks' foreign borrowings was announced in 1987 that the trade surplus began to diminish as exporters were forced to raise their prices because they were unable to speculate (Ranis ed. 1992).

The freeze was brought on by a blowout in the money supply as a result of substantial increases in international reserves due to both the trade surplus and currency speculation. The redistributional costs of sterilisation ultimately required an exchange rate appreciation as well as the abolition of many outward capital controls (to encourage capital outflows and reduce base money) and inward capital controls as they proved to be useless in the face of currency speculation (Appendix 7.3). This is an example of the unsustainability of keeping exchange rates in disequilibrium when short-term capital is mobile.

Indeed, in his study of East Asian economies including Korea, Malaysia, Philippines, Singapore and Thailand, Quirk (1989) found that there had been no sustained and large premium or discount for these East Asian currencies in their black markets for foreign exchange post-1965, although from time to time, some discounts had arisen, indicating temporary overvaluation of the exchange rate in Korea in the early 1970s and the Philippines in the late 1960s and early 1980s.

Apart from temporary overvaluation resulting from a pegged exchange rate and inflation, there is also a claim that overvaluation of the exchange rate can be used as a disinflationary tool; the so-called Exchange Rate Based Stabilisation policy (ERBS). This strategy was used most noticeably in the Southern Cone economies in their (generally recognised as failed) liberalisation attempts during the 1970s. In the case of Chile and Argentina, a downward crawling peg was preannounced (the Tablita) which purposely devalued the domestic currency by less than the inflation differential between it and the United States. In due course, the devaluations were to cease and the exchange rates were to be pegged to the US dollar.

As the traded goods sectors in Argentina and Chile were substantially liberalised at the time, it was hoped that international commodity arbitrage (with a fixed nominal exchange rate acting as a 'nominal anchor') would help reduce domestic inflation. In the event, severe overvaluation of the real exchange rate, with balance of payments crises, recessions and widespread bankruptcies ensued (Kiguel and Liviatan 1992). In Argentina, large fiscal deficits were given as reasons for the failure. In Chile where fiscal surpluses were achieved before and during the period of the Tablita, backward-looking wage indexation and high nominal and real interest rates were considered the main problems (McKinnon 1991). In all of the Southern Cone economies, macroeconomic instability accompanied by rapid capital flight had occurred prior to stabilisation and liberalisation. Exchange controls were obviously unable to stem the capital outflows, and the 'flight' capital was several times the countries' international reserves (Mathieson and Rojas-Suarez 1992). As soon as there were prospects of stabilisation, however, the real domestic interest rates became positive, repatriation of this large amount of capital greatly overvalued the real exchange rate, causing severe problems for the traded goods sectors and monetary policy. Added to this were attempts to use an overvalued nominal exchange rate as inflation control. As in the case of an undervalued exchange rate, short-term movements of international capital made it costly for significant deviations from market rates in the governments' exchange rate management.

In contrast, South Korea successfully disinflated (albeit from an inflation rate of about 20 per cent per year rather than per month) during 1981 and 1984 without using a nominal exchange rate 'anchor'. Although it is argued (McKinnon 1991) that controlled reductions of nominal interest rates in line with inflation prevented a significant inflow of foreign capital and overvaluation of the real exchange rate, the relative lack of a large stock of flight capital waiting for repatriation must have been an important factor contributing to the greater success of the Korean stabilisation. Again, international capital movements required governments to keep exchange rates at equilibrium levels.

Australia in the 1970s also used an overvalued nominal exchange rate under its crawling peg system as an anti-inflationary instrument: '... the exchange rate has at times been held above the "free" market rate as part of a deliberate policy of using it to help reduce inflation and thus, over the medium term, to help restore domestic and external equilibrium' (Australian Treasury 1981). However, the administered system of crawling peg-cum-capital controls became untenable. As pointed out above, the deregulation of the Australian financial sector and the resultant international interest arbitrage brought about channels for evading capital controls. In addition, the resources boom of the early 1980s led to Australian companies building up a large stock of debt denominated in foreign currencies. Not all of this debt was properly hedged so that any expectation of a devaluation (for example expectations during the leadup to the federal election in March 1983) led to an enormous outflow of capital (about A$3 billion or almost 4 per cent of M3). An expected revaluation in December 1983 led to an equivalent of A$1.5 billion of foreign funds being 'booked' by operators to enter the country. Little wonder that the Reserve Bank pointed out: '[f]loating the rate was critical to bringing monetary conditions under control over the second half of 1983/84' (Reserve Bank of Australia 1984). Again, policy regime changes such as financial liberalisation freed up the movements of short-term international capital flows, and forced governments to adopt more flexible and market-oriented exchange rate regimes.

Nor is the causality from policy regime changes in the traded goods sector to the adoption of more flexible exchange rate regimes necessarily one-way. Corden (1993) argues that countries planning substantial foreign trade liberalisation usually precede this with a large currency devaluation. The argument runs that a devaluation would probably lead to an export boom, increasing nominal wages and employment in the tradeable goods sector, and hence make trade liberalisation politically more acceptable. It is therefore entirely consistent that increasing exchange rate flexibility goes hand-in-hand with policy regime changes aimed at achieving outward-looking growth.

Monetary control

The two ends of the spectrum in monetary control are credit market instruments and monetary instruments. Credit market instruments refer to measures that control the availability of credit to the private sector. They typically include ceilings on commercial bank credit to the private sector, credit allocation rules and ceilings on bank loan and deposit rates. Monetary instruments are measures that affect the price and quantity of base money, and typically include open market operations and central bank discount windows. Reserve requirements of commercial banks are somewhere in the middle of this spectrum, directly affecting the size of the money multiplier rather than base money.

McKinnon (1991) argues convincingly that, in a typically repressed economy where the existence of a substantial fiscal deficit leads the government to tax the financial system, either directly through monetising the deficit (inflation tax) and/or indirectly through subsidised interest rates and special credit allocations to favoured sectors, exchange controls on capital inflows and outflows are necessary. As discussed above, however, trade liberalisation tends to weaken the effectiveness of capital controls. Banks in a financially repressed economy therefore would find that their below-market deposit interest rates could not compete with foreign interest rates, and capital outflows would ensue. At the same time, the loss of control over capital inflows would mean that domestic banks could not charge high loan rates on the free (that is undirected) part of their loans as domestic borrowers would simply borrow from abroad. This means that domestic banks would find it increasingly difficult to bear the implicit 'tax' placed upon them by the government. It is therefore not surprising to find that countries which have successfully embarked on trade liberalisation have had their fiscal situation under control, and have therefore had less need to use credit controls as an indirect means of taxing their financial sector (Appendix 7.1).

Furthermore, in the case of Australia and New Zealand between 1975 and 1985, the interaction of credit controls on the one hand, and rapid inflation, large government budget deficits and advances in information technology on the other, resulted in the rapid growth of non-bank financial institutions at the expense of the then regulated banking sector (Leung 1991). Assets of banks as a proportion of total financial sector assets fell to about 40 per cent and 60 per cent in Australia and New Zealand, respectively. In order to regain monetary control, authorities had the choice of either adopting monetary instruments that could affect interest rates more generally in the economy or extending credit market controls to cover the non-bank financial institutions as well as the banks. It was decided that the latter course of action would simply encourage other financial institutions to establish outside the regulatory net, and that the increased efficiency costs of financial disintermediation would outweigh the benefits of such a step. The governments therefore deregulated the domestic financial sector, replacing credit market regulations with more market-oriented monetary instruments. The contributions of a healthy financial sector to efficient resource allocation and economic growth were therefore given priority.

Similar considerations applied to a number of other Asia Pacific economies, such as Indonesia and the Philippines.[6] Real interest rates worldwide were substantially higher in the 1980s than in the 1970s. As a result, the ratio of debt to exports that might have been sustainable in the 1970s became unsustainable in the 1980s. Many developing economies had to rely increasingly on their own savings to finance their development needs (World Bank 1989). Freeing their domestic financial sectors from interest rate controls and credit allocation policies was seen to be important in encouraging the efficient use of investment funds. Initial steps in financial liberalisation, however, opened up channels for international interest arbitrage. Access to short-term capital in turn provided residents with a source of credit from outside the banking system and also created an incentive for the development of financial institutions outside the regulated domestic net (Mathieson 1988). The importance of the informal financial sector to small enterprises in Indonesia has been stressed by McCleod (1991), and the prevalence of finance via the informal Chinese network throughout the region is well recognised in spite of the lack of hard data. These tend to weaken the effectiveness of credit ceilings as a tool of monetary control and encourage the use of monetary instruments that affect interest rates more generally in the economy.

The efficiency argument in favour of financial liberalisation has often been questioned by proponents of the Japan model (for example, Sachs 1987) who claim that subsidised interest rates and directed credit were very much part of the industrial policies on which high growth economies such as Japan, Taiwan and Korea depended. Horiuchi (1984) has shown, however, that during the period of high economic growth in Japan (1953–72), regulated bank deposit rates and central bank discount rates were substantially higher than in the United States, the United Kingdom and West Germany in nominal terms, and higher in real terms as well, if the wholesale price index rather than the consumer price index is used as a deflator (Appendix 7.4).[7] This is certainly consistent with the substantial financial deepening that occurred in Japan during that period, and would indicate that regulated Japanese interest rates were not significantly out of line with rates in economies that did not experience growth on a scale comparable with Japan (McKinnon 1991).

While it is true that regulated deposit rates were consistently lower than the 'free' interbank call rate in Japan during this period, it is not clear that this 'subsidy' went to non-financial industries. While the existence of keiretsu groups comprised of banks and non-financial enterprises would, at first glance, suggest that the interest subsidy had been passed from the banks to the non-financial enterprises in the group, Horiuchi refers to empirical studies indicating that the rapidly growing non-financial enterprises tended to obtain finance from outside the group. Furthermore, the contracted interest rates on bank loans in Japan were rather high compared with those in the United States, the United Kingdom and West Germany (Appendix 7.4), and profits in the Japanese financial sector were also higher than profits in the non-financial sector during this period of high growth. All these facts would seem to indicate that the interest subsidy was, to a large extent, kept by the banks.

During the period of rapid growth in Japan, demand for investible funds consistently exceeded supply (hence the high interbank call rate). Commercial banks frequently exceeded their stipulated ratio of loans to total deposits and had to borrow from the Bank of Japan. It is claimed by proponents of the Japan model that the Bank of Japan directed commercial bank credits to priority industries as part of its conditions for providing the extra funds. Without doubt, this situation of overloan gave the Bank of Japan much more influence in the money market than would otherwise have been the case. Horiuchi argues, however, that it is doubtful whether directed credit through the overloan lever was a conscious government policy as the government acted to diminish the overloan situation in 1962 at a time when Japan was in the process of implementing the National Income Doubling Plan. Under the new system of monetary control introduced in 1962, the Bank of Japan was supposed to engage more in open market operations (buying and selling public bonds) as a means of controlling money supply rather than employing an excessive reliance on 'overloan'. If the Japanese government had been using directed credit as a conscious policy to stimulate economic growth, it would seem that it chose a bad time to diminish the importance of such an instrument.

In short, the postwar rapid growth of Japan seems to have taken place against the background of a financial sector that was much more efficient and less repressed than has been generally claimed by proponents of the Japan model.

In the case of Taiwan, McKinnon (1991) shows that, although there were preferential interest rates available to export loans from the 1950s, real interest rates on these loans were generally positive and substantial (up to 6 per cent). Furthermore, Taiwan's kerb market was better developed and traded in longer-term instruments than most other developing economies, thanks to Taiwan's effective control over inflation. The existence of this market outside the regulated net, together with substantial capital inflow during the 1980s as discussed above, would have rendered credit ceilings quite ineffective. A move towards more flexible exchange rates and market-oriented monetary instruments was inevitable.

Increasing sophistication and deepening in the financial sector therefore go hand-in-hand with outward-looking growth. To this end, government interventions in the financial and foreign exchange markets must be consistent with market imperatives. The challenge is to redefine the role of government and to devise forms of intervention that support developments in the market in order to promote growth. In this regard, an important issue in the literature is sequencing, both in terms of the ordering of economic reforms in general, and of reforms of the financial sector in particular.

Sequencing of economic reforms

As noted above, economies that have successfully embarked on trade liberalisation and outward-looking growth have also had their fiscal situation under control and have embarked, in various degrees, on liberalisation of their domestic financial sectors. It is generally agreed that, as a prior condition to structural reforms, fiscal deficits have to be contained so that governments do not have to rely on inflation tax and other indirect taxes on the financial sector in order to raise revenue.

It is also becoming generally accepted that, in deregulating the domestic financial sector, stringent standards in prudential control of banks (for example, capital adequacy requirements, standardised accounting methods, and well-established commercial laws regarding contracts and bankruptcies) should be established early in the liberalisation process. Otherwise, the more competitive environment created by deregulation could induce banks to lend for projects with unacceptable levels of risk, both in order to increase their market shares and to earn the higher rates of interest associated with inherently more risky projects. This phenomenon of adverse risk selection is enhanced if bank deposits are explicitly or implicitly guaranteed by governments. Banks are then encouraged to lend to risky projects, knowing that in the upswing of the business cycle they will reap the higher interest returns, but in the downswing, their solvency is guaranteed: a moral hazard problem (Villanueva and Mirakhor 1990). The current difficulties facing commercial banking in economies with liberalised financial sectors such as Australia, Japan and the United States and some developing economies such as Indonesia, could be attributed to a lack of prudential supervision early in the liberalisation process.[8]

Furthermore, at the introduction of financial sector deregulation, existing banks typically have longer-term old loans which earn the previously depressed interest rates. Therefore, existing banks are inherently disadvantaged *vis-à-vis* new banks (Mathieson 1979). This is an argument for allowing unrestricted entry of new banks only later in the financial liberalisation process. Alternatively, the old loans could be taken over by the government and subsidised through budget outlays. In the case of Australia, existing banks were given time to merge and rationalise their operations before the entry of new banks. As a result, the existing banks retained and improved their market shares immediately after the entry of new banks.

Perhaps the most contentious part of the sequencing debate relates to the external capital account. McKinnon (1982, 1991) argues that as soon as trade and domestic financial liberalisation policies have shown signs of success, there has usually been a sharp inflow of foreign capital which has either forced an appreciation of the nominal and real exchange rate, or, if the nominal exchange rate was fixed, a rise in the domestic price level. In both cases, the real exchange rate would appreciate, undermining the success of trade reform. Liberalisation attempts by Chile in the late 1970s and South Korea in the mid-1960s both exhibited this phenomenon of real exchange rate overshooting. The policy implication therefore is that the external capital account and, by necessity, the foreign exchange sector, should be deregulated last in the process of economic reforms.

Of course, the overshooting of the nominal and real exchange rates would be exacerbated if there were a tight monetary policy in place so that higher domestic interest rates would induce more capital inflow. Indeed, this was the case in New Zealand in 1985–88 where exchange rate overshooting threatened to undermine the entire reform process. On the other hand, Australia had a fairly lax monetary policy at the time of financial deregulation in the first half of the 1980s. As a result, sequencing in the deregulation of the external capital account was not an issue. It would seem that a tight monetary policy at the time of financial deregulation could be avoided if, as stated earlier, the fiscal policy setting was sufficiently tight prior to the reform process.

McKinnon (1991) argues that much private capital inflow after the start of trade and domestic financial sector liberalisation results from excessive risk-taking on the part of foreign banks because of implicit or explicit guarantees on the part of the governments receiving the capital inflow and the economies where the banks are domiciled. If so, then improved prudential supervision of banks should help reduce this excessive risk-taking. Besides, as most exchange control regulations seem to have become increasingly ineffective in the face of trade and domestic financial sector liberalisation, delaying deregulation of the foreign exchange sector could well be impossible, or at the very least, unacceptably costly.

Apart from reasons of necessity, deregulating international capital flows early in the reform process may well be desirable in that domestic banks would be able to diversify their asset holdings, thereby increasing the financial stability of the system (Mathieson and Rojas-Suarez 1992). In addition, the international diversification of risks and returns on capital could well be an important source of growth. Ongoing economic growth depends on investments in an array of specialised technologies that yield potentially high returns but the developments of which are inherently more risky than investments in existing technologies (Grossman and Helpman 1991). Obstfeld (1992) demonstrates theoretically that for an economy already holding a stock of lower-risk assets, opening to international capital flows would encourage relatively high-yield investments with less certain returns. This development of venture capital becomes more likely because investors are able to hold globally diversified portfolios of assets that allow better management of risky investment. In this way, an open capital account would feed back into and sustain the growth process.

Therefore, as long as the conditions of fiscal restraint and prudential supervision are satisfied, it would seem that the advantages of deregulating the external capital account early in the reform process outweigh the potential costs of exchange rate overshooting.

Successful outward-looking growth strategies inevitably entail the adoption of market-oriented exchange rate regimes and monetary instruments because administered exchange rates and interest rates become both more costly and less necessary. Administered regimes become more costly because trade and financial sector liberalisation undermines the effectiveness of existing capital and credit controls, necessitating more draconian controls with associated higher efficiency costs. Therefore, disequilibrium exchange rate policies (either undervaluation to promote exports or overvaluation to fight inflation) cannot be maintained without incurring the additional costs of greater controls over capital and/or trade.

Administered regimes also become less necessary as successful trade and financial liberalisation requires governments to have in place responsible fiscal policies that do not rely on inflation taxes. There is, therefore, less need to prevent the free movement of capital through controls and less need for direction of bank credit.

Apart from establishing a sound fiscal base and adequate prudential supervision of the financial sector early in the liberalisation process, detailed sequencing of external capital account deregulation is likely to be neither possible nor desirable. The ineffectiveness of capital controls makes sequencing very difficult to implement, while the loss of growth opportunities associated with international diversification of risks and investments makes such sequencing undesirable.

The economies in the Asia Pacific Region that have embarked on significant policy regime changes towards outward-looking growth have experienced greatly increased short-term capital mobility throughout the 1980s. This has resulted in a move towards more flexible exchange rate regimes with reduced controls over international capital movements. The latter, in turn, enables better risk management of capital through global diversification, thereby increasing capital productivity and enhancing the growth process.

Notes to Chapter 7

The author wishes to thank Heinz Arndt, Ron Duncan, Rod Falvey, Anne Krueger, David Robertson, George Fane and Will Martin for their comments on an earlier draft.

[1] Asia Pacific is defined rather broadly to include Sri Lanka, a country that has undertaken significant trade liberalisation and some degree of financial deregulation since the mid-1980s.

[2] An increase in the foreign money supply, for instance, would lead to increased foreign demand for domestic goods, increased foreign prices and decreased foreign interest rates. Under a fixed exchange

rate regime and perfect capital mobility, capital inflow would occur until domestic interest rates were reduced to the lower foreign levels. This would add to the increases in domestic prices and incomes. Under a flexible exchange rate, however, the value of the domestic currency would appreciate, thereby choking off some of the increased foreign demand on domestic goods and services. On the other hand, an external real shock, for instance an increase in foreign government spending, would lead to increased foreign demand for domestic goods, increased foreign prices and increased foreign interest rates. Under a flexible exchange rate regime and perfect capital mobility, domestic currency would depreciate, thereby enhancing the increased foreign demand and pressure on domestic prices and incomes. A fixed exchange rate, on the other hand, would result in an outflow of capital, reducing domestic money supply and prices. The upward pressure on domestic interest rates would also tend to offset the increase in income brought about by increased foreign demand.

3 'Equilibrium' and 'disequilibrium' in exchange rates are conceived in an asset market model where exchange rates are determined by demand and supply of short-term financial assets denominated in different currencies; that is, movements in exchange rates are determined by short-term capital flows. An assumption is made that short-run equilibria converge on long-run purchasing power parity equilibria so that macroeconomic coordination to realign exchange rates is not considered here. Likewise, undervaluation and overvaluation are made with reference to the purchasing power parity exchange rates.

4 Even in the People's Republic of China where dual exchange rates exist, the differential between the official and the secondary market rates has narrowed considerably.

5 Liang and Liang (1988:s86) calculated the purchasing power parity effective exchange rate on exports for Taiwan from 1956 to 1985 and concluded that 'The stable and slightly undervalued nominal exchange rates (during 1982–85) as compared with the purchasing-power-parity effective exchange rates undoubtedly induced producers to continue to expand exports despite the wide fluctuations in currency values of major industrial countries'.

6 The Philippines' policies were probably unsustainable even at the 1970s' interest rates. Higher real interest rates in the 1980s, however, became an additional reason for making the policy regime change.

7 To the extent that financial assets are held as an alternative to, say, real estate, then perhaps the CPI would be an appropriate deflator.

However, if financial assets are held as alternatives to stocks of tradeable goods or foreign exchange as claims on tradeable goods and services, then the WPI would be a more appropriate deflator.

[8] The first-best solution would be the implementation of an appropriately priced deposit insurance scheme.

APPENDIX 7.1

Table A7.1.1: Summary of developments in fiscal, financial and trade sectors for selected Asia Pacific economies, 1980–90

AUSTRALIA

Fiscal situation over the 1980s	Deficit rose to 4% of GDP in 1983–84. Small surplus from 1988.
Financial sector reforms	Abolition of interest rate ceilings, directed credit, and exchange controls in period 1980–85. Floating of dollar in 1983. Entry of new foreign banks in 1985.
Foreign trade reforms	Gradual reduction in tariffs and quotas. In 1988, this process was accelerated.

CHINA

Fiscal situation over the 1980s	Actual budget deficits (2–3% of GDP), but substantial off-budget and state banking system support of state-owned enterprises. Reform of state-owned enterprises recently commenced.
Financial sector reforms	Newly established stock and bond market. Entry of authorised non-bank financial institutions and international banks progressing. Managed float from 1986.
Foreign trade reforms	Substantially reduced control of foreign trade by state agencies. Gradual removal of import barriers; e.g. lifting of import licences and reduction of tariffs on some consumer goods in 1984/85. Removal of export subsidies and greater access to secondary market foreign exchange rate for exporters.

HONG KONG

Fiscal situation over the 1980s	Moderate budget surpluses (1–4% of GDP).
Financial sector reforms	Opening of unified stock exchange in 1986. Reform in 1987 to improve banking system.
Foreign trade reforms	Neutral trade regime. No restrictions.

INDONESIA

Fiscal situation over the 1980s	Deficit rose to 3.5% of GDP in 1986.

| **Financial sector reforms** | Reforms throughout 1980s. Interest credit controls removed. Steps taken to expand money and capital market. In 1988 controls over entry of new banks. Financial deregulation package in 1992 allowed foreigners to buy shares in private commercial banks. |
| **Foreign trade reforms** | Liberalisation: the level of protection, i.e. tariffs, has been reduced. Non-tariff barrier coverage has narrowed. Significant protection remains for the agricultural sector. |

JAPAN

Fiscal situation over the 1980s	Deficits in first half of 1980s, 4–5% of GDP, but surpluses from 1988 onwards.
Financial sector reforms	In 1986, deregulation of interest rate controls and the money market. Increasing emphasis on control of monetary aggregates.
Foreign trade reforms	Radical trade liberalisation for manufactured goods. Accelerated reduction of tariff rates. However, agricultural sector remains highly protected.

KOREA

Fiscal situation over the 1980s	Deficits in early 1980s, but small surpluses towards the end of the decade.
Financial sector reforms	Won pegged to composite of currencies but commercial banks allowed some flexibility to quote rates different from official peg. Between 1981 and 1983, government divested its equity shares in all nationwide city banks. Most preferential interest rates applying to various policy loans were abolished by June 1982. Most bank and non-bank lending rates and some long-term deposit rates were decontrolled, however, they are still very unresponsive to market conditions. Rates on some policy loans were not deregulated, and short-term rates are still controlled.
Foreign trade reforms	Removal of import restrictions began in 1981–82. Tariff reduction program began in 1988, aiming to reduce the 'central tariff rate' from 15% for 64% of total items in 1989 to 8% for 78% of total items in 1993.

MALAYSIA

| **Fiscal situation over the 1980s** | Large deficits in early 1980s (over 10% of GDP). Large reductions made in following years. (Effects moderated by excess saving in private sector.) |

Financial sector reforms	Reforms since 1985. New financial instruments developed. Open market operations increasingly important. Interest rates gradually liberalised. Regulatory system to supervise all financial institutions introduced in 1989.
Foreign trade reforms	Open liberal trade regime. In process of reducing tariffs on a wide range of goods. Some non-tariff barriers but relatively low by international standards.

NEW ZEALAND

Fiscal situation over the 1980s	Reached a deficit of 9.3% of GDP in 1983. Surplus from 1987.
Financial sector reforms	Significant liberalisation from 1984—removal of interest rate ceilings, directed credit, exchange controls and barriers to entry. Exchange rate float. Open market operations used more actively.
Foreign trade reforms	In 1984, phasing-out of export subsidies and import quotas. In 1987, large tariff reductions announced.

PHILIPPINES

Fiscal situation over the 1980s	Deficits peaking at about 5% of GDP in mid-1980s. But considerable off-budget expenditure in the form of Central Bank support of various sectors and enterprises.
Financial sector reforms	Interest rate ceilings removed. Credit controls reduced or eliminated. In 1992, foreign exchange market was deregulated. Restricted entry to new institutions maintained.
Foreign trade reforms	Liberalisation from 1986. Program of tariff cuts in 1991. Many non-tariff barriers remain.

SINGAPORE

Fiscal situation over the 1980s	Budget surplus.
Financial sector reforms	Well-developed financial sector.
Foreign trade reforms	Neutral trade regime. Trade regulations minimal.

APPENDIX 7.2

Table A7.2.1: Empirical studies on capital mobility in the Asia Pacific Region

Author	Chinn and Frankel (1992)
Countries	Australia, Canada, Hong Kong, Japan, Malaysia, New Zealand, Singapore
Test used	Covered interest differential from 1982 to 1992. Three-month money market rates of domestic country and the US were used.
Results	As a group, the mean of the covered interest differential moved from −1% to around zero while standard deviation was near zero.
Author	Faruquee (1991)
Countries	Korea, Singapore, Malaysia and Thailand.
Test used	i = money market rates. i^* = LIBOR on three-month yen deposits. Test of simple interest differential $(i - i^*)$. (Data from 1978–90 broken into two periods: 1978–84 and 1984–90.)
Results	Mean and variance of simple interest differential both declined for the second half of the sample period (1984–1990). This implies greater financial and currency integration with Japan.
Author	Goldsborough and Teja (1991)
Countries	a) Seventeen countries: Australia, Canada, China, Fiji, Hong Kong, Indonesia, Japan, Korea, Malaysia, Mexico, New Zealand, Papua New Guinea, Philippines, Singapore Taiwan, Thailand and the United States. b) Japan, Hong Kong, Malaysia, Singapore Canada, Australia and New Zealand.
Test used	Private domestic savings equals private domestic investment (annual data).
Results	1980–87: less correlation than earlier decades implying greater capital mobility. 1984–87 greater capital mobility than 1980–84.
Author	Haque and Montiel (1990)
Countries	Fifteen countries: Indonesia, Malaysia, Philippines, Sri Lanka, India, Brazil, Guatemala, Jordan, Kenya, Malta, Morocco, Tunisia, Turkey, Uruguay, and Zambia.
Test used	Indirect test of simple interest differential (annual data 1964–87).
Results	For Indonesia, Malaysia, Philippines and Sri Lanka—perfect capital mobility cannot be ruled out.

APPENDIX 7.3

Table A7.3.1: Australia, 1975–91

	Exchange rate arrangements	Capital controls					
		(A)	(B)	(C)	(D)	(E)	(F)
1975	Pegged comp.	*	—	*	*	*	—
1976	Managed float	*	—	*	*	*	—
1977	Managed float	*	—	*	*	*	—
1978	Managed float	*	—	*	*	*	—
1979	Managed float	*	—	*	*	*	—
1980	Managed float	*	—	*	*	*	—
1981	Managed float	*	—	*	*	*	—
1982	Managed float	*	—	*	*	*	—
1983	Managed float	—	—	—	—	—	—
1984	Indep. float	—	—	—	—	—	—
1985	Indep. float	—	—	—	—	—	—
1986	Indep. float	—	—	—	—	—	—
1987	Indep. float	—	—	—	—	—	—
1988	Indep. float	—	—	—	—	—	—
1989	Indep. float	—	—	—	—	—	—
1990	Indep. float	—	—	—	—	—	—
1991	Indep. float	—	—	—	—	—	—

Notes:
Capital controls
(A) Required surrender of export proceeds.
(B) Advanced import deposits.
(C) Limitations or advanced approval on payments for invisibles.
(D) Limitations on foreign currency deposits by residents.
(E) Prior approval required for foreign lending or borrowing by financial institution.
(F) Tax or special reserve requirement on foreign borrowing.
* denotes presence of a particular capital control.
— denotes absence of a particular capital control.
comp.—composite.
indep.—independent.

Table A7.3.2: China, 1975–91

	Exchange rate arrangements	Capital controls					
		(A)	(B)	(C)	(D)	(E)	(F)
1975	Pegged comp.						
1976	Pegged comp.						
1977	Pegged comp.						
1978	Pegged comp.						
1979	Pegged comp.						
1980	Pegged comp.	*	—	*	*	*	—
1981	Pegged comp.	*	—	*	*	*	—
1982	Pegged comp.	*	—	*	*	*	—
1983	Pegged comp.	*	—	*	*	*	—
1984	Pegged comp.	*	—	*	*	*	—
1985	Pegged comp.	*	—	*	—	*	—
1986	Managed float	*	—	*	—	*	—
1987	Managed float	*	—	*	—	*	—
1988	Managed float	*	—	*	—	*	—
1989	Managed float	*	—	*	—	*	—
1990	Managed float	*	—	*	—	*	—
1991	Managed float	*	—	*	—	*	—

Notes: As for Table A7.3.1.

Table A7.3.3: Hong Kong, 1975–91

	Exchange rate arrangements	Capital controls					
		(A)	(B)	(C)	(D)	(E)	(F)
1975	Managed float	—	—	—	—	—	—
1976	Managed float	—	—	—	—	—	—
1977	Managed float	—	—	—	—	—	—
1978	Managed float	—	—	—	—	—	—
1979	Managed float	—	—	—	—	—	—
1980	Managed float	—	—	—	—	—	—
1981	Managed float	—	—	—	—	—	—
1982	Managed float	—	—	—	—	—	—
1983	Managed float	—	—	—	—	—	—
1984	Managed float	—	—	—	—	—	—
1985	Managed float	—	—	—	—	—	—
1986	Managed float	—	—	—	—	—	—
1987	Managed float	—	—	—	—	—	—
1988	Managed float	—	—	—	—	—	—
1989	Managed float	—	—	—	—	—	—
1990	Managed float	—	—	—	—	—	—
1991	Managed float	—	—	—	—	—	—

Notes: As for Table A7.3.1.

Table A7.3.4: Indonesia, 1975–91

	Exchange rate arrangements	Capital controls					
		(A)	**(B)**	**(C)**	**(D)**	**(E)**	**(F)**
1975	Pegged US$	*(1)	*	—	—	*	*(2)
1976	Pegged US$	*(1)	*	—	—	*	*(2)
1977	Pegged US$	*(1)	*	—	—	*	*(2)
1978	Managed float	*(1)	*	—	—	*	*(2)
1979	Managed float	*(1)	*	—	—	*	*(2)
1980	Managed float	*(1)	*	—	—	*	*(2)
1981	Managed float	*(1)	*	—	—	*	*(2)
1982	Managed float	*(1)	*	—	—	*	*(2)
1983	Managed float	*(1)	*	—	—	*	*(2)
1984	Managed float	*(1)	*	—	—	*	*(2)
1985	Managed float	—	—	—	—	*	*(2)
1986	Managed float	—	—	—	—	*	*(2)
1987	Managed float	—	—	—	—	*	*(2)
1988	Managed float	—	—	—	—	*	*(2)
1989	Managed float	—	—	—	—	*	*(2)
1990	Managed float	—	—	—	—	*	*(2)
1991	Managed float	—	—	—	—	*	*(2)

Notes: As for Table A7.3.1 and:
(1) Or open a bank letter of credit.
(2) Only applicable for foreign exchange banks.

Table A7.3.5: Japan, 1975–91

	Exchange rate arrangements	Capital controls					
		(A)	(B)	(C)	(D)	(E)	(F)
1975	Indep. float	—	—	(1)	(2)	*(3)	—
1976	Indep. float	—	—	(1)	(2)	*(3)	—
1977	Indep. float	—	—	(1)	(2)	*(3)	*
1978	Indep. float	—	—	(1)	(2)	*(3)	*
1979	Indep. float	—	—	(1)	(2)	(5)	—
1980	Indep. float	—	—	—	(2)	(5)	—
1981	Indep. float	—	—	—	(2)	(5)	—
1982	Indep. float	—	—	—	(2)	(5)	—
1983	Indep. float	—	—	—	(2)	(5)	—
1984	Indep. float	—	—	—	(2)	(5)	—
1985	Indep. float	—	—	—	(2)	(5)	—
1986	Indep. float	—	—	—	—	(5)	—
1987	Indep. float	—	—	—	—	(5)	—
1988	Indep. float	—	—	—	—	(5)	—
1989	Indep. float	—	—	—	—	(5)	—
1990	Indep. float	—	—	—	—	(5)	—
1991	Indep. float	—	—	—	—	(5)	—

Notes: As for Table A7.3.1 and:
(1) Certain limitations on large payments.
(2) Foreign currency deposits overseas subject to prior approval if not carried out by authorised bank.
(3) Foreign exchange banks subject to controls over their overall net position in foreign currencies.
(4) Payments subject to verification but without limitation.
(5) Generally free but certain transactions require prior notice and waiting period.
(6) Since the Foreign Exchange and Foreign Control Law became effective in December 1980, capital transactions are, in general, permitted unless specifically prohibited.

Table A7.3.6: Korea, 1975–91

	Exchange rate arrangements	Capital controls					
		(A)	(B)	(C)	(D)	(E)	(F)
1975	Pegged to US$	*(1)	*	*	(2)	*	—
1976	Pegged to US$	*(1)	*	*	(2)	*	—
1977	Pegged to US$	*(1)	*	*	(2)	*	—
1978	Pegged to US$	*(1)	*	*	(2)	*	—
1979	Pegged to US$	*(1)	*	*	—	*	—
1980	Managed float	*(1)	—	*	—	*	—
1981	Managed float	*(1)	—	*	—	*	—
1982	Managed float	*(1)	—	*	—	*	—
1983	Managed float	*(1)	—	*	—	*	—
1984	Managed float	*(1)	—	*	—	(3)	—
1985	Managed float	*(1)	—	*	—	(4)	—
1986	Managed float	*(1)	—	*	—	(4)	—
1987	Managed float	*(1)	—	*	—	(4)	—
1988	Managed float	*(1)	—	*	—	(5)	—
1989	Managed float	*(1)	—	*	—	(5)	—
1990	Managed float	*(1)	—	*	—	(5)	—
1991	Managed float	*(1)	—	*	—	(5)	—

Notes: As for Table A7.3.1 and:
(1) Or deposited in foreign exchange accounts in domestic banks.
(2) Certain residents may hold foreign currency deposits at foreign exchange banks.
(3) Borrowings above certain minimum amounts require approval.
(4) Subject to ceilings on conversion of foreign borrowing. All outward bound capital requires approval.
(5) All outward bound capital requires approval.

Table A7.3.7: Malaysia, 1975–91

	Exchange rate arrangements	Capital controls					
		(A)	(B)	(C)	(D)	(E)	(F)
1975	Pegged comp.	(1)	—	(2)			—
1976	Pegged comp.	(1)	—	(2)			—
1977	Pegged comp.	(1)	—	(2)		*	—
1978	Pegged comp.	(1)	—	(2)		(3)	—
1979	Pegged comp.	(1)	—	(2)		(3)	—
1980	Pegged comp.	(1)	—	(2)		(3)	—
1981	Pegged comp.	(1)	—	(2)		(3)	—
1982	Pegged comp.	(1)	—	(2)		(3)	—
1983	Pegged comp.	(1)	—	(2)		(4)	—
1984	Pegged comp.	(1)	—	(2)		(4)	—
1985	Pegged comp.	(1)	—	(2)		(4)	—
1986	Pegged comp.	(1)	—	(2)		(4)	—
1987	Pegged comp.	(1)	—	(2)		(4)	—
1988	Pegged comp.	(1)	—	(2)		(4)	—
1989	Pegged comp.	(1)	—	(2)		(4)	—
1990	Pegged comp.	(1)	—	(2)		(4)	—
1991	Pegged comp.	(1)	—	(2)		(4)	—

Notes: As for Table A7.3.1 and:

(1) Limited exchange control governing reporting and payments structure.

(2) Few restrictions.

(3) If above certain limits.

(4) Banks could borrow freely, but there was a limit on their net foreign
    currency position. Non-banks could borrow freely from abroad sums
    which were less than M$100,000, but they also faced a limit on their net
    foreign currency position.

Table A7.3.8: New Zealand, 1975–91

	Exchange rate arrangements	Capital controls					
		(A)	**(B)**	**(C)**	**(D)**	**(E)**	**(F)**
1975	Pegged comp.	*	—	(1)	*	*	—
1976	Pegged comp.	*	*	(1)	*	*	—
1977	Pegged comp.	*	*	(1)	*	*	—
1978	Pegged comp.	*	—	(1)	*	*	—
1979	Pegged comp.	*	—	(1)	*	*	—
1980	Pegged comp.	*	—	(1)	*	*	—
1981	Managed float	*	—	(1)	*	*	—
1982	Managed float	*	—	(1)	*	*	—
1983	Managed float	—	—	(1)	*	*	—
1984	Managed float	—	—	—	—	(2)	—
1985	Indep. float	—	—	—	—	—	—
1986	Indep. float	—	—	—	—	—	—
1987	Indep. float	—	—	—	—	—	—
1988	Indep. float	—	—	—	—	—	—
1989	Indep. float	—	—	—	—	—	—
1990	Indep. float	—	—	—	—	—	—
1991	Indep. float	—	—	—	—	—	—

Notes: As for Table A7.3.1 and:
(1) Certain payments require Reserve Bank approval.
(2) Limitations on borrowing by corporate entities.

Table A7.3.9: Philippines, 1975–91

	Exchange rate arrangements	Capital controls					
		(A)	(B)	(C)	(D)	(E)	(F)
1975	Managed float	*	—	*	(1)	*	—
1976	Managed float	*	—	*	(1)	*	—
1977	Managed float	*	—	*	(1)	*	—
1978	Managed float	*	—	*	(1)	*	—
1979	Managed float	*	—	*	(1)	*	—
1980	Managed float	*	—	*	(1)	*	—
1981	Managed float	*	—	*	(1)	*	—
1982	Managed float	*	—	*	(1)	*	—
1983	Managed float	*	—	*	(1)	*	—
1984	Indep. float	*	—	*	(1)	*	—
1985	Indep. float	*	—	*	(1)	*	—
1986	Indep. float	*	—	*	(1)	*	—
1987	Indep. float	*	—	*	(1)	*	—
1988	Indep. float	*	—	*	(1)	*	—
1989	Indep. float	*	—	*	(1)	*	—
1990	Indep. float	*	—	*	—	*	—
1991	Indep. float	*	—	*	—	*	—

Notes: As for Table A7.3.1 and:
(1) Certain limitations.

Table A7.3.10: Singapore, 1975–91

	Exchange rate arrangements	Capital controls					
		(A)	**(B)**	**(C)**	**(D)**	**(E)**	**(F)**
1975	Pegged comp.	(1)	—	(2)	*	—	—
1976	Pegged comp.	(1)	—	(2)	*	—	—
1977	Pegged comp.	(1)	—	(2)	(1)	—	—
1978	Pegged comp.	—	—	—	—	—	—
1979	Pegged comp.	—	—	—	—	—	—
1980	Pegged comp.	—	—	—	—	—	—
1981	Pegged comp.	—	—	—	—	—	—
1982	Pegged comp.	—	—	—	—	—	—
1983	Pegged comp.	—	—	—	—	—	—
1984	Pegged comp.	—	—	—	—	—	—
1985	Pegged comp.	—	—	—	—	—	—
1986	Pegged comp.	—	—	—	—	—	—
1987	Managed float	—	—	—	—	—	—
1988	Managed float	—	—	—	—	—	—
1989	Managed float	—	—	—	—	—	—
1990	Managed float	—	—	—	—	—	—
1991	Managed float	—	—	—	—	—	—

Notes: As for Table A7.3.1 and:
(1) Above certain minimum amounts.
(2) Above certain maximum amounts.

Table A7.3.11: Sri Lanka, 1975–91

	Exchange rate arrangements	Capital controls					
		(A)	(B)	(C)	(D)	(E)	(F)
1975	Pegged to pound sterling	*	—	*	*	*	—
1976	Pegged comp.	*	—	*	*	*	—
1977	Indep. float	*	—	(1)	*	*	—
1978	Indep. float	*	—	(1)	*	*	—
1979	Indep. float	*	—	(1)	*	*	—
1980	Indep. float	*	—	(1)	*	*	—
1981	Managed float	*	—	(1)	*	*	—
1982	Managed float	*	—	(1)	*	*	—
1983	Managed float	*	—	(1)	*	*	—
1984	Managed float	*	—	(1)	*	*	—
1985	Managed float	*	—	(1)	*	*	—
1986	Managed float	*	—	(1)	*	*	—
1987	Managed float	*	—	(1)	*	*	—
1988	Managed float	*	—	(1)	*	*	—
1989	Managed float	*	—	(1)	*	*	—
1990	Managed float	*	—	(1)	*	*	—
1991	Managed float	*	—	(1)	—	*	—

Notes: As for Table A7.3.1 and:
(1) Certain payments require exchange control permission.

Table A7.3.12: Taiwan, 1975–91

	Exchange rate arrangements	Capital controls					
		(A)	(B)	(C)	(D)	(E)	(F)
1975	Pegged US$	*(1)	—	*	*	*	—
1976	Pegged US$	*(1)	—	*	*	*	—
1977	Pegged US$	*(1)	—	*	*	*	—
1978	Pegged US$	*(1)	—	*	*	*	—
1979	Managed float	—	—	*	*	*	—
1980	Managed float	—	—	*	*	*	—
1981	Managed float	—	—	*	*	*	—
1982	Managed float	—	—	*	*	*	—
1983	Managed float	—	—	*	*	*	—
1984	Managed float	—	—	*	*	*	—
1985	Managed float	—	—	*	*	*	—
1986	Managed float	—	—	*	*	*	—
1987	Managed float	—	—	(2)	—	*	—
1988	Managed float	—	—	(2)	—	*	—
1989	Managed float	—	—	(2)	—	*	—
1990	Managed float	—	—	(2)	—	*	—
1991	Managed float	—	—	(2)	—	*	—

Notes: As for Table A7.3.1 and:
(1) Minor exceptions.
(2) Maximum amount exists for annual outward remittance for each adult.

Table A7.3.13: Thailand, 1975–91

	Exchange rate arrangements	Capital controls					
		(A)	**(B)**	**(C)**	**(D)**	**(E)**	**(F)**
1975	Other flexible	*	—	(1)	*	*	—
1976	Other flexible	*	—	(1)	*	*	—
1977	Other flexible	*	—	(1)	*	*	—
1978	Other flexible	*	—	(1)	*	*	—
1979	Other flexible	*	—	(1)	*	*	—
1980	Other flexible	*	—	(1)	*	*	—
1981	Other flexible	*	—	(1)	*	*	—
1982	Other flexible	*	—	(1)	*	*	—
1983	Other flexible	*	—	(1)	*	*	—
1984	Other flexible	*	—	(1)	*	(2)	—
1985	Pegged comp.	*	—	(1)	*	(2)	—
1986	Pegged comp.	*	—	(1)	*	(2)	—
1987	Pegged comp.	*	—	(1)	*	(2)	—
1988	Pegged comp.	*	—	(1)	*	(2)	—
1989	Pegged comp.	*	—	(1)	*	(2)	—
1990	Pegged comp.	*	—	—	*	(2)	—
1991	Pegged comp.	*	—	—	—	(2)	—

Notes: As for Table A7.3.1 and:
(1) Some limitations (e.g. on travel).
(2) Some restrictions.

APPENDIX 7.4

Table A7.4.1: Official discount rates, deposit rates, and money market rates (annual average percentage)

	1953–57	1958–62	1963–67	1968–72	1973–77	1978–82
Japan						
Discount rate	6.9	7.1	5.9	5.4	7.1	5.6
Call money rate	8.7	9.6	7.4	7.0	8.6	7.1
Deposit rate[a]	5.1	5.3	5.0	5.0	6.0	5.2
WPI rate of change	1.1	−1.0	1.4	1.3	11.4	5.1
CPI rate of change	3.1	3.6	5.6	5.9	13.1	4.6
United States						
Discount rate	2.4	3.1	4.2	5.2	6.5	11.0
Call money rate	2.1	2.7	4.0	5.4	6.2	10.7
Deposit rate[b]	2.6	3.2	5.0	5.0	5.5	5.7
WPI rate of change	1.0	0.3	1.1	3.6	10.4	9.1
CPI rate of change	1.2	1.5	2.0	4.6	7.7	9.8
United Kingdom						
Discount rate	4.7	4.7	6.4	7.2	11.4	14.5[c]
Call money rate	3.5	4.4	5.2	6.6	9.9	12.2
Deposit rate[d]	2.8	2.7	4.4	4.9	8.2	11.2
WPI rate of change	1.7	1.4	2.3	5.8	17.9	11.4
CPI rate of change	2.9	2.2	3.3	6.6	16.3	12.0
West Germany						
Discount rate	3.8	3.4	3.6	4.7	4.6	5.8
Call money rate	3.7	4.0	3.8	5.3	6.3	7.7
Deposit rate[e]	3.5	2.9	3.1	5.4	6.0	6.8
WPI rate of change	−0.5	0.5	0.9	2.6	6.2	5.4
CPI rate of change	0.9	2.0	2.7	3.5	5.7	5.8

[a] The interest rate on six-month deposits.
[b] The interest rate in time deposits less than US$100,000 (maximum). From 1953 to 1967, the maximum rate on deposits of more than one year.
[c] 1978–80. The Bank of England stopped announcing the minimum lending rate, that is, the discount rate.
[d] The interest rate on deposit accounts at seven days notice (maximum).

Table A7.4.1: _continued_

[e] The interest rate on three-month deposits (maximum).
WPI—Wholesale price index.
CPI—Consumer price index.
Source: Horiuchi, A., 1984, 'The "low interest rate policy" and economic growth in postwar Japan', _The Developing Economies_, 22(4):349-71.

Table A7.4.2: International comparison of prime rates, (average annual percentage)

	Japan[a]		United States[b]		United Kingdom[c]		West Germany[d]	
1953–57	7.8	(1.1)	3.7	(1.0)	5.2	(1.7)	8.4	(−0.5)
1958–62	7.4	(−1.0)	4.5	(0.3)	5.2	(1.4)	7.9	(0.5)
1963–67	6.2	(1.4)	5.2	(1.1)	6.9	(2.3)	8.1	(0.9)
1968–72	5.7	(1.3)	6.7	(3.6)	7.7	(5.8)	9.5	(2.6)
1973–77	6.9	(11.4)	8.4	(10.4)	12.4	(17.9)	10.4	(6.2)
1978–82	6.0	(5.1)	15.2	(9.1)	14.6	(11.4)	11.3	(5.4)

Notes: The numbers in parentheses are rates of changes in the wholesale price index (WPI).
[a] Discount rate of commercial bills eligible for rediscount by the Bank of Japan (more than 3 million yen).
[b] The prime rate.
[c] The interest rate on overdrafts for the prime corporations.
[d] The maximum level of interest rate on overdrafts (until 1966). The interest rate on overdrafts of 1 million deutschmark or less (from 1967).
Source: Horiuchi, A., 1984, 'The "low interest rate policy" and economic growth in postwar Japan', _The Developing Economies_, 22(4):349–71.

Table A7.4.3: Interest rates on bank loans in Japan, (annual average percentage)

	Loan rates covered by formal control: all banks	Loan rates not covered by formal control: all banks	Rate of change in wholesale price index
1953–57	8.2	9.5	1.1
1958–62	7.6	8.9	1.0
1963–67	7.1	8.5	1.4
1968–72	6.9	8.2	1.3
1973–77	7.7	8.8	11.4
1978–82	6.6	7.9	6.1

Notes: Ceilings were imposed on interest rates of short-term (less than one year) bank loans by the Temporary Interest Rate Adjustment Law (1947). Within the legal ceilings, the short-term loan rates were determined by a *de facto* cartel among the private banks. Though interest rates on other loans were exempted from the control, they also were determined by a type of cartel. The Japanese authorities can influence the decision-making of these cartels.

Sources: Horiuchi, A., 1984. 'The "low interest rate policy" and economic growth in postwar Japan', *The Developing Economies*, 22(4):349–71. Extract from McKinnon, R., 1991, *The Order of Economic Liberalization: Financial Control in the Transition to a Market Economy*, Johns Hopkins University Press, Baltimore.

8

Has Development Assistance Aided Development?—The Australian Case

NANCY VIVIANI

The question of whether Australian aid has assisted development is, at one level, a subset of the larger question about what
role aid plays in the development process. In answering this
larger question, economists and political scientists in the 1960s
and 1970s concentrated on the following issues:
- the size of aid, relative to sources of domestic investment and
  the 'savings gap';
- the forms in which the aid was given—for example food aid,
  project aid, and education aid;
- the terms on which the aid was given—its degree of conces-
  sionality and loans versus grants;
- the degree to which it was tied to donor country sourcing
  and the extent to which that practice diminished the value of
  aid to the recipient;
- how well aid projects were implemented by recipients and
  donors; and
- whether the donor's political and commercial interests inherent in the aid transaction undermined the development purposes of the assistance.

Two broad kinds of answers emerged from these earlier
debates. One answer, informed by dependency theory, argued
that aid deepened the dependency of poor countries on the rich,
since it prolonged unequal patterns of exchange and economic
development inherited from the colonial period (Amin 1976;
Hayter and Watson 1985). The other broad answer, from mainstream development economists, was contingent on time and
place: where aid is significant in size relative to other domestic
resources available for development, where its rate of return in
crucial sectors of the economy is positive and where it is implemented effectively, aid can assist development (Bhagwati and
Eckaus eds 1970).

All the issues listed above are still very much on the aid agenda, but the context of the debate about the causes of economic development has shifted substantially. To the earlier question of how much aid matters in development, the answer was that this largely depends on where and how aid is used. In the 1980s, however, the argument about economic development shifted to the role of the state in development and in that debate, the place of aid either disappeared or became quite ambiguous (Hughes ed. 1988a; Islam 1992; Wade 1990).

The shift in the debate on the causes of economic development was forced by a reassessment of the development experiences of countries in East Asia—Japan, Korea, Taiwan, Hong Kong and Singapore (Hughes 1988a; Chowdury and Islam 1993). This reassessment undermined dependency theory, perhaps fatally. It positioned mainstream economists, who stressed freeing domestic markets, liberal trade regimes and a limited government role in social and physical infrastructure as the major causes of rapid economic growth, against political economists who pointed to the important role of the state in directing industry policy and limiting access to domestic markets in these economies (see Islam 1992 for a review of this debate and Wade 1990, for the latter point of view).

In these most recent debates, aid curiously went missing along the way (though George 1988 is an exception). Certainly its role as a boost to capital availability declined as its global volume stabilised. Moreover, private flows and lending became more important than official development assistance in terms of overall foreign resources available to developing economies. In short, except for the very poor countries of Africa, by the late 1980s aid had simply become less important as a source of funds for development. This explains in part why aid is given little space in current debates about the causes of development. Yet, donor countries, including Australia, continue to give substantial amounts of aid, despite the recession in the early 1980s and 1990s. Domestic interests in donor countries debate the uses of aid as strongly as before, and constituencies in international organisations and recipient countries provide a demand for aid funds which is relatively undiminished.

While aid has been moved to the margins of the debate about the causes of development, aid itself remains a major national and international industry, with its own debates still centred on the issues set out above.

Contending Australian approaches

Issues relating to the effectiveness of aid and the place of aid in development have found their way into the public and policy debate in Australia. In this microcosm of the larger debates, some Australian scholars and non-government organisations took up the dependency theme and sustain it today (Burgess 1993; Eldridge 1986). They have called for aid to be concentrated on poverty reduction and basic needs strategies and criticised the Australian government's concentration on aid for economic growth.

Many in Australia oppose this policy prescription. They argue that aid is about boosting economic development, not welfare or consumption for the poor. The following extract from evidence given to a Parliamentary Committee illustrates the opposing arguments.

The Australian Council for Overseas Aid (the peak body for non-government aid organisations):

> Our argument [is] to start with the poverty, to start with the real needs of the people whom we are seeking to help and then add on what is necessary to ultimately achieve the goal. Too often it [aid] focuses on the infrastructure and the large-scale, capital-intensive element of the program and not on the more difficult, more time-consuming, lower amounts of money that are needed to work with the people directly (Joint Committee on Foreign Affairs, Defence and Trade, 1989:295).

The contrary point of view was put by the then Director of the National Centre for Development Studies, Helen Hughes, who told the Committee that 'a grassroots approach to development had been very costly to developing economies in the past ten years':

> I am not very much into helping the poor; I really think it is more important to get development going, particularly in a country which is sufficiently conscious of politics to look after its own poor. What they need are the capital goods, the expertise and the foreign exchange, and out of that will come, in the long run ... very good relations and trade opportunities (Joint Committee on Foreign Affairs, Defence and Trade, 1989:385).

Yet, it is important to put the differences between mainstream economists and the stance taken by some other scholars and non-government organisations into perspective. Aid for development purposes is seen by both as good and as assisting development. The real difference is in their preferences in development strategies and in how aid is used.

The stance of the non-government organisations is firmly grounded in politics: some 70–80 per cent of Australians support the giving of aid (though they would not generally support an increase in aid) and the majority of these support aid as 'welfare for foreigners' not aid to governments (Kelly 1989:8, 39).

While the debates on aid and development in Australia, sketched here, have been studied extensively (see Burgess 1993 for a review), the larger question of the effectiveness of Australian aid in assisting development has not been studied as intensively. Every Australian aid project undergoes a process of review and evaluation, and the Australian International Development Assistance Bureau (AIDAB), the body responsible for implementing Australian aid, has been open about its successes and failures in project aid (AIDAB 1993c). Other forms of aid, food and education aid, have also been evaluated, and policy has shifted as a result.

Yet, despite the relatively large amount of information publicly available on projects in many recipient countries, overall judgments on the effectiveness of Australian aid in assisting development are difficult to make. This is because Australian aid is usually one small factor in a much larger and more complex national development process and no clear connection between aid and development can readily be made.

This discussion tackles the question of the effectiveness of Australian aid in assisting development in the following way. It uses the traditional criteria of size and distribution of aid, the forms of aid, the terms of aid, the degree of tying, the quality of implementation and the relevance of donor interests, to assess the relative effectiveness of Australian aid in five areas:
• aid to Papua New Guinea;
• bilateral projects;
• food aid;
• education aid; and
• the Development Import Finance Facility.

In undertaking this assessment, the costs and benefits to the Australian economy are considered and an attempt is made to assess the costs and benefits in each of these areas of aid to recipients' economic development. In this it is helpful to have some idea of trends in Australian aid over the past five years or so, and some basic information is presented as background (AIDAB 1993e).

Despite the official rhetoric on policy innovation in Australia's aid, the aid program has not changed much in its basic shape over the past five years. New policy moves, especially with respect to aid to Papua New Guinea, population and mixed credits may (the combined use of aid and subsidised loan funds for projects) change this picture in future.

Australia's performance as a donor

The volume and value of Australia's aid

There has been little change in the volume of aid, in real terms since 1989/90 (Table 8.1). The volume of aid in current prices, has grown from A$1.2 billion in 1989/90 to A$1.4 billion in 1993/94. In ranking donors by volume of aid, Australia has fallen (with Norway and Denmark) in the small donors league behind Japan, the United States, France, Germany and some others. Australia supplies about 2 per cent of total world aid flows (Community Aid Abroad 1992:5).

In terms of overall global or regional impact, Australian aid can only be effective at the margin, depending on the size of particular country allocations and the quality of implementation. Since 1945, Australia's aid, in current prices, has totalled A$70 billion. This is a significant sum and its value, relative to other donors, has been enhanced as almost the entire amount has been given on grant rather than loan terms. The largest part of this aid has been given to Papua New Guinea, Australia's former colony. In this respect, there is one case of Australian aid which can pass the volume and value tests of effectiveness.

In relation to Australia's economic capacity, there has been a long-term decline in the value of Australia's aid. Aid was tied to gross domestic product (GDP) growth during the Whitlam years (1972–75) as a matter of policy. It declined steadily as a proportion of GDP over the Fraser years (1976–82), and into the decade of Labor governments (1983–93) it has declined even

Table 8.1: Australia's official development assistance, 1969/70 to 1993/94

	Current prices (A$m)	Constant prices (1990/91) (A$m)	Real change over previous year (%)	ODA/GDP ratio (%)
1969/70	171.5	1,098.6	10.6	0.55
1970/71	180.6	1,090.9	−0.7	0.52
1971/72	200.5	1,128.7	3.5	0.52
1972/73	219.2	1,155.2	2.4	0.49
1973/74	264.9	1,226.4	6.2	0.50
1974/75	334.6	1,271.6	3.7	0.52
1975/76	356.0	1,160.1	−8.8	0.47
1976/77	386.2	1,131.9	−2.4	0.45
1977/78	426.1	1,155.5	2.1	0.46
1978/79	468.4	1,183.7	2.4	0.44
1979/80	508.7	1,170.1	−1.1	0.43
1980/81	568.0	1,180.5	0.9	0.42
1981/82	657.8	1,228.0	4.0	0.43
1982/83	744.6	1,251.7	1.9	0.45
1983/84	931.8	1,465.2	0.7	0.50
1984/85	1,011.4	1,502.9	2.6	0.49
1985/86	1,031.0	1,430.5	−4.8	0.45
1986/87	975.6	1,258.5	−12.0	0.38
1987/88	1,019.6	1,226.8	−2.5	0.36
1988/89	1,194.6	1,319.8	7.6	0.37
1989/90	1,173.8	1,220.6	−7.5	0.33
1990/91	1,261.0	1,261.0	3.3	0.35
1991/92	1,330.3	1,308.3	3.7	0.36
1992/93	1,384.6	1,373.7	3.3	0.36
1993/94	1,402.0	1,359.7	−1.0	0.35

Source: Australian International Development Assistance Bureau, 1993e,
Australia's Development Cooperation Program 1993–94, AGPS, Canberra.

more rapidly as a proportion both of GDP and government
outlays (Figure 8.1). This indicates that party politics do not
determine aid volumes.

For 1993/94, aid is estimated at 0.35 per cent of GDP, a long-
term decline from its peak of 0.55 per cent in 1969/70, and 0.50
per cent in 1983/84. In terms of aid expenditure relative to
national income, in the league table of Development Assistance
Committee donors, Australia stood almost precisely at the mid-
point between Norway, 1.16 per cent of GNP, and Ireland, 0.16
per cent of GNP in 1992 (AIDAB 1993e:50).

Figure 8.1: Trends in aid, government outlays and GDP, 1971/72 to 1992/93

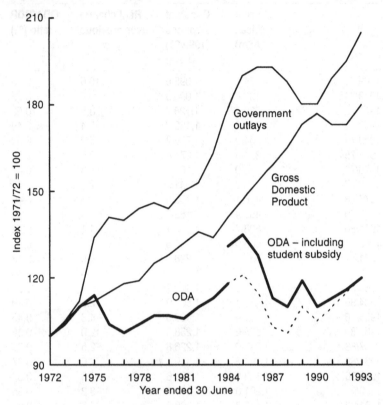

Source: Australian International Development Assistance Bureau, 1993e, *Australia's Development Cooperation Program 1993–94*, AGPS, Canberra.

This long-term decline has little to do with economic conditions. When the nexus between official development assistance
(ODA), GNP and government outlays was broken in around
1975 (and after Australia had pledged to move towards an
ODA/GNP ratio of 0.7 per cent), the annual aid budget again
became a function of the outcome of bureaucratic politics
between the Treasury and the Department of Foreign Affairs
and Trade. Not even the elevation of the commercial aim of
official development assistance in the 1980s could change this
pattern of bureaucratic gridlock outcomes in budgets. This
outcome is unsurprising: Herbert Simon (1958) remarked on it,
and there is a wealth of scholarship from many countries

confirming such patterns (White 1974; Viviani 1979, 1983; Sherlock 1993).

It might be expected, given the pattern of domestic interests in the aid budget (industry, agriculture, education, non-government organisations, and the Department of Foreign Affairs and Trade), that group pressures supported by a favourable public opinion would work to push up the aid budget. But the volume of Australian aid is simply too small to satisfy the range of domestic interests involved. These interests have therefore been competitive, and have not formed a coalition powerful enough to unseat the Treasury's control of the aid budget.

The distribution of Australian aid by region, country and component

There have been some changes in the distribution of Australian aid by region over the past five years (Table 8.2). On a regional basis, only aid to East Asia (due to China) and Other Sub-Saharan Africa has grown significantly in real terms, while there have been declines in aid to South Asia, the Indian Ocean, Southern Africa and the Middle East. These declines are in small parts of the aid program, but they indicate a growing concentration on Asia in recent years.

This relatively stable outcome in the distribution of official development assistance by region is an outcome partly of the pipeline effect (large projects take years to work their way through aid budgets) and partly of the politics of aid. Regional programs have their backers within AIDAB, Department of Foreign Affairs and Trade and outside, and are difficult to shift. The relative stability in the regional direction of aid disguises the greater volatility in the distribution of aid by country. Initiation or completion of large projects does explain some of the movement in the statistics but this is only part of the story (Table 8.2).

Aid to Papua New Guinea (now around one-quarter of total aid) has fallen slightly (A$313 million in 1993/94) in real terms since 1989/90. It has, however, declined steadily as a proportion of total Australian aid and as a proportion of the Papua New Guinea budget. While the effectiveness of Australian aid to Papua New Guinea is discussed below, it is worth noting that this aid is unusual in several respects relative to international aid standards. Papua New Guinea has one of the highest per capita receipts of aid in the world, the volume of aid is

Table 8.2: Total Australian aid flows to major recipients, 1984/85 to 1993/94, (A$m)

Major recipient countries/regions	1984/85	1989/90	1990/91	1991/92	1992/93	1993/94[e]	Average real annual growth rate	
							1984/85 to 1989/90 (%)	1989/90 to 1993/94 (%)[a]
Papua New Guinea	*321.7*	*349.0*	*333.1*	*335.0*	*333.8*	*312.5*	*-5.4*	*-4.4*
SOUTH PACIFIC								
Fiji	16.4	26.1	22.7	29.2	24.3	21.1	2.2	-6.8
Vanuatu	5.6	12.8	14.0	13.2	13.8	13.1	9.8	-1.2
Solomon Islands	8.6	13.7	12.8	14.6	14.1	13.0	2.2	-3.0
Western Samoa	5.3	10.5	12.3	15.7	12.0	11.6	6.8	0.8
Tonga	6.8	10.7	10.8	11.4	10.9	11.5	1.9	0.1
Kiribati	3.4	5.6	4.0	5.2	5.4	4.6	2.9	-6.4
Tuvalu	1.4	2.1	2.4	2.9	2.3	2.2	1.0	-0.6
Other	16.5	30.0	30.7	26.4	36.5	44.2	4.9	8.3
Total South Pacific	*64.0*	*111.6*	*109.7*	*118.7*	*119.4*	*121.3*	*4.1*	*0.3*
SOUTHEAST ASIA								
ASEAN	205.4	219.7	225.0	229.1	256.1	235.9	-5.6	—
Indonesia	76.0	101.3	107.9	115.6	129.4	122.5	-1.4	3.1
Philippines	20.4	31.2	50.1	47.3	48.9	48.0	1.4	9.4
Thailand	30.1	48.1	38.4	38.4	41.8	34.4	2.3	-9.6
Malaysia	64.6	36.4	26.8	26.1	34.9	30.0	-17.0	-6.4
Singapore	10.5	2.8	1.8	1.7	1.1	1.0	-28.5	-24.0

Indochina	16.5	34.9	27.7	40.8	65.8	80.2	8.2	21.0
Vietnam	4.8	17.4	10.0	12.8	28.7	47.5	20.5	26.3
Laos	5.5	8.6	8.4	12.2	16.2	14.8	1.8	12.6
Cambodia	6.1	9.0	8.3	15.8	20.9	17.9	0.6	16.7
Other	20.8	16.2	18.1	9.7	19.6	23.5	-11.4	7.9
Burma	9.1	3.8	0.8	0.2	—	0.6	-21.8	-38.1
Total Southeast Asia	*242.7*	*270.9*	*269.9*	*279.6*	*340.4*	*339.6*	*-4.8*	*4.0*
OTHER REGIONS								
East Asia								
China	34.9	44.1	40.3	60.1	80.9	78.5	-2.4	13.5
Hong Kong	12.7	5.5	4.2	3.6	2.1	:	-21.2	-28.6
Other	1.2	0.9	0.8	0.7	1.0	:	-12.1	2.0
Total East Asia	*48.8*	*50.5*	*45.3*	*64.4*	*79.0*	:	*-6.3*	*14.3*
South Asia								
India	3.4	29.9	38.3	23.0	19.5	23.4	43.8	-7.6
Bangladesh	19.5	37.3	21.0	26.8	15.5	15.9	6.0	-20.6
Sri Lanka	7.0	5.6	6.2	7.2	8.6	9.5	-11.0	12.2
Pakistan	5.4	10.8	6.0	8.4	4.7	5.2	7.0	-18.1
Nepal	2.7	3.4	3.2	3.6	9.0	:	-2.5	36.2
Other	0.8	4.2	7.8	2.4	3.2	:	29.7	-10.1
Total South Asia	*38.8*	*91.2*	*82.4*	*71.5*	*62.4*	:	*10.5*	*-13.2*

Table 8.2: continued

Major recipient countries/regions	1984/85	1989/90	1990/91	1991/92	1992/93	1993/94[e]	Average real annual growth rate	
							1984/85 to 1989/90 (%)	1989/90 to 1993/94 (%)[a]
Indian Ocean								
Mauritius	2.5	4.8	4.1	4.2	4.5	..	6.1	−3.6
Maldives	1.3	2.6	2.1	2.4	2.3	..	7.0	−5.5
Other	1.1	3.0	1.9	2.0	0.8	..	13.8	−36.6
Total Indian Ocean	4.9	10.3	8.1	8.7	7.6	..	8.0	−11.0
Southern Africa								
Mozambique	4.4	13.2	11.8	15.2	16.0	..	16.0	5.0
Malawi	0.5	6.5	6.8	3.6	3.9	..	55.5	−17.0
Zimbabwe	6.0	13.6	6.8	13.5	9.4	..	9.7	−13.0
Tanzania	6.6	9.5	3.9	2.4	2.9	..	0.1	−33.7
Zambia	3.1	2.7	3.4	4.5	4.0	..	−9.4	12.2
Botswana	0.8	4.1	1.9	1.9	1.7	..	29.1	−26.6
Other	2.5	20.5	7.3	14.3	14.8	..	41.8	−11.7
Total Southern Africa	23.9	70.1	42.0	55.4	52.7	..	15.5	−10.5

Other Sub-Saharan Africa								
Ethiopia	23.9	15.3	15.7	21.4	7.1	..	−14.8	−23.8
Kenya	7.8	3.0	3.2	2.7	3.2	..	−23.1	0.6
Sudan	3.6	2.2	2.9	4.6	4.1	..	−15.6	21.2
Uganda	0.5	2.6	0.5	1.0	1.4	..	29.5	−19.9
Other	16.9	5.6	7.9	10.8	23.9	..	−25.3	59.7
Total Other Sub-Saharan Africa	*52.7*	*26.5*	*30.2*	*40.4*	*39.6*	..	*−18.9*	*12.6*
North Africa/Middle East								
Egypt	7.9	14.3	10.2	15.1	4.7	..	4.8	−32.1
Other	5	9.4	12.5	5.7	3.3	..	5.6	−30.6
Total North Africa/Middle East	*12.9*	*23.7*	*22.7*	*20.8*	*8.0*	..	*5.2*	*−31.5*
Rest of World	*2.1*	*6.0*	*5.3*	*3.2*	*4.3*	...	*14.9*	*−11.9*
Total Other Regions	*233.7*	*280.5*	*236.0*	*264.4*	*263.7*	*251.7*	*−3.4*	*−3.6*
Core contributions to multilateral organisations and expenditure in Australia	*148.9*	*200.7*	*312.5*	*333.6*	*271.6*	*276.0*	*−1.2*	*8.9*
Total ODA	*1,011.4*	*1,212.6*	*1,261.0*	*1,331.2*	*1,384.6*	*1,300.2*	*−3.5*	*2.9*

e estimate

a For the period 1989/90 to 1992/93 where data for 1993/94 are not available.

Source: Statistical Analysis and Retrieval Section, Australian International Development Assistance Bureau, Canberra.

large by international bilateral standards and the aid has been delivered by a regular cheque paid into the Papua New Guinea government's budget constituting, until recently, a largely untied grant aid flow.

The volume of aid to the South Pacific region has grown slightly over the past five years. Fiji apparently has not suffered in aid terms for the 1988 coups but there has been some variation across other Pacific island countries (though from small bases).

In Southeast Asia, aid to Indonesia and the Philippines has grown over the past five years. This principally has to do with Australia's political relations with the Association of Southeast Asian Nations (ASEAN). Aid to Thailand, Malaysia and Singapore has fallen significantly, in part because of the shift in student policy from subsidised to fee-paying status but also because these countries have 'graduated' to higher economic levels.

Official aid to Vietnam, cut off in 1979 because of Vietnam's invasion and occupation of Cambodia, has now been resumed and is growing fast. Aid to Laos and Cambodia has grown significantly, the latter related to Australia's political and military involvement in the Cambodian peace process. At the same time, aid to Burma has declined significantly in response to human rights abuses and political repression.

All in all, with respect to Australia's aid to Southeast Asian countries, it seems fair to conclude that the direction (if not the composition) of this aid among countries is a process largely driven by foreign policy and trade considerations. If the distribution is relatively stable among regions, then for individual countries, political considerations (at least in Southeast Asia) are decisive, as is now readily acknowledged in government policy statements (Kerin 1992:8).

Two other shifts in country distribution of aid are also significant. Aid to China (projected at A\$79 million for 1993/94) has grown rapidly in the past five years (up 13.5 per cent a year on average), though there was a hiccup in the growth trend after the Tiananmen Square massacre when new projects were stalled for a time. This shift in focus is largely commercially driven, but it also addresses long-term political and strategic considerations.

Aid to Other Sub-Saharan Africa has grown markedly over the past four years. Total aid to Africa (excluding the Middle East) is slightly less than 10 per cent of total aid and, despite or perhaps because of recurring crises, has not shown much increase in recent years. The decision (AIDAB 1992:64) to close down food aid to Egypt and redirect this to food relief in Southern Africa and poverty programs, again illustrates the shifts within regions alluded to earlier.

It seems clear that while those who direct aid policy cannot do a great deal about its growth or regional distribution, they can move its country distribution to reflect changes in Australia's political and economic interests. This is not to argue that development considerations are neglected in these circumstances (for the money still has to be spent on something); it is simply to acknowledge that it is at the level of country distribution that politics and commercial considerations are most powerful.

Non-government organisations and commercial interests

Bilateral country programs constitute about 60 per cent of total Australian aid. Allocations to emergencies and refugees and to international organisations have increased since 1989/90, substantially so for the latter. Emphasis on community (non-government organisation) programs and support for commercial activities (principally the Development Import Finance Facility) has also increased significantly. Allocations to these activities grew over this period to A$154 million in 1993/94, slightly more than 10 per cent of all aid. The Development Import Finance Facility was budgeted at A$120 million for 1993/94 (AIDAB 1993e:42).

The shift to engaging non-government organisations and commercial firms more directly in the aid program is part of a long-term international and Australian trend. The funding of non-government organisation activities began some 20 years ago and is a product of policymakers' beliefs that non-government organisations can make a significant contribution to grass roots development through harnessing government funds to private funds in development. In Cambodia and Vietnam non-government organisation activities have been crucial in re-establishing these aid relationships. Non-government organisations are also the government's strongest critics and its strongest constituency on foreign aid, so the relationship is ambivalent and highly political.

The relationship between official aid and commercial interests has also shifted considerably over the past five years. The government has always subsidised some private suppliers through tying of aid to goods sourced in Australia and through subsidised insurance of some aid exports. Australian governments in the 1970s were in the forefront of international moves to untie aid, not least as most Australian aid was sourced at home. By the 1980s, the Labor government embarked on new economic policies aimed at restructuring and internationalising Australian industry, with a priority emphasis on transforming exports to Asia (Viviani 1990). Through this move, the limited commercialisation of Australian aid became a plank of government aid policy and of its wider economic policies. The push to increase Australian exports of goods and services through aid met the wall of corrupted aid markets in the Asian region. Japan especially, but also other countries, used their aid programs to a greater or lesser extent to subsidise their companies operating overseas in order to obtain a foothold in lucrative national, international and regional bank projects and services markets (Rix 1990; AIDAB 1993a). Since follow-up contracts from bilateral projects and international contracts give advantages in exports and wider development markets, it was argued that Australian contractors and suppliers were severely disadvantaged in these markets by other countries' subsidies of their firms. Australian policymakers, like their counterparts in other countries, saw mixed credits as the way forward.

The Jackson Committee, which reviewed the Australian aid program in 1984, took the view in 1984 that such mixed credits distorted the development process, that goods supplied under the Development Import Finance Facility should be internationally competitive, and recommended that this program be limited to 5 per cent of total aid (Jackson 1984:13). A decade later, the climate of opinion in government has shifted, not least due to the depth of the Australian recession. While the government stands firm (or almost) against an industry policy that would subsidise exporters, it celebrates the subsidy of Australian exporters through the aid program as leading to a growth in exports (AIDAB 1993a, 1993b). A vigorous debate on this issue is still underway, and is discussed later in more detail.

While any aid program stands on the three principles of development, political interest and commercial interest, and while the government affirms that the overriding goal of aid is sustainable development (AIDAB 1992:iii), it is clear that there has been a significant shift towards commercial interest in

Australia's aid program. Although this is part of an international trend, it also follows the amalgamation of the Department of Foreign Affairs with the Department of Trade in 1987, and the elevation of the private sector to a more important role in economic policy in the 1980s and 1990s.

Other changes in the aid program indicate the government's responsiveness both to emerging international issues and to the domestic politics of aid. The environment (in the form of sustainable development) is now a priority in the program, and 'women in development' has carved out a small but significant place in aid budgets. HIV/AIDS and narcotics have also found a place. The student component has declined rapidly, now largely commercialised in full fee-paying entry. A push to make population a priority in aid has struck a hurdle in the form of one Australian Senator, a Catholic, who happens to hold the balance of power in the Upper House of Parliament.

The government's most recent policy statement, *Changing Aid for a Changing World* (AIDAB 1992), emphasises broad economic growth with a focus on private sector development as the main thrust of policy, allied with a concern for social justice and the human dimension. The aid program and trade strategies are seen as mutually reinforcing, aiming to maximise the benefits to developing economies as well as the returns to Australia.

Yet in reviewing the changes in Australian aid over the past five years, it seems that the defenders of traditional modes of regional distribution of aid and country programs have maintained their position, principally because the development and political interests still largely coincide. They have had to make room for the new claimants—exporters and non-government organisations—and for new issues like the environment and women, but they have managed this by integrating these demands within the traditional structure of the aid program. The newcomers are slowly transforming the aid program from within, but it is a long-term process. The shift from budget support to project assistance in aid to Papua New Guinea will transform that large part of the aid program if it goes ahead as planned. Indochina is a new focus, but it is unlikely to outweigh the emphasis on ASEAN in the medium term. Perhaps the most important change in Australian aid in recent years has been the significant improvement in the professionalism of aid administration, an outcome of the reforms proposed by the 1984 Jackson Committee.

How effective is Australian aid?

The effectiveness of Australian aid in assisting development is assessed by reference to the six traditional criteria listed at the beginning of the discussion: size, terms, forms, tying, quality of implementation and donor interests. These are applied to five widely differing cases. The Director-General of AIDAB has sensibly argued that the aid process contributes to policy dialogue and policy change and to technological transfer (Flood 1993), so some attention will be paid to this aspect also.

Papua New Guinea

On most of these effectiveness criteria, Australian aid to Papua New Guinea ranks highly by international standards. The aid has been, and is, a significant net addition to resources available for Papua New Guinea's development since it gained independence from Australia in 1975. Then, Australian aid constituted nearly one-half of the Papua New Guinea budget, declining to about 13 per cent in 1992/93 (Aopi 1993:4). This proportion remains significant, first because other donors' aid is slight (an effect of the dominance of Australia) and second, because Australian aid operates as a stabiliser in a minerals-based economy subject to severe fluctuations in revenue (Fairbairn 1993).

As mentioned above, the largest part of Australian aid to Papua New Guinea has been given as grant, untied, budget support since 1975. On the three criteria of form, terms and tying, this aid ranks very highly in respect of the recipient gaining the full value of the aid.

Australian aid to Papua New Guinea has not only been exceptional by international standards but, until recently, stood in contrast to the remainder of Australia's aid program which, while on grant terms, was project-based and largely tied to Australian supplies.

In the debate on budget support for Papua New Guinea in the mid-1970s, two arguments were decisive. The first, of principle, maintained that to transform the colonial budget subvention to project aid, given its proportion in the Papua New Guinea budget, would lead to a parallel Australian administration in Papua New Guinea, erosion of Papua New

Guinea sovereignty over development decisions, the *de facto* continuance of Australian neo-colonial control, continuing dependency and poor bilateral relations. The second pragmatic argument was that budget support aid was necessary to maintain government administration in Papua New Guinea, and that neither Australia nor Papua New Guinea had the administrative capacity to manage what would have been a huge project program. It is worth noting also that while Australian aid to Papua New Guinea has been untied, in principle, much of that aid has been sourced in Australia. Australia has supplied at least one-half of Papua New Guinea's imports over this period, enjoying a substantial trade surplus (Aopi 1993:7).

Budget support aid to Papua New Guinea continued to be contested throughout the 1980s and, by 1989, Australia and Papua New Guinea had negotiated a Treaty on Development Cooperation which, when revised in 1992, stated that budget support would be phased out by the end of the decade and would be replaced by an aid program directed to priority sectors such as health, education, infrastructure, the private sector and law and order (AIDAB 1993d:2). The forms of this aid are to include technical assistance, scholarships, projects and so on.

This historic shift in Australian aid to Papua New Guinea, still contested at the highest levels in the Papua New Guinea government (Aopi 1993; Chan 1993), can be explained directly by the remaining two effectiveness criteria—quality of implementation and relevance of donor interests.

With respect to quality of implementation of aid to Papua New Guinea, Australia has played virtually no role, as the aid is a direct subvention to the Papua New Guinea budget. This also means that it is difficult, if not impossible, for AIDAB to account for the uses of this aid to Parliament. The Papua New Guinea government is therefore solely responsible for the quality of implementation, and as this aid is simply one part of its national development program, then the quality of implementation of Australian aid reflects the development progress made by Papua New Guinea since independence.

The Australian government view of this progress is quite clear. Mr Bilney, the Minister for Development Cooperation and Pacific Island Affairs, in November 1993 said:

> Papua New Guinea has made some significant progress in the economic sphere. The Government has established a

reputation for sound macroeconomic management. This reputation has been enhanced by the economy's successful adjustment to the two major shocks of 1989—a sharp downturn in agricultural commodity prices, and the loss of production from Bougainville [gold mine]. I notice in Sir Julius Chan's recent budget speech that gross domestic product is projected by the government to increase by more than 14 per cent this year, largely due to a booming mining sector. This is an impressive achievement by any standard. The challenge now is to make this growth sustainable and to improve the living standards of all Papua New Guineans.

In rising to this challenge, Papua New Guinea faces some major constraints. These include shortages of skilled personnel; poor infrastructure which is compounded by mountainous, rugged terrain; law and order problems; and a rapidly growing, widely dispersed population.

The vast majority of ordinary Papua New Guineans are subsistence farmers. Most of the economic growth since independence has been in the mining sector. Although mining has provided jobs and training for a limited number of people, it is essentially an enclave sector. Links with other sectors—particularly with the subsistence agricultural sector—are weak and growth in the non-mining sectors has been slow.

The result has been that in spite of its abundant natural resources, per capita incomes in Papua New Guinea actually fell in the sixteen years after independence. Although Papua New Guinea is classified as a lower middle income country, its social indicators point to a real standard of living which is closer to that of a low income country. In 1990, annual income per capita was estimated at US$860 but the literacy rate was lower than that of more than half of the world's poorest countries. The average life expectancy for Papua New Guineans of 55 years is well below the average of 62 for the world's poorest countries. Infant mortality rates are still very high at 72 per thousand live births and are comparable with the world's poorest countries.

Added to these discouraging statistics is Papua New Guinea's very high birth rate, which exerts increasing pressure on education and health services and on land. With a rapidly growing population largely dependent on subsistence farming or resource extraction, the consequences of deforestation and land degradation in Papua New Guinea

could be devastating. There is an urgent need for Papua
New Guinea's social indicators to improve.

Each year another fifty thousand young people enter the
job market in Papua New Guinea. Their expectations of
better job opportunities and material wealth draw them
into the urban centres. The result is rising unemployment,
increasing poverty, and problems of law and order. (Bilney
1993:6–8)

The implication of this Australian government view is that
Papua New Guinea has not used its resources (including Australian aid) effectively enough to make progress on what are,
by all accounts, serious development problems. This view of
development in Papua New Guinea finds support in two recent
studies by Stein and Fairbairn (Stein 1991; Fairbairn 1993). It is,
however, vigorously contested by Papua New Guinea senior
officials and ministers, who take a longer-term view, pointing
to the inheritance of problems from the colonial era, the substantial progress in macroeconomic terms made in the difficult
circumstances of Bougainville's attempted secession, and to a
brighter future less dependent on Australian aid (Chan 1993;
Aopi 1993).

The factor missing from these assessments of the effectiveness
of Australian aid in Papua New Guinea's development is the
other, non-quantifiable public goods purchased in part by Australian aid: the sustaining of a democratic political process over
20 years, a high degree of stability in Australia–Papua New
Guinea relations and the development of a productive trilateral
relationship between Papua New Guinea, Indonesia and
Australia. Some of these outcomes have been influenced
strongly by a constructive policy dialogue purchased, at least
in part, by a relaxed aid relationship. This is not to argue that
these achievements would not continue under a different aid
regime. It is rather to argue that without these developments
over the years since independence, the process of economic
development in Papua New Guinea would have been threatened far more extensively.

The charge that Papua New Guinea's development administration has been insufficiently effective can be sustained, at
least in part, on the evidence. Whether an Australian program
of projects and other aid can more effectively address the political and structural economic causes of these failures in development administration remains a moot point.

The final criterion in assessing the effectiveness of Australian aid to Papua New Guinea is the relevance of donor interests. Over the period of budget support aid, Australia's political and security interests in Papua New Guinea have been well served by the aid program which has provided a constructive context for negotiations while preserving Papua New Guinea's sovereignty. It is clear already, that the new form of program aid will reopen this question in a sharp way (Chan 1993).

In the absence of information which identifies the share of Australian exports of goods and services to Papua New Guinea paid for by Australian budget support aid, no clear judgment on Australian commercial interests served by that aid can be made. Despite the consistent pressure by Australian firms to tie Australian aid to Papua New Guinea to Australian sources, it is unlikely, given that Australia is one of Papua New Guinea's major trade partners, that Australian commercial interests have suffered. On the other hand, Papua New Guinea has benefited from having the full value of aid revenue.

This situation will now change as almost all Australian aid to Papua New Guinea will be tied by the end of the decade. As the Minister pointed out, Australian commercial and non-government organisation interests will have increased opportunities in Papua New Guinea in the future (Bilney 1993:15), and this interest must have been one factor in the decision to transform the basis of Australian aid to Papua New Guinea, given the general government policy drive on exports. As with all aid tying, the question arises as to whether such goods and services are delivered at internationally competitive prices. Again, in the absence of data, this remains a moot point.

It is something of an irony that the extremely high quality of Australian aid to Papua New Guinea (on the criteria of size, terms, form and tying) should turn out in the Australian government's view to have been insufficiently effective in its implementation. It is not a surprising irony, given the colonial inheritance, the level of development in Papua New Guinea in 1975, the structural constraints of topography and a subsistence-based economy, and the length of time required to accelerate development in such circumstances. The jury is still out— in the longer run, Australian aid in the first 20 years of Papua New Guinea's independence may very well be seen to have been crucial to its later development.

For the present, Australian aid is much less important to Papua New Guinea than it has been, and in the long run its transformation to project aid may not matter much. It is the decline in the real value of this aid and as a proportion of the Papua New Guinea budget that marks the structural shift in this bilateral relationship.

Bilateral programs

In bilateral programs other than to Papua New Guinea and some South Pacific countries, Australia is a small aid donor. Although almost all aid is grant aid, the sums involved (Table 8.2) are marginal to the overall development of most recipient countries. That said, aid funds are nevertheless significant in terms of some aspects of economic development in some sectors in recipient countries and are important to some sectors of Australian industry.

Applying the criterion of effectiveness is much more difficult, since although size of funds may have a substantial local impact (as in the provision of water resources in some parts of Indonesia), the forms of bilateral projects vary enormously from the straightforward provision of goods, to complex educational upgrading programs. Again the terms of aid are grant, but the provision of aid is tied to Australian sources (though some local and third country sourcing is permitted). The proportion of the total aid program that was tied had risen to 87 per cent in 1991 (Rummery 1993:19).

It is clear that Australia's bilateral project aid benefits both Australia and recipient countries, simply because it involves a government-funded transfer of Australian goods and services for recipients' development programs. The nub of this particular issue is whether this transfer takes place at internationally competitive prices. To the extent that Australian prices are higher, the value of Australian aid to recipient countries is diminished, and Australian suppliers capture a subsidy paid by Australian taxpayers. Even where such subsidised transfers of goods and services result in a significant increase in exports and follow-up contracts for Australian business, an important question remains as to whether this is the most efficient way of going about increasing exports and internationalising Australian business.

Studies of the costs of tying to recipient countries showed costs to be in the order of 20 to 30 per cent, depending on the type of goods and sources supplied (AIDAB 1993a:24). As bilateral country programs make up about 60 per cent or some A$700 million of the total aid program, the costs of tying goods and services to Australian sources may be quite significant as a proportion of that aid.

One example illustrates this: in education projects, the human resource element typically constitutes 70 to 80 per cent of total project costs. These advisory services (now tied to Australian supply at costs significantly above domestic Australian and some competitive overseas prices) are available in some, if not all recipient countries, at significantly lower cost locally. The difference in prices of these services represents a significant loss in the value of the aid project to the recipient countries, and a significant subsidy, by Australian taxpayers, to some Australian individuals. This leads some development planners in recipient countries involved in such projects to argue that the best way to do the job is just to transfer the funds.

A sceptic's response that all aid donors tie aid to a greater or lesser extent is inappropriate since the Australian government continues to make statements indicating that aid helps Australia and developing economies. There is little doubt that many, if not all, Australian exports have become more competitive as a result of aid programs, but to enable informed judgments to be made about the relativities of these benefits, the costs of tying need to be made transparent.

On the criterion of quality of implementation of Australian bilateral projects, it is a fair judgment that the administrative reform of AIDAB, including its country planning and evaluation services, has had a beneficial effect on the overall quality of implementation of aid projects. Also, most developing economies have become significantly better project managers though some failures are readily observed. It is to the credit of AIDAB that an increasing transparency in project evaluations will allow some better founded, independent judgments to be made on the long-term effectiveness of implementation of aid projects. If that can be coupled with transparency on the costs of tying aid, real advances will be possible.

On the criterion of relevance of donor interests, Australia's project aid is, on balance, a positive. Recipient priorities do count in the choice of Australian aid projects, and these have provided a substantial underpinning to wider bilateral relationships. Given Australia's concentration on its own region, these projects provide areas of cooperation at the political and bureaucratic levels not available through other means. As Flood has pointed out, donor groups have been important in the process of policy dialogue and policy reform—as in Indonesia—and as these are one major key to development, aid has been of use in an indirect but influential way (Flood 1993:3).

Food aid

Australian food aid cost A$91 million in 1992/93 (about 6.5 per cent of total aid). It is therefore not large in size, but its distribution can be particularly effective in times of emergency. Of this total, 25 per cent was given bilaterally and the rest through the World Food Program. One-quarter was for direct relief, the remainder being associated with development projects. While such food aid can have the well-known negative effects on local food prices and patterns of agricultural development, these matters are the responsibility of development planners in recipient countries. It is difficult to isolate any such effects relating to Australian food aid.

Food aid is on grant terms and is tied wholly to Australian supply. Since wheat and rice are purchased by AIDAB at prevailing market prices, presumably no element of subsidy occurs here as Australia is an internationally competitive grain exporter. The insurance of food exports through the Export Finance Insurance Corporation may constitute a subsidy as may the carriage of Australian grain on Australian ships, subject to cabotage.

Australian total wheat exports were about A$1.5 billion in 1991, so that food aid purchases, while significant at A$104 million (including rice), are not of major importance in the wheat trade. Nevertheless, AIDAB figures (1992:64) show that these purchases increased wheat growers' incomes by A$1,200 per capita and those of rice growers by A$4,800. These income effects are significant given the difficulties experienced by these rural interests. While food aid is generally not seen as the best form of development assistance (except by Australian farmers), it is one form of Australian aid where recipient countries derive the full benefit of the transfer, and where Australian farmers also benefit.

Education aid

Policy on overseas education shifted significantly following the adoption of the recommendations of the Jackson Committee. Private overseas students, formerly enjoying the benefits of free secondary and tertiary education in Australia, now pay full fees set at 'market' rates, thus contributing income to universities and schools, resulting in additional growth in these educational institutions. In 1993 there were around 65,000 overseas students in Australia of whom some 6,600 were supported by AIDAB scholarships. AIDAB estimates that all these generate some A$1 billion annually in 'export' earnings (AIDAB 1993e:56).

Though the extent of returns to economic development of overseas education are disputed, there is some basic agreement that there is a positive return, if students repatriate. If they do not, these returns accrue to Australia (Harris and Jarrett 1990). Thus student policy interacts closely with migration policy.

Most aid-funded students, it appears, do return home, so there is a net economic return to recipient countries. The case is much less clear with respect to private students, as their movement is not clear from migrant entry statistics. At the least, the 20,000 plus private students from China (most of whom are eventually joined by their families, and are likely to stay in Australia) indicate that these returns will accrue to Australia.

It may be argued that as private overseas students are self- not aid-funded, none of this matters in aid and development terms. However, to the extent that these students do not pay the real cost of their education, universities, other students and ultimately taxpayers, subsidise these costs. It is not clear how far competitive markets for full fee-paying overseas students really do exist in Australian universities, and to the extent that they do not, the much-vaunted A$1 billion in gains to Australia from export of education services may need to be discounted somewhat. On balance it seems reasonable to conclude that aid-funded students benefit both their home countries and Australia, as has always been the case, even if non-economic benefits are not counted. Because of the migration dimension of private students, their case is much less clear-cut.

The Development Import Finance Facility

The Development Import Finance Facility (DIFF) is a form of mixed credit in which aid funds are given in conjunction with soft loans (funded by the Export Finance Insurance Corpora-tion) for specific development projects. In this arrangement two subsidies may occur: one to the Australian supplier of goods and services as supply is tied to Australian sourcing under the DIFF, the other is a non-official development assistance subsidy by the Australian government to the cost of funds lent to the recipient country. Mixed credit arrangements are very impor-tant in development finance in Asia. They are practised com-petitively by all donors and, as a result, the DIFF proportion of total Australian aid has been growing rapidly (to an estimated A$120 million in 1993/94).

On the criterion of effectiveness, the DIFF is not large as a proportion of all Australian aid, its distribution is biased towards China and Indonesia (two of Australia's fastest growing export markets), it is completely tied to Australian sourcing and it is the major vehicle for expanding Australian grant aid volumes to soft loans. AIDAB studies of the program's development impact are largely positive, and its relevance to donor interests in encouraging exports is clear.

This method of financing development has the following effects:

- To the extent that Australian or other suppliers supply goods at higher than internationally competitive prices, the aid budget subsidises those suppliers.
- To the extent that supply prices approach international prices, that aid subsidy is transferred to the recipient country.
- The extent of loan subsidy given by the Export Finance Insur-ance Corporation in financing the Development Import Finance Facility-related loans is a direct transfer to develop-ing economies from Australian taxpayers, outside the aid budget.
- The DIFF subsidies do enable Australian contractors to win contracts they would not otherwise get, and on the evidence, these contracts do result in significant export flows and new contracts.
- The DIFF and other forms of mixed credit do result in the spoiling or corruption of aid and development project markets, and the Organisation for Economic Cooperation and Development (OECD) agreed in 1992 to new rules which would limit that spoiling, by restricting the operation of mixed credits to non-commercially viable projects above A$4 million in value.

• Mixed credit financing can mean that recipient countries undertake lower priority projects that they would not otherwise choose.

This much seems to be agreed by participants in the debate. Yet substantial differences remain, as is clear from the proceedings of a lively seminar on the issue in 1992 (AIDAB 1993a). Russell Rollason, Executive Director of the Australian Council For Overseas Aid, insists that the DIFF is bad aid because its aim is commercial not developmental, it distorts the geographic distribution and sectoral priorities in Australian aid, it is a trade subsidy which prevents developing economies getting a share of the action, and it is an unwanted shift from grants to loans in Australia's aid (AIDAB 1993a:7–10).

On the other hand, two studies presented at the seminar confirmed that the DIFF projects have positive effects both on development in recipient countries and on Australian exports. AIDAB evaluations of nine DIFF projects showed positive benefits in all but one case, in terms of employment creation, infrastructure value, social benefits and amenities, and environmental impact. These studies apparently do not address the relative cost of these benefits as against the same project funded differently. Indeed one estimate given at the seminar was that the price of capital goods, supplied under such mixed credit schemes as the DIFF, is subsidised by around 30 per cent (AIDAB 1993a:24). Data are not available from government sources, however, on the relative prices of goods sourced in Australia and elsewhere.

A 1992 study of the commercial benefits of the DIFF, carried out by the National Institute of Economic and Industry Research (AIDAB 1993a:65–71) showed that the trade creation effects of this program were substantial: A$300 million of these funds led to contracts worth about A$1 billion and these projects resulted in direct exports of A$850 million. Follow-on contracts worth A$129 million had been achieved, and more were expected, leading to projected exports of around half a billion dollars. Further, DIFF projects had a significant impact on the internationalisation of Australian industry in capital goods exports.

Further evidence on the export value of the program appeared in a study of Australia's aid to China. There it was claimed that for every A$100 spent in aid, about A$300 worth of business 'can be confidently expected' to be generated (AIDAB 1993b:7-8). In this the DIFF has even higher rates of return in follow-on business and exports than other forms of aid.

These results are important, given Australia's export drive and they do run in the direction of government policy. Naturally, they are taken by its business supporters as strong evidence that the program more than pays for itself and serves national as well as sectional interests. To the argument that such results would be forthcoming anyway, supporters of the DIFF reply that these contracts would not be won, given that aid markets are already spoiled by subsidised contractors from other countries.

It is clear that the program promotes exports, though its relative impact on the broader picture of improving export performance by Australian manufacturers is not clear (Garnaut 1993a). Spoiled capital goods markets may have to be taken as a given, though the new OECD regulations indicate some shift in policies. It is worth noting that even though agricultural markets are spoiled, Australian farmers can still compete on an unsubsidised basis. It may be possible also that the DIFF, rather than working to make Australian suppliers more competitive in fact prolongs their dependency on subsidy (as is generally the case), and retards business reforms that would otherwise be undertaken.

Given the evidence of positive development outcomes and expanded exports, this issue turns on the evidence as to whether Australian goods and services are supplied at internationally competitive prices. Senior officers of AIDAB (Flood 1993:6) assert that there is no evidence that such goods are not supplied at internationally competitive prices. It might be argued, given the importance of the issue, not only to the DIFF but to bilateral projects and now Papua New Guinea, that it is up to AIDAB, and in its interests, to show that these prices are internationally competitive. As it stands now, there is no substantial evidence either way.

In these circumstances, and given exchanges among economists on this issue, the view advanced by Cuthbertson (AIDAB 1993a:89) that the DIFF is primarily an export subsidy seems appropriate. As such, it does have useful outcomes in both trade and development terms like other export subsidies. As an export subsidy, its proper place is in the trade promotion activities of government. There is a strong argument therefore for removing the program's funds from the aid budget, and locating them with the Export Finance and Insurance Corporation. That move may also be administratively effective, though the development aspects of the program may be downgraded.

The outcome would be that the program would remain as an export subsidy and its value could then be measured against the effectiveness of other forms of export subsidy. AIDAB would lose some 10 per cent of its budget (an unwelcome prospect), and the important political support of one or two sectors of business. The political support of business for the aid program is in any case a double-edged sword. It is literally bought and paid for, and where the price is competitive, as with farmers, there is no problem. Where a significant element of subsidy exists, there is a real political cost to AIDAB in defending the program. The relocation of the DIFF in the overall government budget would not mean a diminution of Australia's efforts to aid development. Rather, the program would be reported to the Development Assistance Committee as a non-official development assistance flow of assistance.

Direct export subsidy schemes appear in aid budgets because policy lines or financial constraints in other, more powerful, areas of government push them into this aid area. To the extent that the Keating government is still focused on reform, the relocation of the DIFF and its open recognition as a direct subsidy to exporters will allow future decisions on its funding to be made without muddying the waters with arguments about its development impact.

Has Australia's development assistance assisted development?

The short answer is yes. It has also assisted Australia's economy and its foreign relations. Using the traditional criteria of size and distribution of aid, the forms and terms of aid, the degree of tying, the quality of implementation and the relevance of donor interests, the following judgments can be made on the available information.

Australian aid to Papua New Guinea has been essential for economic development, for political stability and for sound bilateral relations. While the degree of its effectiveness is disputed and its form will be transformed as a result of this, there can be no doubt that the development record in Papua New Guinea would have been very much worse in the absence of Australian aid, and it is not clear yet whether the move to program aid will improve the effectiveness of Australian aid in Papua New Guinea's development.

There is sufficient evidence to indicate that bilateral programs have been broadly effective in development as the evaluation processes have identified the strengths and weaknesses of a wide range of these. There are ways in which these can be made more effective, and this relates in part to the tying of goods and services to Australian sources, and the processes by which these are supplied. Food aid and education aid, on the record, have also been effective. The impact of student policy on migration policy, however, needs further exploration.

The DIFF is the most contentious form of all Australian aid. The evidence is that it does have a development impact, yet the argument as to its value to recipients, relative to other forms of funding, is unresolved. If it is a plain export subsidy, it should be removed from the aid budget. It is important that those charged with the responsibility for managing Australian aid make available the data on which judgments on this issue can be made.

This analysis of the effectiveness of Australian aid has focused narrowly on the traditional criteria for judging this issue. It is clear from anecdotal evidence that the aid process has a significant impact on the quality of policymaking in development in recipient countries. This dimension of 'aid effectiveness' deserves a separate study.

9

Demographics and Markets— Are there Limits to Export Promotion Strategies?

PHILIPPA DEE AND CHRISTOPHER FINDLAY

Hughes and Woldekidan recently argued that the major challenge of our times was:

> ... enabling people to live at reasonable standards of living ... so that poverty may be largely eliminated (Hughes and Woldekidan 1993:i).

In the following analysis, econometric techniques and a recently developed quantitative model of Asia and the Pacific are applied to examine some aspects of this challenge.

Table 9.1: Income levels, income growth and population growth, selected East Asian economies

	GNP per head 1991 (US$)	Average annual growth rate of GNP per head 1980–91 (%)	Average annual growth rate of population 1991–2000 (%)
Japan	26,930	3.6	0.3
Singapore	14,210	5.3	1.5
Hong Kong	13,430	5.6	0.8
Korea	6,330	8.7	0.8
Malaysia	2,520	2.9	2.2
Thailand	1,570	5.9	1.4
Philippines	730	−1.2	1.9
Indonesia	610	3.9	1.4
China	370	7.8	1.3

Note: World Bank and Chinese official estimates of per capita income in China have been challenged as too low (Garnaut and Ma 1993b).
Source: World Bank 1993a, *World Development Report 1993*, Oxford University Press, Oxford.

Table 9.1 presents data on gross national product (GNP) per head in 1991, and income and population growth projections to the end of the decade for a sample of East Asian economies. Population growth rates range from 0.3 to 2.2 per cent per year. Even relatively low rates of growth imply large absolute changes in population in some countries. For example, they imply roughly 150 million additional people in China, 32 million in Indonesia and 12 million in the Philippines by the end of the century.

Hughes and Woldekidan's challenge highlights the connections between population growth and standards of living. High population growth rates will make it more difficult for some of these economies to maintain growth in per capita incomes. Population growth itself, however, is not independent of income levels and income growth. It is often hypothesised that higher rates of economic growth and rising incomes per head will lead to a fall in population growth rates. Hughes and Woldekidan (1993:7) stress this connection: 'economic growth is the most important determinant of the demographic transition'.

The question is how economic growth can be accelerated to a rate significantly faster than population growth so that the 'underdevelopment trap' can be broken and population growth rates be reduced.

While there may be a connection between income levels and population growth, the effect may take some time to appear (Easterlin 1968; Simon 1977). Even relatively rapid growth of income per head in the East Asian economies with high rates of population growth will not help meet the challenge in the immediate term. How to maintain rates of productivity growth is still an issue.

Concerns, therefore, lie with the connections between demographic trends and economic growth over a shorter time period than that over which natural forces are likely to bring down rates of population growth. Taking rates of population growth as given, the question then is what rate of productivity growth must be realised over the next decade or so, in a sample of developing economies, in order for them not to slip backwards. A comparison of these estimates and recent experience of productivity growth can provide some indication of the ease with which these economies can meet the challenge that Hughes and Woldekidan outline.

One feature of demographic trends over the next decade is the very large increases in total population expected in some of the East Asian economies. Another feature is the changing age composition of the population, not just in the East Asian economies but also in some of the industrialised economies such as Japan. Estimates of the changing composition of the populations in various regions over the next decade are presented in Figure 9.1.

Changes in the age structure of a population can potentially have a significant impact on economic growth. One important connection is between the age structure of the population, the overall savings propensity, the consequent rate of global capital accumulation and therefore the rate at which incomes can increase. The connection between age structures and savings rates is quantified below and a multi-country economic model is used to draw out some of the implications for income levels and capital flows in East Asia.

It is found that while the shifting demographic characteristics in East Asia and elsewhere will, in principle, affect savings rates, the orders of magnitude over the next decade are relatively small. The result implies that concerns are misplaced about the impact of population ageing on the capacity of East Asian economies to maintain high income growth rates over the next decade.

The major issue in meeting Hughes and Woldekidan's challenge is therefore the rates of productivity growth that can be expected over the decade alongside the growth in the total population. Estimates of real income growth in the economies of the region, based on prospective rates of population and labour force growth and historical rates of productivity growth are reported.

The relationship between per capita income levels and productivity growth, with a focus on the low-income economies in the region, is also considered. The question addressed is how much productivity growth rates must increase in order for real per capita incomes to double in those economies whose current GNP per head is less than US$3,000. These results are then compared with the recent experience of those economies to quantify the extent of Hughes and Woldekidan's challenge.

Figure 9.1: Demographic projections, 1990–2000

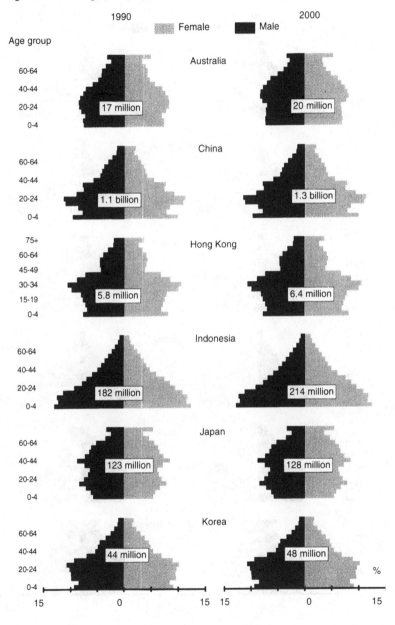

Figure 9.1: (continued)

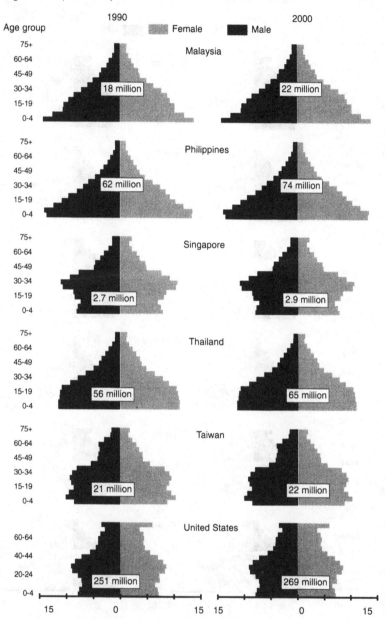

Source: Bulatao, R.A., et al., 1990, *World Population Projections 1989–90*, Johns Hopkins University Press, Baltimore.

Demographics and savings rates

Econometric estimation of a savings relationship permits identification of the effects of the changing age structure of the population on the propensity to save. The hypothesis is that
household savings rates depend on the age of the heads of the
household: people of working age will save while those of
retirement age will dissave. The hypothesis is tested in a cross-
sectional context for the pragmatic reason that while there may
be noticeable changes in the demographic structure of a single
economy over time, there is more variation in demographic
structures across countries at a point in time. The results therefore have a long-run flavour.

There are a number of factors other than demographics which
will influence savings rates. One of these, potentially, is income
per head.

The relationship between income per head and savings is
complex.[1] That between income and the absolute level of
savings is likely to be positive but it is not clear whether savings
will grow faster or slower than income. It is therefore not clear
whether savings will rise or fall with income per head.

One early approach to answering this question was to distinguish between sources of income. It was assumed that there was
a higher propensity to consume out of labour income than out of
income from capital. This distinction was stressed in the early
growth literature (the Kaldor savings function discussed in
Branson 1972:407). The distinction implied that changes in the
aggregate savings rate could be generated via changes in the composition of labour and non-labour income. But in an open economy
context, the hypothesis gives no clear prediction as to the sign of
the dependence between savings rates and per capita incomes.

Another approach has been to look at savings behaviour in
a lifetime context. In the life-cycle hypothesis (Ando and Modigliani 1963), consumers spend according to their anticipated
lifetime earnings. Current consumption therefore depends not
just on current income but also expected future income as well
as the stock of other assets. In some empirical tests of the life-
cycle hypothesis, expected income has been proxied by the
growth rate of income in recent periods so that in econometric
work, income growth has been included alongside current
income levels (Leff 1969).

In the model estimated below, only current income is included as an explanatory variable. No distinction is made between sources of income. Tests for the effects of income growth rates were run but the results were not significant and the equations are not reported.

Several other factors are omitted from the model specification.

First, no distinction is made between public and private savings. One interpretation of this approach is that household preferences are over national savings relative to national income, and that a policy decision to reduce public sector savings would, in the absence of associated changes in national income, be undone by a compensating reaction by the private sector. In fact, the compensation may not be one for one. The World Bank (1991) suggests that less than one-half of an increase in public savings obtained by cutting government consumption would be offset by lower private savings, and slightly more of the increase in public savings obtained by raising taxes would be offset by lower private savings. The Bank concludes that cutting public deficits will raise national savings.

This argument suggests that it may be important in the short term to distinguish public from private savings. But if cutting public deficits eventually raises national income, the significance of the distinction may be less important in the longer term.

The model specification also makes no allowance for the effects of financial market reform and its impact on real interest rates. The implicit assumption is that there is a global capital market and the real returns to saving are the same worldwide. Financial market distortions in some economies, however, can lead to low or negative real interest rates which have been associated with low growth (World Bank 1991), one possible reason being that they reduce savings rates, another that they lead to a misallocation of investment funds. In principle, the effect of higher real interest rates on savings is ambiguous. The empirical evidence, summarised in World Bank (1991), is that the effect is positive but small.

Finally, differences in preferences for bequests are ignored, as are cross-country differences in social security systems and the tax treatment of savings. The latter may be captured indirectly, however, to the extent that the nature of taxation systems and the presence of social security systems are broadly correlated with national incomes across countries.

The model specification is that the national savings rate S (national savings as a percentage of GDP) depends on GDP per capita *gdppc*, the proportion of the population that is of working age (15–64) *popw*, and the proportion of the population that is of retirement age (65 and over) *popr*. Savings rates are expected to be positively related to *popw* and negatively related to *popr*. Essentially, the objective is to explain savings rates by income per head and the dependency ratio, although some writers have noted that savings rates would also depend on the specific age of the working age population (Ruggles 1993; Yotopoulos and Nugent 1976).

Two functional forms are tested, one in log form and the other using the raw data but with the reciprocal of the income variable (note the samples differ). All data come from the World Bank (1992a). The results are shown below (t statistics in brackets).

$$\ln(S) = -13.647 - 0.18 \ln(gdppc) + 3.90 \ln(popw) - 0.49 \ln(popr)$$
$$\quad (3.12) \quad (2.14) \qquad (3.34) \qquad (1.98)$$

$$R^2 = 0.34 \qquad (n=88)$$

$$S = 36.3 - 2139.4 \, (1/gdppc) + 1.07 \, popw - 0.77 \, popr$$
$$\quad (2.55) \quad (4.21) \qquad (4.03) \qquad (2.02)$$

$$R^2 = 0.43 \qquad (n=104)$$

The value of R^2 is below 50 per cent in each case so there is substantial variation around the line. Apart from the problem of omitted variables, there is also a problem with the data. Savings are calculated as a residual and the data are therefore subject to considerable measurement error. As the notes to the tables in the data source point out, savings are estimated by deducting national consumption from gross domestic product (GDP), both themselves estimates. Because the serious measurement error occurs in the dependent variable, the R^2 is expected to be low but the coefficient estimates are not necessarily biased.

One final econometric problem is that the causation is assumed to be one-way, from income to savings. Yet there is clearly a link the other way, especially in the longer term. Many studies (for example Horioka (1990), summarised in box 6.3 in the World Bank (1991)) point to a positive relationship between

savings and growth. As noted, there is also a longer term connection between savings, growth and the demographic variables. The presence of these simultaneity problems suggests the
coefficient estimates are likely to be biased, but as Mankiw,
Romer and Weil (1992) note in a recent test of the reverse causality, finding appropriate instrumental variables to correct the
problem is extremely difficult when the behavioural context is
so broad.

The results suggest no clear relationship between the savings
rate and income per head. The income variable is significant in
both equations but the sign is sensitive to the functional form.
The log specification gives a negative sign, although the elasticity is small (less than 0.2). The other functional form implies
a positive relationship between savings rates and income per
head.

The results on the demographic variables are more stable.

The elasticities in the first equation have the expected signs.
The estimates suggest that a 1 per cent change in the proportion
of the population of working age will raise the savings rate by
4 per cent. The elasticity for the population of retirement age is
-0.5.

In the second equation, each percentage point rise in the population of working age adds about one percentage point to the
average savings rate. There is sample variation in the working
age population of around $+/-10$ points which implies that this
is a significant source of variation in savings rates across
countries.

Each unit rise in the percentage of the population of retirement age causes the savings rate to fall by about 0.8 points.
There is sample variation in the proportion of the population
in retirement of $+/-9$ points. This too is a significant source of
variation in savings rates.

The above results can be combined with projected changes in
the age structure of the population in individual economies
over the next decade to predict what the demographic changes
might mean for national savings rates. The results derived
using the parameter estimates from the second equation above
are shown in Table 9.2. The population projections are taken
from a source which takes account of expected migration patterns as well as fertility rates, mortality rates and so on.
Expected migration patterns largely account for the projected
increase in the working age population in the United States.

Table 9.2: Changes in dependency ratios and implied changes in savings rates, 1990–2000

	Proportion of population working age (%)		Proportion of population of retirement age (%)		Change in savings rate (% points)
	1990	2000	1990	2000	1990–2000
Australia	67	68	11	11	0.8
New Zealand	67	67	11	11	0.6
Canada	68	69	11	12	0.1
United States	66	67	12	12	1.1
Japan	70	68	12	15	−5.2
Korea	68	70	5	7	1.0
European Union	68	67	14	16	−1.9
Indonesia	60	64	4	5	3.7
Malaysia	59	61	4	4	1.7
Philippines	57	63	3	4	5.7
Singapore	72	72	6	7	−0.7
Thailand	63	66	4	5	3.5
China	68	67	6	7	−2.3
Hong Kong	69	69	9	10	−1.9
Taiwan	66	70	6	8	3.3
Rest of the world	57	59	5	5	1.8

Source: Calculations based on Bulatao, R.A., et al., 1990, *World Population Projections 1989–90 edition*, Johns Hopkins University Press, Baltimore.

The results show that over the next decade, the expected changes in national savings rates are relatively small, largely because demographic trends have a conflicting impact on national savings rates in many countries. In Korea, Taiwan and all but one of the ASEAN (Association of Southeast Asian Nations) economies, for example, a growing proportion of retirement age people is more than offset by a growing proportion of working age people. This is consistent with the ageing of their 'triangular' shaped population structures shown in Figure 9.1. For these economies, savings rates are projected to increase. Thus there is no apparent reason why these economies should, in the short term, face a growth constraint from a lack of domestic funds for investment purposes.

Nevertheless, some of these economies have also borrowed steadily from overseas to fund domestic investment. Of possibly more concern to their future development is the projected decline in savings rates in some of the industrialised economies, particularly Japan and the European Union. Declining savings rates are projected to be a feature of economies with a growing proportion of retirement age people, along with a stagnant or declining proportion of people of working age. The question remains whether the projected increases in savings rates in many of the East Asian economies will be swamped by the reductions in savings rates in some of the industrialised economies.

The Salter model

Prospects for GDP growth in East Asia will, in the first instance, depend on growth in employment, capital stocks and productivity. Changes in world savings rates may constrain the total pool of world savings available for investment purposes. These changes may also influence the dependence of individual economies on overseas borrowing. This will affect debt-service obligations and the extent to which income generated in a region is retained by the residents of that region. It is useful to look at the basic forces for future GDP growth before considering how changes in savings rates around the world would modify the story. The Salter model can be used to make GDP and income growth projections for the East Asian economies, using forward projections of population and labour force growth and past patterns of productivity growth.

Salter is a computable general equilibrium model of the world economy originally developed by the Australian Industry Commission for the Australian Department of Foreign Affairs and Trade (Jomini et al. 1994). It models the production and consumption patterns of 37 separate industry/commodity groups in 16 regional economies—Australia, New Zealand, Canada, the United States, Japan, Korea, the European Union, Indonesia, Malaysia, the Philippines, Singapore, Thailand, China, Hong Kong, Taiwan and the rest of the world. It also shows how the 16 regional economies are linked through trade.[2] Finally, it explains how production, consumption and trade patterns throughout the world would adjust to change via the responses of relative prices and regional incomes.

One feature of the model is that it employs the Armington assumption that domestic and imported commodities in each region are imperfect substitutes for one another, although the treatment is slightly more flexible than Armington's (1969) original. Armington assumed the elasticity of substitution between domestic commodities and imports from each source to be equal. The Salter model uses a nested substitution structure, allowing the substitution parameters between different sources of imports to be specified independently of the substitution parameters between domestic commodities and the aggregate bundle of imports. This nesting structure allows for different implicit elasticities of substitution between domestic goods and imports from various sources.

The Armington specification determines the way in which exports from one region are seen to compete with exports from other regions and with domestically produced commodities in each regional market, based on relative prices. Changes in relative prices, in conjunction with changes in regional incomes, in turn determine how volumes of interregional trade change in response to economic circumstances. Because the model keeps track of price changes it can also make corresponding projections for each region's terms of trade. The Armington specification means that terms of trade changes can arise from several sources. These effects are important in the later interpretation of results.

The first source is through changes in average world prices of traded commodities, and whether the region is initially a net importer or a net exporter of those commodities. If the region is either a net exporter of commodities whose prices rise, or a net importer of commodities whose prices fall, its terms of trade would tend to improve.

In a model in which traded commodities are distinguishable by source, and in which commodities from different sources are imperfect substitutes, the prices which a particular region receives for its exports or pays for its imports may deviate from the world average. If a region has a particularly large expansion in exports of a commodity to a particular destination, the price it receives is likely to rise by less, or fall by more, than the average world price. This will make a further negative contribution to the region's terms of trade. On the other hand, a region which experiences a particularly large expansion in imports from a particular source may be able to pay a price which rises by less than the world average price, or falls by more. This will make a further positive contribution to a region's terms of trade.

The Salter model is normally used to produce conditional projections of the impact of policy changes at some single point of time in the future. Such projections would show how future levels of production, consumption and trade in each region would differ from what they would otherwise be. They would normally abstract from changes in population and technology that generate an underlying growth path, simply considering the deviation from that path at some point in the future as a result of the policy change. By contrast, the focus of the current exercise is on changes in population and technology and the underlying growth they generate. It abstracts from policy changes that also affect the growth path. However, it is still important to stress that the results reported here are conditional projections. They are not predictions.

As noted, the main sources of GDP growth in a region are growth in labour, capital and total factor productivity. Salter is like other neoclassical models in that it does not explain how improvements in total factor productivity occur. It can nevertheless trace through the impact of historical levels of total factor productivity growth on activity levels and real incomes in each region.

Nor does Salter explain the growth of labour supply, since over the longer term this reflects population growth and demographic changes that are not captured in the model. But Salter can assess the impact on regional economies of projected labour supply growth in each region, as measured by growth in the working age population. It can also assess the impact of total population growth on the size and commodity composition of demand in each region. Households in each region not only substitute between sources of commodities, but also between commodities themselves. The commodity composition of their demand is guided by a linear expenditure system, which recognises that as incomes per household rise, each household will tend to spend a higher proportion of their total budget on commodities and services whose demand is income elastic.

Unlike some neoclassical models, Salter makes provision for unemployment, so that growth in the working age population need not translate one for one into growth in employment. The approach here is to abstract from year-to-year cyclical influences and changes in participation rates, both of which might cause employment growth to deviate from growth in the working age population. It is assumed that the two will keep in step over the next decade. Real wages in each region are assumed to adjust if necessary to ensure this occurs.

The final source of regional GDP growth lies in increases in capital stock. The Salter model makes allowance for the way capital is accumulated in each region and how it can move between regions over the longer term. Thus, while Salter recognises capital growth as a source of GDP growth, the model provides its own estimates of the capital growth to be expected from changes occurring elsewhere. In the model, the world capital stock will grow in response to total factor productivity growth or increases in labour supply—both of which will tend to boost the profitability of capital—but is constrained by the pool of world savings available for investment purposes.

The model initially assumes constant private and government savings rates in each region. In a separate experiment, the effects of changes in the age structure of the population on national savings rates in each region are assessed.

The world capital stock is allocated between industries and regions in the longer term so as to eliminate abnormal returns to capital. The model keeps track of the extent to which capital growth in each region can be financed by that region's national savings, or whether the region also needs to borrow from overseas. The additional capital adds to the region's productive capacity, but foreign debt-service payments are deducted from GDP in order to measure national income, that portion of the returns from activity in a region retained by the residents of that region.

Table 9.3 shows the projected annual average growth in total and working age populations in each region expected over the period 1990 to 2000. It also shows the average annual growth in total factor productivity which might be expected over the same period. These are historical productivity growth rates and are used to derive the base case results. The implications of variations in those rates are discussed below.

Measuring total factor productivity growth is typically subject to a number of limitations in data and method. For most countries, several different sources of estimates for total factor productivity growth could be found. The particular estimates recorded in Table 9.3 were chosen either because they were thought to be the most reliable, or because they were relatively conservative and therefore likely to be more representative of longer-term trends. They are not always the most recent estimates available. Selection in all cases was restricted to published estimates based on historical experience.

Table 9.3 records negative total factor productivity growth for several regions. The negative estimate recorded for Canada is a weighted average of estimates for separate industrial

Table 9.3: Average annual population growth 1990–2000 and historical total factor productivity growth, (per cent)

	Growth in working age population	Growth in total population	Growth in total factor productivity
United States	0.84	0.70	0.90
Canada	0.86	0.75	−0.04
European Union	0.03	0.13	1.30
Japan	0.03	0.34	1.70
Korea	1.26	0.94	3.14
Taiwan	1.49	0.81	5.15
China	1.07	1.27	2.53
Hong Kong	0.89	0.96	1.30
Indonesia	2.29	1.62	1.80
Malaysia	2.42	2.10	1.80
Philippines	2.73	1.80	−0.51
Singapore	0.83	0.75	−0.60
Thailand	2.01	1.42	1.70
Australia	1.47	1.35	0.50
New Zealand	0.78	0.67	0.60
Rest of the world	2.32	2.00	—

Sources: Population growth projections are taken from Bulatao, et al. (1990). Total factor productivity growth figures for Australia, New Zealand, Japan and the European Union are from Englander and Mittelstadt (1988). Other sources are Rao and Preston (1983) for Canada; Kendrick (1992) for the United States; Kim and Park (1985) for Korea; Ikemoto (1986) for Indonesia, Malaysia and Thailand; Austria (1992) for the Philippines; Kim and Lau (1992) for Singapore and Hong Kong; Li, Gong and Zheng (1992) for China; and Ho (1992) for Taiwan. The value for the rest of the world was chosen judgmentally based on World Bank (1991) estimates that productivity growth has been negative in Africa and Latin America, but positive in a broad group comprising Europe, Middle East and North Africa.

sectors, which show that Canada's poor productivity performance has been concentrated in its agricultural and mining sectors. Englander and Mittelstadt (1988) also report negative overall productivity growth for Canada. The negative productivity estimate for Singapore is supported by Young (1992), who argues that Singapore's rapid GDP growth has been generated by increases in factor inputs whereas Hong Kong's rapid GDP growth has been generated by productivity improvements. Kim and Lau's (1992) estimates for these economies are nevertheless chosen in preference to Young's because they are more conservative.

The estimates for several other economies deserve comment. Annual productivity growth estimates for China vary widely, from −4.2 per cent for the 1980–84 period (McGuckin et al. 1992) to 6.2 per cent for the 1981–89 period (Ho 1992). It is likely that China's productivity growth has indeed varied markedly over time. The figure shown in Table 9.3 was estimated over a relatively long time period but was thought to be a conservative indicator of sustainable longer-term trends.

Finally, the productivity growth estimate for Taiwan is not the most conservative that could be found. The alternative annual estimate of 1.3 per cent from Kim and Lau (1992) probably underestimates Taiwan's productivity growth relative to other regions. However the estimate used does affect the growth rate attributed to Taiwan in the projections reported below.

East Asian growth prospects

The estimates in Table 9.3 show the forces for growth that might be expected over the next decade if productivity growth remains at its historical average. Based on these, the Salter model provides estimates of the corresponding regional growth in real GDP, real income, capital stocks, and so on. The results are shown in Table 9.4.[3]

The projected annual average growth rates for real GDP in all regions (except Taiwan) are lower than have been achieved over the past decade. Part of the reason is that over the past decade, most regions have been able to generate employment growth in excess of growth in the working age population. Part of this is due to cyclical factors, and part is due to upward trends in participation rates among the working age population. The model abstracts from both these influences. If the upward trends in participation rates continue then the forces for GDP growth over the next decade will be stronger than projected here.

Growth in GDP is projected to be accompanied by even faster growth in real exports, at least among countries that can

Table 9.4: Projected annual average growth in selected national aggregates[a]

	Real GDP	Real exports	Terms of trade	Net interest income from abroad	Real national income[b]	Real per capita income
Australia	1.73	2.41	0.40	−0.15	1.82	0.47
New Zealand	0.97	0.40	0.82	0.20	1.48	0.81
Canada	0.02	−1.10	0.63	0.38	0.66	−0.09
United States	1.68	2.17	0.20	−0.09	1.77	1.07
Japan	2.54	3.38	−0.05	−0.07	2.67	2.33
Korea	7.18	8.74	−1.44	−1.65	5.68	4.74
European Union	1.60	1.30	−0.01	0.04	1.79	1.66
Indonesia	4.53	6.14	−0.58	−1.75	3.03	1.41
Malaysia	4.49	4.54	−0.41	−1.03	3.55	1.45
Philippines	0.39	−1.81	1.23	0.32	1.08	−0.72
Singapore	0.66	0.85	0.90	0.10	2.64	1.89
Thailand	3.47	4.20	−0.29	−0.77	2.87	1.45
China	4.90	5.69	−0.61	−0.31	4.51	3.24
Hong Kong	2.39	2.81	0.45	−0.44	2.51	1.55
Taiwan	14.28	14.80	−3.18	−3.09	11.33	10.52
Rest of the world	1.01	−0.56	0.46	0.28	1.51	−0.49

[a] All variables are measured in percentage changes, except for net interest income from abroad which is in percentage points worth of national income.
[b] Defined as net national product (GNP net of depreciation) deflated by the national (household plus government) consumption price index.
Source: Salter model projections based on historical experience.

maintain a reasonable rate of total factor productivity growth. With further trade liberalisation over the next decade the growth in export volumes could be expected to be even greater. Economies with reasonable rates of total factor productivity growth are also projected to maintain reasonable trade balances, so their imports are projected to grow broadly in line with exports. This helps to create the markets for exports of other economies. There are, however, limits to the gains from export-oriented growth strategies. The projected very rapid growth in export volumes in some East Asian economies is predicted to generate some decline in their terms of trade. These terms of trade declines help to explain why growth in real income is projected to be lower than growth in real GDP in some economies.

The results also suggest that economies that can maintain a reasonable rate of productivity growth will remain attractive destinations for global investment funds. They will be able to build up their capital stocks, possibly even at the expense of economies in which productivity growth is low. They may incur additional debt-service obligations in the process, but in no case does their projected decline in net interest income from abroad jeopardise their growth in real income.[4]

By contrast, some of the low productivity growth economies can cushion their real incomes by increasing their overseas investment and/or reducing their external debt. The results suggest that Canada and the Philippines fall into this category, with worsening balance of trade deficits being covered by improved net income from abroad. Several of the economies with medium productivity growth are also projected to have a net increase in net interest income from abroad.

Overall, the results suggest that despite significant increases in population in some economies, productivity improvements maintained at historical rates will ensure that they remain competitive, both in product markets and in the global market for capital. They will remain sufficiently competitive, at least over the next decade, to combat diminishing returns to fixed factors, particularly land, and to enjoy at least some growth in incomes per head.

Although the results for the capital account of the balance of payments are not shown, they suggest that in the absence of declines in domestic savings rates, Japan and the European Union will continue to help finance the net capital growth occurring elsewhere. The econometric projections presented earlier in this chapter, however, suggest that declines in savings rates can be expected in these economies, driven by demographic forces that will increase dependency ratios over the next decade. The question remains whether these demographic changes are likely to jeopardise growth in the East Asian economies.

To test the significance of these projected changes in savings rates throughout the world, the Salter model was used to generate an alternative growth scenario. Again this took account of the prospective changes in total and working age populations and the historical rates of total factor productivity growth in each region, but also assumed that household and government savings rates would change over a ten-year horizon by the amounts shown in Table 9.2. As suggested in the introduction, the results showed the incremental impact of the changes in savings rates to be trivial. For example, they were projected to reduce Japan's annual net capital outflow by an amount equal to 0.006 percentage points of GDP and to reduce annual real GDP growth in Indonesia by 0.005 per cent. Even if simultaneity problems in the econometric estimation had led to coefficients being biased downward by a factor of one-half, the Salter projections suggest that the true implied changes in savings rates would still be trivial.

These results highlight the point that the availability of finance is not the main issue. The main issue is the extent to which the funds available are employed in a productive fashion.

Improving East Asian living standards

Although real per capita incomes are projected to increase in most East Asian economies over the next decade, the projected growth rates based on historical rates of productivity growth are modest.

Hughes and Woldekidan (1993) stressed that strong, sustainable economic growth is the most potent force available to raise living standards and alleviate poverty. Rates of poverty are still high in the poorer East Asian economies. No reliable estimates of poverty are available for China, but estimates suggest poverty rates of 18 per cent in Malaysia, 24 per cent in Thailand, 23 per cent in Indonesia and 59 per cent in the Philippines. These compare with poverty rates of less than 10 per cent in Korea, Taiwan and Hong Kong (Bautista 1990).

The challenge, particularly for the poorer East Asian economies, is to accelerate growth and make more rapid improvement in living standards. The analysis of this paper suggests the process need not be jeopardised by population growth nor changes in the age structure over the next decade. The key will be faster productivity growth.

But is the necessary productivity growth achievable? If the poorer East Asian economies with per capita incomes of less than US$3,000 are to double their per capita incomes over the next decade, they need to raise their average annual per capita income growth from the projected rates of between −0.7 and 3.2 per cent in Table 9.4 to 6.9 per cent.

Results from the Salter model in Table 9.4 suggest the challenge will not be easy. There are several aspects to the problem. One is achieving higher productivity growth. The second is the terms of trade effects and increased debt-service obligations. The economies with faster productivity growth appear able to maintain their competitiveness on product markets without jeopardising living standards, so long as other countries are growing at a reasonable rate. But the terms of trade declines they experience and the increased debt-service obligations they acquire are more serious when they accelerate their growth to rates much faster than elsewhere. There are at least some limits to export promotion strategies and from the perspective of their terms of trade, the poorer East Asian economies will continue to have an important stake in productivity growth and economic growth prospects elsewhere.

Additional Salter model results suggest that in the absence of improved productivity performance elsewhere, the poorer East Asian economies would need to improve their annual average productivity performance to around 4 per cent per annum to be able to double their per capita incomes by the end of the century. In other words, it would require more than double the historical rate of around 1.7 to 1.8 per cent (Table 9.3) in Indonesia, Malaysia, and Thailand. It would require China to increase its historical productivity performance by a factor of more than one-half. It would require a significantly greater improvement than either of these cases in the Philippines. The task is not trivial, but some of the East Asian economies have reached such rapid productivity growth for periods in the past.

Living without poverty

Within a time frame in which population growth is constant, this chapter has examined several aspects of the Hughes and Woldekidan challenge—to enable people to live at reasonable standards of living.

Even without population growth as given, the changing age composition of the population could affect economic growth through its impact on savings rates. While in principle the effect of ageing populations is important, particularly in the economies of Japan and the European Union, its empirical significance over the time frame considered here is small. The implication is that the availability of funds for investment is not likely to be the major constraint on growth in East Asia.

The issue is the scope to maintain or increase productivity growth. In this regard, the East Asian economies face a major challenge. Productivity growth at historical rates is likely to lead to relatively modest growth in real incomes per capita. Removing poverty in the lower income economies will require much more rapid productivity growth than historical experience.

Even with more rapid productivity growth, there are limits to export-oriented development strategies. One is the challenge to manage any additional debt-service obligations. While increased foreign debt could be avoided by endeavouring to raise domestic savings rates by policy means, the substitution of foreign debt for lower consumption at home would not necessarily assist the consumption levels and well-being of the poor—the target of Hughes and Woldekidan.

The other risk is of significant terms of trade declines associated with rapid export growth. This is less likely the faster the growth in trading partners' economies. Thus the economies of East Asia continue to have a strong interest in each other's productivity performance, as well as in productivity growth in the industrial nations. Such productivity growth creates a 'virtuous cycle' that helps relax some of the constraints to economic growth in any one region.

Notes for Chapter 9

The views expressed in this discussion do not necessarily reflect those of the Australian Industry Commission or the Australian Department of Foreign Affairs and Trade. The authors would like to acknowledge the assistance of Stephen Brown, Roberta Wise and Wu Yanrui.

[1] For extensive reviews of the literature on the determinants of savings rates see Schmidt-Hebbel, Webb and Corsetti (1992) and Chandavarkar (1993). This literature is not conclusive on the effects of dependency ratios on saving. A simple model is used here to derive parameters used in subsequent modelling work.

2 A significant share of China's trade with other regions occurs through Hong Kong. In order to better capture China's 'true' trade linkages in the Salter database, available data on Hong Kong's re-exports by source and destination were converted back to direct trade between the ultimate source and final destination countries. Thus the Salter database is able to record at least some of the trade between China and Taiwan, for example, but the conversion also means that the activity levels recorded for Hong Kong are exclusive of its *entrepôt* activity and the small margin it earns thereon.

3 The average annual population and total factor productivity growth estimates from Table 9.3 were first converted to cumulative ten-year growth rates, then used to obtain model projections for cumulative growth in the endogenous variable corrected for lineansation error. Table 9.4 reports these model results reconverted to an average annual basis. The total factor productivity growth estimates for each region were introduced into the model as uniform improvements in the productivity of all primary factors—labour, capital and land—in all industries in that region. The exception was in Canada where the sector-specific estimates that underlie the overall figure of Table 9.3 were used directly. The results are not sensitive to the assumption that total factor productivity growth affects the productivity of all primary factors. An alternative growth scenario in which overall total factor productivity growth was assumed to affect only the productivity of labour in each region produced results very close to those in Table 9.4.

4 The real income results shown in Table 9.3 are calculated exactly, but for interpretive purposes it is useful to note that real income as defined can also be approximated as follows:
$\%\triangle$ (real income) = $\%\triangle$ (real GDP) + S_T. $\%\triangle$ (terms of trade) + $\triangle$ (net interest income from abroad as percentage of national income), where S_T is the share of exports (or imports) in GDP. The relationship between changes in net interest income from abroad and changes in a region's capital stock is not one for one because some of an increase in capital can be financed from domestic savings as real incomes rise, even with savings rates fixed. The projected changes in net interest income from abroad also take account of induced changes in the world bond interest rate.

10

Sustaining China's Remarkable Exports and Growth Performance

YONGZHENG YANG

China's foreign trade performance has been strong since the economic reform process began in late 1978, in line with experience in the newly industrialising economies. Exports grew at an annual rate of 16.7 per cent between 1978 and 1992, and imports grew at a slightly lower rate of 15.4 per cent. By 1992, China's exports had reached US$85 billion, amounting to 20 per cent of official GDP (*People's Daily*, Overseas Edition, 25 June 1993). As a result of this tremendous growth, China became the eleventh largest trading nation in the world in 1992, up from thirty-second in 1978. Not only has China become a more open economy, the country is now a major player in the world market.

China's strong export growth has been maintained for 15 years, despite economic boom and bust cycles. The tragic events of June 1989 did not stop export expansion. One naturally wonders what has driven this strong growth and if it is sustainable. This is not the first time these questions have been raised. Back in the 1980s, many people cast doubt on China's ability to sustain its export growth on the grounds that the strong growth in the first half of the 1980s was a result of the initial opening-up of the Chinese economy and that such effects were one-off in nature (World Bank 1988). A new round of economic reforms in 1992 and 1993 has resulted in hyper-growth and increasing inflation.

The issue of sustainability also arises from rapid changes in the world market. The outcomes of the Uruguay Round trade negotiations and increasing regionalism in world trade have significant implications for China (World Bank 1993e). Continuous Sino-US disputes over China's most-favoured-nation status have increased the uncertainty that a changing world market has brought about. While demand constraints are certainly important in the examination of China's growth prospects, this discussion examines domestic policy issues only.

In order to assess the sustainability of China's export growth from a supply-side perspective, analysis needs to go beyond the boom and bust cycles to an examination of the fundamentals on which the economy has been operating. Such an exercise entails detailed investigation of the mechanisms of China's export growth. It is difficult to generalise the mechanisms nationwide because policies often differ across regions or sectors of the economy. Nevertheless, some of the essential features and trends of China's trade policies can be identified. These features and trends seem to have been the fundamental forces behind China's overall export growth, while regional and sectoral differences in policies are likely to be more important in explaining variations in export performance across regions and sectors.

The aim of the following analysis is twofold. First, an attempt is made to define the links between China's export growth and changing patterns of trade to its ongoing economic reforms. Second, the fundamental forces driving export growth are examined.

Economic reform and export performance

Three basic constraints had to be overcome when China embarked on its export drive in the late 1970s:
- more economic incentives had to be given to enterprises;
- exporters had to be exposed to correct price signals so that resources could be allocated more efficiently; and
- enterprises had to become accountable for their profits and losses and to have greater autonomy in responding to price incentives.

The initial boost to China's exports occurred in late 1978 when reforms leading to production responsibility systems and price increases for farm products expanded agricultural production tremendously. Abundant supply of agricultural products fuelled growth of the non-agricultural sector, especially light industries which were heavily dependent on the supply of raw materials from the rural sector. Shortages of consumer goods which prevailed until the late 1970s disappeared rapidly. Under the old trade system exports only occurred when there was abundant supply. The rapid growth provided the first opportunity for China to increase its production of labour-intensive light manufactures. Abundant supply of agricultural products also helped maintain a stable macroeconomic environment by keeping inflation down (World Bank 1990a).

In the early 1980s central planners concentrated on an oil-oriented export strategy. Light manufactured products were not considered potentially promising exports. This approach was reinforced by the buoyant demand for petroleum in the world market. Despite chronic energy shortages in the domestic economy, exports of crude petroleum increased rapidly in the first half of the 1980s. By 1986 it was obvious that domestic petroleum production was unable to sustain this rapid growth due to constraints in investment and the slower than expected development of new oil fields. The sharp fall in oil prices in 1986 also had drastic adverse effects on the oil-oriented export strategy.

The bias towards primary commodity exports was, however, intrinsic in the domestic price system. As the result of a heavy-industry-oriented development approach, primary commodities were underpriced to provide low-cost inputs to the industrial sector (Anderson 1990b). At the same time, manufactured products were overpriced. This was largely accomplished by arbitrary pricing and a turnover tax system (Sun 1992; Zhang 1993). The more processed a product, the more heavily it was taxed. More recently, as reforms have proceeded, low domestic prices for primary commodities have been maintained by export taxes and licensing (World Bank 1993e). Depressed domestic prices made export of primary products attractive (Lin and Yang 1992). In 1980, for example, while the average cost of exports was yuan 2.5 per US dollar, the cost for oil and coal was yuan 1 per US dollar (Yan 1982). At the prevailing exchange rate of yuan 1.5 per US dollar, foreign trade corporations which handled the export of these products made a huge profit.

The turnaround in oil exports and rapid growth of light industries provided a unique opportunity for China to shift its exports from primary to manufactured goods (Table 10.1). Chinese planners began to realise the potential of labour-intensive manufactured exports. Priority was provided to light industries in resource allocation, and exports were encouraged. Measures to encourage light industry included targeted

Table 10.1: Composition of Chinese exports in terms of factor intensity, 1965–91, (per cent)

	1975–79	1980–84	1985–89	1990–91
Agriculture-intensive	47.5	24.0	18.7	12.1
Capital-intensive	17.0	15.3	20.5	26.7
Labour-intensive	27.0	33.6	46.6	52.7
Minerals-intensive	8.4	27.1	14.3	8.5

Notes: Commodity classifications used in this table are based on Krause (1982), shares of various categories may be biased because of double-counting of Hong Kong re-exports of Chinese products. Given that re-exports are of similar commodity composition to overall Chinese exports, however, these biases are likely to be minimal. Details of double-counting of re-exports will be discussed later.
Source: International Economic Databank, The Australian National University, Canberra.

investment, preferential credit allocation and higher foreign exchange retention rates (Yang 1992; World Bank 1993e). The accelerated growth of labour-intensive manufactured exports more than compensated for the decline in exports of crude petroleum, ensuring that China's total exports continued to grow rapidly.

Reforms to the trade regime

Foreign trade corporations

Structural adjustment in the domestic economy provided an initial impetus to the growth and changing composition of exports. The sustained growth and structural change of the past 15 years, however, have been driven by profound changes in the trade regime as well as in overall economic conditions.

One of the first important measures aimed at increasing the efficiency of the Chinese trade regime was the decentralisation of foreign trade management. The number of foreign trade corporations increased rapidly throughout the 1980s from 12 in 1978 to 600 in 1984 (Gao 1993), and to 1,000 in 1986 (World Bank 1988). By 1991, there were more than 4,000 foreign trade corporations, despite a rationalisation in 1990 which saw over 1,000 foreign trade corporations abolished (MOFERT 1993:39;

Lardy 1992b). In addition, since 1983 a large number of producing enterprises have gained the right to directly export and import their own products. The government has indicated a desire for further increases in the number of such enterprises. At present there are 1,390 enterprises which have this right (*People's Daily*, Overseas Edition, 9 February 1993, 25 May 1993). The granting of rights to conduct foreign trade has favoured large state firms. This means that, although the number of enterprises holding such rights is limited, they are nevertheless important in terms of output and exports. Foreign-invested firms also enjoy this right. Another important, though often overlooked, channel used to avoid the state monopoly on external trade has been internal trade among enterprises in different regions. For example, firms in Beijing sell their products to firms in Shenzen, which have the right of direct exporting. Often firms have their own representatives in Shenzen. It is not surprising, therefore, that of the 4,000 foreign trade corporations nationwide, over one-fifth are located in the five special economic zones (Shenzen, Xiamen, Zhuhai, Shantou, Hainan) (MOFERT 1993:39). Such 'informal' channels of exporting have further weakened official control.

Foreign exchange retention

An incentive for internal trade was created by different rates of foreign exchange retention for various regions. Up to 1990, retention rates were much higher in the special economic zones and Guangdong province. Higher retention rates also applied to export earnings from clothing, handcrafts, electronics and machinery in 1988 (Gao 1993). This resulted in increasing levels of internal exports from low to high retention rate regions. Labour and capital were drawn into these high retention rate regions from the rest of the country. While internal trade may have increased China's overall exports, such growth did not come without losses of allocative efficiency. Obviously, an alternative and more efficient way to increase national output and exports would have been an equal retention rate across regions. This would have prevented the transport costs associated with the internal trade.

In 1990, the foreign exchange retention policy was reformulated on the basis of product lines, and variations in the retention rate across regions were removed. While the retention rate on earnings from most products is now 80 per cent, electronics, machinery and science and technology products are accorded a 100 per cent retention rate (World Bank 1993e). While this policy change may have removed geographic discrepancies in incentives, it has created new, albeit less severe, distortions.

Despite these drawbacks, foreign exchange retention has provided a powerful incentive to exporting enterprises. Exports are determined at the margin by the weighted average of the official exchange rate and the secondary exchange rate, which has been consistently higher than the former (Table 10.2). The overvalued official exchange rate effectively becomes a specific tax on exports (Martin 1990; World Bank 1993e). In fact, before the abolition of export subsidies in 1991, exporting enterprises were able to obtain a marginal revenue higher than the weighted average of the official and secondary market exchange rates as the result of higher foreign exchange retention of above-plan exports and subsidies (Sun 1992:75).

Table 10.2: Official and secondary market exchange rates, 1978–92, (yuan/US$)

	Official exchange rate	Secondary market exchange rate
1978	1.68	—
1979	1.55	—
1980	1.50	—
1981	1.70	3.08
1982	1.89	3.08
1983	1.98	3.09
1984	2.29	3.08
1985	2.93	3.23
1986	3.43	5.00
1987	3.72	5.70
1988	3.72	6.32
1989	3.76	5.91
1990	4.78	5.75
1991	5.32	5.90
1992	5.51	6.50

Sources: Gao Xiaoguang, 1993, China's Foreign Exchange Regime and its Impact on Exports and Growth, PhD dissertation, National Centre for Development Studies, The Australian National University, Canberra; Zhang Xiaoguang, 1993, China's Trade Pattern and International Comparative Advantage, PhD dissertation, National Centre for Development Studies, The Australian National University, Canberra.

Foreign exchange markets

Foreign exchange retention created a need for foreign exchange markets. The government responded by gradually introducing foreign exchange swap markets around the country. There have, however, been some restrictions on entry to these markets. Before December 1991, only foreign-invested and authorised domestic enterprises could sell foreign exchange in the markets. Again, large state enterprises were favoured. Since 1992, sales of foreign exchange have been virtually unrestricted. Price ceilings for foreign exchange were imposed until 1988. They were reintroduced briefly between February and May 1993 when high inflation led to a sharp depreciation of the renminbi (about 40 per cent). It is not known, however, how binding these restrictions were. Judging by the fact that the secondary exchange rate was able to appreciate when the official exchange rate depreciated (Table 10.2), the price ceilings were perhaps not too far from the equilibrium exchange rate.

Foreign exchange swap markets have played a key role in China's trade reforms and growth. With increasing competition among foreign trade corporations, increased prices for tradeable goods as a result of the secondary exchange rate have been passed on to producing enterprises. Thus, not only do the markets provide greater incentives to exporters, but they also direct foreign exchange to more efficient users by forcing importers to pay marginal or nearly marginal costs for foreign exchange. The secondary rate also provides a guide to the level of the official exchange rate, making the decision on the rate less difficult and quicker. Further expansion of the swap markets will particularly benefit small, non-state enterprises in the coastal areas which are often trade-oriented, but have little access to foreign exchange for imports through official allocations.

Increases in retention rates and the inflow of foreign investment have led to rapid expansion in foreign exchange swap markets. In 1988, transactions of foreign exchange in swap markets reached US$6.3 billion, or 18 per cent of China's imports (Gao 1993:45). By 1992, transaction volumes totalled US$25.1 billion, an increase of 46.5 per cent from 1991. This was equal in value to 31 per cent of imports in 1992 (*People's Daily*, Overseas Edition, 16 January 1993).

In addition to the foreign exchange swap markets, Hong Kong currency is circulating in China, particularly in the south, as is other foreign exchange. It has been reported that one-fifth of Hong Kong currency is now circulating in China (*Bulletin*, 26 May 1993, cited in *China News Digest*, 27 June 1993). Holdings of foreign currency in Chinese banks by individuals reached US$8.5 billion in 1992, and it was believed that significantly more was circulating outside banks (*China News Digest*, 30 September 1992). In 1992 US$400 million of foreign exchange held by individuals was traded in foreign exchange swap markets (*People's Daily*, 16 February 1993).

Further reforms have been proposed by the government. It has been announced that the authorities will improve foreign exchange markets (including integration of regional swap markets); deepen reforms in foreign exchange retention and use of foreign exchange; reduce direct but strengthen indirect control of foreign exchange; and put domestic and foreign firms on an equal footing with respect to foreign exchange (*People's Daily*, Overseas Edition, 20 February 1993). Although these proposals are vague, they seem to be in the right direction.

The ultimate goal for China is, however, to have a single, fully convertible, market-determined exchange rate. On 1 January 1994 the dual exchange rate system was replaced by a unified exchange rate based on the swap market rate. This brings the exchange rate reform much closer to its logical destination. Attempts to bring renminbi exchange rates to a reasonable level began with the introduction of an internal settlement rate in 1981. As the official exchange rate was overvalued, the internal settlement rate did provide extra financial incentives to exporters (Sun 1992). The internal settlement rate was abolished in 1985 when the official exchange rate was devalued to the level of the internal settlement rate to form a single official exchange rate. Nevertheless, the government realised that it was necessary to have flexible and realistic exchange rates to maintain export growth. Inflationary pressure throughout the 1980s forced the Chinese government to continuously devalue the renminbi in order to maintain export competitiveness (Table 10.2).

Reduced levels of protection

In a market-oriented economy, exchange rates are fundamentally determined by demand and supply of foreign exchange even if a fixed exchange rate regime prevails. Both demand and supply are influenced by trade interventions, such as tariffs. In the pre-reform era, China's exchange rate was determined largely independent of trade barriers. In addition, at any given exchange rate, exports and imports were taxed or subsidised so that border prices were not transmitted into the domestic economy. Consequently, trade barriers did not affect production decisions to any significant extent. With the weakening of planning since the late 1970s, however, trade policy has become important to production and trade decisions. In 1984, an import agency system was introduced (Sun 1992). This system gradually expanded to include export activities as well, although the use of the system has been less widespread in the latter case (World Bank 1993e). Under this arrangement, foreign trade corporations charge commissions and end-users of imports pay importing costs. Thus, international prices, trade barriers and exchange rates all play an important part in the effective exchange rate formation.

China's trade policy involves trade taxes and a complex system of quantitative restrictions. Quantitative restrictions are progressively being replaced by trade taxes. A large number of exports, mostly primary products, are taxed. Part of the rationale behind the imposition of these export taxes has been to take advantage of the optimum export taxes that China seems to enjoy in certain products, most noticeably food exports to Hong Kong and exports of a number of mineral products, such as tungsten. A number of manufactured products, particularly semi-processed products such as yarns and fabrics, are also subject to export taxes. Chinese officials admit that excessive export taxes often tend to reduce China's market share in Hong Kong. As a result, competition from other countries has to be constantly monitored.

Tariffs are perhaps the most important trade tax. Chinese tariff levels are quite high by developing country standards, despite several reductions in the recent past (World Bank 1993e). Following a typical developing country protection pattern, tariff levels tend to increase with the degree of processing. Manufactured products tend to be more protected than primary products (World Bank 1988; Zhang and Warr 1990; Zhang 1993). In 1984, tariff rebates were introduced, and with the abolition of export subsidies in 1991, rebates on indirect and value added taxes were also introduced (Sun 1992). Rebates have substantially reduced export costs. In the case of tariff rebates, while the import-weighted nominal tariff rate has been around 32 per cent since the mid-1980s, actual revenue collections from tariffs have been very low, largely as a result of tariff rebates. In 1986, actual tariff collections were only 10 per cent of import values (World Bank 1993e:60), and in 1992, the rate dropped to less than 4 per cent (*People's Daily*, Overseas Edition, 9 January 1993). Smuggling is partly responsible for the low tariff revenue collections (World Bank 1993e).

Recent GATT-motivated reforms

As trade has intensified and the Chinese economy become increasingly dependent on the world market, China has expanded its diplomacy to guard its trade and other interests. After regaining membership of the World Bank and the International Monetary Fund in 1980, China formally lodged an application in July 1986 to re-enter the GATT (General Agreement on Tariffs and Trade). A series of trade reforms has been introduced in support of China's attempts to regain GATT membership. Sino–US disputes over trade, human rights and China's arms sales have probably also accelerated trade reforms.

In the beginning of 1991, export subsidies were removed, state monopoly was further reduced and exporting enterprises became accountable for their profits and losses. At the end of 1992, the number of products subject to export licensing and quotas was reduced by more than 50 per cent (*International Business*, 29 January 1992, *People's Daily*, Overseas Edition, 31 January 1992). The share of products subject to licensing in total exports fell from 66 per cent to 31 per cent, and control of licensing and quotas was further decentralised to lower-level governments. On the import side, tariffs were reduced for 225 commodities in 1991 (*People's Daily*, Overseas Edition, 31 January 1992). In 1992, tariffs were cut for 3,371 items, leading to a reduction of the average tariff level by 7.3 percentage points. At the same time, regulatory tariffs introduced in 1985 were abolished, the list of products for import substitution was abolished, and the number of commodities under import licensing was reduced by more than 50 per cent from the 1986 level. To increase the transparency of the trade system, a few dozen internal policy documents concerning imports were published for the first time. It was also announced that China would remove two-thirds of import licensing in five years (World Bank 1988:22; *People's Daily*, Overseas Edition, 20 March 1993).

It is clear from the above discussion that important reforms have occurred in China's trade regime, although substantial distortions are still in place. China still suffers efficiency losses from variable tariff rates across commodities, excessive and sometimes redundant licensing, trade plans/control, fragmented foreign exchange markets and partial foreign exchange retention among other distortions (World Bank 1993e). Nevertheless, the anti-export bias inherited from the central planning era has been substantially reduced by continuous depreciation of the renminbi, the introduction of foreign exchange retention and secondary foreign exchange markets, and the lowering of trade barriers.

The macroeconomic environment

The performance of China's export sector cannot be adequately explained without examining domestic macroeconomic conditions. International experience shows that macroeconomic conditions are vital to export growth (Hughes 1985; Fischer 1993). To examine China's macroeconomic policy, one has to take into account the reforms of the past 15 years.

Price reforms and inflation

Chinese enterprises have in general enjoyed increasing autonomy and become more price-responsive. The price system itself has undergone substantial reforms. Price reforms began with agricultural products, and were then applied to manufactured consumer goods. The number of agricultural products which were subject to state pricing was reduced to seven by the late 1980s. For manufactured consumer goods, price control was removed from 800 items leaving just over 30 items covered by late 1992. Recently, price reforms have focused on industrial inputs. In September 1992, prices for 593 production materials and services were freed of price control (*People's Daily*, Overseas Edition, 2 September 1992). This is said to be the largest step forward in price reforms in the past decade, bringing down the total number of inputs subject to price control from 737 at the end of 1991 to 89.

Among the 89 products still subject to price control, price ceilings for above-plan output have been abolished. Flexibility in pricing is allowed. Thirty-four products are still subject to state-fixed prices and the remaining 55 are only subject to guidance in price setting. After the September 1992 price reforms, the proportion of production materials and services still subject to state price control dropped from about 50 per cent in 1986 to 20 per cent (*People's Daily*, Overseas Edition, 18 March 1993).

An economy in transition from a centrally planned to a market-oriented system is prone to inflation because prices under central planning are often distorted and price adjustments normally entail price increases (World Bank 1990a). Cost-push inflation is thus inevitable if macroeconomic policy is not prudent. Export growth is unlikely to be sustained if inflation runs high. Continuous price reforms generated much higher overt inflation than prevailed during the pre-reform era in China. Authorities have responded by continuous devaluations of renminbi and increases in foreign exchange retention (Sun 1992). In such an inflationary environment, exports will be discouraged and imports encouraged, if exchange rates are not flexible enough.

In order to examine whether such an anti-export bias has occurred, one needs to compare effective exchange rates for exports and imports. Details of trade taxes and subsidies are required for such comparisons. Due to the non-transparency of trade restrictions and the extent of non-price barriers in the Chinese trade regime, reliable estimates of subsidies for either exports or imports are extremely difficult to obtain. The closest data to effective exchange rates for exports are fragmented statistics on average export costs (Table 10.3). Combined with the weighted average of the official and secondary market exchange rates, these statistics provide a crude indication of the prices of exportables relative to domestic sales or importables.

Before the introduction of the internal settlement rate in 1981, average export costs were consistently higher than the weighted exchange rate. This means that without substantial subsidies the export sector as a whole would have suffered considerable losses. The introduction of the internal settlement rate in 1981 did seem to cover export costs. In 1985 when inflation was running high, average export costs again exceeded the

Table 10.3: Average cost of foreign exchange earnings, China, 1978–92, (yuan/US$)

	Weighted exchange rate	Average export cost
1978	1.68	2.50
1979	1.55	2.40
1980	1.50	2.31
1981	3.08	2.48
1982	3.08	2.67
1983	3.08	3.02
1984	3.08	2.79
1985	3.01	3.20
1986	3.84	3.50
1987	4.46	4.20
1988	4.86	4.15
1989	4.93	5.15
1990	5.23	5.87
1991	5.73	. .
1992	6.37	. .

Sources: Weighted average exchange rates are from World Bank, 1993e, *China: Foreign Trade Reform: Meeting the Challenge of the 1990s*, World Bank, Washington, D.C.; average export costs are from Zhang Xiaoguang, 1993, China's Trade Pattern and International Comparative Advantage, PhD dissertation, National Centre for Development Studies, The Australian National University, Canberra; and Sung, Y.W., 1991a, 'Explaining China's export drive: the only success among command economies', *Occasional Paper*, 5, Hong Kong Institute of Asia-Pacific Studies, The Chinese University of Hong Kong.

weighted exchange rate. In the following three years, export costs again seemed to be fully covered by the weighted exchange rate. This situation was again reversed in 1989 and 1990 as the result of substantial increases in the average export cost. Throughout the 1978–90 period, however, the gap between the weighted exchange rate and the average export cost appears to have narrowed. If tax rebates are taken into account in the estimation of average export cost, profits without subsidies for more efficient exporters are conceivable.

For a long time, Chinese authorities have used average export costs as a basis for setting exchange rates (Sun 1992; *Economic Daily*, 8 June 1993). This has several drawbacks. The exchange rate is a marginal price, not an average price. Marginal export costs could be considerably higher than average costs when there are resource (particularly capital) constraints on the economy. Thus, indexing exchange rates to average export costs almost inevitably leads to an overvaluation of the domestic currency. Indexation itself could be a difficult task. Presumably, accurate average export costs can only be calculated at the end of each year, and exchange rate adjustments will have to be based on the previous year's export cost estimates. More fundamentally, average costs are endogenous variables depending on exchange rates. Thus, to base exchange rates on average exchange costs is self-defeating. In an inflationary environment, it is particularly difficult to index exchange rates to average export costs. In an economy characterised by boom and bust cycles, it is even more difficult.

Exchange rate policy

As the anti-export bias in China's trade system seems to have fallen over time, the competitiveness of Chinese exports in the world market should improve. Real effective exchange rates have been used to analyse changes in China's export competitiveness (World Bank 1990a, 1993e; Gao 1993). All three studies used official (including the internal settlement rate) exchange rates in their estimation of real effective exchange rates. As argued, however, by Byrd (1987), Sicular (1988) and Martin (1990), market prices have become marginal prices for Chinese enterprises and, in particular, the weighted averages of official and secondary exchange rates are the relevant exchange rates for estimating real effective exchange rates, rather than the official exchange rates (World Bank 1993e). In fact, as noted earlier, many enterprises may have faced an exchange rate higher than the weighted exchange rate because of higher foreign exchange retention rates for above-plan exports before 1991 and subsidies associated with the fulfilment of export plans (Sun 1992). This argument is further strengthened by the fact that large amounts of foreign currencies are being circulated in black markets, particularly in South China, where export growth has been most dynamic.

Nevertheless, real effective exchange rates based on both official and secondary market exchange rates are estimated (Table 10.4). For China, consumer price indexes are used in the calculations while wholesale price indexes are used for China's 28 major trading partners. Edwards (1989) suggests that there are advantages in using consumer price indexes for the home

Table 10.4: Real effective exchange rates (export-weighted), China, 1978–92
(1978 = 100)

	Based on official rates	Based on secondary rates
1978	100.0	100.0
1979	100.3	100.2
1980	104.2	104.2
1981	117.8	213.0
1982	125.8	204.9
1983	124.6	194.1
1984	143.4	192.3
1985	166.1	182.9
1986	191.2	278.0
1987	209.3	320.2
1988	188.7	320.2
1989	169.3	265.8
1990	221.4	266.2
1991	245.5	271.9
1992	250.2	294.8

Source: International Monetary Fund, *International Financial Statistics*, various
volumes, extracted from International Economic Databank, The Australian
National University, Canberra.

country and wholesale price indexes for partner countries, and
that this combination is more likely to show the competitiveness of the home country in tradeable goods in relation to its
non-tradeable goods. Both the World Bank (1990a) and Gao
(1993) followed this approach. Wherever wholesale price
indexes were not available, producer price indexes of various
kinds were used.

Gao (1993) argues that inflation is not adequately represented
by official consumer price indexes published by the Chinese
State Statistical Bureau. As an alternative, price indexes for
agricultural procurements and consumer price indexes multiplied by a factor of 2.5, based on the estimate of Feltenstein and
Fahadian (1987), were used. Given that Feltenstein and Fahadian's estimate was based on data for 1955-83 (inflation has not
been suppressed to the same extent since 1983), and that the
factor 2.5 only represented the degree of inflation suppression
and actual prices did not necessarily increase by this much, the
usefulness of this estimate for real effective exchange rate estimation is questionable.

In the first three years of economic reform (1978–80), despite an appreciation of the renminbi, real effective exchange rates depreciated slightly as a result of low inflation (Table 10.4). Between 1981 and 1987, the official exchange rate depreciated substantially. Relative macroeconomic stability during this period meant that the renminbi also depreciated in real terms. High inflation in 1988 and 1989 caused sharp appreciation of the renminbi in real terms, despite continued devaluations. As austerity policies were introduced in late 1989, real effective exchange rates started to depreciate again, at a rate similar to the official rate. Real effective exchange rates based on secondary market rates followed a similar trend over the period 1978–92, but provided much more favourable exchange rates for tradeable goods.

Sensitivity analysis was performed with regard to China's inflation rates. It was found that, based on the official exchange rate, the real effective exchange rate would have not depreciated at all had actual inflation (measured by consumer price indexes) been 1.2 times higher than the officially published rates. Based on the secondary market rate, the actual inflation rate would have to be 1.4 times higher than the official inflation estimates for the real effective exchange rate to have been unchanged over the period 1978–1992. Experiments were conducted to test the sensitivity of the estimates of real effective exchange rates to import-weighted measures of China's trading partners' exchange rates. Exports, before redistribution of Hong Kong's re-exports, were also used as alternative weights in these calculations. The resulting differences were marginal.

The fluctuations in the real effective exchange rate over time highlight the increasing importance of the macroeconomic environment to China's export sector. When real effective exchange rates appreciated in 1988 and 1989, imports surged while export growth slowed. This period was unlike 1978–80; export growth did not slow down when real effective exchange rates were appreciating. This may be due to the fact that the Chinese economy at that time was still very much under central planning and exports were not driven by financial incentives. Export growth therefore continued, albeit at a cost of greater state subsidies.

The impact of macroeconomic conditions on trade is also evident from the boom-bust cycle in the first half of 1993. As a result of high inflation and slow adjustments in the official exchange rate, export growth decelerated from 18 per cent in 1992 to 4.4 per cent while import growth remained high (*China News Digest*, 7 July 1993). The main reasons for the slowing of export growth, according to Wu Yi, Minister of Foreign Economic Relations and Trade, were: strong domestic demand; price increases in the domestic market, leading to increases in the cost of exports; inadequate funds for the procurement of exportable goods; inadequate transport services; and disorder of export management (*People's Daily*, Overseas Edition, 9 June 1993). These are clearly the symptoms of an overstretched economy.

Monetary policy

Various measures have been taken by the government to prevent exports from sliding, for example, higher priority for exporting enterprises in loans and transport, but these can only relieve the short-term problems. Some fundamental problems are unlikely to be overcome. One key area seems to be the financial system. On the supply side of the system, the Chinese central bank, the People's Bank of China, has been unable to control the money supply. It was estimated that between 1984 and 1992, money supply was growing at a rate of 28 per cent while the economy was growing at 8 to 9 per cent per annum in real terms (Zhang 1993). The inability of the central bank to control the money supply largely results from its susceptibility to political influence. Following the decentralisation of the banking system, local branches of Chinese banks have been effectively hijacked by local governments to serve local requirements. National financial policies have been put aside.

On the demand side, the weak accountability of state enterprises and local governments means that demand for credit is often excessive, particularly in times when expansionary policies and financial deregulation are pursued. This is exacerbated by repressed and sometimes even negative interest rates. Credit allocation is also skewed to state enterprises for ideological and historical (central planning) reasons. Although state enterprises siphon a large portion of resources, they seem to be the least efficient. Their huge financial losses drain government revenues, contributing to fiscal deficits which are, in turn, being monetised (Ma 1992). As in 1988–89, inflation in the first half of 1993 seems to have been investment-pushed. In 1988–89, investments were often unproductive, adding little output in the short run. Similar investments may have been repeated in 1993 (*People's Daily*, Overseas Edition, 10 July 1993).

It seems clear that fundamental reforms to the financial sector have to be carried out if macroeconomic stability is to be maintained in the longer run. These reforms are intertwined with enterprise reforms, which in turn depend upon changes in other areas, such as the establishment of a social security system to deal with the problems arising from labour market reforms. In addition, government fiscal policy needs to be tightened to bring budget deficits under control (Garnaut and Ma 1993a). While these reforms are vital, detailed discussion is beyond the scope of this chapter.

Fundamental forces driving export growth

The above analysis confirms that reforms have substantially reduced the anti-export bias in China's trade system. While state enterprises seem to have responded to the new export environment and, until recently, were largely responsible for export growth, it is the non-state sector that has moved most forcefully to take advantage of reforms.

Rural industries

Just as the initial impetus to export growth was from rural China, one of the leading sources of export expansion has also come from rural China. Township enterprises have emerged as the most dynamic force in China's export drive. Exports from these enterprises grew at an annual rate of 32 per cent between 1985 and 1992, nearly twice as fast as the national average. As a result of such rapid growth, township enterprises accounted for nearly one-third of China's total exports in 1992, up from 14 per cent in 1985 (*Economic Daily*, 14 June 1993; Lardy 1992a).

Township enterprises specialise in labour-intensive manufactured exports (Table 10.5). They dominate China's exports of clothing and account for substantial portions of the nation's exports of other labour-intensive manufactured exports. Rural exports are moving away from farm produce to manufactures.

Table 10.5: Shares of township enterprises in national export procurements, 1988–90, (per cent)

	1988	1989	1990
Clothing	49.6	65.2	72.0
Handcrafts	39.0	43.1	45.0
Chemicals	23.6	36.3	27.3
Silk	21.4	25.1	24.3
Other light manufactures	19.3	22.8	28.5
Textiles	16.4	19.2	21.9
Machinery	16.2	19.6	21.8
Food	27.1	19.3	15.5
Minerals	13.6	15.9	15.5
Other farm products	16.3	9.2	10.4
Others	32.7	61.1	24.5

Source: Editorial Board of ACTE, 1992, *Almanac of China's Township Enterprises 1991*, Agriculture Press, Beijing.

With increasing land constraints and low labour costs this trend is likely to continue for some time before township enterprises move into manufacturing of more sophisticated products.

Unlike their state counterparts, township enterprises have expanded without significant subsidies. They are accountable for their own profits and losses. In many respects, they are disadvantaged. They usually do not have access to raw material supplies at low prices via the planning system. Instead, they have to buy materials from markets where prices tend to be higher. In addition, these enterprises tend to have low priority in capital allocation from the state-monopolised banking system. Many rely on savings of their own or loans from the secondary financial market, where interest rates are very high (Cheng 1992). Township enterprises often suffer from infrastructure shortages in areas such as power supply and transport services. They are often forced to pay extra to maintain supplies. It was reported that tens of thousands of township enterprises in the Pearl River Delta had to pay nearly three times the official price to ensure power supply by installing their own diesel-powered generators; some obtain their power supply from Hong Kong at twice the official price (*Economic Daily*, 14 June 1993).

The major advantage of township enterprises is, however, that their managers have the right to make most important decisions in their operation. Due to their small scale and lower levels of government interference, they are more flexible in responding to market conditions. As noted earlier, they also tend to concentrate on labour-intensive products and maximise the returns of their scarce capital resources. Many take advantage of tax holidays in the first three years of establishment. They reward hard work and skills. As a result, a large number of underpaid skilled workers have been attracted to township enterprises. They are quick in adapting to new technologies. Eighty per cent of China's patents have been bought by township enterprises in recent years (*Economic Daily*, 16 June 1993).

China's rural entrepreneurs have transformed the Chinese economy. In 1978, their share in China's industrial output was negligible. In 1992, the output of township enterprises was more than 1,000 billion yuan, accounting for one-third of national industrial output. In 1991, 85 per cent of the increase in rural net income was generated by township enterprises (Chen 1993). The enterprises employed over 100 million people in 1992, or more than one-fifth of rural labour, equivalent to the total increase in employment in the urban sector in the past 30 years. Every year, township enterprises absorb one-half of the surplus labour in rural China. In the Pearl River Delta, labour shortages have drawn millions of workers from other regions (*People's Daily*, Overseas Edition, 5 January 1993; *Economic Daily*, 13 June 1993).

Foreign-invested firms

Another dynamic force behind China's export expansion is foreign investment. Reforms of the trade regime, and the economy in general, have attracted rapid inflow of foreign investment (Yang 1993). There are over 70,000 foreign-invested firms in China, of which 47,000 were established in 1992 (*People's Daily*, Overseas Edition, 20 March 1993). These firms have invested US$178.4 billion, of which foreign capital accounts for US$68.7 billion. A dominant portion of foreign investment has come from Hong Kong (Yang 1993). More recently, Taiwanese and Korean investment has surged as well. In fact, China has become the largest destination for Taiwanese investment (*People's Daily*, Overseas Edition, 4 May 1993).

From a low base in the early 1980s, exports from enterprises with foreign investment reached US$17.4 billion in 1992, or one-fifth of China's total exports (Table 10.6). Foreign-invested enterprises ran a US$9 billion trade deficit in 1992, but this was largely due to the purchase of investment goods (*International Business*, 9 February 1993). In addition, large foreign exchange savings have been earnt through import substitution. Although statistics are not available, these savings could be substantial in areas such as transport equipment and machinery.

Table 10.6: Exports by China's more market-oriented sectors, 1985–92, (US$ billion)

	Township enterprises	Foreign-invested firms	Special economic zones	Economic and technological development zones	National total
1985	3.9	0.3	1.3	0.04	27.4
1986	4.5	0.5	1.8	0.05	30.9
1987	5.1	1.2	3.0	0.11	39.4
1988	8.0	2.5	4.2	0.41	47.5
1989	10.1	4.9	7.0	0.51	52.5
1990	12.5	7.8	8.0	0.69	62.1
1991	16.2	12.1	9.6	1.14	71.9
1992	26.7	17.4	12.4	1.47	85.0

Sources:
Township enterprises: Lardy, N.R., 1992a, 'Chinese foreign trade', *The China Quarterly*, 131, Special Issue: The Chinese Economy in the 1990s, September; *Nongye Jingji Wenti (Issues in Agricultural Economics)*, No. 1 1993:35, for 1991; *Economic Daily*, 14 June 1993, for 1992;
Foreign-invested firms: Lardy (1992a:711) for 1985 to 1990; *International Business*, 9 February 1993, for 1991 and 1992;
Special economic zones: Editorial Board of ASEZ, 1991, *Almanac of China's Special Economic Zones and Coastal Economic and Technology Development Zones 1990*, Reform Press, Beijing, up to 1989; MOFERT, 1993, *Almanac of China's Foreign Economic Relations and Trade 1992/3*, China Advertising Pty Ltd, Hong Kong, for 1990; *People's Daily*, 19 February 1993, for 1991 and 1992;
Economic and technology development zones: Editorial Board of ASEZ, 1991, *Almanac of China's Special Economic Zones and Coastal Economic and Technology Development Zones 1990*, Reform Press, Beijing, 1985 to 1989; MOFERT, 1993, *Almanac of China's Foreign Economic Relations and Trade 1992/3:79*, China Advertising Press Pty Ltd, Hong Kong, 1990 and 1991; 1992 figure is based on the growth rate of special economic zones.

Exports by foreign-invested firms largely consist of processed goods. In 1992 these goods accounted for 88 per cent of total exports by those firms that had foreign investment. Eleven coastal provinces accounted for 97 per cent of the total exports, and the five special economic zones accounted for 30 per cent. Manufactures dominated the exports (94 per cent) and machinery and electronics accounted for more than one-third (US$6 billion) of the total value of exports. Other major exports included tape recorders, television sets, transport containers, cameras, textiles, clothing, toys, bicycles, telephones, plastic products and bags. Textiles and clothing exports amounted to US$4.9 billion, or 19 per cent of national textile and clothing exports. Exports of shoes reached US$2.0 billion, or one-half of total national shoe exports.

A large proportion of the exports has been produced by informal foreign investment, particularly in the coastal regions. Such informal foreign investment includes compensation trade, assembling, equipment and machinery leasing, and export processing. These types of informal foreign investment have become an important form of technology transfer and a driving force for China's export growth in the coastal regions, particularly along the southeast coast where people have close ties with Hong Kong, Taiwan, Macau and Southeast Asian countries (Yang 1992). In 1988, exports based on processing accounted for 23 per cent of total exports, and since then this share has doubled (World Bank 1993e:11). It was reported that informal Hong Kong capital alone employed three million mainland workers in the Pearl River Delta (*The Bulletin*, 27 May 1993, cited in *China News Digest*, 27 June 1993). More recently, the Republic of Korea has become an important source of informal foreign investment, particularly in the northeast part of the country. Foreign firms not only provide scarce capital, but perhaps more importantly, management skills and export markets. While many foreign investments aim at the huge domestic markets, informal investments are more export-oriented.

Special economic zones

The four special economic zones (Shenzen, Xiamen, Zhuhai and Shantou) set up since 1979 have also played an important part in China's export drive. This is not so much due to the export growth in the zones themselves, but rather due to the flexibility they have introduced to the rest of China through internal trade, as noted above. Total trade by special economic zones in 1992 amounted to US$24 billion, 14.7 per cent of national trade (*People's Daily*, Overseas Edition, 18 February 1993). Exports were $12.4 billion, 15 per cent of national exports; imports were $12 billion. It should be noted, however, that exports from special economic zones may include products originating in other parts of the economy.

Economic and technological development zones

A large number of economic and technological development zones have been set up by local governments. These normally enjoy similar status to special economic zones. Most of the zones have not generated much export capacity, and perhaps never will, due to their poor infrastructure and management. Large resources may have been wasted in these zones, and the central government is now trying to rationalise them. Figures shown in Table 10.6 only include fourteen more established zones. They are Dalian, Qinhuangdao, Tianjin, Yantai, Qingdao, Lianyungang, Nantong, Minxing, Hongqiao, Caohejing, Ningpo, Fuzhou, Guangzhou and Zhanjiang. Unlike most other zones, these have emerged as an increasingly important source of exports.

Combined contribution of non-state enterprises

Although there is considerable overlapping in the trade statistics presented in Table 10.6, the combined contribution of township enterprises, foreign-invested firms and special economic zones to China's exports has been substantial and increasing rapidly. More importantly, their contribution to incremental exports is much greater as a result of their rapid growth. Preliminary estimates of their marginal contribution have been made. It was reported that in 1991 about 79 per cent of exports by coastal regions were attributable to foreign-invested firms (MOFERT 1993:79). According to a report by *International Business* (9 February 1993), foreign-invested firms contributed 30 per cent of exports from special economic zones. Further, Dan (1993) reported that 30 per cent of exports by economic and technological development zones were from foreign-invested firms. Application of these ratios for 1985–92 permits elimination of the overlap between exports by township enterprises, foreign-invested firms, special economic zones and economic and technological development zones (Table 10.7). These estimates may overcorrect for earlier years, as overlap between the four sectors was smaller in those years.

It is clear from Table 10.7 that most of China's export growth in recent years has come from the more market-oriented sectors. They were responsible for more than 80 per cent of annual growth in 1992. The largest contribution among these sectors has come from township enterprises (63 per cent). In some years (1989 and 1992), it seems that the rest of the economy experienced negative export growth: in these years, export growth was entirely from these more market-oriented sectors.

This pattern of export growth is not surprising given the process and sequencing of reforms and the macroeconomic environment they have created. Agricultural reforms initiated in the late 1970s have created a market-oriented rural economy. Although the farming sector seems to have largely exhausted its reform-generated potential for rapid growth in output, the liberal economic environment in rural China has proven equally conducive to non-farming activities, in some ways magnified by the relatively poor performance of the urban state sector. The inflow of foreign investment, initially to the special economic zones and later to the rest of the country, has provided a further boost to what was already one of the most dynamic sectors of the economy.

These developments have all occurred in a rapidly liberalising economic environment. State monopoly is disappearing, and competition is increasingly fierce among exporters. China's wool war, cotton war, cashmere war, coal war, and so on, are at least partly fuelled by such competition in the presence of residual restrictions on domestic trade (Sun 1992). Prices for raw materials have been raised sharply in recent years, leaving the state supply system unable to cope with non-state competition. Less dynamic regions have been moved to erect regional trade barriers to prevent goods from flowing to areas where marginal returns are higher. All these factors seem to suggest that exporters have been responding to the reform-created environment.

Given the continuous liberalisation outlined in the previous discussions, one would expect that most Chinese enterprises are

Table 10.7: Contribution of different sectors to export growth, 1985–92, (US$ billion)

	Township enterprises (1)	Foreign-invested firms (2)	Special economic zones[a] (3)	Economic and technological (4)	Sum of (1) + (2) + (3) + (4) (5)	National exports (6)	(5) as a % of (6) (7)	Share of increment of (6) (8)
1985	3.08	0.21	1.34	0.03	4.66	27.4	16.99	—
1986	3.56	0.35	1.84	0.03	5.78	30.9	18.71	32.17
1987	4.03	0.84	3.01	0.08	7.96	39.4	20.19	25.59
1988	6.32	1.75	4.17	0.29	12.53	47.5	26.38	56.48
1989	7.98	3.43	7.04	0.36	18.81	52.5	35.83	125.56
1990	9.88	5.46	8.04	0.48	23.86	62.1	38.42	52.57
1991	12.80	8.47	9.59	0.80	31.66	71.9	44.03	79.59
1992	21.09	12.18	12.40	1.03	46.70	85.0	54.94	114.86

Notes: The following adjustments have been made:
Original township figures in Table 10.6 are multiplied by 0.79 (MOFERT, *Almanac of China's Foreign Economic Relations and Trade, 1992/3*, China Advertising Pty Ltd, Hong Kong, 1993).
Original figures for foreign-invested firms in Table 10.6 are multiplied by 0.7 (*International Business*, 9 February 1993).
Original figures in Table 10.6 for economic and technology development zones are multiplied by 0.7 (Dan, Jun, 'Woguo jingji jishu kaifaqu de fazhan ji duice', *Economic Discussions*, (*Wingji Zongsheng*), 1993, 3:40–2).
[a] Figures exclude Hainan for 1985–89.
Sources: As for Table 10.6.

facing largely market-determined prices at the margin. This is particularly true for rural township enterprises, foreign-invested firms and special economic zones. It is therefore not surprising that these sectors have responded most rapidly to economic reforms, given that township enterprises and foreign-invested firms have always, by and large, been accountable for their profits and losses.

A time of major change

Due to the reforms of the past 15 years, the Chinese economy is now largely operating in a market-determined environment, despite some continuing central planning and extensive distortions in both commodity and factor markets. As prices for 80 per cent of output are established freely, markets have become the dominant determinant of resource allocation. With the burgeoning of collective, private and foreign-invested firms throughout the country, labour markets are also becoming increasingly flexible.

Reforms have brought fundamental changes to the trade sector. Increasing foreign exchange retention, the introduction and expansion of secondary foreign exchange markets, devaluations of the renminbi, tax rebates for exports and reductions in trade barriers have all helped to put Chinese exporting enterprises in an unprecedented favourable position. The rising number of enterprises engaging in direct international trade and growth of foreign investment and township enterprises have introduced increasingly vigorous competition.

China's trade pattern has thus been shifting in the direction of its comparative advantage. This has involved rapid growth of labour-intensive manufactured exports in the past 15 years. Perhaps more importantly, reforms have led to a macroeconomic environment where the anti-export bias from the central planning era is diminishing and the real effective exchange rate of the renminbi has depreciated almost continuously. This seems to have led to sustained growth of exports, despite considerable inflation and reductions in, and then the removal of, export subsidies.

The more market-oriented areas of the economy, namely, township enterprises, foreign-invested firms and special economic zones, have been able to take advantage of these developments more fully than have state enterprises, and have become the driving force behind China's strong export growth in recent years. The change towards labour-intensive manufactured products also seems to have occurred as a result of the rapid expansion of exports from these areas.

There is still much room for increased efficiency in the export sector through further reforms. Despite resource allocation being primarily by market forces, the remaining distortions are severe in the form of state plans, dual and multiple prices (until early 1994 including multiple exchange rates), quantitative restrictions, variable levels of taxes, fragmentation of the economy and state monopoly. Not only have these distortions led to sub-optimal export patterns at the margin, but they have also created massive rent-seeking activities and consequent corruption of government officials.

Further sustained export growth will largely depend on the performance of non-state enterprises, which in turn depends on macroeconomic stability. Instability in the macroeconomy will not only create booms and busts, but will also impede further microeconomic reforms, vital to increasing overall economic efficiency, as well as the performance of the trade sector. To this end, it seems essential that fundamental reforms occur in the more rigid parts of the economy, namely, the financial sector, state enterprises and the state labour sector.

Notes to Chapter 10

The author wishes to thank David Wall, Xiaoguang Zhang, Will Martin, Dong Fureng, Yiping Huang, Guonan Ma and Weiguo Lu for their comments on this chapter.

11

Commodity Terms of Trade and Instability

RON DUNCAN

> It would thus appear reasonable to conclude that there is
> little basis in casual empiricism or crude cuts of the statis-
> tics to indicate that instability in export earnings, prices,
> or quantities have *prima facie* been a problem. Clearly,
> more careful theoretical work will be necessary if under-
> standing of the instability phenomenon is to increase
> (Krueger 1984b:565).

There has been a large amount of analysis dealing with the
effects of terms of trade and export revenue instability on the
growth of developing economies. However, cross-country
studies have given inconclusive results. Some find that export
instability appears to have negative effects on growth (Coppock
1962; Glezakos 1973; Lancieri 1978). Others conclude that instability is a positive factor (Knudsen and Parnes 1975; Lim 1980;
Yotopoulos and Nugent 1976). It is, of course, arguable that
these studies are not contradictory: export earnings instability
may have positive effects on savings rates (in line with the permanent income hypothesis) or negative effects on growth if the
instability leads to misallocation or waste of resources. Many
other cross-country studies have been unable to come to a conclusion one way or the other about the effects of export instability on growth (Kenen and Voivodas 1972; MacBean 1966;
Maizels 1968; Moran 1983; Tan 1983; Voivodas 1974). Specific
general-equilibrium country studies which have developed
detailed structural models (linking analysis of the macroeconomy with specific commodity sectors and international
commodity markets) have also been carried out (Adams and
Behrman 1982; Lasaga 1981; Lim 1974; Obidegwu and Nziramasanga 1981; Priovolos 1981; Reynolds 1963; Stein 1977). Nevertheless, these studies do not arrive at a firm and general

conclusion regarding the effects of export earnings instability on economic growth.

There could be many reasons why these studies have failed to agree on the effects of export earnings instability on growth. These include measurement problems (for example, choice of an appropriate index of instability), sampling problems (for example, choice of countries or time interval), inadequate structural formulations (for example, differentiation among countries according to economic structures), and so on. An assumption of uniformity in the responses to export earnings instability does seem unwarranted, however.

Recent work by McCarthy and Dhareshwar (1992) showed that the impact of adverse external shocks (including terms of trade, interest rate and global demand shocks) on developing economies, and of terms of trade shocks in particular, is large: commonly equivalent to 10 per cent or more of gross domestic product (GDP). McCarthy and Dhareshwar also examined how countries have responded to these external shocks. They noted what they believed was a tendency for favourable shocks to be regarded as permanent and for unfavourable shocks to be seen as temporary. They found that the size and impact of the shock depended on factors such as degree of openness, export/import composition and size of external debt. The adjustments undertaken varied considerably, with some countries relying on additional external financing, others giving more emphasis to export promotion and others emphasising import substitution. They raised questions as to the impact of the various instruments and whether there is a correct response to shocks.

A related, microeconomic issue, which has also been the subject of long debate, is the question of whether farmers in developing economies misspend commodity boom incomes. Deaton (1992) has summarised this debate. Of more recent research interest have been the questions of whether governments misspend the proceeds of commodity booms, and the extent of benefits and costs ensuing from developing economy governments' attempts to stabilise farmers' incomes. Studies by Bevan, Collier and Gunning (1989), Cuddington (1989), Davis (1983), Rajaram (1985) and Tanzi (1986) found that most of the developing economies they analysed responded to commodity booms by undertaking unsustainable expenditure programs. An exception described by Cuddington was Cameroon. Recent papers by Hill (1991) and Cuddington and Hill (1992) find that the government of Botswana appears to have behaved sensibly by saving unexpected increases in export earnings from its diamond sector, its major export earner.

The inconclusiveness about whether instability has an adverse effect on growth seems to have resulted in a tentativeness on the part of economists towards taking a position on what course developing economies should follow with regard to terms of trade or export revenue instability. Of those bold enough to offer specific policy advice, such as Balassa (1988), Cuddington (1989) and Tanzi (1986), this has usually been premised on the permanent income hypothesis. In reaction to temporary windfalls from commodity price increases which do not change the country's permanent income, their recommendation is to smooth consumption by using the windfall to pay off foreign debt, purchase foreign assets (to be held as a buffer fund), or invest domestically, providing the investment spending is limited to the windfall.

However, recently, improved understanding of the behaviour of primary commodity prices in international markets has raised serious doubts about this set of recommendations. The results of recent research on commodity prices and related implications for policy advice about volatility in the terms of trade are outlined here. In particular, the implications for policy advice of financial openness and the use of financial markets for commodity risk management purposes are explored. In addition some other issues are considered. For example, is there a tendency to regard price shocks as permanent or temporary, and is the response similar in the public and private sectors? And, is there a tendency to regard positive shocks as permanent and negative shocks as temporary?

Primary commodity price behaviour and implications for policy

From the recent work of Cuddington and Urzúa (1989), Deaton (1992), Deaton and Laroque (1992), Gersovitz and Paxson (1990), Gilbert (1983), Trivedi (1989, 1992), Williams and Wright (1991), and Wright and Williams (1990), understanding of the behaviour of primary commodity price series measured in real

terms is now considerably improved. The important characteristics can be summarised as follows:

- shocks are persistent in the short run (often lasting several
  years), that is, prices behave like random walk series in the
  short to medium term;
- over the very long run, real prices are strongly mean-reverting[1]; and
- positive (increases in prices) shocks are more frequent and
  larger than negative shocks, a phenomenon which appears to
  be due to the fact that storage cannot be negative. The large
  increases in prices occur when stocks are low and there is an
  adverse supply or positive demand shock.

Less well established is that instability in food commodity
prices arises mostly from supply shocks (weather, disease),
whereas shocks in raw material prices (except for energy)
derive mostly from demand shocks.

As Deaton (1992) has argued, these characteristics have
strong implications for policy instruments such as price stabilisation schemes.

Given the actual behaviour of commodity prices, which are
very strongly autocorrelated at high frequencies and revert to
their means only slowly, it is quixotic to recommend any simple
permanent income rule or compensation scheme as in Balassa
(1988). The swings are too large, too sustained and too uncertain. The accumulation of reserves over booms would be very
large, very expensive and almost certainly politically infeasible
(Deaton 1992:14).

Deaton's recommendation for policy is a rather sobering one:

> To the extent that the sharp upward spikes in commodity
> prices are driven by clearly stationary shocks, such as
> abnormal weather conditions or industrial disputes, it
> makes sense to try to smooth them out, not to adjust con-
> sumption and investment, and to accumulate the proceeds
> in a compensation fund, the balance of which can be used
> to fund consumption and investment over the long run. It
> is in this case that the permanent income rule is appropri-
> ate. However, except in such cases ... price changes should
> be treated as permanent, and fundamental adjustments
> made. Although it is typically the case that prices will
> eventually revert to their long-run norms, the process is so
> long and so uncertain that attempts to ignore fluctuations

by holding consumption and investment on their long-run growth paths are doomed to fail (Deaton 1992:16).

But as Deaton warns, and as experience has shown over and over, it is rarely obvious that a price run-up or fall will be temporary. As Deaton points out, even the 1976–79 coffee price boom, which was due to a severe frost in Brazil, was perceived as long-lived and resulted in large-scale plantings in many countries. Thus, adherence to Deaton's recommendation means that all shocks must be regarded as permanent. This would be certain to lead to unsustainable consumption and investment levels. The policy choice, however, is not as restricted as these essentially opposing sets of recommendations imply.

The World Bank has recently given attention to encouraging developing economies to reduce their exposure to commodity price uncertainty by transferring it externally through the use of financial markets (futures, options, swaps), and in this way stabilising (or, rather, smoothing out) the revenue streams of both producers and governments (which often rely heavily on export taxation) (Claessens and Duncan 1993). The possibility of using such instruments offers the opportunity of giving less pessimistic advice than does Deaton. Moreover, if such instruments are used, the very difficult task of deciding whether a price movement is permanent or transitory becomes unnecessary and the adjustment to price shocks less costly.

Wright and Williams (1990) showed that even using a simple uncorrelated price mechanism with a stationary mean, the likelihood of generating a sequence of observations which would lead to the depletion of funds in a stabilisation scheme was significant. Research by Larson and Coleman (1991) showed that with a price series following a log-normal random walk (stochastic mean) or one with a mixed stochastic-deterministic price process (mean-reverting) the use of simple futures or options hedging strategies can greatly reduce the variability of stabilisation fund revenues and payments, and thus extend the life of the stabilisation scheme, but not offer immortality. Claessens and Varangis (1993) demonstrated that use of options hedging would perform better than an oil stabilisation fund in Venezuela in removing short-period oil price volatility and at lower cost. Given the existence of 'fat tails' in the oil price distribution (as in many commodity prices), use of market instruments which trade away the spikes, such as options, appear to be much more cost-effective than holding low-yielding assets in reserves. They argue, however, that an oil stabilisation fund could be complementary in smoothing the long-run stream of government revenues (oil revenues comprise over 80 per cent of government revenues in Venezuela).[2] Moreover, the hedging program would likely lengthen the life of the, necessarily smaller, stabilisation fund.

Given the often-high volatility of government revenues in developing economies, due to their dependence on commodity taxes, reducing exposure to this risk should be a major concern.[3] The work cited above shows that this is possible where futures markets exist.[4] The risk management activity can be carried out either by the government or by the commodity producer (as with crude oil or minerals producers) in a manner which will hedge the share of revenues going to the government (Claessens and Coleman 1991).

Given, however, that the government makes no attempt to stabilise or smooth international prices on behalf of producers or consumers, or does so poorly, the effectiveness of the private sector's behaviour depends on their response to price shocks and on their ability to manage their price risk exposure. The carrying out of this latter activity depends heavily on the absence of government-imposed wedges between international and domestic prices and on the absence of impediments to international currency movements (Coleman and Jones 1993; Duncan 1992).

Are terms of trade shocks seen as permanent or temporary?

Bevan, Collier and Gunning (1987) showed that in Kenya, which has negligible export taxes on coffee, private coffee farmers saved about two-thirds of the windfall from the 1976–79 coffee price boom. This indicates, consistent with the permanent income hypothesis, that they regarded the sharp price increase as transitory. In a later paper Bevan, Collier and Gunning (1989) show that the Kenyan government had low investment rates on the share of the windfall that it received. While the government did not share directly in the windfall (through export taxes), it did benefit indirectly through increases in sales taxes and import taxes (and thus eventually appropriated nearly 65 per cent of the windfall, Bevan, Collier and Gunning 1989:365). The government appears to have regarded the price rise as permanent. As Bevan, Collier and Gunning (1989:364) report: '... the government did not merely spend its windfall income but transformed a temporary increase in expenditures into a permanent (or at least long-lived) one'.

Bevan, Collier and Gunning (1989) conclude that if the Kenyan government had appropriated the windfall directly through export taxes, and hence stabilised farmers' incomes, but had acted similarly in its expenditures, the overall result would have been even more disastrous. This touches on the question of whether governments should stabilise producers' revenues through export taxes or fixed producer prices set by government marketing boards if they cannot be trusted to make appropriate savings and investment decisions in situations of unstable prices.

Kenya is unusual in that most other developing economy governments have directly appropriated a large share of the price booms of their most important export commodities through progressive export taxes or public ownership. But, as shown by Cuddington (1989), Davis (1983), Rajaram (1985) and Tanzi (1986), the Kenyan government expenditure response is not unique. The only exceptions which these authors found of sound government policies, as defined by the permanent income hypothesis, were Botswana and Cameroon (see above). Thus, it is clear that the proper comparison for what the private sector does or may do is what governments actually do in situations of unstable prices and revenues and it appears from these studies that in the main they do not follow sound policies in response to commodity price shocks.

Deaton (1992) suggested, however, that government response may not be as poor as earlier research had found. He carries out a test of the response to commodity price shocks in national income, consumption, investment, government expenditure and net exports in 35 African countries. His results lead to the tentative conclusion that:

> Positive shocks to export prices appear to generate a good deal of economic growth, and they do it by stimulating what appears to be productive investment. Although there

is indeed evidence of an asymmetric response, with investment and (ultimately) GDP expanding more in response
to price increases than they decline in response to price
falls, and although this asymmetry is consistent with the
common observation that governments spend in response
to booms but cannot contract during slumps, the expansionary phase still has the positive effects listed above
(Deaton 1992:33).

These results held up when the countries were split into high
and low export-taxers, which supports the idea that governments act as sensibly as the private sector. There was, however,
a difference between mineral (usually enclave) and non-mineral
(usually small farmer) activities. Movements in prices of minerals, including crude oil, had little effect on output. This is
consistent with the notion that governments consume most dis-
cretionary income from mineral production.

To test whether terms of trade shocks are regarded as permanent or transitory, and whether responses differ between the
private and public sectors, the analytical framework of Hall's
(1978) life-cycle, permanent income, hypothesis is adopted. This
hypothesis states that individuals select a level of consumption
in each period based on expected lifetime income, rather than
on current income. Thus, current consumption is best forecast
by lagged consumption (that is, it follows a random walk with
time-varying drift) while savings are a function of income in
each period. According to the permanent income hypothesis,
the appropriate response to an export revenue shock depends
upon its effects on permanent income. If the shock is temporary, so that the change in permanent income is small, the
appropriate response to a boom is seen as saving a large share
of the increased income, or borrowing to maintain consumption
during a fall in income.

Hall analysed US consumption behaviour using unit root tests
of consumption measured in levels and logarithms. Because of the
low power of unit root tests, and because most macroeconomic
variables are found to be non-stationary, Hall's test tends to be
biased towards accepting the permanent income hypothesis.

An alternative test of the permanent income hypothesis when
both consumption and income are non-stationary uses the Euler
equation:

$$\Delta c_t = k + \theta \Delta y_t + \varepsilon_t$$

where c_t is consumption, k is a constant term, y_t is income and ε_t is white noise. The permanent income hypothesis holds when θ is found to be not statistically different from zero. The specification of the test equations given below follows Flavin (1981), who redefined Δy_t as the innovations in income (that is, the unexpected deviations from its long-run univariate time series process), and Cuddington and Hill (1992) who included lagged Δy_t in the equation:

$$\Delta c_t = k + \theta_0 \Delta y_t + \theta_1 \Delta y_{t-1} + \theta_2 \Delta y_{t-2} + \varepsilon_t$$

Inclusion of lags on the income (or, in this case, export revenue) innovation appears to be desirable to avoid a possible source of bias towards accepting the permanent income hypothesis. A strong form of the permanent income hypothesis holds when θ_0, θ_1 and θ_2 are jointly found to be not statistically different from zero. The long-run univariate time series process of Δy_t is assumed to be AR(3).

Instead of looking at instability in income, instability in export revenue, an important part of income in most developing economies, and one which can be treated as largely exogenous, is considered (see Table 11.1 for export revenues of developing economies expressed as a share of GDP on average over the period 1971–91). The set of 42 developing economies included in the analysis is shown in Table 11.1. As well as showing export revenues as a share of GDP, Table 11.1 lists these economies' most important export commodity and the share of export revenue this commodity earned in 1985. To see the importance which the main exporting commodity and petroleum or petroleum product imports play in the movement of the oil-importing countries' (those whose main export is not crude oil) terms of trade, each oil-importing country's terms of trade was regressed against the international price of the main export commodity and the international price of petroleum. As can be seen from the R^2 measures in column five of Table 11.1, these two prices explain a large part of the movement in the terms of trade in all but two cases. In the case of Equatorial Guinea, cocoa exports are almost as important as timber, and in Mauritius the importance of sugar has declined substantially as manufactured exports have grown rapidly.

For the crude oil exporters, the crude oil price alone explains a large part of variability in terms of trade, except for Congo, Mexico and Syria. The main reason for the low R^2 for these

Table 11.1: Developing economies' major commodity exports

	Share of exports in GDP (1971–91) (%)	Main export commodity	Main export as share of total exports in 1985 (%)	R² for main export in terms of trade (1965–91)ᵃ	Volatility of export revenues (1970–92)ᵇ
Algeria	26.1	Crude oil	42.7	0.98	25.9
Benin	24.3	Cotton	37.5	0.84	18.8
Burundi	10.8	Coffee	69.0	0.94	27.3
Chile	24.7	Copper	36.9	0.97	14.9
Colombia	15.5	Coffee	33.8	0.95	10.8
Congo	46.2	Crude oil	72.9	0.01	24.5
Costa Rica	32.8	Coffee (2)	21.3	0.83	9.3
Côte d'Ivoire	37.5	Cocoa	36.1	0.78	14.4
Ethiopia	11.9	Coffee	64.7	0.96	14.1
Equatorial Guinea	38.8	Timber	52.8	0.07	21.0
Fiji	47.0	Sugar	51.9	0.93	10.3
Gabon	54.3	Crude oil	59.5	0.80	24.5
Ghana	13.5	Cocoa	43.7	0.89	30.2
Guyana	64.9	Metal ores	32.6	0.63	19.3
Honduras	29.9	Bananas	46.3	0.67	9.7
Kenya	27.0	Coffee	32.8	0.76	11.4
Kuwait	65.7	Crude oil	53.5	0.99	31.7
Liberia	53.5	Iron ore	31.7	0.92	7.1
Madagascar	14.5	Coffee	32.7	0.72	10.4
Malawi	24.9	Tobacco	67.0	0.81	15.9
Mali	14.9	Cotton	76.5	0.95	13.3
Mauritania	45.4	Iron ore (2)	38.7	0.83	17.1
Mauritius	52.9	Sugar	34.1	0.27	14.9
Mexico	12.1	Crude oil	31.6	0.05	14.6
Nicaragua	28.0	Coffee	43.8	0.66	21.6
Nigeria	21.8	Crude oil	92.9	0.70	34.2
Papua New Guinea	40.4	Metal ores	49.8	0.61	20.6
Paraguay	19.3	Cotton	41.1	0.94	16.9
Rwanda	11.6	Coffee	85.2	0.93	24.8
Saudi Arabia	57.1	Crude oil	70.2	0.99	32.4
Somalia	15.9	Meat	55.3	0.93	27.5
Sri Lanka	27.9	Tea	27.3	0.88	15.8
Sudan	9.8	Cotton	30.9	0.92	19.7
Suriname	51.2	Metal ores	66.5	0.78	12.8

Table 11.1: *continued*

	Share of exports in GDP (1971–91) (%)	Main export commodity	Main export as share of total exports in 1985 (%)	R² for main export in terms of trade (1965–91)ᵃ	Volatility of export revenues (1970–92)ᵇ
Syria	17.9	Crude oil	47.0	0.02	20.1
Tanzania	15.9	Coffee	42.9	0.66	14.4
Togo	46.7	Phosphate rock	49.7	0.81	24.8
Uganda	11.5	Coffee	93.2	0.97	38.9
Uruguay	19.9	Wool	25.7	0.92	9.0
Venezuela	26.0	Metal ores	40.1	0.99	23.3
Zaire	17.3	Copper	37.2	0.90	20.6
Zambia	38.0	Copper	82.9	0.99	24.0

ᵃ For oil-importing countries, i.e., those whose main export is not crude oil, the R^2 is from an equation regressing the international price of the main export commodity and the international price of petroleum on the terms of trade of each country. For oil-exporting countries, the R^2 is from a regression of the international crude oil price on the terms of trade.
ᵇ Volatility is defined as the standard deviation of percentage changes.
2—number two export commodity.
Source: The International Economic Databank, The Australian National University.

countries is the recent development of their oil sectors. If the regression is restricted to the 1974–91 period, the R^2 changes to 0.94, 0.70 and 0.24, respectively.

The volatility of export revenues for these countries for the period 1970–92 is shown in the last column of Table 11.1. The highest volatilities are registered mainly by crude oil exporters, although some coffee exporters also experience high volatilities. In most cases, high volatilities are associated with high export concentrations, although this is not always so, as evidenced by Ethiopia, Fiji, Ghana, Malawi and Mali. This implies that the export portfolio of these countries provides some cross-hedging of prices or that they are smoothing their export revenue stream in some other way.

The volatilities of private and government consumption expenditures for these countries are shown in Table 11.2. It is

Table 11.2: Volatility of consumption expenditures in developing countries, 1970–92

	Volatility of consumption expenditure[a]	
	Private (%)	Government (%)
Algeria	14.4	14.4
Benin	9.5	12.8
Burundi	9.9	13.5
Chile	20.6	22.5
Colombia	8.0	10.9
Congo	18.2	9.9
Costa Rica	17.9	20.9
Côte d'Ivoire	12.1	13.9
Ethiopia	7.7	13.2
Equatorial Guinea	13.7	10.1
Fiji	9.1	12.5
Gabon	19.7	21.7
Ghana	9.8	18.1
Guyana	21.7	28.7
Honduras	9.1	12.9
Kenya	7.3	15.4
Kuwait	12.3	10.4
Liberia	8.7	15.7
Madagascar	12.1	11.9
Malawi	12.0	9.1
Mali	10.4	14.8
Mauritania	13.2	19.4
Mauritius	7.0	9.2
Mexico	18.6	21.4
Nicaragua	29.2	37.6
Nigeria	24.5	33.8
Papua New Guinea	8.3	8.1
Paraguay	15.0	20.6
Rwanda	13.0	24.5
Saudi Arabia	18.7	22.9
Somalia	17.7	51.5
Sri Lanka	13.7	15.1
Sudan	17.3	26.5
Suriname	31.4	14.3
Syria	14.5	22.8
Tanzania	16.6	24.9
Togo	23.1	17.8
Uganda	27.1	54.9
Uruguay	18.3	23.3
Venezuela	17.4	18.9

Table 11.2: *continued*

	Volatility of consumption expenditure[a]	
	Private (%)	Government (%)
Zaire	13.5	20.7
Zambia	26.5	16.1

[a] For definition of volatility see Table 11.1.
Source: The International Economic Databank, The Australian National University.

of interest to note that, for the majority of countries, consumption volatilities are reasonably low, for both private and public consumption, and that private consumption variability is lower than government, but not by much. There are 16 countries where government consumption volatility is much larger than private consumption (greater than 5 percentage points difference) and nearly all are in Africa. There are also cases where private consumption is more variable than government. In some of these cases looked at, however, the quality of the data raises suspicions.

Initial tests on the permanent income hypothesis are reported in Table 11.3. The coefficients on the unexpected change in export revenues in the current period (no lags included in the regression) are shown for private and government consumption.[5] In most countries the coefficient is not significantly different from zero and the permanent income hypothesis cannot be rejected. Where the permanent income hypothesis is rejected, it is usually rejected for both private and government consumption.

In Table 11.4 results are reported from equations which include two lags on the unexpected deviation. Only results for coefficients on the lags which are significant or near to significant are reported. Cases where the permanent income hypothesis is rejected in Table 11.3 are mostly confirmed. Inclusion of the lags, however, does lead to rejection of the permanent income hypothesis for about ten additional countries, in most of these the hypothesis is rejected for government consumption only. According to Table 11.4, there are 13 countries in which the permanent income hypothesis is rejected for private consumption: Chile, Costa Rica, Côte d'Ivoire, Equatorial Guinea, Fiji, Mexico, Nigeria, Paraguay, Somalia, Sri Lanka, Sudan,

Table 11.3: Regression results on test of permanent income hypothesis for impact of unexpected change in export revenue variable on private and government consumption

	Coefficient on unexpected change in export revenue			
	Private consumption		Government consumption	
Algeria	0.14	(1.2)	0.01	(0.11)
Benin	0.09	(0.87)	−0.005	(0.04)
Burundi	0.10	(1.2)	0.09	(0.77)
Chile	0.47	(1.91)	0.55	(2.01)*
Colombia	0.00	(0.00)	−0.07	(0.31)
Congo	−0.04	(0.24)	−0.12	(1.31)
Costa Rica	0.92	(3.01)*	1.05	(2.95)*
Côte d'Ivoire	0.23	(1.64)	0.12	(0.75)
Ethiopia	−0.09	(0.74)	0.41	(2.32)*
Equatorial Guinea	0.10	(0.58)	0.25	(1.69)
Fiji	0.32	(2.37)*	0.59	(2.74)*
Gabon	0.05	(0.26)	0.17	(1.03)
Ghana	−0.02	(0.23)	0.21	(1.88)
Guyana	0.11	(0.43)	0.03	(0.09)
Honduras	0.31	(1.68)	0.24	(0.88)
Kenya	0.08	(0.66)	0.24	(0.84)
Kuwait	0.003	(0.04)	0.07	(0.90)
Liberia	−0.24	(1.13)	0.40	(1.31)
Madagascar	0.21	(1.07)	0.11	(0.58)
Malawi	0.29	(1.90)	−0.03	(0.20)
Mali	0.33	(1.45)	0.39	(1.27)
Mauritania	0.01	(0.06)	0.31	(1.22)
Mauritius	0.28	(3.20)*	0.22	(1.71)
Mexico	0.64	(3.03)*	0.76	(3.20)*
Nigeria	0.36	(2.53)*	0.19	(1.00)
Papua New Guinea	0.18	(1.59)	0.27	(3.04)*
Paraguay	0.42	(2.61)*	0.27	(1.09)
Rwanda	0.15	(1.24)	0.20	(0.92)
Saudi Arabia	−0.08	(0.60)	0.09	(0.65)
Somalia	−0.22	(1.00)	−0.55	(1.15)
Sri Lanka	0.61	(4.86)*	0.46	(2.66)*
Sudan	0.21	(1.27)	0.56	(1.56)
Suriname	−0.36	(0.57)	−0.07	(0.24)
Syria	0.40	(2.80)*	0.56	(3.18)*
Tanzania	0.31	(1.35)	0.36	(1.11)
Togo	−0.47	(2.82)*	−0.09	(0.62)
Uganda	0.67	(6.18)*	0.77	(10.54)*
Uruguay	0.65	(1.83)	0.62	(1.26)
Venezuela	0.06	(0.40)	0.14	(0.91)

Table 11.3: *continued*

	Coefficient on unexpected change in export revenue			
	Private consumption		Government consumption	
Zaire	−0.01	(0.11)	0.09	(0.45)
Zambia	0.16	(0.72)	0.05	(0.34)

Notes: t statistics are shown in brackets.
* indicates significance at the 95% confidence level.

Uganda and Uruguay. There are 18 countries for which the hypothesis is rejected for government consumption, including eight of the above.

How valid are the test results? One means to examine this is to compare them with other investigations. Consider Kenya which has been studied in detail by Bevan, Collier and Gunning (1989) in respect of the response of private and public consumption and savings to the 1976–79 coffee boom. As summarised earlier, they found the private sector to regard the shock as temporary while the government appropriated a large part of the windfall indirectly in later years and spent it as though the shock was seen as permanent. This is consistent with the Kenyan results in Table 11.4. The coefficients on the current and lagged innovation variable for government consumption are significantly different or close to significantly different from zero. The only inconsistency is the significant two-year lagged coefficient on private consumption. It would be of interest to check the results with detailed experiences in other countries. From the information reported in Cuddington (1989) and McCarthy and Dhareshwar (1992), however, it is not possible to do so.

To examine whether there is a different response to booms and busts in export prices and if the response differs between the private and government sectors, the unexplained deviations from the AR(3) process imposed on the export revenue data were split according to whether they were positive (price increases) or negative (price decreases) and the permanent income tests repeated. The results are presented in Table 11.5.

The possible responses can be put into four sets:
• price increases are regarded as permanent while price declines are regarded as transitory (this is claimed to be common behaviour);

Table 11.4: Regression results on tests of permanent income hypothesis on
private and government consumption for lagged changes in
export revenues

		Coefficients on unexpected changes in export revenues						F test
		t		t − 1		t − 2		
Algeria	(p)	0.03	(0.15)					0.15
	(g)	−0.03	(0.17)					0.07
Benin	(p)	0.17	(1.26)					0.79
	(g)	0.006	(0.03)					0.03
Burundi	(p)	0.09	(0.86)					0.32
	(g)	0.01	(0.05)					0.68
Chile	(p)	0.68	(2.49)*	0.48	(1.96)*			2.08
	(g)	0.44	(1.48)	0.42	(1.59)			5.60
Colombia	(p)	−0.03	(0.14)					0.04
	(g)	−0.10	(0.35)					0.29
Congo	(p)	0.18	(1.38)					0.63
	(g)	−0.08	(0.77)					1.23
Costa Rica	(p)	1.50	(2.78)*					1.82
	(g)	1.80	(2.91)*					2.04
Côte d'Ivoire	(p)	0.38	(2.05)*	0.27	(1.44)	0.50	(2.51)*	1.52
	(g)	0.10	(0.44)			0.58	(2.30)*	1.41
Ethiopia	(p)	−0.05	(0.19)					0.48
	(g)	0.59	(2.50)*					0.23
Equatorial	(p)	1.10	(3.07)*	−0.55	(2.17)*			3.23
Guinea	(g)	0.46	(2.25)*	−0.23	(1.60)			4.11
Fiji	(p)	0.21	(1.29)	0.51	(3.18)*	0.29	(1.73)	13.70
	(g)	0.62	(1.78)					0.97
Gabon	(p)	0.13	(0.73)					4.77
	(g)	0.18	(0.85)	0.48	(2.13)*			2.41
Ghana	(p)	0.05	(0.70)					0.34
	(g)	0.30	(2.24)*	0.24	(1.82)			4.28
Guyana	(p)	0.07	(0.17)					0.10
	(g)	−0.13	(0.13)	0.94	(2.21)*	−0.59	(1.52)	1.65
Honduras	(p)	0.34	(1.25)					0.73
	(g)	0.65	(1.82)	0.53	(1.44)			1.96
Kenya	(p)	0.17	(1.21)			0.54	(3.16)*	0.16
	(g)	0.30	(1.87)	0.29	(1.83)	0.39	(1.97)*	1.07
Liberia	(p)	0.66	(1.23)					1.39
	(g)	2.34	(3.65)*					2.52
Madagascar	(p)	0.38	(0.99)					0.80
	(g)	0.57	(1.78)					1.06
Malawi	(p)	0.25	(1.49)					1.38
	(g)	−0.02	(0.10)					0.82
Mali	(p)	0.36	(1.53)					0.45
	(g)	0.56	(2.11)*					3.28

Table 11.4: *continued*

		Coefficients on unexpected changes in export revenues			F test
		t	t − 1	t − 2	
Mauritania	(p)	0.07 (0.27)			3.49
	(g)	0.11 (0.25)			0.83
Mauritius	(p)	0.09 (0.37)			3.91
	(g)	−0.06 (0.17)			2.11
Mexico	(p)	0.79 (4.10)*	0.51 (2.70)*	−0.50 (2.55)*	2.68
	(g)	0.94 (3.98)*	0.58 (2.48)*	−0.42 (1.73)	2.75
Nigeria	(p)	0.33 (1.78)			2.92
	(g)	0.10 (0.43)			2.24
Papua New	(p)	0.42 (1.28)			2.05
Guinea	(g)	0.32 (1.22)		0.50 (1.80)	1.74
Paraguay	(p)	0.42 (1.95)	0.55 (2.27)*	0.76 (2.86)*	0.56
	(g)	0.38 (1.13)	0.98 (2.60)*		0.99
Rwanda	(p)	·0.09 (0.66)			0.63
	(g)	−0.20 (0.88)			0.21
Somalia	(p)	−0.35 (2.63)*			0.33
	(g)	−0.90 (1.90)	2.86 (3.71)*		12.07
Sri Lanka	(p)	0.72 (4.37)*			9.54
	(g)	0.58 (2.66)*			2.52
Sudan	(p)	0.18 (0.98)	0.76 (3.56)*		2.69
	(g)	0.56 (1.32)			0.75
Syria	(p)	0.20 (1.17)	0.33 (1.79)		4.14
	(g)	0.42 (1.82)	0.55 (2.25)*	0.97 (2.34)*	4.28
Tanzania	(p)	0.30 (0.87)			0.53
	(g)	0.54 (1.16)			0.65
Togo	(p)	−0.22 (0.90)			6.98
	(g)	0.42 (2.72)*	0.69 (4.36)*	0.26 (1.96)*	1.93
Uganda	(p)	0.80 (4.36)*			7.27
	(g)	0.80 (12.19)*	−0.24 (3.48)*	0.18 (2.27)*	6.39
Uruguay	(p)	0.59 (1.33)	1.17 (2.96)*		4.90
	(g)	0.80 (1.62)	1.35 (3.06)*		5.89
Venezuela	(p)	0.08 (0.30)			0.47
	(g)	0.14 (0.46)			0.71
Zaire	(p)	−0.04 (0.13)			0.53
	(g)	−0.46 (0.94)			0.10
Zambia	(p)	0.55 (1.19)			0.93
	(g)	0.27 (1.11)			0.24

Notes: t statistics are shown in the brackets.
p prefers to private consumption.
g refers to government consumption.
* indicates significance at the 95% confidence level.

Table 11.5: Results on test of asymmetric response to export revenue shocks

	Coefficient on unexpected changes in export revenue			
	+ inc. shock		− inc. shock	
	Private	Government	Private	Government
Algeria	0.05 (0.22)	−0.34 (0.96)	0.20 (0.90)	−0.25 (1.11)
Benin	0.03 (0.19)	−0.16 (0.81)	0.05 (0.13)	0.08 (0.23)
Burundi	−0.13 (0.28)	−0.53 (1.72)	0.50 (3.61)*	−0.33 (0.78)
Chile	0.34 (0.57)	0.87 (1.58)	0.74 (1.02)	1.13 (1.45)
Colombia	0.18 (0.40)	−0.22 (0.41)	−0.27 (0.86)	−0.11 (0.21)
Congo	−0.18 (0.55)	−0.10 (0.52)	0.38 (0.77)	−0.004 (0.02)
Costa Rica	0.75 (2.48)*	1.10 (2.11)*	5.91 (3.24)*	6.31 (3.02)*
Côte d'Ivoire	0.08 (0.25)	0.15 (0.52)	1.53 (2.12)*	0.19 (0.18)
Equatorial Guinea	1.33 (2.45)*	0.62 (1.34)	0.37 (0.75)	−0.07 (0.29)
Ethiopia	−0.05 (0.15)	0.20 (0.44)	−0.12 (0.32)	0.10 (0.23)
Fiji	0.75 (1.06)	1.47 (1.90)	−0.02 (0.04)	0.74 (0.93)
Gabon	−0.22 (0.45)	−0.18 (0.48)	−0.30 (0.86)	−0.03 (0.05)
Ghana	0.13 (0.66)	0.50 (1.64)	−0.21 (1.30)	0.23 (0.82)
Guyana	0.53 (0.71)	0.51 (0.50)	0.13 (0.19)	0.12 (0.14)
Honduras	0.42 (1.41)	0.92 (1.64)	−0.84 (1.18)	−0.44 (0.46)
Kenya	0.12 (0.63)	0.39 (1.48)	−0.87 (1.94)	−0.65 (1.32)
Liberia	0.87 (1.37)	1.65 (1.79)	0.41 (0.61)	1.74 (1.58)
Madagascar	−0.43 (0.40)	0.83 (0.94)	0.34 (0.63)	0.27 (0.51)
Malawi	0.25 (1.18)	0.13 (0.65)	0.96 (2.82)*	−0.36 (0.74)

Mali	-0.32	(0.74)	0.11	(0.14)	0.44	(0.83)	0.50	(0.75)
Mauritania	-0.04	(0.16)	0.51	(0.91)	-0.39	(0.45)	-1.17	(1.94)
Mauritius	0.31	(2.74)*	0.42	(2.44)*	0.88	(1.45)	0.35	(0.53)*
Mexico	0.98	(2.12)*	1.12	(2.10)	1.68	(17.20)*	1.81	(3.87)*
Nicaragua	1.34	(5.94)*	0.65	(3.47)*	1.23	(1.33)	1.61	(1.39)
Nigeria	0.30	(1.74)	0.19	(0.55)	0.77	(1.48)	0.43	(0.65)
Papua New Guinea	0.04	(0.51)	0.33	(3.38)*	0.19	(0.48)	0.08	(0.27)
Paraguay	0.05	(0.15)	0.53	(1.12)	0.03	(0.03)	-0.89	(0.62)
Rwanda	0.04	(0.16)	0.14	(0.23)	-0.59	(1.35)	-0.67	(0.93)
Somalia	-0.14	(0.11)	7.19	(1.60)	-0.09	(0.12)	0.14	(0.13)
Sri Lanka	0.14	(0.66)	0.26	(0.78)	0.98	(3.90)*	0.86	(1.83)
Sudan	-0.32	(0.62)	1.06	(1.72)	0.20	(0.47)	0.67	(1.05)
Syria	-0.10	(0.34)	0.28	(0.68)	0.68	(2.86)*	1.04	(1.69)
Tanzania	-0.59	(1.08)	-0.39	(0.26)	0.66	(1.17)	0.47	(0.64)
Togo	-0.83	(4.05)*	-0.22	(1.46)	-0.96	(2.20)*	-0.82	(1.55)
Uganda	2.59	(11.02)*	4.20	(1.01)	0.88	(8.05)*	0.76	(4.25)*
Uruguay	1.22	(1.24)	1.68	(1.28)	0.58	(0.70)	0.17	(0.22)
Venezuela	0.002	(0.005)	0.08	(0.17)	0.35	(0.79)	0.30	(0.66)
Zaire	0.08	(0.14)	0.55	(0.52)	-0.12	(0.51)	-0.11	(0.47)
Zambia	0.49	(0.54)	0.81	(2.14)*	0.05	(0.08)	-0.16	(0.54)

Notes: t statistics are in the brackets.

The + inc. shocks are the positive residuals from the AR(3) process on the export revenue series.

The − inc. shocks are the negative residuals from the AR(3) process on the export revenue series.

- price increases and decreases are believed to be permanent;
- increases are believed to be transitory while declines are believed to be permanent (a pessimistic, risk-averse strategy); and
- increases and decreases are believed to be transitory.

The results in Table 11.5 are generally consistent with those in Table 11.4, with most coefficients insignificant, indicating consistency with the permanent income hypothesis (that is, positive and negative shocks are regarded as transitory). The cases where the permanent income hypothesis is rejected are also generally consistent with the results reported in Table 11.4. These are cases which fall into each of the first three categories listed above.

- In the first category, increases are permanent while declines are temporary (the optimistic case). The private sectors in Equatorial Guinea, Fiji and Liberia follow this behaviour, while there are eight governments which do so, Ghana, Honduras, Kenya, Mauritius, Papua New Guinea, Somalia, Sudan and Zambia.
- The tendency to regard all shocks as permanent is shared by the private sectors in Costa Rica, Mauritius, Mexico, Nicaragua, Nigeria and Uganda, as well as by the government sectors in Chile, Costa Rica, Liberia, Mexico and Nicaragua.
- Those taking the pessimistic view that price increases are transitory while price declines are permanent include the private sectors in Benin, Côte d'Ivoire, Malawi, Sri Lanka and Syria, and by the government sectors of Sri Lanka, Syria and Uganda.

The role of financial markets

Improved understanding of the process underlying the behaviour of primary commodity prices has shown, in stark relief, the uncertainty about whether commodity price movements are temporary or permanent. The recommendation that the private and public sectors should follow a policy dictated by the permanent income hypothesis (i.e., not adjusting consumption to the temporary shocks but using buffer funds to smooth consumption) is based on the assumption that whether a shock is temporary or permanent is known at the time. Deaton (1992) and others have shown that this is seldom likely to be the case.

Yet Deaton's recommendation of adjusting consumption to the shocks seems to put too little weight on the mean-reversion properties of these series. Policy advice should be shifted to a more practical basis; to acknowledge that scope exists in financial markets for smoothing consumption streams, whether private or government. This is not to say that adjustments do not have to be made to sustained or permanent shifts in commodity prices, but that financial markets offer the opportunity to smooth this transition and to do so without decisions having to be made on the basis of whether the price shock is temporary or permanent. The opportunity to use financial markets depends very much on the financial openness of the economy.

The evidence from the cross-country analysis is that private and government consumption behaviour is much more consistent with the permanent income hypothesis than might be believed from earlier studies which may have concentrated more on some of the exceptions. This may mean that there is some knowledge as to whether shocks are temporary or permanent and this is acted upon appropriately; or that hedging mechanisms are used to smooth, without the need to know the nature of the shocks. The latter explanation is preferred. The mechanisms used for such smoothing are not known, but it is suspected that the financial openness of an economy has a bearing on the effectiveness and cost of smoothing activity. The World Bank's program of assistance to developing economies on the use of financial markets for hedging commodity price risks provides evidence that many countries have substantial barriers against the use of futures markets and the international transfer of funds (Duncan 1992).

The regression results show, however, that of this group of developing economies there is a substantial number (13) in which the private sector is treating temporary shocks as permanent and an even larger number (18) in which the government is acting in this manner. Further, there is evidence of different behaviour towards temporary price increases and decreases by both private and public sectors. This points to the need for education about the behaviour of commodity prices in international markets; an endeavour which can be undertaken with more confidence now that understanding of this subject has improved.

To conclude, it may well be that more financially open economies have less adjusting to do in response to external shocks, in the sense that the price shocks are hedged. If financial liberalisation is necessary for the full range of hedging instruments to be available, it is putting the private sector at a disadvantage (relative to operating in other countries) if financial liberalisation is not carried out in conjunction with the opening up of the trading sector. In fact, lack of financial openness may explain some poor supply responses to trade sector liberalisation. Financial openness would also appear to reduce the need for government stabilisation mechanisms and the many problems associated with them, including the direction of accumulated funds to other purposes. For these various reasons, there appears to be a good case for pushing harder for faster financial liberalisation.

Notes to Chapter 11

[1] As Deaton (1992) points out, this finding is contrary to widespread results showing that real commodity prices are I(1). Deaton argues that these results have arisen because of the low power of the unit-root tests. A similar challenge to the existence of unit roots in real GNP has recently been published (Rudebusch 1993).

[2] It has been suggested that the establishment of such stabilisation funds provides positive externalities, such as an increase in confidence and a reduction in costs of resource adjustment (Gilbert 1992; Cuddington 1989). These do not appear, however, to be sufficient reasons to establish stabilisation funds when the private sector and government can hedge.

[3] Tanzi (1986:89) estimates that 'more than 50 per cent of the tax revenue of developing countries may be directly related to the foreign sector'.

[4] Of course, the ability to engage in such *ex ante* smoothing of incomes is limited by the existence of suitable hedging instruments and the length of the horizons over which existing financial instruments (such as futures and options) extend.

[5] The regression equation is $\Delta c_t = k + \theta_0 er_t + \varepsilon_t$ where Δc_t is the difference in logs of annual consumption, and Δer_t is the residual from the AR(3) process on the difference in logs of export revenues.

12

Agricultural Policy: Constraints to Development

KYM ANDERSON

The experience of the world's fastest growing economies this century, Japan and the four newly industrialised economies of Hong Kong, Singapore, South Korea and Taiwan, gives rise to the question of whether a comparative disadvantage in agriculture was a factor in their growth. These economies are all poorly endowed with natural resources and, in particular, have very little arable land per capita. By contrast, among the slowest growing of the more industrialised economies this century have been land-abundant Argentina, Australia and New Zealand, not to mention the slow-growing poorer agrarian economies of Latin America and Sub-Saharan Africa. Indeed, for a sample of 27 countries and country groups spanning the world, the coefficient of correlation between an index of agricultural comparative advantage and the GDP growth rate for 1970–91 was 0.39 (which is statistically significant at the 5 per cent level). The countries and country groups (which together account for all countries of the world other than the non-Asian former Council for Mutual Economic Assistance (COMECON) countries) and the index of comparative advantage used are shown in Figure 12.1.[1]

This discussion explores one aspect of the statistically supported hypothesis that a comparative advantage in agriculture is a constraint on economic growth. Relatively poor growth performance is not due to poor managerial performance of farmers, for countless analyses have shown them to be no less efficient than non-farmers. Nor does it have to do solely with the fact that agricultural relative to industrial terms of trade fluctuate widely around a long-run downward trend, although that fact certainly enters the present story indirectly.[2] Rather, the focus is on the choice of policies affecting the rural sector: if societies systematically demand, and governments supply

Figure 12.1: Relationship between agricultural taxation/protection and a country's per capita income and agricultural comparative advantage, 1980–82[a]

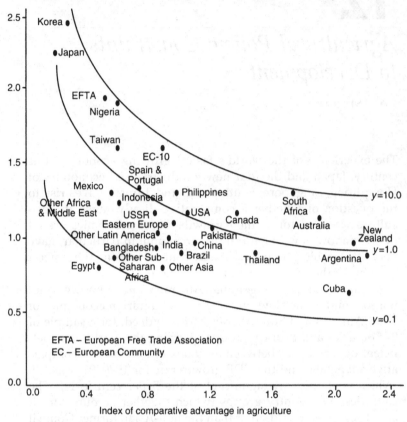

Index of comparative advantage in agriculture

Notes:

[a] The nominal protection coefficient (*npc*) is the weighted average ratio of domestic producer prices to border prices for grains, livestock products and sugar, valued at official exchange rates (and so understating the degree of effective taxation of agriculture in those developing economies with industrial protection and over-valued exchange rates). The index of agricultural comparative advantage (*ca*) is the ratio of what domestic production and consumption would be in the absence of the country's food price distortions (as estimated by the Tyers/Anderson model of world food markets). The fitted curves shown correspond to the indicated ratios of national per capita income to its global average (*y*). The regression equation relating these three variables for the 30 country and country groups shown is:

$$npc = 0.22 - 0.51ca + 0.11y \qquad R^2 = 0.83$$
$$\quad\;\; (8.7) \quad (-10.7) \quad (5.6)$$

Source: Tyers, R. and Anderson, K., 1992, *Disarray in World Food Markets: A Quantitative Assessment*, Cambridge University Press, Cambridge:76–7.

policies which cause agriculture to contribute less than its potential, then it would not be surprising to observe slower growth in those economies with a relatively heavy reliance on agriculture (that is, those with an above-average comparative advantage in agriculture, given their income level).

The discussion begins with an examination of evidence relating to the pattern and extent of intersectoral bias in public policies. The available empirical evidence, which is now considerable, reveals a clear policy bias in low-income economies against the rural sector. It also reveals a gradual weakening in that policy bias as economies develop, but more so in densely populated economies (where for some the bias is now distinctly in favour of farmers) and least so in those economies that retain a comparative advantage in agriculture.

Why this systematic pattern of distortions to incentives occurs is the question then addressed. This is an area in which economists are only beginning to shed some light, so the discussion is necessarily more exploratory and less definitive than that which precedes it. Even so, this new economics of politics, together with the new economics of public finance, does provide insights as to why the above-mentioned intersectoral biases in policies are observed and supports the view of Stigler (1975) that policies 'adopted and followed for a long time, or followed by many different states, could not usefully be described as a mistake'. Public finance considerations contribute partly to the explanation, including as to why among high-income economies it is those with the strongest comparative advantage in agriculture that support farmers least. But mostly the policy bias is the outcome of an unequal distribution of incentives to influence the policy formation process among interested groups. Not only are costs of collective action much greater for rural than urban groups (especially in low-income economies), but there are large inequalities between groups in the net benefits per capita from the particular price-distorting policies adopted. On the one hand, industrialists are highly favoured and farmers are hurt relatively little in low-income agrarian economies where agriculture is effectively taxed; while on the other hand, farmers gain substantially (at little cost to others) in industrialised economies from policies that favour agriculture relative to industry.

The question of what is or could be done to improve on the present situation is addressed. It would be easy to be fatalistic

and answer: 'nothing', but in fact, several important developments are altering patterns of policy bias for the better. Some
suggestions as to how to accelerate that process of reform conclude the chapter.

The pattern and extent of intersectoral policy bias

Nations need to be governed and governments require
resources. Taxation is therefore inevitable. As well as having to
decide who and how much to tax, governments have the power
to decide how to spend those tax revenues and whether to
introduce or change policies that may not directly affect public
finances but nonetheless affect producer, consumer and investor incentives. In aggregate, those public policies help determine the level, growth and distribution of national economic
welfare. They also affect welfare in other nations to the extent
that they influence the international terms of trade.

With the usual assumptions including the absence of externalities, national economic welfare is maximised for a small
open economy if free markets are allowed to operate and non-
distortionary transfers via taxes and subsidies are feasible and
costless to administer (Corden 1974). The relationship between
actual prices and quantities and their free market levels is therefore of concern. One of the reasons governments choose to set
prices at other than free market levels might be that the above
underlying assumptions do not correspond to the real world.

Any policy that causes prices and quantities to be at other
than their free market levels will be said to have introduced a
distortion, for want of a better word. Three sets of such distortions are considered here: distortions to the prices of goods and
services, distortions to the allocation of factors between sectors,
and distortions affecting changes in the available quantity and
quality of productive factors (especially human capital).

Product price distortions

The stock of estimates of the extent to which domestic producer
and consumer prices differ from international prices for farm

products relative to non-farm tradeables has grown substantially during the past decade or so. The broad picture that emerges from those empirical studies is summarised in the following points.

- Developing economies tend to underprice farm products whereas industrialised economies tend to overprice them (Johnson 1991; Tyers and Anderson 1992).
- The underpricing of farm products in developing economies is effectively accentuated by the protection those economies provide their industrial sectors and the overvaluing of their currencies. As Krueger, Schiff and Valdes (1988) show, this indirect taxation of agriculture is typically much more important than the more-easily estimated direct underpricing (Table 12.1).
- Ironically, as economies develop and agriculture's relative importance in terms of output, employment, wealth and votes declines, the price-policy bias against agriculture tends to disappear. This happened for the United Kingdom in the eighteenth century, for several other Western European economies in the nineteenth century, and for Japan at the turn of this century (Anderson 1983; Kindleberger 1975; Lindert 1991; McCalla 1969; Stuart 1992; Tracy 1989). It happened only in recent decades in North America, however, and for Australasia it took until the 1990s.
- These gradual changes away from underpricing farm relative to non-farm products have continued beyond the point of neutrality and are resulting in growing overpricing of farm products in many industrialised economies. For Western Europe the average tariff on food roughly equalled that for manufactures in 1927, at just under 30 per cent, but by the early 1960s it had fallen below 15 per cent for industrial goods and had risen to more than 50 per cent for food (Tyers and Anderson 1992: Table 2.2). This trend continued and, if anything, accelerated in the 1980s, so that currently the nominal rate of (tariff plus non-tariff) protection to Western European agriculture averages around 90 per cent (Table 12.2) while manufacturing tariffs average about 5 per cent.[3] In East Asia the changes have been even faster. Protection from rice imports began as soon as Japan's rice self-sufficiency dropped below 100 per cent at the turn of the century. During the interwar period, the trade policy was extended to include the colonies of Korea and Taiwan, but even that was

Table 12.1: Estimated nominal indirect rates of taxation of agricultural
production due to industrial and exchange rate policies and
nominal direct rates of taxation of non-staple farm products:
selected industrialising economies, 1975–79 and 1980–84

	Indirect rate of taxation		Direct rate of taxation		
	1975–79	1980–84	1975–79	1980–84	
Argentina	16	37	..	..	
Brazil	32	14	..	..	
Chile	−22	7	..	..	
Colombia	25	34	7	5	(coffee)
Côte d'Ivoire	33	26	31	21	(cocoa)
Dominican Rep	18	19	15	32	(coffee)
Egypt	18	14	36	22	(cotton)
Ghana	66	89	−26	−34	(cocoa)
Korea	18	12	..	..	
Malaysia	4	10	25	18	(rubber)
Morocco	12	8	..	..	
Pakistan	48	35	12	7	(cotton)
The Philippines	27	28	11	26	(copra)
Portugal	5	13	..	..	
Sri Lanka	35	31	29	31	(rubber)
Thailand	15	19	..	..	
Turkey	40	35	−2	28	(tobacco)
Zambia	42	57	−1	−7	(tobacco)
Unweighted average	24	27	12	14	

Source: Krueger, A.O., Schiff, M. and Valdes, A., 1988, 'Agricultural incentives
in developing countries: measuring the effects of sectoral and economywide
policies', *World Bank Economic Review*, 2(3):255–72.

able to keep the empire self-sufficient in food only by raising
the tariff equivalent of the import restrictions to more than
50 per cent by the latter 1930s (Table 12.3).[4] After postwar
reconstruction, Japan continued to raise agricultural protection, and Korea and Taiwan, while initially adopting the standard low-income-economy pattern of price distortions
against agriculture, soon followed suit (Table 12.4), as have,
more recently, numerous other middle-income economies
including several in Southeast Asia and now China.

In short, there are strong positive correlations between the
extent of price policy discrimination against farmers and both

Table 12.2: Nominal rates of assistance to agriculture in industrialised economies, 1979–91, (per cent, based on producer subsidy equivalents)[a]

	1979–81	1982–84	1985–87	1988–91
European Union	58[b]	50[b]	85	84
EFTA	. .	113[c]	180	176
Japan	133	170	250	190
United States	19	28	56	33
Canada	32	41	79	48
Australia	10	16	16	13
New Zealand	22	37	28	6
All OECD	41	45	79	73

[a] The border price plus the per unit producer subsidy equivalent, expressed as a percentage of the border price for each commodity, and averaged across commodities using production valued at border prices as weights. The European Union rates include national government assistance as well as that provided by the Common Agricultural Policy.
[b] EC–10.
[c] 1979–85.
EFTA—European Free Trade Association.
OECD—Organisation for Economic Cooperation and Development.
Source: OECD, 1992, *Monitoring and Outlook of Agricultural Policies, Markets and Trade*, OECD, Paris.

the degree of poverty in a country and its agricultural comparative advantage. These are shown graphically and econometrically in Figure 12.1 for 30 countries and country groups spanning the world. The correlation between support for, and comparative disadvantage in, agriculture is also evident among the industrialised economies (Table 12.5). Table 12.5 also suggests that the rate of increase in agricultural price support is correlated positively with the rate of overall economic growth and negatively with the change in agricultural comparative advantage (as indicated in Table 12.5 by the rate of farm relative to non-farm labour productivity growth).

Finally, the gradual change over time in the distortions to domestic relative prices in favour of farmers reduces import demand and increases supplies of farm products for export, thereby putting increasing downward pressure on the international terms of trade facing farmers. In so far as those policies also attempt to stabilise domestic food prices, they add to the

Table 12.3: Rice self-sufficiency and agricultural taxation/protection in Japan, Korea and Taiwan, 1883–1938

	Rice self-sufficiency (%)		Share of Japan's rice consumption from Korea and Taiwan (%)	Nominal rate of rice protection in the Japanese empire (%)	Net direct taxation of Japanese industries as a percentage of sectoral income	
	Japan	Japanese empire			Agric.	Non-agric.
1883–87	101	101	—	. .	22	2
1888–92	101	101	—	. .	16	1
1893–97	99	99	—	. .	12	1
1898–02	97	97	1	. .	12	2
1903–07	91	92	1	9	11	5
1908–12	96	98	2	21	12	6
1913–17	95	99	3	27	13	4
1918–22	91	96	5	14	9	5
1923–27	87	97	9	11	10	5
1928–32	89	99	12	26	7	4
1933–37	83	100	17	45	3	4
1938	84	100	18	84	. .	. .

Source: Anderson, K., Hayami, Y. and George, A., 1986, *The Political Economy of Agricultural Protection: East Asia in International Perspective*, Allen & Unwin, Sydney; Anderson, K. and Tyers, R., 1992, 'Japanese rice policy in the interwar period: some consequences of imperial self-sufficiency', *Japan and the World Economy*, 4(2):103–27.

Table 12.4: Nominal rates of assistance to agriculture in Japan, Korea and Taiwan, 1955–82 (per cent)

	Japan	Korea	Taiwan
1955–59	44	−15	−21
1960–64	68	−5	2
1965–69	87	9	2
1970–74	110	55	17
1975–79	147	129	36
1980–82	151	166	55

Source: Anderson, K., Hayami, Y. and George, A., 1986, *The Political Economy of Agricultural Protection: East Asia in International Perspective*, Allen & Unwin, Sydney.

Table 12.5: Indicators of agricultural assistance, comparative advantage and economic growth in industrialised economies, 1960–87

	Real GDP growth (% pa) (1960–85)	Nominal rate of assistance to agriculture (%)		Relative price of agricultural products domestically as a percentage of relative international price (1961–65 = 100)			Agri-cultural land per capita (ha) 1985	Food self-sufficiency (%) 1985	Growth in value added per employee in agriculture relative to non-agriculture (1960–85)
		1965–75	1975–83	1960–69	1970–79	1980–87			
North America and Australia	2.1	10	15	101	108	99	3.6	125	2.4
Western Europe	2.7	50	55	102	108	119	0.4	106	1.7
Japan, Korea and Taiwan	5.9	90	150	108	135	161	0.05	78	0.9

Source: Anderson, K., Hayami, Y. and George, A., 1986, *The Political Economy of Agricultural Protection: East Asia in International Perspective*, Allen & Unwin, Sydney.

instability of international food prices around their long-run
trend. What proportions of that downward trend and of the
amplitude of the fluctuations around the trend (Figure 12.2) can
be attributed to policy developments in the past is a moot point.
But one recent empirical study suggests that as of 1990, agricultural protection and insulation policies in industrialised
economies alone reduced international food prices by one-fifth
and raised the coefficient of variation of real international food
prices by almost one-half (Tyers and Anderson 1992: Tables 6.9
and 6.14). The long-run downward trend suggests that if a government were to aim to keep the level of real domestic food
prices constant, then the policy actions of other governments
alone would, *ceteris paribus*, require it to raise continually its
level of support for farm prices.

Distortions to the allocation of factors and prices of farm inputs

Perhaps the main factor–market distortion that affects the rural
sector of developing economies has to do with the adoption of
minimum wages above market-clearing levels for many non-
farm jobs. In many developing economies this has resulted in
labour earnings in urban areas several times those in rural
areas, far more than enough to compensate for differences in
costs of living and the amortised cost of moving to an urban
area. While the number of jobs available in the formal urban
sector will be smaller the higher is the institutionally set wage,
this does not necessarily mean more labour is available in the
rural sector at a lower wage: the high wage in the formal sector
attracts migrants from the countryside who join a pool of urban
unemployed waiting hopefully for one of those high-wage jobs.
The net effect can be to reduce available labour in, and output
of, the rural sector and the economy generally, as shown by
numerous variations of the original Harris–Todaro analysis (for
example Corden 1974; Sah and Stiglitz 1992).

It is true that some developing economies provide subsidised
farm credit (and subsidised irrigation and modern farm inputs
such as fertiliser), but to control their fiscal cost such programs
typically involve rationing. At best they provide a small offset
to the negative effect on farm output of the distortions to
product prices, while at the same time adding to the inequality
of incomes in rural areas.[5]

Figure 12.2: Real international food prices, 1900–92 (1977–79 = 100)[a]

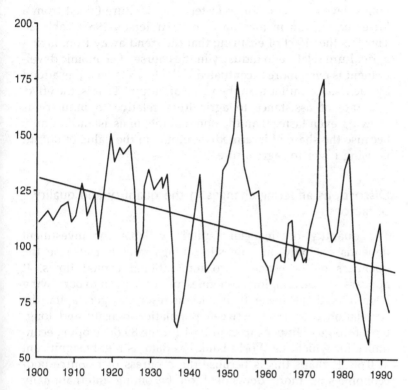

[a] An index of export prices in United States dollars for cereals, meats, dairy
  products and sugar, deflated by the United States producer price index
  (primarily for industrial products), with weights based on the importance of
  each product in global exports, 1977–79.
Source: Author's calculations based mainly on price series made available by
the World Bank's Economic Analysis and Projections Department, see
Grilli, E. R. and Yang, M. C., 1988, 'Primary commodity prices, manufactured
goods prices and the terms of trade of developing countries: what the long run
shows', *World Bank Economic Review,* 2(1):1–48.

Incidentally, the increasing use of purchased inputs as economies develop occurs much faster in agriculture (albeit from a lower base) than in manufacturing (Anderson 1987: Table 2). This has the effect of ensuring that the trend away from taxing agriculture relative to industry in the course of economic development is even more accentuated if the focus is on value added by each sector rather than the value of output. That is, the effective rate of assistance to agriculture relative to industry is growing even faster than the nominal rate of assistance, simply because the share of intermediate inputs in the value of output is rising faster for agriculture.

Distortions affecting changes in the quantity and quality of factors

The quantity of financial capital available for investment depends not only on domestic savings rates but also on the openness of an economy to international capital flows. It appears that developing economies are more open to borrowing from abroad the fewer their natural resources per capita: the correlation coefficient between population density and long-term foreign debt per capita in 1991 for the 85 developing economies for which the World Bank has data, is highly significant at 0.66. Perhaps this is because the progress of resource-poor economies is more dependent on becoming internationally competitive in manufacturing, and success in that sector is perceived to depend more on imported capital and know-how than on success in farming. To the extent that the inflowing capital is used wisely and thus boosts economic growth, this would be another reason to expect a positive correlation between resource poorness and economic growth rates.

Government policies also have an impact on incentives to improve the quality of productive factors. In the case of land, developing economy agriculture often suffers through uncertainty over the extent that governments might undersupply institutions to establish clear rural land-use rights (as and when traditional systems of allocating access break down), and/or threaten to or incompletely undertake land reforms. Risk-averse investors will spend less on improving land the greater is such uncertainty.

Agriculture also contributes less than it could to economic growth in so far as government policy fails to ensure that the gap between the private and social rates of return to investments in land-enhancing agricultural research is bridged. That gap exists because it is technically difficult for a private agent to capture all the returns from biological research: an improved seed variety, once released by a breeder, can be quickly reproduced by others. As a consequence the social rate of return from much agricultural research far exceeds the private rate. Even though the expenditure on agricultural research as a proportion of the value of farm output has been rising steadily over time, it is still relatively small in developing economies (Table 12.6). Moreover, available empirical studies suggest agricultural research policies go only a small way towards closing the gap between social and private returns to agricultural research and that at the margin, and in developing economies especially, the social rate of return still far exceeds the opportunity cost of available funds (Ruttan 1983).

Possibly even more important are the effects of government policies on investments in health and education. Typically, government expenditure per capita on schooling and on health programs and facilities is heavily biased in favour of urban areas.[6]

Table 12.6: Agricultural research expenditure as a percentage of agricultural output value, 1959–80[a]

	1959	1970	1980
Low-income economies	0.15	0.27	0.50
Lower middle-income economies	0.29	0.57	0.81
Upper middle-income economies	0.29	0.54	0.73
High-income economies	0.68	1.37	1.50

[a] The greater research expenditure share in higher-income economies would be even more apparent if international rather than domestic prices had been used to calculate the value of agricultural output, given the across-country pattern of price distortions reported above, but less apparent if value added rather than the value of output had been used as the denominator, since the value added share of farm output falls as economies develop (from around three-quarters in very low-income economies to around one-quarter in very industrialised economies).

Source: Judd, M.A., Boyce, J.K. and Evenson, R.E., 1986, 'Investing in agricultural supply: the determinants of agricultural research and extension', *Economic Development and Cultural Change,* 35(1):77–114.

In the case of education this means that children in rural areas receive fewer years and a lower quality of schooling than do urban children, and significant numbers of rural children in low-income economies do not even complete primary school. Yet the rate of return to primary education is far higher than that from higher levels of education (Table 12.7).

This suggests a gross misallocation of government resources from both efficiency and equity perspectives. From an efficiency viewpoint such underinvestment is undesirable because better-educated people adapt better and more quickly to change (Schultz 1975). That is, better-educated farmers are better managers in a modernising (as distinct from traditional) agricultural sector (Schultz 1964; Jamison and Lau 1982). But more importantly it also means that better education in rural areas would enable children to take advantage of off-farm employment opportunities more quickly and easily. Schultz (1961) has argued also that underinvestment in rural education is inappropriate from an equity viewpoint, because farm families bear a disproportionately large share of the costs of adjustment that accompany economic progress: not only does the agricultural sector decline in relative terms over time; for reasons explained in Johnson (1991) and Anderson (1987), but the absolute number of workers on farms eventually declines (not least because of the above-average availability to this sector of labour-saving techniques and machines). Yet despite these arguments, which if anything suggest there should be a bias in education spending in favour of the rural sector, the opposite policy bias is observed.

Table 12.7: Average rates of return from investment in education in developing economies, (per cent)

	Social			Private		
	Primary	**Secondary**	**Tertiary**	**Primary**	**Secondary**	**Tertiary**
Africa	26	17	13	45	26	32
Asia	27	15	13	31	15	18
Latin America	26	18	16	32	23	23

Source: Psacharopoulos, G., 1985, 'Returns to education: a further international update and comparison', *Journal of Human Resources*, 20(4):583–604.

On explaining the pattern of intersectoral policy biases

Why is it that governments in developing economies hold down the relative price of farm products and underinvest in two of the most obvious sources of economic growth in agrarian economies, namely, agricultural research and education in rural areas? And why is this bias against agriculture reduced as an economy develops, but least so for economies that retain an agricultural comparative advantage? To explain these intersectoral policy biases and their changes over time, analysts have focused on one or more of at least four sets of considerations. They have to do with public finance, the costs of collective lobbying action by different interest groups, and with the benefits to those groups, and to politicians, from having a particular policy bias.

Public finance considerations

Public finance specialists have long pointed out that an important assumption in the theory of distortions—that government revenue for the provision of public goods and for redistributing welfare can be costlessly raised and distributed—is less valid in practice the poorer and more agrarian is an economy (Stiglitz 1987; Sah and Stiglitz 1992). For example, it may be prohibitively expensive to collect a head tax or land tax in rural areas of low-income economies, or to distribute small amounts of cash to urban slum dwellers. For that reason the greater allocative benefits of using first-best rather than nth-best policy instruments for raising government revenue and redistributing welfare in the absence of such administrative costs need to be weighed against the greater administrative costs associated with first-best rather than nth-best instruments (n>1). As well, the higher per capita cost of providing rural areas with health and education services, and with transport and communications infrastructure (because of less scope for exploiting economies of scale), may help explain the lower government expenditures per capita on those services in rural areas as compared with urban regions.

Useful though this new public finance literature is in fine-tuning the ranking of policy instruments that are appropriate under various conditions, such considerations go only a small way towards explaining the intersectoral policy biases summarised above. Costs of collecting income and wealth taxes in low-income economies may require greater reliance on indirect taxes, and collection cost differentials may justify tax collection at the border rather than as sales or excise taxes. It is therefore not surprising to find that agriculture is taxed (directly and indirectly) more in economies where farming is an export sector, nor (as Krueger, Schiff and Valdes 1988 found) that within the farm sector of developing economies (and Australia) the import-competing sub-sectors are less discriminated against than the exporters.

But why is the offsetting of the protective effect of an import restriction on manufactures by a tax on (what is often only a small number of) local producers so rarely seen? Why in low-income economies are quantitative restrictions or prohibitions on imports of industrial products used rather than tariffs, if revenue collection is the motive for restricting trade? And in what sense is it equitable in developing economies to favour urban households by artificially lowering food prices when this is at the expense of much poorer rural households, and in industrialised economies to favour farmers in proportion to their output, which is effectively what happens when price and trade policies are used as a means of raising farm incomes?

Answers to these questions are more likely to be found by exploring the differences in costs and benefits enjoyed by pertinent interest groups from lobbying politicians, and the differences between policy regimes in enhancing the government's prospects of remaining in power.

Costs of lobbying for an intersectoral policy bias

Mancur Olson was the first to explore systematically the implications of differential costs of collective action on policy outcomes (Olson 1965, 1986). In a low-income agrarian economy the costs of farmers acting collectively to become informed and lobby for a more favourable policy regime tend to be prohibitively high.[7] Free-rider problems, low levels of education and low-quality transport and communications infrastructure all militate against farmers taking collective action. In contrast, urban capitalists are relatively well educated, politically articulate, small in number, have larger sales per firm than farmers, and are often located in cities within easy reach of people in government. Hence their costs of becoming informed and lobbying are comparatively low. They are also able to enlist the support of urban workers and unemployed people, most notably in the form of threatened or actual riots should food price rises be contemplated by the government.

In the course of an economy's development, however, the costs of collective action decrease more for farmers than for most urban residents. This occurs in part because the difference between urban and rural transport and communication costs narrows. But more importantly it occurs because a way emerges for farmers to reduce substantially their free-rider problem, while in urban areas that problem increases. As farmers gradually commercialise their activities, they perceive income-earning opportunities in supplying farm inputs and marketing farm output. They also often fear exploitation by the middle-persons who emerge to supply those services. Thus farmer associations or cooperatives form. Once established, these organisations are able to lobby on behalf of farmers at relatively low cost, despite the large number of relatively small farms involved in agriculture. Furthermore, established cooperatives (and other suppliers of farm input and output marketing services) have a vested interest in lobbying not only on behalf of farmers but also on their own behalf. This adds to the effective demand for policies favouring agriculture (including subsidies on fertiliser, farm credit, etc.). In contrast, the increasing value of the time of urban workers and the declining relative importance of food prices in their real incomes, plus their greater incentive to free-ride as the urban population swells, makes them less inclined to support protests against food price increases as economies develop. As well, urban capitalists become more numerous and their interests become more diffuse, adding to difficulties in acting collectively.

Benefits from lobbying for an intersectoral policy bias

In seeking to explain the tendency for incentive distortions to move gradually from taxing to favouring farmers relative to industrialists in the course of economic development, an even more important part of the explanation is to be found by examining the domestic distributional effects of policy interventions. Those effects can be summarised as follows.

Consider first a small country facing exogenously determined international prices, a country whose polity cannot influence or be influenced by other countries. Assume the economy has three sectors (agriculture, industry and non-tradeables) with sector-specific capital and intersectorally mobile labour. If it is a low-income agrarian economy with the majority of its workforce involved in semi-subsistence farming, a policy-induced increase in the price of food would have a large impact on the demand for labour, thereby substantially raising wage rates. Yet this wage hike could be insufficient to offset the increase in the cost of living for labourers, who spend a large proportion of their income on food and non-tradeables (the price of which would also rise). Even more importantly, the rise in wages very substantially reduces the income of industrial capitalists. The latter therefore have an incentive to incite labourers to oppose farm assistance policies and instead support a policy regime favouring industry (urban jobs) over agriculture. Furthermore, the magnitude of the gain per farmer, following an increase in the relative price of farm products, would be small compared with the loss for industrial capital owners. The net gain to landholders would be small because of a rise not only in the cost of their consumption of food (in opportunity cost terms if they produce their own) and non-tradeables, but also in their wage payments in so far as they are net buyers of farm labour services. Together these would erode much of the increased return to farm assets.

A recent simulation study suggests that lowering the price of farm relative to industrial products in such a low-income agrarian economy could result in the proportional loss to farmers being only one-tenth of the proportional gain to industrial capitalists (Anderson 1993). When capitalists' relative gain is added to the fact that in such an economy the cost of collective lobbying action by a small group of urban capitalists is far smaller than those costs for peasant farmers (who are poorly served with transport and communications infrastructure), plus the superficial appeal of the arguments for infant industry protection, it is not surprising that policies favouring industry over agriculture are observed in low-income economies.

In industrialised economies where agriculture accounts for a very small share of production, employment and consumption expenditure, the skew in the income distribution effects of distorting the relative price of farm products is the reverse. Raising farm product prices has little effect on wages, on the price of non-tradeables, on returns to industrial capital, or on household expenditure. Hence non-farm groups, including industrial capitalists, have little incentive to oppose farm-support policies. With farmers' inputs receiving only a small fraction of farm sales revenue (most of it being absorbed by purchased intermediate inputs, unlike in low-income economies), net farm income and asset values are boosted very considerably in percentage terms by agricultural price-support policies. The above-mentioned simulation study suggests that the proportional gain to farmers from a policy-induced increase in the relative price of farm products could be seven times the loss to industrial capitalists in such an economy, and more than five times the proportional gain to farmers in the low-income agrarian economy.

Given these vast differences between high-income and low-income economies in the incentives for different producers to lobby for policies that favour their sector, it is understandable that there are strong demands on governments to alter gradually their country's policy regime in the course of their economic development, from discriminating against, to favouring, farmers. But why is it in the interests of governments to satisfy that demand, given the high cost of distorting incentives in terms of national output and income forgone?

Net benefits to the government from supplying an intersectorally biased policy regime

Governments choose policies not only with overall efficiency and aggregate national economic welfare in mind, but also in response to the non-economic concerns of the community at large, as well as to concentrated political pressures from vested interest groups. It is understandable that non-farmers in those economies with a comparative disadvantage in agriculture (the densely populated economies of Western Europe and Northeast Asia) are more tolerant of support for agriculture; partly because they are more concerned about security of food supplied from abroad, because their farmers have come under strong pressure to stop farming (and from a base of smaller-scale agriculture than in the more sparsely settled areas of the Americas and Australasia), and because, unlike the food-exporting economies, high-income food-importing economies

(which included much of Western Europe until half a generation ago), they could assist farmers without budgetary outlays,
simply by imposing levies on food imports. In contrast, governments in the land-abundant countries such as the Americas
and Australasia find it relatively costly in terms of political
support to assist export-oriented farmers because that necessarily involves overt outlays from the Treasury in the form of
at least export subsidies, whereas their import-competing
industries can be supported relatively covertly with import controls which add to, rather than reduce government revenue,
and at the same time appear to contribute to diversifying the
economy and reducing its reliance on fickle primary export
markets.[8]

Policy implications

The above discussion suggests that one of the contributors to
the fact that there is a negative correlation across countries
between their agricultural comparative advantage and economic growth rate has been an intersectoral policy bias against
agriculture. That policy bias is evident in all but the most industrialised economies and, even among the industrialised economies, it has lingered longest in those that have retained a
comparative advantage in farm products.

Wouldn't the fact that the densely populated industrialised
economies have chosen to change gradually to a price-policy
bias in favour of agriculture lead one to expect them to grow
slower, because of this opposite policy distortion? Certainly
theory suggests they should grow slower than if their policy
regime against agriculture had been replaced by one that was
intersectorally unbiased. But four other points need to be recognised. First, the bias in favour of farmers, documented above,
relates only to output prices. Available evidence suggests the
policy bias against rural areas in terms of underinvestment in
agricultural research and in schooling continues in these countries (albeit to a lesser extent). This more or less offsets the positive price policy bias. Second, the relative size of the farm
sector being helped in high-income economies is far smaller
than the relative size of the farm sector being harmed in the
low-income economies by the choice of price and trade policies.
Hence the negative impact on the latter economies' GDP

growth would be relatively greater than it would on the former's. Third, because developing economies with an agricultural comparative disadvantage tax agriculture less (Figure 12.1), and begin to reduce intersectoral policy bias at an earlier stage of economic development (see Tables 12.3 and 12.4 for some Asian examples), they would be expected to grow faster than other economies with similar starting incomes per capita. Finally, growth in the use of agricultural protection by the advanced industrialised economies worsens the terms of trade for those economies with an agricultural comparative advantage, slowing their GDP growth further.

Is there any possibility of reducing the policy distortions to incentives?

One might be tempted to conclude that the political economy of policy distortions makes attempts to reduce them a lost cause, that in any case the dampening effect on international prices of agricultural protection in high-income economies is offset by the taxing of farmers in low-income economies, and that low-income-economy farm households will eventually be compensated, via the gradual reversal of the policy bias, as their national economies develop. But such conclusions must be rejected on several grounds.

First, while it happens to be the case, according to one set of estimates (Tyers and Anderson 1992: Table 6.9), that the international price-depressing effect of agricultural protection policies in high-income economies almost fully offsets the international price-raising effect of price discrimination against agriculture in low-income economies, that is not true of the effects of those policies on the stability of international prices. On the contrary: the same empirical study suggests developing economy policies are even more destabilising of international prices than are industrialised economy policies. Indeed if both groups of countries ceased to insulate their domestic food markets from international fluctuations, the need for such insulation would disappear because international food price fluctuations would then be smaller than those currently experienced in the domestic insulated markets of almost all countries (Tyers and Anderson 1992: Tables 6.14 and 6.15).

Second, it can take generations for the gradual change from effectively taxing to subsidising the rural sector to come about through normal domestic political economy forces. The view that this provides intertemporal equity not only requires a stretched notion of a multigenerational welfare function, but also ignores the fact that throughout that process, while relative prices are distorted and other inefficient policies are in place, the economy's output level and growth rate are less than they need be. The experience of China post-1978 shows how enormous those opportunity costs can be: not only did the raising of farm prices towards international levels and the move from the collective to the household responsibility system allow China's agricultural output to increase by more than 50 per cent in six years, but the savings generated by that farm income growth allowed massive investments in rural industrialisation, the combined effect of which contributed to a doubling of the country's GDP in less than a decade.

And third, the 'do nothing' conclusion should be rejected because it is possible to influence the domestic political market so as to reduce past policy biases. Certainly, the production and dissemination of empirical information on the costs and adverse distributional consequences of policy biases has played a role in strengthening opposition to them. But there have also been two sets of international forces that have gradually influenced domestic political markets in favour of policy reform: international aid and loan organisations, and multilateral trade/economic integration agreements.

The roles of international aid/finance organisations

Various international aid and loan organisations have had, and continue to have significant effects in reducing the policy biases against agriculture in developing economies. Banks, of course, are one such force. The aid and loan packages of the World Bank and its regional affiliates, together with the International Monetary Fund, for example, are being offered on increasingly strict conditions that require economically sound macroeconomic, trade and sectoral policies. Also, the private banks that lend to developing economies were severely affected by the failure of many of those economies to repay loans in the 1980s, and so they are even more anxious than the World Bank and the International Monetary Fund to see less distortionary, growth-enhancing policies in place before extending loans.

A lesser-known positive influence on developing economy agriculture is the so-called Consultative Group on International Agricultural Research. Starting with the highly successful initiative of the Rockefeller Foundation to establish cereal breeding research stations in Mexico and the Philippines a generation ago, various other private donors, national aid agencies and groups such as the World Bank formed the Consultative Group on International Agricultural Research; it involves a network of more than a score of new international agricultural research centres throughout the world. Given the above-mentioned gross underinvestment in agricultural research in developing economies and the political reasons for it, this initiative is having a major impact on agriculture's contribution to overall economic growth in those countries, of which the green revolution of the 1960s was but a beginning.

The contributions of multilateral trade/economic integration agreements

Just as the use of a political market framework is helpful in explaining why governments impose trade barriers and other domestic distortions, so it can be helpful in explaining why governments are more inclined to reduce trade barriers multilaterally rather than unilaterally (Hillman and Moser 1992; Grossman and Helpman 1992). Suppose the climate of public opinion in a country shifts against protectionist policies, for example because of new information showing those policies to be more costly and inequitable than was previously perceived. It will pay the government to liberalise trade somewhat in response to that shock to the political market, but the net political benefit to the government will be greater (or cost will be less) if other countries can be enticed to liberalise at the same time. The following two illustrations show why. First, in the case of the United States–European Union farm trade dispute where both economies subsidise their exports, the extra political benefit would come from the fact that domestic farm prices would have to fall less to reach the international price level (and hence would harm domestic farm interests less) the more the other economy lowered its farm subsidies, because the latter would raise international food prices. And second, in the case of the United States–

Japan trade dispute, lowering protection against imports of
United States rice would hurt the Japanese government less
if, in return for losing political support from rice farmers, it
gained support from domestic manufacturers because of
fewer threats to their access to US markets, and vice versa
for the United States' government. Hence the demand for
bilateral, minilateral and multilateral trade negotiations, and
for an institution such as the GATT.

The most significant minilateral agreements to form free
trade areas or customs unions, the European Union and the
European Free Trade Association (EFTA), have worsened the
relative price of farm products in international markets because
Western Europe's external agricultural protection levels have
risen while those to manufacturing have fallen. Furthermore,
the enlargements of the European Union from six to nine
members in the early 1970s, and to 12 members in the early
1980s, resulted in a ratcheting upwards of Europe's average
level of farm protection. The opposite effect is likely (though
not certain) if/when some of the remaining EFTA members join
the European Union later this decade, as their current levels of
farm price support exceed those in the European Union. And
the demands for access to the high-priced Western European
food markets by farmers in Central and Eastern Europe also
will make it more difficult politically for governments in the
West to retain present policies (Hamilton and Winters 1992;
Anderson and Tyers 1993).

To date, the GATT's success, following seven rounds of multilateral trade negotiations, has been confined mainly to lowering tariffs on manufactures. That too has contributed to a
worsening of the international terms of trade faced by farmers.
But the recently concluded eighth round, the Uruguay Round,
brings agriculture under the GATT for the first time. Effective
implementation of the new agreement will boost economies
with an agricultural comparative advantage because of several
features of the agreement. It will:
• lead to the tariffication of agricultural support measures,
  reducing the degree of insulation between domestic and
  international food markets and thereby lowering fluctuations
  in the latter;
• slow and hopefully reverse the long-run upward trend in
  agricultural protection rates in advanced industrialised economies, and lock-in the reforms to prevent backsliding (which
  makes it more significant than just the 'MacSharry' proposed

reforms to the European Union's Common Agricultural Policy, not least because the latter might otherwise be less than fully implemented);

- make it more difficult for middle-income economies, including the former centrally planned economies, as and when they join the GATT, to follow the advanced industrialised economies' example of increasing agricultural protection as their economies develop;
- ensure that US export subsidy payments are lowered and reduce the probability of further farm export subsidy wars which, with tariffication, would reduce fluctuations in international food prices;
- strengthen the GATT rules against the use of sanitary and phytosanitary provisions as substitute trade barriers; and
- thus, most likely, raise the average level of the relative price of farm products in international markets, since liberalisations in other product areas (textiles, services) addressed in the Uruguay Round are likely to be smaller.

For all these reasons and others (particularly the pressures to reduce unilaterally the policy bias against agriculture in developing economies and Australasia, the regional integration pressures in Europe to lower agricultural protection levels there, and the multilateral pressure via the Uruguay Round that has also put pressure on East Asia to open its food markets), one can be cautiously optimistic that the years ahead will be kinder to economies with a comparative advantage in agriculture than have recent decades—especially the past ten years. Such is the interdependence of the world economy that these pressures and their accompanying reforms could well boost growth in countries with an agricultural comparative disadvantage as well, but at least countries with a comparative advantage will be better off than if farm policy reforms did not occur.

Notes to Chapter 12

[1] The countries and country groups (which together account for all countries of the world other than the non-Asian former COMECON countries) and the index of comparative advantage used are shown in Figure 12.1. Real GDP growth data are from the World Bank's *World Tables 1993*. Three of the 30 observations had to be ignored because of a lack of GDP growth data, namely, the former USSR, other Eastern Europe countries and Cuba. The

correlation coefficient is even higher at −0.45 if only 1970–80 GDP growth data are used.

2   A downward trend in the relative price of food may be a reflection of relatively rapid technological progress in agriculture. In the United States, for example, total factor productivity growth since the late 1940s has been nearly four times as fast in farming as in the private non-farm sectors (Jorgenson and Gollop 1992). Agricultural-exporting economies might therefore be expected to have performed well, were it not for the fact that globally the demand for farm products is price and income inelastic so that consumers rather than farmers are the major beneficiaries.

3   It is true that non-tariff barriers to trade in some manufactures have grown as tariffs on imports of manufactures have come down, but evidently these have been insufficient to prevent rapid growth in manufactures trade. Indeed the global trade-to-GDP ratio has risen from less than one-fifth in the late 1930s to more than one-third today (Anderson and Blackhurst 1993: Appendix), even though much of GDP is non-tradeable internationally. How much of that rise is due to the drop in international transport and communications costs and in the value added share of output is a moot point, but it is probably much less than 100 per cent.

4   Notice also from Table 12.3 that the rate of direct taxation net of direct subsidies to agriculture, as a share of farm income, dropped steadily as Japan's industrialisation proceeded, to below the rate applying to non-farm sectors by the end of the 1930s.

5   Such inputs may in any case be justified on efficiency grounds if their use involves positive externalities. Sah and Stiglitz (1992:120–1) mention several possible externalities, including the likelihood that neighbouring farmers benefit freely from watching the early adopters of a new technology.

6   For documentary evidence of this type of bias in Papua New Guinea, for example, see the results presented by Jarrett and Anderson (1989).

7   This affects farmers' demands not only for favourable prices but also for more support for such things as agricultural research, schools and health clinics. Presumably, since several years elapse before a pay-off from agricultural research is obvious, such public investments are even less likely to be provided than higher farm prices (Anderson 1981).

8   On the importance of this cosmetic attraction in the history of the political economy of Australia's intersectoral policy bias, see Anderson and Garnaut (1987).

13

Environmental Constraints on Development and International Rules

DAVID ROBERTSON

The incorporation of environmental considerations into policies to promote economic development has been slow. This should not be surprising because the environment does not have high priority in countries where poverty is extant and survival is exigent, making economic growth the principal objective of government policies. In other words, developing economies would be expected to show a strong time preference for consumption now rather than conservation for future generations (Tisdell 1988). Nevertheless, environmental and natural resource constraints may become serious medium-term issues if resources are not appropriately priced. Depletion of a country's environmental endowment must eventually impede its development (GATT 1991).

For developing economies, domestic environmental problems have most relevance. These can be effectively managed using domestic economic policies: internalising externalities, establishing legal property rights or introducing environmental and health standards and regulations. Such measures to overcome market or policy failures are consistent with Helen Hughes' view that domestic policies are the key to development success (Hughes 1989a).

Increasingly, global treaties and pressures from some international environmental lobby groups seek to constrain developing economies' choices about the use of national resources (forests, minerals, land, water, etc.) in the development process. Pressures take the form of threats to discriminate in trade and attempts to override sovereign rights over national resources in order to protect 'global commons' and to preserve biodiversity and fragile landforms. Some developing economies are beginning to resist these political pressures because of the constraints they impose on their potential development.

Frictions between developing and industrialised economies were evident at the United Nations Conference on the Environment and Development Summit (June 1992), as they were at the 1972 United Nations Conference on the Environment (Beckerman 1992). Suspicions have been obvious at follow-up meetings resulting from the United Nations Conference on the Environment and Development (UNCED) agreements.

Developing economies face environmental constraints on their economic growth at three levels:

- public choice in national policies to achieve ecologically sustainable development;
- transborder (bilateral) measures to contain environmental degradation; and
- global treaties and international rules.

A brief analysis of domestic policy alternatives will highlight some of the issues surrounding the search for efficient environmental policies in developing economies. The implications of global environmental policies for developing economies are then explored.

Environmental policies in developing economies

Promoting economic growth and reducing poverty have priority over environmental concerns in developing economies. The first requirement of environmental policies, therefore, is that they should be cost-effective and promote economic efficiency. Given the variety of endogenous and policy-induced distortions in developing economies, these are often difficult objectives to achieve.

It is well established (Cropper and Oates 1992) that environmental degradation occurs because of market failure, and that the optimal policy should involve internalisation of external costs or benefits. In many developing economies policy failure has been an equally prevalent factor in damage to the environmental endowment.

- Development policies that subsidise water consumption, fertilisers, pesticides and energy-use may cause serious pollution damage or costs (Eskeland and Jimenez 1992).
- Subsidies paid to cattle and soya farmers in Brazil led to

massive destruction of Brazilian forests (Binswanger 1987).
- Failure to charge for rural roads or replacement costs thereof has caused over-exploitation of forests, land and water.
- Inappropriate pricing policies for agricultural output have caused desertification in Africa, salination from subsidised irrigation and soil loss from poor land management.
- Agricultural sectors have also suffered from distortions created by inappropriate macroeconomic policies and import-substitution strategies.

Whether caused by market failure or policy failure, public intervention is necessary to mitigate environmental damage. The interventions may be:
- market-based measures, intended to influence private production or consumption;
- command and control instruments to regulate production or consumption activities; or
- direct government involvement in the form of spending on clean-up activities.

In developing economies, public finance is seldom available for cleaning up environmental damage. The choice between the other two categories will depend on the effectiveness of market competition, the susceptibility of the problem to regulatory measures and the costs of monitoring. Administrative difficulties associated with regulation in many developing economies seem likely to render market measures the most effective instruments. One attraction of taxes to correct externalities in developing economies is that they raise revenue while improving economic efficiency.

In practice, environmental externalities take many forms: toxic emissions from industrial plants, soil loss after excess logging, river pollution from intensive agriculture, overgrazing of pastures, etc. The analysis that follows is based on pollution of air or water from an industrial plant. The analysis is easily adapted to any problem of externalities.

Pollution is a negative external effect of production (or consumption) which imposes costs on the community. The market provides no inducement to restrict the externality since the costs (damages) are not borne by the perpetrator. The optimal solution would be to tax or charge the polluting activity to encourage reduction of the externality, up to the point where the marginal social costs equal the marginal social benefits (Pigou 1920). (The alternative of a subsidy paid for abatement is not generally suitable for developing economies because it depends on raising revenue elsewhere in the economy.) In 1972, the Organisation for Economic Cooperation and Development (OECD) countries adopted the polluter-pays principle which states that if producers are made responsible for external costs they will be encouraged to abate their pollution.

Where polluters and victims are few, full information is available and negotiating costs are low, Coase (1960) showed that proper allocation of property rights could establish equilibrium between polluters and those suffering the pollution. Those affected by the externality will negotiate with the perpetrator to allow some pollution, at a price. The price will depend on consumers' perceived costs to the producer of pollution and the costs of pollution abatement. This market solution to the pollution problem may avoid government intervention (except to establish legal property rights) as long as property rights are easily identifiable and negotiations are inexpensive (for example, where logging causes siltation of a river used for tourism and recreational fishing a negotiated solution should be feasible). Government intervention will be necessary where the number of owners involved makes negotiations impossible.

Command and control measures (for example a requirement for output filters on machinery to reduce emissions) restrict emissions at source and remove the opportunity to trade in pollution rights. Setting and enforcing standards for production and consumption processes and equipment has been the most popular externality control instrument in OECD countries (Opschoor and Vos 1989). In practice, source-specific restraints cause variations in costs among polluters, whereas market-based measures are cost-effective. Where pollution levels differ among plants the charge will influence each according to the costs of abatement. Plants will employ anti-pollution equipment up to the point where the marginal cost of such equipment equals the charge for non-compliance with directives on pollution levels. Despite the evidence that price measures are more cost efficient than command and control methods, governments seem to prefer regulations because they are more certain of their effects. (It seems also to satisfy environmental groups who reject the idea of selling rights to pollute.) Developing economies experience difficulties monitoring pollution because of the expense and technological complexity of required equipment.

Indirect instruments may be adopted where monitoring or enforcement are difficult. For example, taxes on coal and other energy inputs may be used as proxies for taxes on emissions. These may cause distortions because there is no fixed relationship between inputs and the many kinds of outputs.

Whatever mix of market measures and regulations is adopted to reduce environmental degradation, income distribution will be affected. Pollution controls may most benefit the urban poor, although the price effects of anti-pollution measures may also fall on them (for example a petrol tax may raise bus fares). The political economy of environmental policies will play a major role in the incidence of costs and benefits in the community (Meier 1990). Large industries may be able to persuade governments to tailor taxes or charges so that their incidence is disproportionately borne by small businesses in non-traded sectors. Alternatively, farmers may obtain exemptions from fuel taxes on the grounds that food prices will be kept down or exports facilitated.

Transborder pollution (acid rain or river pollution) introduces the additional complication of separate jurisdiction for polluters and sufferers. The polluter-pays principle would be difficult to apply, unless the polluters accepted responsibility. If the upstream polluters refuse to take responsibility, the victims may have to bribe them to abate the pollution. This victim-pays approach will benefit both parties.

Global environmental issues

For 20 years, environmental problems were regarded as national concerns or related to transborder issues, and the analysis in the previous section provided the appropriate approach. Since the mid-1980s, however, attention has shifted to global issues. On the one hand, scientific evidence has accumulated to suggest that global commons such as the atmosphere, oceans and biodiversity may be being used unsustainably. On the other hand, environmental activists seem to have decided that by appealing for global strategies they attract more popular support for environmental issues than they get from local communities. After all, most local issues involve costs for residents to correct externalities or pay for clean-ups. Global issues do not obviously bear on living standards or incomes. Moreover, predictions of global disaster capture the imagination. Forebodings of ozone depletion, loss of biodiversity and climate change have raised the profile of environmentalists and their associated green political parties.

The 1992 UNCED meeting in Rio demonstrated that global environmental issues have been accepted into international politics. It is not clear that the Rio Declaration or Agenda 21 gave the environment priority over economic, trade or development issues, but political pressures for the pre-eminence of environmental issues have increased. Developing economies have been much discomfited by this turn of events and by some of the proposals discussed at UNCED and later United Nations meetings.

Developing economies' concerns are of three types.

- New global treaties have provisions that restrict independence of action and impose costs on development. These provisions infringe on property rights over natural resources (for example protection of tropical forests, preserving biodiversity, etc.) and employ the threat of trade sanctions to enforce the treaties.

- Threats to amend the General Agreement on Tariffs and Trade (GATT) provisions to permit discriminatory trade policies on environmental grounds, including extraterritorial application of national laws and environmental standards (i.e. whether or not imports can be restricted to enforce one country's environmental policies on other countries); this could close markets against developing economies' exports.

- UNCED produced draft agreements on climate change and preserving biodiversity; it extended the Global Environment Facility to give financial support for investment and technical assistance relating to global environmental targets.

In countries where large proportions of the population live in poverty, global environmental concerns carry little weight. In as much as the global treaties introduce new constraints on prospects for economic development they are not welcome. A major concern of developing economies' governments is that many negotiations on correcting environmental damage take place without their being properly represented.

For example, the OECD is giving much attention to environmental issues. Horizontal committees, where environmental problems are examined with other OECD committees (for example trade and environment, industry and environment, etc.), have been formed. It has become the practice for industrialised economies examining GATT issues in the OECD to devise a proposal to put before negotiating groups (for example trade in services in the Uruguay Round). The same seems likely to happen on trade and environment issues. The OECD Ministerial Council approved new procedural guidelines on integrating trade and environmental policies in June 1993 (OECD 1993). The Council also approved a large program of follow-up work for the trade and environment committee. Although the work program calls for consultation with developing economies, the main recommendations will be formulated by OECD countries.

If the OECD committees recommend amendments to the GATT articles on procedures relating to environmental measures, developing economies could have difficulties changing these recommendations. Certain environmental principles suggested by the OECD indicate the kind of thinking in its committees:

- precautionary principle: where there are threats of serious or irreversible damage, lack of full scientific certainty should not be used as a reason for postponing measures to prevent environmental degradation;
- priority of prevention: decision-making should favour the prevention of environmental degradation over after-the-fact remediation of environmental degradation and provide for environmental safeguards, where necessary; and
- policy integration: enhancing integration of environmental and trade policy decision-making is called for.

Applied by national governments to their own sovereign resources these principles are unexceptionable, but if applied extraterritorially using trade measures they would impose severe restrictions on development.

The Rio meeting of UNCED revealed that in some cases developing economies have different views on environmental issues from those accepted in industrialised economies and propagated by 'green' non-government organisations. For example, Organisation of Petroleum Exporting Countries' views on climate change and use of hydrocarbon fuels and Malaysia's attitudes to felling tropical timber are at odds with opinion held by many others. To be effective, decisions on global environmental issues will require universal application. Developing economies' willingness to participate needs to be considered; enforcing standards or policies using trade restrictions or other economic measures could engender resentment and be self-defeating.

Implications of global environmental treaties for development

Trade restrictions have been incorporated into several global environment treaties, as a measure to achieve compliance or as trade sanctions to persuade non-signatories to adopt the treaties. The GATT group on environmental measures and international trade has found 17 multilateral agreements that have trade provisions (GATT 1991:24). Most instances where trade restrictions have been used concern protection of flora and fauna, and are non-controversial.

The most significant treaties that permit restrictive trade measures are:

• The 1987 Montreal Protocol on substances which deplete the ozone layer (55 signatories) contains provisions to use trade restrictions against non-signatories. Import bans on chloro-fluorocarbons from non-signatories were effective from January 1990 and exports of chloro-fluorocarbons to non-signatories were banned from January 1993. Imports containing chloro-fluorocarbons are banned and by 1994 further trade restrictions may be introduced on products made using chloro-fluorocarbons and halons. Developing economies were accorded a ten-year grace period to achieve the chloro-fluorocarbon targets. The 1990 London Protocol accelerated the phase-out of chloro-fluorocarbons, but retained the dispensation for developing economies.

• The 1975 Convention on International Trade in Endangered Species of wild fauna and flora justifies use of trade restrictions (compliance is voluntary). A listing as an endangered species requires members to ban all commercial trade in that species. A threatened species requires a trade permit system administered by exporting countries. Trade in ivory was banned in 1989 to protect the African elephant. This has cast doubt on the effectiveness of bans, because it has encouraged poaching and smuggling of a valuable resource. (Questions are being raised by developing economies about the compatibility of these Conventions on International Trade in Endangered Species trade measures with GATT Article XX.)

- The 1989 Basel Convention on the control of transboundary movements of hazardous wastes and their disposal. This Convention is still awaiting ratification by some major industrial countries. The aim of this Convention is to regulate shipment of wastes by ensuring that the importer has information about the content and has the capacity to dispose of the material in an environmentally sound manner. The responsibility applies to both exporter and importer and depends on trade controls to be effective. Trade with non-signatories is subject to the same conditions and may be banned.

The trade measures authorised by these global treaties are neither compatible with GATT Article I (most-favoured-nation treatment), nor with general exceptions under Article XX. So far, no measure employed under global treaties has been brought as a complaint to the GATT. Given the protective nature and general acceptability of these global agreements, complaints to the GATT seem unlikely. Most of the major economic powers are parties to these global treaties as well as to the GATT. As long as this 'gentlemen's agreement' exists, many trade officials believe that it will be possible to avoid making amendments to GATT articles to permit exceptions on environmental agreements (GATT 1991:26).

Nevertheless, a gentlemen's agreement should not be pushed too far. The drafting of a Convention on Climate Change could bring objections from developing economies if carbon taxes, or something similar, threatened to raise their industrial costs, or if trade restraints were authorised to enforce compliance. China (not yet a member of the GATT) rejected the Montreal Treaty, and with other developing economies would be expected to be reluctant to accept the Convention on Climate Change. Developing economies' sensitivity to measures mentioned in connection with the draft forestry agreement at UNCED also indicates that a complaint to the GATT may not be far away.

The two draft global treaties adopted at the Earth Summit, conventions on climate change and protection of biological diversity, represent an extension of global strategies. Existing global treaties on chloro-fluorocarbons, waste disposal and protection of species have limited scope. That they contravened commitments in other treaties (for example the GATT) could be overlooked because of their narrow, specialised coverage. The new conventions are all-embracing. Although their provisions are not yet clear, any actions to restrict emissions such as carbon dioxide and nitric acids will have widespread effects on industries' costs and their locations. Similarly, protection of biodiversity will restrict access to natural resources and specific regions (forests, lakes, minerals) in many countries. Both will impact on national sovereignty. Developing economies could oppose such inroads into property rights regarded as essential for development. Even if grace periods for implementation are granted to developing economies, there could be tensions.

Tensions with the General Agreement on Tariffs and Trade

Environmental groups have made the GATT a target in their campaign to give prominence to environmental issues of all kinds. GATT rules prevent the use of discriminatory trade measures, whether tariffs, quantitative restrictions or export subsidies. All these have been advocated at one time or another to support environmental objectives, for example improvements in forest management or preservation of natural resources (minerals) (Arden-Clarke 1992; S.A.F.E. Alliance 1992). The environmental lobbies regard existing trade treaties, especially the GATT, as restraining governments from following environmentally friendly policies. Instances cited include Denmark's law on reusable containers for beer and soft drinks and Germany's laws on disposal of packaging materials and eco-labelling of products. These cases create new costs which discriminate against foreign suppliers. The GATT Working Group on environmental measures and international trade is considering all three cases on its current agenda.

Why have trade and environmental policies become closely linked (for example, OECD procedural guidelines, 1993)? After all, environmental problems arise one way or another from decisions about consumption and production, whereas international trade policy is limited to cross-frontier transactions. Trade liberalisation is a means to increase economic opportunities, a fact increasingly recognised by developing economies.

That efficiency gains from trade permit a given output/consumption to be obtained using fewer resources seems not to be understood by green lobbies.

Some specific links can be drawn between trade and the environment. Changes in any one policy will affect economic behaviour generally. A change in trade policy alters the volume and location of global production and consumption, and among other things may affect the environment. This link, however, is not simple. Some environmental groups believe there is a positive connection between economic growth and environmental degradation (Shrybman 1990; Arden-Clarke 1992). But increasing living standards raise consciousness about the environment and increase the resources that the community can make available for pollution abatement and conservation (GATT 1991). It is not a simple relationship but one involving positive feedbacks through technology, consumer preferences, etc.

The major attraction of trade policy to environmental lobbies seems to be its potential for use as an instrument for achieving particular goals. Using discriminatory import measures to force other countries to adopt stricter environmental codes, applying subsidies to production of environmental control equipment, or restricting exports to conserve natural resources are all regarded as acceptable by environmental groups (Arden-Clarke 1992). Economists' arguments that trade measures are second-best policies for dealing with externalities in consumption or production are ignored (Johnson 1965; Lloyd 1992; Snape 1992). The theory of externalities and public goods explains that tax and subsidy measures acting directly on the cause of the distortion are the efficient option.

Environmentalists see principles of non-discrimination and reciprocity in trade treaties as impediments to environmental protection. Policies designed to internalise externalities are perceived by industries as affecting the international competitiveness of domestic industries. Internalising externalities using taxes or introducing regulations raises costs to domestic industries and this imperils exports and increases competition for import-competing industries. A subsidy on exports or an increase in protection for the import-competing sector would compensate for the environmental protection, but GATT commitments do not allow that. Hence attempts by environmental lobbies (aided and abetted by protectionists) to amend the GATT rules.

So far, the cost effects of environmental policies have worked in favour of industries in developing economies which have given less attention to pollution control and to protection of the environment than OECD countries. Some industrialised economies' politicians have described developing economies as pollution havens (Dean 1992).

Studies by Leonard (1988) and Tobey (1990) show little evidence of the industry flight expected to follow from the introduction of new environmental protection strategies. Use of pollution control measures has not had significant effects on industrial costs. The 2 to 3 per cent increments such measures generate have been swamped by other changes affecting production costs, such as wage increases, exchange rate variations, technology change, etc. In addition, political and economic uncertainties have had more influence on location decisions than have the costs of environmental measures.

A World Bank study (ed. Low 1992) found that the intensity of pollution increased in developing economies in the 1970s and 1980s. It was not possible, however, to establish whether this had been caused by migration of dirty industries from developed economies, or instead represented the rapid economic growth of developing economies over this period. The latter would be consistent with the observation that the pollution intensity of output declines as incomes rise beyond a certain level and the share of manufacturing in total output declines. Low and Yeats (1992) show that dirty industries increased their intensity in developing economies' exports in the past two decades. But they showed also that the growth in the index of dirty industries was much less in developing economies with open trading policies.

In spite of the empirical evidence that environmental policies have little effect on trade flows and the observation that trade itself is seldom the source of environmental damage (Sorsa 1992), conflicts continue between environmentalists and the trading system (the GATT). The emphasis given to trade and environment in the OECD indicates that these conflicts represent a point of maximum friction for environmental lobbies. This should be worrying for developing economies which could face new discrimination in trade, if the most-favoured-nation treatment (GATT Article I) were relaxed.

Eco-dumping has become a concern in industrialised economies where environmental policies have taken hold. This term describes imports from producers in countries with low environmental standards which have a cost advantage over products from countries with high environmental standards. Environmentalists claim that countervailing duties against 'unfair' trade should be allowed to protect high environmental standards. Without such protection, it is argued, the high standard countries would be subject to pressure to lower their standards, whereas if penalty tariffs were levied against less environmentally aware governments they would be encouraged to raise environmental standards. This approach is naive. Products may be manufactured in many ways, using a wide variety of inputs from different countries. Globalisation of production requires trade in all kinds of components so countervailing duties would require schedules of trade measures to compensate for environmental cost differences. Isolating environmental cost advantages from all other cost differences would be virtually impossible. (The US Congress considered an International Pollution Deterrence Bill in 1991 which would have amended US trade laws so that failure of foreign manufacturers to enforce effective environmental policies would be regarded as a subsidy. No allowance was made, however, for low US energy prices!)

The use of discriminatory countervailing duties, if permitted under GATT Article VI and the Tokyo Round Anti-dumping and Subsidy Codes, could represent a serious threat to developing economies' exports. Apart from the threat of raising barriers against exports regarded as receiving eco-subsidies, such measures would greatly increase uncertainties about future changes in trade conditions as new environmental policies are introduced in industrialised economies. Moreover, once such an environmental breach in the GATT rules occurred, capture by protectionist lobbies would become a danger. Arguments over cost differences such as low-wage labour and different programs of social welfare would be put forward as valid arguments for new protection against competitive imports from newly industrialising economies (such arguments are gaining currency in European Union circles).

Another threat to developing economies' sovereignty was raised by the suggestion that trade bans should be applied to imports of tropical timber from regions where sustainable forest management techniques were not in use. The Netherlands and Austria have proposed such bans. As only around 15 per cent of forest clearing is for timber, the remainder being mostly slash-and-burn clearing for farming, trade bans are inappropriate. (In Indonesia, a ban on exports of timber discriminated in favour of inefficient local wood processors resulting in greater use of logs and more logging (Braga 1992).) Nevertheless, the rapid deforestation in the Amazon and Southeast Asia may persuade environmentalists to try again to obtain trade barriers as a lever to reduce deforestation. Already some UN programs and some aid projects through the World Bank have been suspended or revised under pressure from green groups. (The Sardar Sarovar dam project in India was suspended on environmental grounds.)

The two fundamental criticisms of GATT rules by environmentalists are:

- that most-favoured-nation treatment and national treatment prevent the use of trade protection measures to support domestic environmental laws; and
- that the GATT agreement on technical barriers to trade (Standards Code) cannot be used to establish international environmental standards (that is harmonisation of environmental standards).

Article XX of the GATT allows trade protection to safeguard public policies in the areas of morals, health, etc. Two clauses of that article have special significance for environmentalists. Although the environment is not specifically mentioned, Article XX(b) allows trade measures 'necessary to protect human, animal or plant life or health', and Article XX(g) refers to 'conservation of exhaustible natural resources, if such measures are made effective in conjunction with restrictions on domestic production or consumption'. The main issue of uncertainty about using these clauses to justify trade measures used for environmental reasons relates to extraterritoriality.

Only six cases have been referred and decided under these clauses using GATT dispute settlement procedures (Petersmann 1993). The infamous 1991 Mexican–US, tuna–dolphin case upset environmental groups worldwide. Mexico complained about a US ban on imports of yellow-fin tuna caught off Mexico using purse-seine nets. The US ban was based on US laws to protect dolphins which feed with the tuna. US tuna fishermen were upset by the GATT panel's decision because they would have benefited from the protection! The GATT panel's report on the tuna–dolphin case found that the US import ban did not meet the conditions of Article XX. To be justified under the article, measures must: meet the GATT definitions; be necessary or be the least trade-distorting measures available; and be applied without discrimination. Thus Article XX requires the use of the most efficient policies that attack the source of the problem, not just the easiest instrument to apply, as border measures often are.

The conditions for using Article XX are strict and environmental groups want to change them to make use easier. This would enable extraterritorial application of domestic laws and allow pressure to be brought to bear on countries to raise their environmental standards. Unfortunately, extraterritorial application could be used to spread discriminatory protection for commercial reasons. Nevertheless, if the GATT contracting parties wanted to amend the GATT rules this could be done by consensus. Alternatively, waivers could be granted under Article XXV (two-thirds majority) in specific cases where environmental measures were deemed to require supporting trade measures (GATT 1991).

Environmental groups also argue directly for international harmonisation of environmental standards. Proposals for international harmonisation neglect the many national differences in pollution absorption capacities, social choices about acceptable levels of pollution and resource use, administrative capacities to implement policies, and the costs arising from the policies (Robertson 1992).

The Tokyo Round agreement on technical barriers to trade (Standards Code) was designed to prevent standards being used as non-tariff barriers to trade. The Code is applied only by its 40 signatories, and its precise standing in the GATT is unclear. It promotes harmonised international standards, as defined by international standards organisations, to reduce trade distortions, but the GATT does not determine international standards. The Uruguay Round negotiations on the Code have incorporated environmental interests into the redrafted Standards Code in two ways (Dunkel Draft Final Act). First, the environment is mentioned with health and safety as a valid reason for enforcing national technical standards. This appears to provide scope for environmental standards to be used to restrict trade. Second, the draft Code includes 'processes and production methods' within technical regulations. If importing countries were allowed to prescribe the production methods for

acceptable imports, opportunities for discrimination and protection would increase. During 1991, the Uruguay Round negotiating group on technical standards clawed back some ground
by referring to 'products and related processes and production
methods'. It remains to be seen how the final Uruguay Round
agreement turns out.

Developing economies' governments are beginning to regard
these pressures exerted to amend the GATT rules and to influence their domestic policies as eco-imperialism. Most of the
global environmental problems have been caused by development in industrialised economies and they are responsible for
pollution threats to the atmosphere. The property rights of
developing economies are being infringed by green sermons
from the rich countries. Developing economies resent being
asked to restrict their trade and development to overcome these
problems. They are sometimes concerned by the emphasis
given to the environment by the rich when there is so much
poverty in their populations.

Financial assistance for environmental protection

The 1992 Earth Summit produced the Rio Declaration and
Agenda 21, which form the basis for future agreements on environment and development. In addition, two draft conventions
were approved, one on climate change and one on biodiversity,
subject to an enlargement and reconstruction of the Global
Environment Facility to support developing economies' efforts
to comply with the two new conventions.

In the year following UNCED some progress was made with
the new conventions. The first meeting of the Commission for
Sustainable Development (in New York, June 1993) to oversee
the agreements was largely procedural.

Developing economies' participation in the global conventions approved in Rio will depend on an operational Global
Environment Facility (GEF). The funding and management of
the GEF is still under discussion. At the Participants Meeting
in Beijing (May 1993), concerns were expressed by the United
States and the developing economies about representation on
the management and the secretariat, and about control over

approval of GEF projects. That meeting finished one day early and the GEF seems likely to develop into a UN political wrangle.

The GEF pilot phase (1990–93) is nearing completion, with the initial US$1.3 billion pledge being largely committed by the end of 1993. The GEF has three coordinating agencies, the World Bank, United Nations Environment Program and United Nations Development Program. The GEF provides finance (grants and conditional lending) for investments and technical assistance to contribute to protection against global environmental degradation: climate change, biodiversity, ozone depletion and international waters. (More than 80 per cent of funds have been allocated so far to counteracting global warming and protecting biodiversity.) It is intended that the GEF should finance additional costs to developing economies arising from the two new global conventions. Separate financial provisions included in the Montreal Protocol are administered by the GEF although applied to ozone protection.

The acceptable and cost-effective operation of the GEF is probably a prerequisite for developing economies' participation in the new global treaties (Robertson 1990). Its role will have to expand to satisfy developing economies that the burden for protecting the global commons does not fall on them. It was pointed out in Rio that revenues from any carbon taxes imposed in OECD countries should be transferred to developing economies to help them to reduce pollution and emissions.

The volume of resources needed by developing economies to overcome their environmental problems is subject to exaggeration and overestimation depending on the targets set for the environment. Even so, World Bank estimates, which seem reasonably based, indicate that vast sums must be diverted from industrialised economies over the next decade (World Bank 1992a).

The World Bank estimates that US$37–42 billion is needed for local and national problems, which have priority in developing economies. Investments to maintain growth in agricultural and output growth will amount to US$20–25 billion (Table 13.1). If global environmental concerns such as climate change are accorded greater priority, additional outlays to improve fuel efficiency and to install renewable energy sources will add to these costs, subject to the form of any carbon tax and distribution of the revenue. Any projections of this kind

Table 13.1: Estimates of environmental restoration costs in 2000, (1990 US$ billion per year)

Investment in water and sanitation	10
Reducing emissions from coal-fired power stations	7
Reducing motor vehicle pollution	10
Reducing industrial pollution	10–15
Agriculture and forest programs	20–25
Family planning and education	8
Total	60–75

Source: World Bank, 1992a, *World Development Report 1992*, Oxford University Press, Oxford:Table 9.1.

are difficult but the *World Development Report, 1992* (World Bank 1992a) indicates costs are about equivalent to present overseas development assistance from OECD donors (OECD 1993). In other words, to the extent that the financial burden for environmental improvement has to be met from the budgets of industrialised economies, OECD donors would have to increase their present ODA/GNP ratios from 0.35 per cent towards the United Nations' overseas development assistance target of 0.7 per cent.

As developing economies' growth rates improve they will be able to increase resources applied to national problems, such as health, sanitation and water. Much of the cost will be paid for by producers and consumers if economic policy instruments are introduced to internalise externalities. At the same time, important programs on education and family planning will probably require more funding than *World Development Report, 1992* (World Bank 1992a) estimates. Restoring water quality and soil loss will require major public works. At least US$25 billion in additional aid will be required by the end of the 1990s, one-third higher than present levels.

The demand for financial transfers from industrialised economies to improve environmental performance in developing economies will be large. At the same time, industrialised economies require investment in their own infrastructures and environmental programs, as well as supporting reconstruction in former socialist economies. Unless much larger transfers are made, it is unlikely that developing economies will contribute to the various global environmental targets. The alternative is to wait until their own living standards reach levels where the environment becomes a priority for them.

Meeting developing economies' concerns

Developing economies are openly fearful that trade restrictions may be used to force them to meet environmental targets set by industrialised economies and implemented through new global treaties. Threats to amend the GATT rules to allow trade discrimination by industrialised economies to extend the effectiveness of their environmental laws and policies are not taken lightly. At the same time, some developing economies resent intrusions into their domestic affairs and infringements of sovereign rights over their national resources, evident in proposed new global environment treaties and in proclamations by green groups.

Global treaties intended to coerce countries into adopting particular environmental policies and targets are unlikely to achieve the desired goals. Historically, trade sanctions have generally been unsuccessful (Hufbauer and Schott 1985). Moreover, economic theory establishes that trade policy instruments are inefficient for dealing with domestic economic distortions, such as environmental externalities (Lloyd 1992).

Where environmental priorities differ, as they often do between developing and industrialised economies, targeted improvements are more likely to be attained through cooperation than through threats and sanctions. Concerns with global issues (climate change, biodiversity, oceans and ozone) are most evident in industrialised economies, while developing economies are more concerned with domestic issues, such as health, water quality and sanitation. If industrialised economies wish to attract developing economies' interest in global issues, there is a good case for compensation in the form of financial or technology transfers. Private sector actions such as debt-for-nature swaps and private aid flows may help.

The main burden of transfers must fall on overseas development assistance programs. If most weight is given to developing economies' domestic environmental concerns, the type of aid increases set out by the World Bank would be required before developing economies contribute much to global environmental targets. This would require a major increase in overseas development assistance from OECD economies in the 1990s.

As the scope of new global treaties increases, their overlap with existing treaties such as the GATT will reach proportions that require reconciliation. The prospects for a 'Green Round' of GATT negotiations are increasing. The dangers of such negotiations being captured by protectionists do not seem to concern environmental lobbies. In ensuring that GATT principles remain in place the major developing economies have made their interests clear.

Although global treaties have captured the high ground of environmental politics, the enthusiasm evident among environmental lobbies in industrialised economies is unlikely to be echoed in many developing economies. The expressed concerns of the communities are unlikely to be matched by real resources, when the economic costs become evident. (Media polls are a poor indicator of financial support.) Already, some industrialised economies' governments are reconsidering their commitments to the Convention on Climate Change. Some European countries are reassessing the economic implications of carbon taxes (favoured by the European Community Commission). The effects of new taxes on industrial costs have become sensitive during the recession. The Clinton Administration, on the other hand, seems to be more forthcoming about overseas development assistance increases than the Bush administration was at UNCED, although, again, the talk is likely to be ahead of resource commitments allowing for other policies.

The UNCED outcome is reminiscent of United Nations Conference on Trade and Development debates in the 1970s on the new international economic order. The emphasis at UN meetings is on drafting agreed texts, with little attention given to the practicality of provisions or to devising effective instruments. The negotiating process at UNCED and in subsequent drafting of the new global treaties is complicated by the breakdown of old G77 alliances.

Developing economies' priorities will play a key role in the introduction of any new global environmental treaties and in the types of instruments they will include.

Bibliography

Adams, F.G. and Behrman, J., 1982. *Commodity Export and Economic Development: the commodity problem, goal attainment and policy in developing countries*, Lexington Books, D.C. Heath, Lexington, Mass.

AIDAB, see Australian International Development Assistance Bureau.

Amin, S., 1976. *Unequal Development: An Essay on the Social Formations of Peripheral Capitalism*, Month Rev. Press, New York.

Amsden, A., 1989. *Asia's New Giant: South Korea and Late Industrialisation*, Oxford University Press, New York.

Anderson, K., 1981. 'Politico-economic factors affecting public agricultural research investment in developing countries', in M.A. Bellamy and B.L. Greenshields (eds), *The Rural Challenge*, Gower, London.

——, 1983. 'Growth of agricultural protection in East Asia', *Food Policy*, 8(4):327–36.

——, 1987. 'On why agriculture declines with economic growth', *Agricultural Economics*, 1(3):195–207.

——, 1990a. *Changing Comparative Advantage in China: Effects on Food, Feed and Fibre Markets*, OECD, Paris.

——, 1990b. 'China's economic growth, changing comparative advantages and agricultural trade', *Review of Marketing and Agricultural Economics*, 58(1):56–75.

——, 1992. 'Europe 1992 and the Western Pacific Economies', *Economic Journal*, 101(November):1538–52.

——, 1994. 'Lobbying incentives and the pattern of protection in rich and poor countries', *Economic Development and Cultural Change* 42(1), October.

—— and Blackhurst, R. (eds), 1993. *Regional Integration and the Global Trading System*, Harvester-Wheatsheaf, London.

——, Hayami, Y. and George, A., 1986. *The Political Economy of Agricultural Protection: East Asia in International Perspective*, Allen & Unwin, Sydney.

____ and Garnaut, R., 1987. *Australian Protectionism: Extent, Causes and Effects*, Allen & Unwin, Sydney.

____ and Hege, Norheim, 1992. *Is World Trade Becoming More Regionalised?*, General Agreement on Tariffs and Trade Secretariat, Geneva.

____ and Tyers, R., 1992. 'Japanese rice policy in the interwar period: some consequences of imperial self-sufficiency', *Japan and the World Economy*, 4(2):103–27.

____ and ____, 1994. 'Implications of EC expansion for European agricultural policies, trade and welfare', in R. Baldwin, P. Haaparanta and J. Kiander (eds), *Expanding European Regionalism: The EC's New Members*, Cambridge University Press, Cambridge, 1994.

Ando, A. and Modigliani, F., 1963. 'The "lifecycle" hypothesis of saving: aggregate implications and tests', *American Economic Review*, 53:55–84.

Aopi, G., 1993. 'Towards 2000: the economic impact on Papua New Guinea of the changing aid relationship—the Papua New Guinea perspective', Address to the PNG Aid Forum, Brisbane, 29 November.

Arden-Clarke, C., 1992. *International Trade, GATT and the Environment*, World Wildlife Fund, Geneva.

Ariff, M. and Hill, H., 1985. *Export Oriented Industrialisation: The ASEAN Experience*, Allen & Unwin, Sydney.

Armington, P.S., 1969. 'A theory of demand for products distinguished by place of production', *IMF Staff Papers*, 16(1): 159–78.

Arndt, H.W., 1965. 'Australia—developed, developing or midway?', *The Economic Record*, 41(95):318–40.

____, 1987. *Economic Development: The History of an Idea*, University of Chicago Press, Chicago.

Australian Council for Overseas Aid, 1992. *Aid for a Change*, ACFOA, Canberra.

Australian International Development Assistance Bureau (AIDAB), 1992. *Australia's Overseas Aid Program 1992–1993*, AGPS, Canberra.

____, 1993a. *Development with a DIFFerence*, AGPS, Canberra.

____, 1993b. *The Commercial Benefits from Development Cooperation with China*, AGPS, Canberra.

____, 1993c. *Evaluation Series*, AIDAB, Canberra.

____, 1993d. *Project Profiles: PNG and Australia*, AIDAB, Canberra.

____, 1993e. *Australia's Development Cooperation Program 1993–94*, AGPS, Canberra.

Australian Treasury, Dept of, 1981. *Economic Paper 9*, AGPS, Canberra.

Austria, M.S., 1992. Aggregate Productivity in the Philippines Economy, PhD dissertation, The Australian National University, Canberra.

Aw, Bee-Yan, 1991. 'Singapore', in D. Papageorgiou, M. Michaely and A. Choksi (eds), *Liberalizing Foreign Trade, Korea, the Philippines, and Singapore*, Basil Blackwell, Cambridge, Mass.:309–428.

Balassa, B., 1985. *Change and Challenge in the World Economy*, Macmillan, London.

——, 1986. 'Japan's trade policies', *Weltwirtschaftliches Archiv*, 122(4): 745–90.

——, 1988. 'Temporary windfalls and compensation arrangements', *Policy, Planning and Research Working Paper*, 28, World Bank, Washington, D.C.

Baldwin, R.E., 1969. 'The case against infant industry tariff protection', *Journal of Political Economy*, 77(3):295–305.

Bates, R.E., 1983. *Markets and States in Tropical Africa*, University of California Press, Berkeley.

Bates, R.H. and Krueger, A.O. (eds), 1993. *Political and Economic Interactions in Economic Policy Reform: Evidence from Eight Countries*, Basil Blackwell, Oxford.

Bautista, R.M., 1990. 'Poverty alleviation, economic growth and development policy in East Asia', *NCDS Working Paper*, 90/54, National Centre for Development Studies, The Australian National University, Canberra.

——, Hughes, H., Lim, D., Morawetz, D. and Thoumi, F., 1983. *Capital Utilization in Manufacturing in Developing Countries*, IBRD, Oxford University Press, New York.

Beckerman, W., 1992. 'Economic growth and the environment: whose growth? whose environment?', *World Development*, 20(4):481–96.

Bergsten, C.F. and Noland, M., 1993. *Reconcilable Differences? United States–Japan Economic Conflict*, Institute for International Economics, Washington, D.C.

Bevan, D.L., Collier, P. and Gunning, J.W., 1987. 'Consequences of a commodity boom in a controlled economy: accumulation and redistribution in Kenya, 1975–83', *World Bank Economic Review*, 1(3):489–513.

——, 1989. 'Fiscal response to a temporary trade shock: the aftermath of the Kenyan coffee boom', *World Bank Economic Review*, 3(3):359–78.

Bhagwati, J., 1978. 'Anatomy and consequences of exchange control regimes', *Foreign Trade Regimes and Economic Development*, Vol. 11, National Bureau of Economic Research, Cambridge, Mass.

——, 1988. 'Export-promoting trade strategy: issues and evidence', *The World Bank Research Observer*, 3(1):27–57.

____, 1992. Regionalism vs. multilateralism: an overview, Paper presented at the World Bank–CPER conference on New Dimensions in Regional Integration, Washington 2–3 April.

____ and Eckaus, R. (eds), 1970. *Foreign Aid*, Penguin, London.

Bilney, G., 1993. Papua New Guinea and Australia: a developing partnership, Address to PNG Aid Forum, Brisbane, 29 November.

Binswanger, H.P., 1987. 'Brazilian policies that encourage deforestation in the Amazon', *World Bank Environment Department Working Paper*, 16, World Bank, Washington, D.C.

Braga, C.A.P., 1992. 'Tropical forests and trade policy: the case of Indonesia and Brazil', in Patrick Low (ed.), *International Trade and the Environment*, World Bank Discussion Paper, 159, Washington, D.C.

Branson, W.H., 1972. *Macroeconomic Theory and Policy*, Harper & Row, New York.

Brittan, Sir Leon, 1992. The role of industrial and competition policies in a world of megacompetition, Davos, Switzerland, 3 February.

Brown, W., 1990. 'Trade deals a blow to the environment', *New Scientist*, 10 November:12–13.

Brundtland, G.H., 1987. *Our Common Future*, World Commission on Environment and Development, Penguin, London.

Bulatao, R.A., Bos, E., Stephens, P.W. and Vu, M.T., 1990. *World Population Projections 1989–90 Edition*, Johns Hopkins University Press, Baltimore.

Bulletin, The, 26 May 1993.

Burgess, M., 1993. 'Aid and third world development', *Current Affairs Bulletin*, 69(12).

Byrd, W.A., 1987. 'The impact of the two-tier, plan/market system in Chinese industry', *Journal of Comparative Economics*, 11(3):295–308.

Carvalho, J.L. and Haddad, C., L.S., 1981. 'Foreign trade strategies and employment in Brazil', in A.O. Krueger, L.B. Hal and N. Akrasanee (eds), *Trade and Employment in Developing Countries, 1, Individual Studies*, University of Chicago Press for the National Bureau of Economic Research, Chicago:29–82.

Chan, Sir Julius, 1993. Keynote Address, Paper presented at the PNG Aid Forum, Brisbane, 29 November.

Chandavarkar, A., 1993. 'Saving behaviour in the Asia-Pacific Region', *Asian-Pacific Economic Literature*, 7(1):9–24.

Chen, Xiwen, 1993. 'Jieguo biange yu buju tiaozheng: xiangzhen qiye fazhan de xin jieduan' (Structural change and geographical adjustment: a new phase of development for township enterprises), *Nongye Jingji Wenti (Issues in Agricultural Economics)*, 1:31–35.

Chenery, H.B. and Strout, A., 1966. 'Foreign assistance and economic development', *American Economic Review*, 56(4):679–733.

Cheng, Enjiang, 1992. 'Financial reforms and the role of credit co-operatives in China's rural economic development', Paper presented at the Fifth Annual conference of the Chinese Economic Association, University of Adelaide, Adelaide, November 12–13, 1992.

Chia Siow Yue, 1993. ASEAN economic development strategies: a comparison with the Asian NIEs, Paper presented at the *Trans-Pacific conference*, Centre for Pacific Rim Studies, University of California, Los Angeles.

China News Digest, various issues.

Chinn, M. and Frankel, J., 1992. 'Financial links around the Pacific rim: 1982–1992', in R. Glick (ed.), *Exchange Rate Policies in Pacific Basin Countries*, Proceedings of a conference at the Reserve Bank of San Francisco, 16–18 September, 1992.

Cho, Y. and Khatkhate, D., 1989. 'Lessons of financial liberalization in Asia: a comparative study', *World Bank Discussion Paper*, 50, World Bank, Washington, D.C.

Chowdury, A. and Islam, I., 1993. *The Newly Industrialising Economies of East Asia*, Routledge, London.

Christensen, S.R. et. al., 1992. Institutional and political bases of growth-inducing policies in Thailand, World Bank, Washington, D.C.

Claessens, S. and Coleman, J., 1991. 'Hedging commodity price risks in Papua New Guinea', *Policy, Research and External Affairs Working Paper*, 749, World Bank, Washington, D.C.

_____ and Duncan, R.C., 1993. *Managing Commodity Price Risk in Developing Countries*, Oxford University Press, Oxford.

_____ and Varangis, Panos, 1993. 'Oil price instability, hedging and an oil stabilization fund: the case of Venezuela', International Economics Department, World Bank, Washington, D.C. (mimeo).

Coase, R., 1960. 'The problem of social costs', *Journal of Law and Economics*, 3:1–44.

Cole, D. and Lyman, P., 1971. *Korean Development, The Interplay of Politics and Economics*, Harvard University Press, Cambridge, Mass.

Coleman, J. and Jones, C., 1993. 'Commodity price stabilization, insurance and the role of public policy', World Bank, Washington, D.C. (mimeo).

Collins, S., 1991. 'Saving behavior in ten developing countries', in D. Bernheim and H. Shoaven (eds), *National Savings and Economic Performance*, University of Chicago Press, Chicago.

Community Aid Abroad, 1992. *Review*, CAA, Melbourne.

Coombs, H.C., 1981. *Trial Balance: Issues of my Working Life*, Sun Papermac, South Melbourne.

Cooper, Richard, 1974. 'Worldwide versus regional integration: is there an optimal size of the integrated area?', *Yale Economic Growth Center Discussion Paper*, 220, Yale.

Coppock, J.D, 1962. *International Economic Instability*, McGraw-Hill Publishing Company, New York.

Corbo, V. 1992. *Developing Strategies and Policies in Latin America: A Historical Perspective*, ICS Press, San Francisco.

Corden, W.M., 1974. *Trade Policy and Economic Welfare*, Clarendon Press, Oxford.

_____, (ed.), 1985. 'Exchange rate protection', in W.M. Corden (ed.), *Protection, Growth and Trade: Essays in International Economics*, Blackwell, Oxford:271–87.

_____, 1993. 'Exchange rate policies for developing countries', *Economic Journal*, 103:198–207.

Cropper, M.L. and Oates, W.E., 1992. 'Environmental economics: a survey', *Journal of Economic Literature*, XXX(June):675–740.

Cuddington, J., 1989. 'Commodity export booms in developing countries', *World Bank Research Observer*, 4(2):143–65.

_____ and Hill, C.B., 1992. 'Diamond booms in Botswana and the permanent income hypothesis', *Georgetown University Department of Economics Working Paper*, 92–10, Georgetown University.

_____, and Urzúa, C.M., 1989. 'Trends and cycles in the net barter terms of trade: a new approach', *Economic Journal*, 99:426–42.

Dan, Jun, 1993. 'Woguo jingji jishu kaifaqu de fazhan ji duice' (The development and strategies of China's economic and technological development zones), *Jingji Zongheng (Economic Discussions)*, 3:40–2.

Davis, J.M., 1983. 'The economic effects of windfall gains in export earnings, 1975–78', *World Development*, 2(2):119–39.

Dean, J.M., 1992. 'Trade and the environment: a survey of the literature', in P. Low (ed.), *International Trade and the Environment, World Bank Discussion Paper*, 159, World Bank, Washington, D.C.

_____, Desai, S. and Riedel, J. 1993. *Trade Policy Reform in Developing Countries, A Review of and the Evidence Since 1985*, World Bank, Washington, D.C. (unpub.).

Deaton, A.S., 1992. 'Commodity prices, stabilization, and growth in Africa', *Princeton University Research Program in Development Studies Discussion Paper*, 166, 24 December.

_____ and Laroque, G., 1992. 'On the behavior of commodity prices', *Review of Economic Studies*, 59(1):1–24.

Diaz-Alejandro, C., 1965. 'On the import-intensity of import substitution', *Kyklos*, 18(3):495–511.

Dooley, M. and Isard, P., 1980. 'Capital controls, political risks, and deviations from interest-rate parity', *Journal of International Economics*, 12:257–76.

Dornbusch, R., 1992. 'The case for trade liberalization in developing countries', *Journal of Economic Perspectives*, 6(1):69–85.

—— and Edwards, S., 1989. 'The macro economics of populism in Latin America', *World Bank Working Paper*, 316, World Bank, Washington, D.C.

Drysdale, P., 1988. *International Economic Pluralism: Economic Policy in East Asia and the Pacific*, Columbia University Press, New York and Allen & Unwin, Sydney.

——, 1991. 'Open regionalism: a key to East Asia's economic future', *Pacific Economic Papers*, 197, Australia–Japan Research Centre, The Australian National University, Canberra.

—— and Elek, A. 1992. 'China and the international trading system', *Pacific Economic Papers*, 214, Australia–Japan Research Centre, The Australian National University, Canberra.

—— and Garnaut, R., 1982. 'Trade intensities and the analysis of bilateral trade flows in a many-country world', *Hitotsubashi Journal of Economics*, 22(2):62–84.

—— and ——, 1989. 'A Pacific free trade area?' in J.J. Schott (ed.), *More Free Trade Areas?*, Institute of International Economics, Washington, D.C.

—— and ——, 1993. 'The Pacific: an application of a general theory of economic integration' in C.F. Bergsten and M. Noland (eds), *Pacific Dynamism and the International Economic System*, Institute for International Economics, Washington, D.C.

Duncan, R.C., 1992. Commodity futures and risk management for developing countries: the World Bank's experience, Paper presented at the Nikkei Commodity Futures Symposium, *New Era of Commodity Futures Markets*, Tokyo, 7 December.

Easterlin, R.A., 1968. *Population, Labour Force and Long Swings in Economic Growth*, Harper & Row, New York.

Economic Daily, various issues.

Economic Planning Board, 1987. *Korea Statistical Yearbook 1986*, Seoul.

Economist, Survey, 19 October, 1992:5.

Economist Intelligence Unit, 1988. *China, Japan and the Asian NICs: Hong Kong and Macau, Singapore, South Korea, Taiwan—Economic Structure and Analysis*, EIU, London.

Editorial Board of ASEZ, 1991. *Almanac of China's Special Economic Zones and Coastal Economic and Technology Development Zones 1990*, Reform Press, Beijing.

Editorial Board of ACTE, 1992. *Almanac of China's Township Enterprises 1991*, Agriculture Press, Beijing.

Edwards, S., 1984. *The Order of Liberalization of the External Sector in Developing Countries*, Essays in International Finance 156, Princeton.

_____, 1989. 'Real exchange rates in the developing countries: concepts and measurements', *NBER Working Paper*, 2950.

Eldridge, P. (ed.), 1986. *Australian Overseas Aid: Future Directions*, Croom Helm, Sydney.

Elek, A., 1992a. 'Pacific economic cooperation: policy choices for the 1990s', *Asian-Pacific Economic Literature*, 6(1):1–15.

_____, 1992b. 'Trade policy options for the Asia Pacific region in the 1990s: the potential of open regionalism', *American Economic Review, Papers and Proceedings*, 82(2):74–8.

_____, 1992c. Regionalism in the world economy: implications for AFTA and ASEAN trade policy, Paper presented at the 17th conference of the Federation of ASEAN Economic Associations, *AFTA and Beyond*, Surabaya, Indonesia, November 15–17, 1992.

_____, 1993. Asia Pacific economic cooperation: opportunities and risks for a new initiative, Paper presented at the Asia-Australia Institute Asia Leaders Forum, *APEC in Asia*, 28–29 June, 1993.

Englander, A.S. and Mittelstadt, A., 1988. 'Total factor productivity: macroeconomic and structural aspects of the slowdown', *OECD Economic Studies*, 10:7–56.

Eskeland, G.S. and Jimenez, E., 1992. 'Policy instruments for pollution control in developing countries', *World Bank Research Observer*, 7(2), July:145–69.

European Community Council, Regulation No. 4064/89, 21 December 1989, *Official Journal of the European Community*, No. L 395, 30 December.

Fairbairn, T.I., 1993. 'Recent developments' in AIDAB, *The Papua New Guinea Economy: Prospects for Sectoral Development and Broad Based Growth*, AIDAB, International Development Issues, No. 30, AIDAB, Canberra.

Faruquee, H., 1991. Dynamic capital mobility in Pacific Basin developing countries: estimation and policy implications, *IMF Working Paper*, 115, International Monetary Fund, Washington, D.C.

Feldstein, M. and Horioka, C., 1980. 'Domestic savings and international capital flows', *Economic Journal*, 90:314–29.

Feltenstein, A. and Fahadian, Z., 1987. 'Fiscal policy, monetary targets, and price level in a centrally planned economy: an application to the case of China', *Journal of Money, Credit and Banking*, 19(2):138–56.

Finger, J.M., 1991. 'Development economics and the General

Agreement on Tariffs and Trade' in J. de Melo and A. Sapir (eds), *Trade Theory and Economic Reform: North, South, and East: Essays in Honour of Béla Balassa*, Basil Blackwell, Cambridge, Mass.

——, 1992. 'GATT's influence on regional trade arrangements', Paper presented at the World Bank–CPER conference, *New Dimensions in Regional Integration*, Washington, 2–3 April.

Fischer, S., 1993. 'Does macroeconomic policy matter?: Evidence from developing countries', *ICEG Occasional Paper*, 27, International Center for Economic Growth, ICS Press, San Francisco, California.

Flavin, M., 1981. 'The adjustment of consumption to changing expectations about future income', *Journal of Political Economy*, 89:974–1009.

Flood, P., 1993. 'Discussant's paper', Hughes *Festschrift*, The Australian National University, August.

Food and Agriculture Organisation, 1992. *Production Yearbook*, FAO, Rome.

Frank, C.R. Jr, Kwang Suk Kim and Westphal, L.E., 1975. *Foreign Trade Regimes and Economic Development, Vol. 7: South Korea*, Columbia University Press for the National Bureau of Economic Research, New York.

Frank, I., 1980. *Foreign Enterprises in Developing Countries*, Johns Hopkins University Press, Baltimore.

——, 1989. 'Comments' in J.J. Schott (ed.), *Free Trade Areas and U.S. Trade Policy*, Institute for International Economics, Washington, D.C.:85–9.

——, 1991. *Breaking New Ground in U.S. Trade Policy*, Westview Press, Boulder.

Frankel, J., 1991. 'Is a Yen bloc forming in Pacific Asia?' in R. O'Brien (ed.), *Finance and the International Economy, The AMEX Bank Review Prize Essays*, Oxford University Press, Oxford.

——, 1992. 'Is Japan creating a Yen bloc in East Asia and the Pacific?', Paper presented at the NBER conference, *Japan and the U.S. in Pacific Asia*, Del Mar, CA, 3–5 April.

——, 1993. 'Is Japan creating a Yen bloc in the Pacific', in R. Garnaut and P. Drysdale (eds), *Asia Pacific Regionalism: Readings in International Economic Relations*, Harper Educational, Sydney.

Fukusaku, K., 1992. 'Economic regionalism and intra-industry trade: Pacific Asia perspectives', *OECD Development Centre Technical Papers*, 53, Paris, February.

Gao Xiaoguang, 1993. China's Foreign Exchange Regime and Its Impact on Export and Growth, PhD dissertation, National Centre for Development Studies, The Australian National University, Canberra.

Garnaut, R. 1972. Australian Trade With Southeast Asia: A Study of
    Resistances to Bilateral Trade Flows, PhD dissertation, The
    Australian National University, Canberra.
____, 1991a. 'Exchange rate regimes in the Asian-Pacific region',
    Asian-Pacific Economic Literature, 5(1):5–26.
____, 1991b. 'The market and the state in economic development:
    applications to the international system', Singapore Economic
    Review, 36(2):13–26.
____, 1994. 'The floating dollar and the Australian structural
    transition', Economic Record, 70:80–86.
____ and Ma Guonan, 1992. China's Grain Economy, Australian
    Government Publishing Service, Canberra.
____ and ____, 1993a. 'Economic growth and stability in China',
    Journal of Asian Economics, 4(1):5–24.
____ and ____, 1993b. 'How rich is China?: evidence from the food
    economy', Australian Journal of Chinese Affairs, 30:121–46.
General Agreement on Tariffs and Trade, (GATT), 1991. International
    Trade, 1990-91, Vol. 1, GATT, Geneva.
____, 1993. Focus: GATT Newsletter, No. 100 (July), GATT, Geneva.
George, S., 1988. A Fate Worse than Debt, Penguin, New York.
Gersovitz, M. and Paxson, C.H., 1990. 'The economies of Africa and
    prices of their exports', Princeton Studies in International Finance,
    68, Princeton University, Princeton.
Gilbert, C.L., 1984. 'Efficient market commodity price dynamics',
    Commodity Studies and Projections Division Working Paper,
    1984–85, World Bank, Washington, D.C.
____, 1992. 'Commodity markets, commodity futures and
    international commodity policy', Department of Economics,
    University of London Paper, 248, Queen Mary and Westfield
    College, London.
Glezakos, C., 1973. 'Export instability and economic growth: a
    statistical verification', Economic Development and Cultural Change,
    21:670–8.
Gold, T.B., 1986. State and Society in the Taiwan Miracle, M.E. Sharpe
    Inc., New York.
Goldsborough, D. and Teja, R., 1991. Globalization of financial
    markets and implications for Pacific Basin developing countries,
    IMF Working Paper, 34, International Monetary Fund,
    Washington, D.C.
Grilli, E. 1994. 'Economic growth, income distribution and poverty in
    developing countries: the evidence', in E. Grilli and D. Salvatore
    (eds), Economic Development Handbook, North-Holland,
    Amsterdam.
____ and Yang, M.C., 1988. 'Primary commodity prices,
    manufactured goods prices, and the terms of trade of

developing countries: what the long run shows', *World Bank Economic Review*, 2(1):1–48.

Grossman, G. and Helpman, E., 1991. *Innovation and Growth in the Global Economy*, MIT Press, Cambridge, Mass.

———, 1992. 'Trade wars and trade talks', Princeton University, Princeton (mimeo).

Hall, R., 1978. 'Stochastic implications of the life cycle permanent income hypothesis: theory and evidence', *Journal of Political Economy*, 86(6):971–87.

Hamilton, C. and Winters, L.A., 1992. 'Opening up international trade in Eastern Europe', *Economic Policy*, 7(14):78–116.

Haque, N. and Montiel, P., 1990. Capital mobility in developing countries—some empirical tests, *IMF Working Paper*, 117, International Monetary Fund, Washington, D.C.

Harberger, A., 1988. 'Growth, industrialization and economic structure: Latin America and East Asia compared', in H. Hughes (ed.), *Achieving Industrialization in East Asia*, Cambridge University Press, Cambridge:164–94.

Hare, P., 1992. 'Europe', *Oxford Review of Economic Policy*, 8(1):82–104.

Harris, G. and Jarrett, F., 1990. *Educating Overseas Students in Australia: Who Benefits?*, Allen & Unwin, Sydney.

Hayter, T. and Watson, C., 1985. *Aid: Rhetoric and Reality*, Pluto, London.

Hill, C.B., 1991. 'Managing commodity booms in Botswana', *World Development*, 19(9):1185–96.

Hillman, A.L. and Moser, P., 1992. Trade liberalization as politically optimal exchange of market access, Paper presented at the fifth ERWIT conference, Lisbon, 24–28 June.

Hirshman, A., 1957. 'Economic policies in underdeveloped countries', *Economic Development and Cultural Change*, 5(4):362–70.

Ho, C.S., 1992. 'Comparison of aggregate productivity trends between Taiwan and the Chinese mainland', Paper presented at the conference, *Productivity, Efficiency, and Reform in China's Economy*, Chinese University of Hong Kong, Hong Kong.

Horioka, C.Y., 1990. 'Why is Japan's household saving rate so high?: a literature survey', *Journal of the Japanese and International Economies*, 4:49–92.

Horiuchi, A., 1984. 'The "low interest rate policy" and economic growth in postwar Japan', *The Developing Economies*, 22(4):349–71.

Hudec, R.E., 1987. *Developing Countries in the GATT Legal System*, Thames Essay 50, Gower for the Trade Policy Research Centre, London.

Hufbauer, G.C. (ed.), 1990. *Europe 1992: An American Perspective*, The Brookings Institution, Washington, D.C.

_____ and Schott, J., 1985. *Economic Sanctions Reconsidered: History and Current Policy*, Institute for International Economics, Washington, D.C.

Hughes, E. and Hare, P., 1992. 'Industrial policy and the restructuring of Eastern Europe', *Oxford Review of Economic Policy*, 8(1):82–104.

Hughes, H., 1964. *The Australian Iron and Steel Industry 1848–1962*, Melbourne University Press, Melbourne.

_____, 1968–71. Letters to Heinz W. Arndt.

_____, 1971. 'The manufacturing sector', in Asian Development Bank, *Southeast Asia's Economy in the 1970s*, Longman, London.

_____, 1972. 'Assessment of policies towards direct foreign investment', in P. Drysdale (ed.), *Direct Foreign Investment in Asia and the Pacific*, The Australian National University Press, Canberra.

_____, 1980. 'The prospects of ASEAN countries in industrialised country markets', in Ross Garnaut (ed.), *ASEAN in a Changing Pacific and World Economy*, Australian National University Press, Canberra.

_____, 1984. 'External debt problems of developing countries', in R. Bautista and S. Naya (eds), *Energy and Structural Change in the Asia Pacific Region*, The Philippines Institute for Developing Studies, Manila.

_____, 1985. 'Policy lessons of the development experience,' *Group of Thirty, Occasional Paper*, 16, New York.

_____, 1986. 'The political economy of protectionism in eleven industrial countries', in R. Snape (ed.), *Issues in World Trade Policy: GATT at the Crossroads*, Macmillan, London.

_____, (ed.), 1988a. *Achieving Industrialization in East Asia*, Cambridge University Press, Cambridge.

_____, 1988b. 'Explaining the Differences Between the Growth of Developing Countries in Asia and Latin America in the 1980s', *NCDS Working Paper*, 88/3, National Centre for Development Studies, The Australian National University, Canberra.

_____, 1989a. 'Towards clarity and common sense', in S. Naya, M. Urrutia, S. Mark and A. Fuentes (eds), *Lessons in Development: A Comparative Study of Asian and Latin American Countries*, ICS Press, San Francisco:259–78.

_____, 1989b. 'Agricultural development, growth and equity: 30 years of experience', *NCDS Reprint Series*, 1, National Centre for Development Studies, The Australian National University, Canberra.

_____, (ed.), 1992. *The Dangers of Export Pessimism: Developing Country*

Exports to Industrial Markets, International Center for Economic Growth, San Francisco.

——, 1993a. 'East Asia: is there an East Asian model?', *Economics Division Working Papers*, 93/4, Research School of Pacific Studies, The Australian National University, Canberra.

——, 1993b. 'Development policies and development performance', in E. Grilli and D. Salvatore (eds), *Handbook of Economic Development*, North-Holland, Amsterdam.

—— and You Poh Seng, 1969. *Foreign Investment and Industrialization in Singapore*, Australian National University Press, Canberra.

—— and Woldekidan, B., 1993. Improving social welfare in developing countries: a fifty year perspective, Paper presented at the conference, *Individual and Social Wellbeing*, National Centre for Development Studies, The Australian National University, Canberra.

Ikemoto, Y., 1986. 'Technical progress and level of technology in Asian countries, 1970–80: a translog index approach', *The Developing Economies*, 24(4):368–90.

International Business, various issues.

International Economic Databank, The Australian National University, Canberra.

International Labor Organisation (ILO), 1992. *Yearbook of Labor Statistics*, ILO, Geneva.

International Monetary Fund (IMF), 1976–78. *Exchange Restrictions— Annual Report*, Washington, D.C.

——, 1979–92. *Exchange Arrangements and Exchange Restrictions— Annual Report*, IMF, Washington, D.C.

——, various years. *International Financial Statistics*, IMF, Washington, D.C.

Irwin, D.A., 1992. 'Multilateral and bilateral trade policies in the world trading system: an historical perspective', Paper presented at the World Bank–CPER conference, *New Dimensions in Regional Integration*, Washington, 2–3 April.

Islam, I., 1992. 'Political economy and East Asian economic development', *Asian-Pacific Economic Literature*, 6(2): 69-101.

Jackson, R.G. et al., 1984, *Report of the Committee to Review the Australian Overseas Aid Program*, (The Jackson Report), AGPS, Canberra.

James, W.E. and McCleary, R., 1992. 'The US response to increasing regionalism: a Pacific perspective', in M.G. Plummer and W.E. James (eds), *Europe and Asia in the 1990s*.

Jamison, D.T. and Lau, L.J., 1982. *Farmer Education and Farm Efficiency*, The Johns Hopkins University Press, Baltimore.

Jarrett, F.G. and Anderson, K., 1989. *Growth, Structural Change and Economic Policy in Papua New Guinea: Implications for Agriculture*,

National Centre for Development Studies, The Australian
National University, Canberra.

Johnson, B.C., 1983. *Development in South Asia*, Penguin Books, New
York.

Johnson, D.G., 1991. *World Agriculture in Disarray*, St Martins Press,
New York.

Johnson, H.G., 1965. 'Optimal trade interventions in the presence of
domestic distortions', in R.E. Baldwin et al. (eds), *Trade, Growth
and the Balance of Payments*, Essays in honor of Gottfried
Haberler, North-Holland, Amsterdam.

Joint Committee on Foreign Affairs, Defence and Trade, 1989.
*A Review of the Australian International Development Assistance
Bureau and Australia's Overseas Aid Program*, AGPS, Canberra.

Jomini, P., Zeitsch, J.F., McDougall, R., Welsh, A., Brown, S.,
Hambley, J. and Kelly, J., 1991. *Salter: A General Equilibrium
Model Of The World Economy, Volume I, Model Structure, Database
And Parameters*, Industry Commission, Canberra.

_____, McDougall, R., Watts, G. and Dee, P.S., 1994. *The Salter Model
of the World Economy: Model Structure, Database and Parameters*,
Industry Commission, Canberra.

Jorgenson, D.W. and Gollop, F.M., 1992. 'Productivity growth and
US agriculture: a postwar perspective', *American Journal of
Agricultural Economics*, 74(3):745–56.

Judd, M.A., Boyce, J.K. and Evenson, R.E., 1986. 'Investing in
agricultural supply: the determinants of agricultural research
and extension', *Economic Development and Cultural Change*, 35(1):
77–114.

Julius, D., 1990. *Global Companies and Public Policy: The Growing
Challenge of Direct Investment*, The Royal Institute of International
Affairs, London.

Kelly, J., 1989. *Australians' Attitudes to Overseas Aid*, AGPS, Canberra.

Kendrick, J.W., 1992. 'Why was US economic growth in the 1980's
not stronger?', *Southern Economic Journal*, 59(1):104–7.

Kenen, P.B. and Voivodas, C., 1972. 'Export instability and economic
growth', *Kyklos*, 25:791–804.

Kerin, J., 1992. *Changing Aid for a Changing World*, AIDAB, Canberra.

Khan, M. and Villanueva, D., 1991. 'Macroeconomic Policies and
Long-Term Growth: A Conceptual and Empirical Review', *IMF
Working Paper*, 28, International Monetary Fund, Washington,
D.C.

Kiguel, M.A. and Liviatan, N., 1990. 'The inflation-stabilization
cycles in Argentina and Brazil', *World Bank Working Paper*, 443,
World Bank, Washington, D.C.

_____ and _____, 1992. 'Nominal anchors, stabilization and growth:
some thoughts on high-inflation economies' in V. Corbo et al.

(eds), *Adjustment Lending Revisited: Policies to Restore Growth*,
World Bank, Washington, D.C.

Kim, J., and Lau, L.J., 1992. The sources of economic growth of the
newly industrialized countries on the Pacific rim, Paper
presented at the conference, *Economic Development of the Republic
of China and the Pacific Rim in the 1990s and Beyond*, Taipei,
Taiwan.

Kim, K. and Park, J., 1985. *Sources of Economic Growth in Korea:
1963-1982*, Korean Development Institute, Seoul.

Kim Kwang Suk, 1991. 'Korea', in D. Papageorgiou, M. Michaely
and A.M. Choksi (eds), *Liberalizing Foreign Trade, Korea, the
Philippines, and Singapore*, Basil Blackwell, Cambridge,
Mass.:1–131.

Kindleberger, C.P., 1975. 'The rise of free trade in Western Europe,
1820–75', *Journal of Economic History*, 35(1):20–55.

Knudsen, O. and Parnes, A., 1975. *Trade Instability and Economic
Development*, Lexington Books, D.C. Heath, Lexington, Mass.

____, ____ and Yotopoulos, P.A., 1976. 'A transitory approach to
export instability', *Food Research Institute Studies*, XV:91–108.

Kojima Kiyoshi, 1975. 'Japan and the future of world trade policy',
in C.F. Bergsten (ed.), *Toward a New World Trade Policy: The
Maidenhead Papers*, Lexington Books, Lexington, Mass.

Krause, B.L., 1982. *United States Policy Towards the Association of
Southeast Asian Nations*, The Brookings Institution, Washington,
D.C.

Krueger, A.O., 1977. Growth, distortions, and patterns of trade
among many countries, Frank D. Graham Memorial Lecture,
Princeton University.

____, 1978. 'Liberalization attempts and consequences', *Foreign Trade
Regimes and Economic Development*, Vol. 10, National Bureau of
Economic Research, Cambridge, Mass.

____, 1980a. *The Foreign Sector and Aid*, Harvard University Press,
Cambridge.

____, 1980b. 'Trade, policy as an input to development', *American
Economic Review*, 70(2), Papers and Proceedings (May):288–92.

____, 1984a. 'Comparative advantage and development policy twenty
years later', in M. Syrquin, L. Taylor and L.E. Westphal (eds),
Economic Structure and Performance, Academic Press, Orlando, Fl.:
135–56.

____, 1984b. 'Trade policies in developing countries', in R.W. Jones
and P.B. Kenen (eds), *Handbook of International Economics*, Vol 1.,
North-Holland, Amsterdam.

____, 1984c. 'Problems of liberalization', in A. Harberger (ed.), *World
Economic Growth*, ICS Press, San Francisco.

____, 1990. 'Economists' changing perceptions of government', *Weltwirtschaftliches Archiv*, 126(34):417–31.

____, 1991. Ideas underlying early development policy, Paper presented at the Institute for Policy Reform, March.

____, 1993. *The Political Economy of Political Reform in Developing Countries*, MIT Press, Cambridge, Mass.

____, (forthcoming). 'East Asian experience and endogenous growth theory', in A.O. Krueger and T. Ibo (eds), *Lessons from East Asia*, NBER–East Asia Seminar on Economics, Vol 4, University of Chicago Press, Chicago.

____, Schiff, M. and Valdes, A., 1988. 'Agricultural incentives in developing countries: measuring the effect of sectoral and economywide policies', *World Bank Economic Review*, 2(3):255–72.

Krugman, P., 1991. 'The move to free trade zones', *Federal Reserve Bank of Kansas Review*, December.

____, 1992. Regionalism vs. multilateralism: analytical notes, Paper presented at the World Bank–CPER conference on Regional Integration, Washington, 2–3 April.

Kuo, S.W.Y., 1983. *The Taiwan Economy in Transition*, Westview Press, Boulder.

Kuznets, P., 1988. 'An East Asian model of economic development: Japan, Taiwan and South Korea', *Economic Development and Cultural Change*, 36(3):S11–S43.

Lancieri, E., 1978. 'Export instability and economic development: a reappraisal', *Banca Nazionale del Lavoro Quarterly Review*, 125: 135–52.

Lardy, N.R., 1992a. 'Chinese foreign trade', *The China Quarterly*, 131, Special Issue: The Chinese Economy in the 1990s, September: 691–720.

____, 1992b. *Foreign Trade and Economic Reform in China: 1978-1990*, Cambridge University Press, Cambridge, New York.

Larson, D.F. and Coleman, J., 1991. 'The effects of option-hedging on the costs of domestic price stabilization schemes', *Policy, Research and External Affairs Working Paper*, 653, World Bank, Washington, D.C.

Lasaga, M., 1981. *The Copper Industry in the Chilean Economy: An Econometric Analysis*, Lexington Books, D.C. Heath, Lexington, Mass.

Lawrence, R., 1987. *Imports in Japan: Closed Markets or Closed Minds?*, Brookings Papers on Economic Activity 2:517–554.

____, 1991. 'How open is Japan?' in P. Krugman (ed.), *Trade with Japan: Has the Door Opened Wider?*, University of Chicago Press, Chicago.

Lee Sheng-yi, 1990. *Money and Finance in the Economic Development of Taiwan*, Macmillan, Hampshire.

Lee Tsao Yuan (ed.), 1991. *Growth Triangle: The Johor–Singapore–Riau Experience*, Institute of South East Asian Studies, Singapore.

Leff, N.H., 1969. 'Dependency rates and savings rates', *American Economic Review*, 59:886–96.

Leonard, H.J., 1988. *Pollution and the Struggle for the World Product*, Cambridge University Press, Cambridge.

Leung, S., 1991. 'Financial liberalization in Australia and New Zealand', in S. Ostry (ed.), *Authority and Academic Scribblers: The Role of Research in East Asian Policy Reform*, International Center for Economic Growth, San Francisco.

Li, J., Gong, F. and Zheng, Y., 1992. Productivity and China's economic growth, Paper presented at the conference, *Productivity, Efficiency and Reform in China's Economy*, The Chinese University of Hong Kong, Hong Kong.

Liang, K. and Liang, C., 1981. 'Trade strategy and the exchange rate policies in Taiwan', in W. Hong and L. Krause (eds), *Trade and Growth of the Advanced Developing Countries in the Pacific Basin*, Korea Development Institute, Seoul.

———, 1988. 'Development policy formation and future priorities in the Republic of China', *Economic Development and Cultural Change*, 36(3):s67–s101.

Lim, D., 1974. 'Export instability and economic development: the example of West Malaysia', *Oxford Economic Papers*, 26(1):78–92.

———, 1980. 'Income distribution, export instability and savings behaviour', *Economic Development and Cultural Change*, 28(2):359–64.

Lin Shujuan and Yang Yongzheng, 1992. 'China's exports: performance and issues', in Helen Hughes (ed.), *The Dangers of Export Pessimism*, ICS Press, San Francisco, California.

Lincoln, E.J., 1990. *Japan's Unequal Trade*, The Brookings Institution, Washington, D.C.

Lindert, P.H., 1991. 'Historical patterns of agricultural policy', in C.P. Timmer (ed.), *Agriculture and the State: Growth, Employment and Poverty*, Cornell University Press, Ithaca.

Lipsey, R.G., 1960. 'The theory of customs unions: a general theory', *The Economic Journal* 70(Sept):496–513.

Little, I.M.D., 1982. *Economic Development: Theory, Policy, and International Relations*, Basic Books, New York.

———, 1989. 'An economic reconnaissance', in W. Galenson (ed.), *Economic Growth and Structural Change in Taiwan*, Cornell University Press, Ithaca:448–508.

Liviatan, N., 1990. 'Brazil', *World Bank Working Paper*, 443, Washington, D.C.

Lloyd, P.J., 1992. 'The problem of optimal environment policy choices', in K. Anderson and R. Blackhurst (eds), *The Greening of World Trade Issues*, Harvester-Wheatsheaf, London.

Low, P. (ed.), 1992. *International Trade and the Environment*, World Bank Discussion Paper, Washington, D.C.

_____ and Yeats, A., 1992. 'Do "dirty" industries migrate?', in P. Low (ed.), *International Trade and the Environment*, World Bank Discussion Paper 159, Washington, D.C.

Ma Guonan, 1992. 'Budget deficits and fiscal policy targets in China', *Working Paper, Centre for Chinese Political Economy*, Macquarie University, Sydney.

MacBean, A.I., 1966. *Export Instability and Economic Development*, Allen & Unwin, London.

Maizels, A., 1968. 'Review of export instability and economic development', *American Economic Review*, 58:575–80.

Mankiw, N.G., Romer, D. and Weil, D.N., 1992. 'A contribution to the empirics of economic growth', *Quarterly Journal of Economics*, 107(2):407–37.

Martin, J.W., 1990. 'Two-tier pricing in China's foreign exchange market', *China Working Paper*, 90/4, National Centre for Development Studies, The Australian National University, Canberra.

Mason, E.S., Perkins, D.H., Kwang Suk Kim and Cole, D.C., 1980. *The Economic and Social Modernization of the Republic of Korea, Studies in the Modernization of the Republic of Korea, 1945–1975*, Harvard University Press, Cambridge.

Mason, M., 1992. *American Multinationals and Japan: The Political Economy of Japanese Capital Controls, 1894–1980*, Harvard University Press, Harvard.

Mathieson, D., 1979. 'Financial reform and capital flows in a developing economy', *International Monetary Fund Staff Papers*, 26(Sept):450–89.

_____, 1988. 'Exchange rate arrangements and monetary policy', *IMF Working Paper*, 14, International Monetary Fund, Washington, D.C.

_____, 1990. 'Financial market integration and exchange rate policy', *IMF Working Paper*, 2, International Monetary Fund, Washington, D.C.

_____ and Rojas-Suarez, L., 1992. 'Liberalization of the capital account: experiences and issues', *IMF Working Paper*, 46, International Monetary Fund, Washington, D.C.

McCalla, A., 1969. 'Protectionism in international agricultural trade', *Agricultural History*, 43(3):329–44.

McCarthy, F.D. and Dhareshwar, A., 1992. 'Economic shocks and the global environment', *World Bank Policy Research Working Paper*, 870, World Bank, Washington, D.C.

McCleod, R., 1991. 'Informal and formal sector finance in Indonesia: the financial evolution of small business', *Savings and Development*, 15(2):187–209.

McDougall, R., 1993. 'Incorporating international capital mobility into Salter', *Salter Working Paper*, 21, Industry Commission, Canberra.

McGuckin, R.H., Nguyen, S.V., Taylor, J.R. and Waite, C.A., 1992. 'Post-reform productivity performance and sources of growth in Chinese industry: 1980–85', *Review of Income and Wealth*, 38(3): 249–66.

McKinnon, R., 1973. *Money and Capital in Economic Development*, The Brookings Institution, Washington, D.C.

_____, 1982. 'The order of economic liberalization: lessons from Chile and Argentina', *Carnegie-Rochester Conference Series on Public Policy*, 17(Autumn):159–86.

_____, 1991. *The Order of Economic Liberalization: Financial Control in the Transition to a Market Economy*, Johns Hopkins University Press, Baltimore.

Meier, G.M., 1990. 'Trade policy, development, and the new political economy', in R.W. James and A.O. Krueger (eds), *The Political Economy of International Trade*, Blackwell, Oxford.

Mikesell, R.F. and Zinser, J.E., 1973. 'The nature of the savings function in developing countries: a survey of the theoretical and empirical literature', *Journal of Economic Literature*, 11:1–26.

Milner, H. (1991). A three bloc trading system, Paper presented at the IPSA conference, Buenos Aires, Argentina, 20–25 July.

MOFERT, 1993. *Almanac of China's Foreign Economic Relations and Trade 1992/3*, China Advertising Pty Ltd., Hong Kong.

Montiel, P.J., 1993. 'Capital mobility in developing countries', *World Bank Policy Research Working Paper*, 1103, World Bank, Washington, D.C.

Moran, C., 1983. 'Export fluctuations and economic growth', *Journal of Development Economics*, 12:195–218.

Moreno, R., 1993. 'Exchange rate policy and insulation from external shocks: the experiences of Taiwan and Korea, 1970–1990', *Working Paper*, 3, Centre for Pacific Basin Monetary and Economic Studies, San Francisco.

Myint, H. 1971. 'Overall report' in Asian Development Bank, *Southeast Asia's Economy in the 1970s*, Longman, London.

Nam Chong Hyun, 1980. 'Trade and industrial policies, and the structure of protection in Korea', in W. Hong and L.B. Krause (eds), *Trade and Growth of the Advanced Developing Countries in the Pacific Basin*, Korea Development Institute, Seoul:187–211.

Ng Chee Yuen and Pang Eng Fond (eds), 1993. *The State and*

Economic Development in the Asia Pacific, Institute of Southeast
  Asian Studies, Singapore.
Nogues, J. and Quintanilla, R., 1992. Latin America's integration and
  the multilateral trading system, Paper presented at the World
  Bank–CPER conference, *New Dimensions in Regional Integration,*
  Washington, D.C., 2–3 April.
Noland, Marcus, 1992. Protectionism in Japan, Paper presented at
  the *Open Economies Review* 4, Washington, Institute for
  International Economics.
Obidegwu, C.F. and Nziramasanga, M., 1981. *Copper and Zambia: An
  Econometric Analysis,* Lexington Books, D.C. Heath, Lexington,
  Mass.
Obstfeld, M., 1992. 'Risk-taking, global diversification, and growth',
  NBER Working Paper, 4093, National Bureau of Economic
  Research, Cambridge, Mass.
OECD, see Organisation for Economic Cooperation and
  Development.
Okuno, M. and Suzumura K., 1986. 'The economic analysis of
  industrial policy: a conceptual framework through the Japanese
  experience', in H. Mutoh, S. Sekiguchi, K. Suzumura and
  I. Yamazawa (eds), *Industrial Policies for Pacific Growth,* Allen &
  Unwin, Sydney.
Olson, M., 1965. *The Logic of Collective Action,* Harvard University
  Press, Cambridge.
——, 1986. 'The exploitation and subsidization of agriculture in
  developed and developing countries', in A. Maunder and
  U. Renborg (eds), *Agriculture in a Turbulent World Economy,*
  Dartmouth, London.
Opschoor, J.P. and Vos, H., 1989. *The Application of Economic
  Instruments for Environmental Protection in OECD Member
  Countries,* OECD, Paris.
Organisation for Economic Cooperation and Development (OECD),
  1991. *DAC Annual Report,* OECD, Paris.
——, 1992. *Monitoring and Outlook of Agricultural Policies, Markets and
  Trade,* OECD, Paris.
——, 1993. OECD Ministerial Council Meeting Communiqué, OECD,
  Paris.
Pacific Basin Economic Council (PBEC), 1992. *North American Free
  Trade: Implications for International Business,* San Francisco, PBEC
  Secretariat.
Pangestu, M., 1991. 'Macroeconomic management in the ASEAN
  countries', in M. Ariff (ed.), *The Pacific Economy: Growth and
  External Stability,* Allen & Unwin, Sydney.
Pearson, C., 1992. 'Trade and environment: seeking harmony', OECD
  Economic Directorate, Version II, January.

People's Daily, Overseas Edition, various issues.

Petersmann, E.W., 1993. 'International trade law and international environmental law', *Journal of World Trade*, 27(1), February:43–81.

Petri, P., 1991. 'Japanese trade in transition: hypotheses and recent evidence' in P. Krugman (ed.), *Trade with Japan: Has the Door Opened Wider?*, University of Chicago Press, Chicago.

Pezzey, J., 1989. 'Economic analysis of sustainable growth and sustainable development', *World Bank Working Paper*, 15, World Bank, Washington, D.C.

Pigou, A.C., 1920. *The Economics of Welfare*, Macmillan, London.

Polasek, M. and Lewis, M., 1985. 'Australia's transition from crawling peg to floating exchange rate', *Banca Nazionale del Lavoro Quarterly Review*, June:187–203.

Priovolos. T., 1981. *Coffee and the Ivory Coast: An Econometric Study*, Lexington Books, D.C. Heath, Lexington, Mass.

Psacharopoulos, G., 1985. 'Returns to education: a further international update and comparison', *Journal of Human Resources*, 20(4):583–604.

Quirk, P., 1989. 'Issues of openness and flexibility for foreign exchange systems', *IMF Working Paper*, 3, International Monetary Fund, Washington, D.C.

Rajaram, A., 1985. *Commodity Price Booms and the Exchange Rate: Exchange Rate Overvaluation in Sub-Saharan Africa*, World Bank, Special Office for African Affairs, Washington, D.C.

Ranis, G. (ed.), 1992. *Taiwan: From Developing to Mature Economy*, Westview Press, Boulder, CA.

Rao, P.S. and Preston, R.S., 1983. 'Inter-factor substitution and total factor productivity growth: evidence from Canadian industries', *Discussion Paper*, 242, Economic Council of Canada, Ottawa.

Reserve Bank of Australia (RBA), 1984. *Annual Report*, AGPS, Canberra.

Reynolds, C.W., 1963. 'Domestic consequences of export instability', *American Economic Review*, 53(2):93–102.

Riedel, J., 1988. 'Economic development in East Asia: doing what comes naturally?', in H. Hughes (ed.), *Achieving Industrialization in East Asia*, Cambridge University Press, Cambridge.

——, 1993. 'Vietnam: on the trail of the tigers', *The World Economy*, 16(4):401–22.

Rix, A., 1990. *Japan's Aid Program: A New Global Agenda*, AGPS, Canberra.

Robertson, D., 1990. 'The global environment: are international treaties a distraction?', *The World Economy*, 13(1):111–27.

——, 1992. 'Trade and the environment: harmonization and technical standards', in Patrick Low (ed.), *International Trade and the Environment*, World Bank Discussion Paper, Washington, D.C.

Robertson, W., 1938. 'The future of international trade', *Economic Journal*, March:5.

Romer, P.M., 1992. 'Two strategies for economic development: using ideas and producing ideas', Proceedings of the World Bank Annual Conference on Development Economics, 1992, Supplement to *The World Bank Economic Review* and *The World Bank Research Observer*:63–91.

Rudebusch, G.D., 1993. 'The uncertain unit root in real GNP', *The American Economic Review*, 83(1):264–72.

Ruggles, R., 1993. 'Distinguished lecture in economics and government: accounting for savings and capital formation in the United States, 1947–1991', *Journal of Economic Perspectives*, 7(2):3–18.

Rummery, A., 1993. 'Australian Aid to Papua New Guinea', *Current Affairs Bulletin*, 69(12):

Ruttan, V.W., 1983. *Agricultural Research Policy*, University of Minnesota Press, Minneapolis.

Sachs, J., 1987. 'Trade and exchange rate policies in growth-oriented adjustment programs', *NBER Working Paper*, 2226, National Bureau of Economic Research, Cambridge, Mass.

S.A.F.E. Alliance, 1992. *Food Fit for the World?*, Public Health Alliance, London.

Sah, R.K. and Stiglitz, J.E., 1992. *Peasants Versus City Dwellers: Taxation and the Burden of Economic Development*, Clarendon Press, Oxford.

Saxonhouse, G., 1992. Trading blocs, Pacific trade and pricing strategies of East Asian firms, Paper presented at the World Bank–CPER conference, *New Dimensions in Regional Integration*, Washington, 2–3 April.

Schmidt–Hebbel, K., Webb, S. and Corsetti, G.L. 1992. 'Household saving in developing countries: first cross-country evidence', *World Bank Economic Review*, 6(3): 529–47.

Schultz, T.W., 1961. 'A policy to redistribute losses from economic progress', *Journal of Farm Economics*, 43(3):554–65.

_____, 1964, *Transforming Traditional Agriculture*, Yale University Press, New Haven.

_____, 1975, 'The value of the ability to deal with disequilibria', *Journal of Economic Literature*, 13(3):827–46.

Scitovsky, T. 1990. 'Economic development in Taiwan and South Korea,' in L. Lau (ed.) *Models of Development*, ICS Press, San Francisco:127–81.

Setboonsarng, S., (unpub.). 'Thailand', World Bank, Washington, D.C., 1980.

Sheard, P., 1992. 'Keiretsu and closedness of the Japanese market: an economic appraisal', *Discussion Paper*, 273, The Institute of Social and Economic Research, Osaka University, June.

Sherlock, S., 1993. 'Australia's Overseas Aid Program', *Current Affairs Bulletin*, 69(12).

Shrybman, S., 1990. 'International trade and the environment: an environmental assessment of GATT', *The Ecologist*, Vol. 20:30–1.

Siamwalla, A. and Setboonsarng, S., (unpub.). 'Trade exchange rate and agricultural pricing policies in Thailand', World Bank, Washington, D.C., 1980.

Sicular, T., 1988. 'Plan and market in China's agricultural commerce', *Journal of Political Economy*, 96(2):283–307.

Simon, H., Guetzkow, H., 1958. *Organisations*. J. Wiley, New York.

Simon, J.L., 1977. *The Economics of Population Growth*, Princeton University Press, Princeton.

Snape, R.H., 1992. 'The environment, international trade and competitiveness', in K. Anderson and R. Blackhurst (eds), *The Greening of World Trade Issues*, Harvester-Wheatsheaf, London.

Sorsa, P., 1992. 'GATT and environment', *The World Economy*, 15(1): 115–37.

Stein, L., 1977. 'Export instability and development: a review of some recent findings', *Banca Nazionale del Lavoro Quarterly Review*, 122:279–90.

——, 1991. *Papua New Guinea: Economic Situation and Outlook*, AGPS, Canberra.

Stigler, G.J., 1975. *The Citizen and the State*, University of Chicago Press, Chicago.

Stiglitz, J.E., 1987. 'Some theoretical aspects of agricultural policies', *World Bank Research Observer*, 2(1):43–60.

Stuart, C., 1992. 'Corn laws and modern agricultural trade policy', *Seminar Paper 524*, Institute for International Economic Studies, Stockholm.

Summers, L.H., 1991. Regionalism and the world trading system, Paper presented at the Kansas Hole conference, *Free Trade Areas*, Federal Reserve Bank of Kansas City, August.

Sun Fanghong, 1992. The Role of Foreign Exchange Policy in China: An Historical Perspective. PhD dissertation, School of Economic and Financial Studies, Macquarie University, Sydney.

Sung, Y. W., 1991a. 'Explaining China's export drive: the only success among command economies', *Occasional Paper*, 5, Hong Kong Institute of Asia-Pacific Studies, The Chinese University of Hong Kong.

——, 1991b. *The China–Hong Kong Connection: The Key to China's Open Door Policy*, Cambridge University Press, Cambridge.

——, 1992 'The economic integration of Hong Kong, Taiwan and South Korea with the mainland of China', in R. Garnaut and Liu

Guoguang (eds), *Economic Reform and Internationalisation: China and the Pacific Region*, Sydney, Allen & Unwin.

Takatashi, I., 1993. 'A Pacific perspective for the President', *International Economic Insights*, January/February.

Tan, G., 1983. 'Export instability, export growth and GDP growth', *Journal of Development Economics*, 12:219–27.

Tanzi, V., 1986. 'Fiscal policy responses to exogenous shocks', *American Economic Association Proceedings*, 76(2):88–91.

Tinbergen, J., 1984. 'Development cooperation as a learning process', in G.M. Meier and D. Seers (eds), *Pioneers in Development*, Oxford University Press for the World Bank, Oxford:315–31.

Tisdell, C., 1988. 'Sustainable development: differing perspectives of ecologists and economists, and relevance to LDC's', *World Development*, 16(3):373–84.

Tobey, J.A., 1990. 'The effects of domestic environmental policies on patterns of world trade: an empirical test', *Kyklos*, 43(2):191–209.

Tracy, M., 1989. *Agriculture in Western Europe: 1880–1988*, Harvester-Wheatsheaf, London.

Trivedi, P.K., 1989. 'The prices of perennial crops: the role of rational expectations and commodity stocks', in L.A. Winters and D. Sapsford (eds), *Primary Commodity Prices: Economic Models and Policy*, Cambridge University Press, Cambridge.

____, 1992. Tests of some hypotheses about the time series behavior of commodity prices, *Indiana University Working Papers in Economics*, 92-026, Bloomington, Indiana.

Tseng, W. and Corker, R., 1990. *Financial Liberalization, Money Demand, and Monetary Policy in the SEACEN Countries during the 1980s*, International Monetary Fund, Washington, D.C.

Tyers, R. and Anderson, K., 1992. *Disarray in World Food Markets: A Quantitative Assessment*, Cambridge University Press, Cambridge.

United Nations, various years. *Economic Survey of Asia and the Far East*, United Nations, New York.

United Nations, various years. *Yearbook of National Accounts Statistics*, United Nations, New York.

United Nations, 1992. *World Investment Report: Transnational Corporations as Engines of Growth*, United Nations, New York.

United Nations Development Programme (UNDP), 1992. *Human Development Report*, Oxford University Press, New York.

United Nations Industrial Development Organisation (UNIDO), 1986. *Industrial Policy in East Asia, 1950-1985*, Monograph IS.636, Vienna.

United States Department of Commerce, 1993. *Summary of U.S. International Transactions*, 15 June.

Villanueva, D. and Mirakhor, A., 1990. 'Strategies for financial reforms: interest rate policies, stabilization, and bank supervision in developing countries', *IMF Staff Paper*, 37(3):509–36.

Viner, J., 1950. *The Customs Union Issue*, Carnegie Endowment, New York.

Viviani, N., 1979. 'The problems of aid administration and policy formulation among western countries', in R. Shand and H. Richter (eds), *International Aid*, ANU Press, Canberra.

———, 1983. 'Aid policies and programmes' in P. Boyce and J. Angel (eds), *Independence and Alliance*, Allen & Unwin, Sydney.

———, 1990. 'Foreign economic policy', in C. Jennett and R. Stewart (eds), *Hawke and Australian Public Policy*, Macmillan, Melbourne.

Voivodas. C., 1974. 'The effect of foreign exchange instability on growth', *Review of Economics and Statistics*, 56:410–12.

Wade, R. 1988. 'The role of government in overcoming market failure: Taiwan, Republic of Korea and Japan', in H. Hughes (ed.), *Achieving Industrialization in East Asia*, Cambridge University Press, Cambridge:129–63.

———, 1990. *Governing the Market: Economic Theory and the Role of Government in East Asian Industrialization*, Princeton University Press, Princeton.

Westphal, L., 1990. 'Industrial policy in an export-propelled economy: lessons from South Korea's experience', *Journal of Economic Perspectives*, 4(3):41–59.

Whalley, J., 1992. Regional trade arrangements in North America: CUSTA and NAFTA, Paper presented at the World Bank–CPER conference, *New Dimensions in Regional Integration*, Washington, 2–3 April.

White, J., 1974. *The Politics of Foreign Aid*, The Bodley Head, London.

Williams, J.C. and Wright, B.D., 1991. *Storage and Commodity Markets*, Cambridge University Press, Cambridge.

Winters, A., 1992. The European Community: a case of successful integration?, Paper presented at the World Bank–CPER conference, *New Dimensions in Regional Integration*, Washington, 2–3 April.

World Bank, 1976. *World Tables*, Johns Hopkins University Press, Baltimore.

———, 1987. *World Development Report 1987*, Oxford University Press for the World Bank, New York.

———, 1988. *External Trade and Capital*, World Bank, Washington, D.C.

———, 1989. *World Development Report 1989*, Oxford University Press for the World Bank, Washington, D.C.

———, 1990a. *China: Macroeconomic Stability and Industrial Growth under Decentralized Socialism*, World Bank Country Study, Washington, D.C.

_____, 1990b. *Social and Economic Indicators,* Johns Hopkins University Press, Baltimore.

_____, 1991. *World Development Report, 1991: The Challenge of Development,* Oxford University Press for the World Bank, Washington, D.C.

_____, 1992a. *World Development Report, 1992: Development and the Environment,* Oxford University Press for the World Bank, Washington, D.C.

_____, 1992b. *Social and Economic Indicators,* Johns Hopkins University Press, Baltimore.

_____, 1993a. *World Development Report 1993,* Oxford University Press for the World Bank, Washington, D.C.

_____, 1993b. *World Bank Policy Research Bulletin.*

_____, 1993c. *Sustaining Rapid Development in East Asia and The Pacific,* World Bank, Washington, D.C.

_____, 1993d. *Strategies for Rapid Growth: Public Policy and the East Asian Miracle,* World Bank, Washington, D.C.

_____, 1993e. *China: Foreign Trade Reform: Meeting the Challenge of the 1990s,* World Bank, Washington, D.C.

_____, 1993f. *The East Asian Miracle: Economic Growth and Public Policy,* World Bank, Washington, D.C.

_____, 1993g. *Global Economic Prospects and the Developing Countries,* World Bank, Washington, D.C.

Wright, B.D. and Williams, J.C., 1990. The behavior of markets for storable commodities, Paper presented at the *34th Annual conference of Australian Agricultural Economics Society,* University of Queensland, Brisbane.

Xu Xinpeng, 1993. Economic cooperation relations between Taiwan and Fujian, Guangdong Provinces, Paper presented at the conference, *Taiwan in the Asia-Pacific in the 1990s,* 1–2 April 1993, Australian National University, Canberra.

Yamazawa, I., 1992. 'On Pacific economic integration', *Economic Journal,* 102(415):1519–29.

Yan Zongda, 1982. *Zhonggong chukou maoyi de yanjiu (Exports of the Communist Party of China),* Chinese Academy of Economic Research, Taipei.

Yang Gang, 1993. The Impact of Direct Foreign Investment on Manufactured Exports from China, 1979–1990, PhD dissertation, National Centre for Development Studies, Australian National University, Canberra, Canberra.

Yang Yongzheng, 1992. The Impact of the Multifibre Arrangement on World Clothing and Textile Markets with Special Reference to China, PhD dissertation, National Centre for Development Studies, Australian National University, Canberra.

Yoo Jung-ho, 1990. 'The industrial policy of the 1970s and the evolution of the manufacturing sector in Korea', *KDI Working Paper 9017*, Korea Development Institute, Seoul.

Yotopoulos, P.A. and Nugent, J.B., 1976. *Economics of Development: Empirical Investigations*, Harper & Row, New York.

Young, A., 1992. 'A tale of two cities: factor accumulation and technical change in Hong Kong and Singapore', in O.J. Blanchard and S. Fischer (eds), *NBER Macroeconomics Annual 1992*, MIT Press, Cambridge, Mass.

Zhang, J., 1993. 'Factors behind China's inflation', *Australian Financial Review*, 23 June:19.

Zhang Xiaoguang, 1993. China's Trade Pattern and International Comparative Advantage, PhD dissertation, National Centre for Development Studies, Australian National University, Canberra.

____ and Warr, P.G., 1990. 'China's trade patterns and comparative advantage', in Chinese Students' Society for Economic Studies, *China: Trade and Reform*, National Centre for Development Studies, The Australian National University, Canberra.

Index

Adams, F.G., 271
adverse risk selection, 167
Africa, *xvi*, 194, 204; income, 60; price
  policy, 321
agricultural comparative advantage,
  293, 299
agricultural protection, 313
agricultural research, 305
agricultural sector, 37, 236
aid, 193, 194, 195, 200, 207, 314
aid distribution, 200
aid effectiveness, 195, 196, 208, 211
aid policy, 205
aid volume, 204
Albania: manufacturing sector, 50
Algeria: commodity exports, 280;
  consumption, 282, 284, 286;
  demography, 41; exports, 288;
  investment, 52; manufacturing
  sector, 48; savings, 51, 52
Amazon: deforestation, 332
Amsden, A., 76, 79
Anderson, K., 246, 294, 297, 300, 301,
  302, 304, 306, 310, 313, 316, 318
Ando, A., 227
Aopi, G., 208, 209, 211
APEC countries, 130; open trade, 150;
  regional development, 148; regional
  forum, 145; regionalism, 132; trade,
  139; trade liberalisation, 132
Arden-Clarke, C., 328, 329
Argentina, 293; cereal, 45;
  employment, 49; financial
  instability, 54; fiscal deficit, 161;
  industrial output, 49; inflation, 54;
  investment, 52; manufactures, 49;
  savings, 52; taxation of agricultural
  production, 298; tubers, 45
Ariff, M., 100

Arndt, H.W., *xviii*, *xix*
ASEAN countries, 204, 207; capital,
  99; capital-intensive industries, 94;
  credit, 99; debt-service, 97;
  economic success, 81; education, 83;
  employment, 86; exchange rate, 85;
  export manufacturing, 97; export-
  oriented industrialisation, 137;
  exports, 86; financial liberalisation,
  99; financial sector, 99; foreign
  direct investment, 94, 95, 97;
  foreign investment policy, 96;
  growth, 137; heavy industries, 94;
  industrialisation, 86; industry
  policy, 87; inflation, 85; interest
  rates, 85; interest rates, 99;
  investment, 94, 99; macroeconomic
  stabilisation, 85; manufactures, 86;
  policy reform, 84; primary
  commodity exports, 83; regional
  security, 147; role of government,
  76; savings, 99; state enterprises,
  101, 102; structural adjustment, 85
Asia Pacific: capital, 152, 153, 157,
  158, 170; capital, 176; covered
  interest differential, 155; exchange
  rates, 151, 152, 153, 158, 170;
  financial integration, 155; financial
  liberalisation, 159; financial sector,
  152; financial sector liberalisation,
  157; foreign trade, 152; free trade,
  149; free trade region, 148; interest
  rates, 151, 152; intra-regional trade,
  138; investment, 137, 157; outward
  looking policy, 158; reform, 152;
  regionalism, 144, 149; savings, 157;
  trade liberalisation, 149, 159
Asia Pacific Economic Cooperation
  (APEC countries), *xxi*